The Personalist Ethic and the Rise of Urban Korea

This book reviews South Korea's experiences of kŭndaehwa (modernization), or catching up with the West, with a focus on three major historical projects – namely, expansion of new (Western) education, industrialization and democratization. The kŭndaehwa efforts that began in the last quarter of the nineteenth century have now fully transformed South Korea into an urban industrial society. In this book, we will explore the three major issues arising from the kŭndaehwa process in Korea: How was the historical transformation made possible in the personalistic environment? How personalistic is modern Korea? And how difficult is it to build an orderly public domain in the personalistic modern Korea, and how do Koreans respond to this dilemma of modernization? As an examination of modernization as well as Korea, this book will appeal to students and scholars of Korean studies, sociology, politics and history.

Chang Yun-Shik is Emeritus Professor in the Department of Sociology at the University of British Columbia, Canada.

Routledge Advances in Korean Studies

For a full list of titles in this series, please visit www.routledge.com

29 **Leader Symbols and Personality Cult in North Korea**
The Leader State
Jae-Cheon Lim

30 **The Failure of Socialism in South Korea**
1945–2007
Yunjong Kim

31 **Nouveau-riche Nationalism and Multiculturalism in Korea**
A Media Narrative Analysis
Gil-Soo Han

32 **Understanding Korean Public Administration**
Lessons Learned from Practice
Edited by Kwang-Kook Park, Wonhee Lee and Seok-Hwan Lee

33 **Modern Korea and Its Others**
Perceptions of the Neighbouring Countries and Korean Modernity
Vladimir Tikhonov

34 **Samsung, Media Empire and Family**
A Power Web
Chunhyo Kim

35 **The Korean Tradition of Religion, Society and Ethics**
A Comparative and Historical Self-Understanding and Looking Beyond
Chai-sik Chung

36 **Change and Continuity in North Korean Politics**
*Edited by Adam Cathcart, Robert Winstanley-Chesters
and Christopher Green*

37 **The Personalist Ethic and the Rise of Urban Korea**
Chang Yun-Shik

The Personalist Ethic and the Rise of Urban Korea

Chang Yun-Shik

LONDON AND NEW YORK

First published 2018
by Routledge
2 Park Square, Milton Park, Abingdon, Oxon OX14 4RN

and by Routledge
711 Third Avenue, New York, NY 10017

Routledge is an imprint of the Taylor & Francis Group, an informa business

© 2018 Chang Yun-Shik

The right of Chang Yun-Shik to be identified as author of this work has been asserted by him in accordance with sections 77 and 78 of the Copyright, Designs and Patents Act 1988.

All rights reserved. No part of this book may be reprinted or reproduced or utilised in any form or by any electronic, mechanical, or other means, now known or hereafter invented, including photocopying and recording, or in any information storage or retrieval system, without permission in writing from the publishers.

Trademark notice: Product or corporate names may be trademarks or registered trademarks, and are used only for identification and explanation without intent to infringe.

British Library Cataloguing-in-Publication Data
A catalogue record for this book is available from the British Library

Library of Congress Cataloging-in-Publication Data
Names: Chang, Yunshik, author.
Title: The personalist ethic and the rise of urban Korea / Chang Yun-Shik.
Description: Abingdon, Oxon ; New York, NY : Routledge, 2018. | Series: Routledge advances in Korean studies ; 37 | Includes bibliographical references and index.
Identifiers: LCCN 2017037394 | ISBN 9781138097902 (hardback) | ISBN 9781315104676 (ebook)
Subjects: LCSH: Korea (South)—Economic conditions. | Korea (South)—Social conditions. | Korea (South)—History. | Urbanization—Social aspects—Korea (South)
Classification: LCC HC467 .C366 2018 | DDC 330.95195—dc23
LC record available at https://lccn.loc.gov/2017037394

ISBN: 978-1-138-09790-2 (hbk)
ISBN: 978-1-315-10467-6 (ebk)

Typeset in Times New Roman
by Apex CoVantage, LLC

For Sungbon

Contents

Acknowledgments		viii
Introduction		1
1	Chosŏn Dynasty Korea	10
2	Korea in transition 1876–1945: Kŭndaehwa efforts before liberation	51
3	Growth of new (Western) education	84
4	Industrialization	110
5	Democratization	162
6	Urbanization and the expansion of the public domain	209
	Conclusion	246
	Index	258

Acknowledgments

I am indebted to many people in producing this book.

As it should be obvious from the book, I draw heavily on the work of Ronald Dore. Less obvious are the many insights I gained from his other works not cited here. I particularly appreciate Dore's help in formulating the concept of the personalist ethic in the form of lengthy comments on the papers I sent him and suggestions for revisions and additional readings.

I acknowledge receipt of financial support from the Korea Foundation for this book project and the Social Sciences and Humanities Research Council of Canada for other research projects related to this one, without which it would have been impossible to produce this book.

Daniel A. Bell, Lew Sok Chun, Michael Kew, Kim Uchang, Elvi Whittaker, and Yi Chaeyol commented on parts of the manuscript, for which I am very grateful. The uncommonly constructive review by an anonymous reader from Routledge proved to be most useful to me in revising it into the final version.

My thanks also go to Namlin Hur, Hyunho Seok, and Jaibong Hahm for inviting me to workshops they organized to present my ideas on the personalist ethic.

I have benefitted from numerous conversations I had with Donald Baker on Korean history and society over the years, and he has also helped me to translate a number of Korean phrases and sentences into English.

Encouragement I received from the late Alan Crawford, Neil Guppy, Namlin Hur, Steven Hugh Lee, Bob Ratner, Kristin Sopotiuk, Joseph Stefanich, Eui-Young Yu, and Elvi Whittaker served as pressure to finish writing the manuscript.

I was fortunate to have able research assistants, Jeong Lee, Sarah Lee, Jeongun Park, and Yoon Kyung Kim while preparing the manuscript.

I should specifically mention with gratitude Kim Aeryŏng in Korea for locating and sending me source materials in Korean; Vanessa LeBlanc for her careful editing of the manuscript which made the book more readable, orderly, and balanced; Kee Young Choi for his help in solving whatever problems I had with my personal computers; and Stephanie Rogers at Routledge for her humane professionalism.

Above all, I cannot thank my wife, Sungbon, enough for her support and intuitive comments on various points I made in the book. I dedicate it to her.

Introduction

This book reviews South Korea's experiences of kŭndaehwa (modernization) or catching up with the West with a focus on three major historical projects – namely, expansion of new (Western) education, industrialization and democratization. The kŭndaehwa efforts that began in the last quarter of the nineteenth century have now fully transformed South Korea into an urban industrial society.

At the time of Liberation in 1945, 70 percent of the Korean population was illiterate; only a small portion of the population had any school education. In the last decade of the twentieth century, both primary and junior high school education in South Korea were made compulsory. Senior high school education was not made compulsory, but it is nearly universal, and the majority of high school graduates (80 percent) advance to colleges or universities. As of 2011, the percentage of the Korean adult population aged 25–64 who graduated high school was higher (81 percent) than that of the average of the Organisation for Economic Co-operation and Development (OECD) (75 percent).

The South Korean economy evolved into a capitalist market economy, carving out a niche in the global market. The average annual economic growth rate was 9 percent during the development plan period (1964–1985). The growth of per capita income was dramatic, increasing to US$20,000 in 2011 from US$60 in 1960. South Korea now ranks fourteenth in the world for gross national product (GNP) and tenth for volume of trade or exports. At the end of the colonial period, the proportion of the labour force engaged in farming was 80 percent; it was down to 5 percent by 2000. Agriculture is no longer considered the foundational industry of the country. The age-old tenancy system was dismantled with land reforms in the first decade after Liberation. People now choose occupations in the job market, thereby achieving higher social standing. The consumer market has expanded rapidly, providing people with various goods, services and lifestyles to choose from.

The Republic of Korea was officially born in 1948 with the adoption of a democratic constitution. Unlike the aforementioned projects in which the state and civilians fully cooperated, the democratization process was stalled for almost four decades by two authoritarian presidents who refused to step down after the end of their terms and revised the constitution in order to stay in office longer (or permanently). Through civilian struggles and three major uprisings by civilian

2 *Introduction*

opposing forces, democracy returned in 1987. Election of the president and National Assembly members by popular vote was resumed, and the three government branches were separated. Autonomy was granted to local administrations to form self-governments through popular election. Pro-government organizations were released from government control, and ruling parties were no longer under the direct influence of the president. The freedom of the press was fully guaranteed for the media. Labour unions have regained their autonomy and, together with student activists and Christian churches, actively function as pressure groups.

Moreover, Korean democracy is currently going through a consolidation process. Firstly, institutionalization of political conflict is slowly taking place. Although the National Security Law is still in effect, the ideological distinction between conservatives (strongly anti-communistic and anti-North Korea) and progressives (less hostile or more conciliatory toward the north) is firmly established. The spectrum of political orientation may not extend very widely yet, but Korea is finally becoming a pluralistic society ideologically. Secondly, constitutionalism and human rights are deliberately promoted. The birth of the Constitutional Court in 1998 and the National Human Rights Committee in 2001 are cases in point. Thirdly, the non-governmental organization (NGO) sector has grown rapidly. Many of these civic organizations monitor the activities of the government administrators and politicians, promote the public good and are engaged in the legislative process by formulating and submitting bills to the National Assembly.

What South Korea has accomplished with the modernization project has been widely recognized and extolled. The economic development of Korea has been touted as "a miracle on the side of the Han River." Eric Hobsbawm praised it "as spectacular an industrial success story as any in history" (1994: 362, quoted in Kim Uchang (2006:221)). Alice Amsden, the economist, considers Korea as "Asia's next giant" (1989). The sociologist Michael Seth regards what Korea has also accomplished in the field of school education as the "Educational Revolution" (Seth 2002: 2). Frank Gibney, the former *LA Times* reporter, hailed the democratic development as a "quiet revolution" (1992).

But early foreign observers had different opinions about the feasibility of the "kŭndaehwa" of Korea. The American missionary doctor Horace Allen wrote to the American secretary of state on the eve of the Russo-Japanese War (1905),

> These people (Koreans) cannot govern themselves. They must have an overlord as they had for all time. . . . Let Japan have Korea outright if she can get it. . . . I am no pro-Japanese enthusiast, as you know, but neither am I opposed to any civilized race taking over the management of these kindly Asiatics for the good of the people and the suppression of oppressive officials, the establishment of order and the development of commerce.
>
> (Quoted in Duus 1995: 189)

Sydney Webb, father of British Fabianism, wrote in 1911 that he had seen a nation of 12 million "dirty, degraded, sullen, lazy and religionless savages who slouch around in dirty white garments of the most inept kind and who live in filthy mud

Introduction 3

huts" (quoted in Wade 2002). During the Korean War, the Indian diplomat Vengali Menon, head of the UN Special Delegation, said, "How can a rose blossom from a garbage dump?" General Douglas MacArthur, the then commander of the UN Forces fighting in Korea, declared, "This country has no future. This country will not be restored even after a hundred years."[1]

How then was this historical transformation, considered impossible by many foreign observers, brought to fruition? How does one account for it? Each of the three major kŭndaehwa processes – educational, economic and democratic – has been explored by both Korean and foreign scholars. But few attempts have been made to understand the process by which Korea broke away from its Confucian past and evolved into a new Westernized society in such a short period of time. We, therefore, analyze these three development processes as an interrelated phenomenon. We should take notice of the fact that while the economic and educational development of Korea has been state led, civilians have led the democratic development. Still, they occurred jointly and were nearly simultaneous.

In doing so, we should first take notice that pursuit of modernity in South Korea stands in sharp contrast to that of the West. Though Korean kŭndaehwa efforts have been concentrated on catching up with the West by learning from them and importing their institutions and organizations, they were not accompanied by the emergence of individualism[2] as it did in the West and as predicted by modernization theorists (e.g., Parsons 1971: 12–13). The modern urban Korean continues to remain as a relational being, not an independent being in isolation. Personal relationship is widely valued, and deliberate efforts are being made to widen individual personal networks by creating new ties and cultivating interpersonal solidarity. Emphasis on personal ties (or relations) and mutual help, rather than autonomy, prevails in South Korea. In fact, there is a strong sense of animosity to individualism, and market development has had the effect of making Koreans even more personalistic than in the past.

The personalist ethic

Personalism or the personalist ethic is a concept unfamiliar to scholars as well as laymen. It is the mode of social conduct prevalent in Korea in the past as well as present, or the remnant of the Confucian and rural communal ethic. Though urban Koreans are basically personalists, they do not identify themselves as such. It is about time that this widely practiced normative pattern of social behavior or habits of mind that constitutes the moral basis of the urban community be conceptually recognized and given a label for analytic purposes. The following is my codification of this social norm based on long personal observations as a native of that society, and I use it as the key concept in explaining the kŭndaehwa experiences of Korea. I will therefore discuss it in some detail in the rest of this chapter.

The personalist ethic[3] refers to the mode of conduct that governs social relations in the domain of personal networks in which members know each other personally and tend to interact with others as whole persons, not as partial persons or nameless role players. It began as the mores of the small rural community or

4   *Introduction*

hamlet as farming was adopted as the dominant mode of production in ancient times and was incorporated into the semiformal Confucian communal ethic when Chosŏn Korea imported the community compact system (hyangyak) from China in the early sixteenth century. (For more on this, see Chang (unpublished)).

The person here is close to the person Redfield previously defined – namely, "myself in another form, his qualities and values are inherent in him and his significance is not merely one of utility" (1947: 301).

The person's relation with close others is characterized by a strong sense of mutual aid, mutual indebtedness and obligation, mutual trust and mutual attachment and feelings.

Mutual help among friends and acquaintances in the form of physical labour, financial assistance, gifts, emotional support or personal favor is an unforced but expected and obligatory act. Assistance thus given creates a debt that needs be reciprocated in the future, and failure to do so may be interpreted as an act of severing ties. Furthermore, in the close relationship of personal bonds, one is encouraged to seek out advice and help. In Korea, failure to involve one's close friend in making a decision on important matters – whether marrying off children, sending sons to a city for advanced studies, planning to have a concubine, buying more land or cows, repairing thatches and so on – may easily hurt his feelings or make the friend feel unwanted. In other words, there is a mutual expectation to consult on matters that might in another cultural context, such as in Canada, be considered entirely private. In Canada, minding one's own business is condoned as much as minding other people's business is frowned upon. Individualism is a concept native to the West and carries pejorative overtones of selfishness in Korean society. Reciprocating help received from close others requires giving spontaneously rather than in a way calculated to pay off the personal debt engendered by the help received. One does not pay off the personal debt completely for paying off the personal debt implies ending personal relationships. The bondage with close others is not to be severed ever, and friends and acquaintances always remain mutually indebted.

As such, the indebtedness or obligation is an indebtedness or obligation to a specific person. Non-fulfilment of this obligation would likely cause displeasure or distress to this specific person (Dore 1958: 254). The sense of mutual indebtedness or obligation is more widely known as ŭiri (giri in Japanese). The maintenance of ŭiri relations became an end in and of itself. To say that a person does not know ŭiri is a direct, negative reflection on his personality. Ŭiri has long been regarded as one of the foremost virtues in Korea, as it has been in Japan.

The ŭiri relation is a relation of mutual trust. In the ŭiri relationship, one develops a strong sense of trust in close others. That is to say, he or she feels confident that his or her close others – kin members, friends and acquaintances – would not do something that would be considered an act of betraying him or her, or negatively affect their personal relationships. Ŭiri is valued so strongly that one does not easily refuse to oblige requests for help or cooperation – including bending rules – from close others.

While one gives and receives help to and from the close others continuously over a long period of time, both parties are likely to have the feeling of mutual

Introduction 5

attachment or become sensitive to each other's feelings in their interactions. One may risk a great deal in ignoring the other's feelings for impersonal ends. This tendency to be susceptible to human feelings (injŏng' e yakhada) develops into an inclination to share others' feelings or emotions – anger, hate, fear, love or pity. In Parsonian terminology, the personalistic relationship is affectionate rather than affectionately neutral. Being affectionally neutral or impersonal to close others is considered withdrawing chong (affection), which in turn is regarded as a form of expressing displeasure or an intention of severing ties.

The personalist ethic, the code of conduct in the small face-to-face rural community in the pre-modern era, survived the assault of urbanization. Urban Koreans have not become individualists as sociologists had predicted, but they remain personalists.

Though, in contrast to life in the rural village, kin members, friends and close acquaintances in the city often do not live in the same neighborhoods or work at the same places, they make conscious efforts to maintain their kinship or personal bonds through various forms of interaction: for example, chatting to each other on the phone; exchanging gifts on special occasions such as birthdays, weddings or New Years' Eve; visiting each other at home or in the hospital when they are sick; meeting for coffee, meals or drinks; going fishing or sightseeing, golfing or meeting regularly for whatever reason. Personalistic Koreans get together with friends for the sake of being together, or purposely create such occasions, more often than individualistic Canadians.

City residents may withdraw from this circle of friends or close acquaintances if they so wish. But informal personal ties, mutual trust, reciprocal obligation and indebtedness are highly valued in and of themselves and expected to be maintained even at the expense of self-interest. In interpersonal relations based on the norm of mutual obligation, one may act according to one's own will, but also according to that of others who will assume partial responsibility for acts not of their own doing.

The binding force of personalism makes disengagement from these relationships difficult, as that would violate the norm of mutual obligation. Hence, urban Koreans are neither free from their personal ties nor completely alienated from others. They are not a lonely face in a crowd (Riesman 1950), nor are they likely to be "bowling alone" (Putnam 2000). They are most emphatically part of a tightly clustered inner group of personal acquaintances and are well protected from the tendency to become depersonalized and alienated – the tendency that followed the individuation process in the West.

In the city, one also belongs to a multitude of closely knit circles or networks. Within these, one counts on the help of intimate others in achieving one's personal ends, and intimate others are obliged to render assistance when requested. As such, mutual obligation and indebtedness within a personal network inevitably works as a factor in restricting one's autonomy. Being perpetually indebted to others, one is expected to repay personal favors one owes.

Mutual help does have the effect of making it easier for one to achieve one's personal ends; it may even be argued that two people helping each other can accomplish more than each of the two can separately.

6 *Introduction*

When mutual help is emphasized and easily available, one may also readily seek help for one's personal affairs rather than managing them on one's own or standing on one's own feet. The personalist is prone to be more reliant on close others than self-reliant. Reliance on close others for one's own personal affairs helps avoid full responsibility for one's failure. One may blame close others for one's suffering from failure.

The personalist ethic, with its emphasis on personal intimacy and attachment or commitment thus has a tendency to blur the distinction between oneself and others within a network and makes the network a cohesive group. This helps develop a strong sense of "we" among the insiders of the network against those outside of it. When there is a visible leader, a network becomes identified with his (usually) name, and each member is commonly referred to as that leader's man. Moreover, if any member of a network gets engaged in competition against or feuds with outsiders, the entire network quickly comes to his aid.

A correlate of such a sense of we-ness based on strong binding forces is a weak sense of the self as a free independent being. Freedom is a Western concept imported after the port opening in 1876. The concept of freedom became closely associated with the lost homeland after Korea was colonized by Japan in 1910. Freedom or independence to Koreans meant more the Wilsonian idea of self-determination of nations, the idea partly responsible for the 1919 independence movement, than individual autonomy. In democratic Korea, freedom largely means freedom in the public domain that the constitution guarantees for citizens or public men – freedom of the press and expression, freedom of association, freedom of movement, freedom of beliefs, etc. The idea has not entered the personal network domain as a behavioral norm. Koreans remains personalists in the personal network domain. They are keenly aware of what close others think of their behavior and are apt to seek support in making decisions. Hence, they are less likely to insist on being autonomous and self-assertive, or standing up for their rights and self-interests even at the expense of social harmony; adhere to principle or conviction, or doing what they think is right without seeking approval of his close others – that is to say, being morally consistent or "true to thyself"; or value privacy in the sense of being left alone in one's personal space and guard it against external invasion (I am indebted to Dore 1991, 1992 for this section).

The sense of self is weaker in the vertical relation than in the horizontal relations, as one is less likely assert oneself in front of one's elder or superior. Children tend to depend on their parents' help. Students rarely ask their teachers questions in the classroom, and it is almost a taboo for a disciple to disagree with or criticize their teacher's ideas expressed in public lectures or published works. Once, the author's American friend made a remark in a private group discussion: "Here in America, one's disciple is one's best critic." The same cannot be said about personalist Korea. Doing so is considered an act of disrespect of the authority of one's teachers.

Personal networks may continue to flourish in cities as a preserve of the traditional norm of mutual help. But, aside from this expressive dimension, there is

Introduction 7

also an instrumental side. Personalist urban Koreans clearly appreciate the economic and status implications of the personal network. To know someone well, as discussed earlier, implies a mutual personal obligation. In urban life, unlike in a small, closed, rural community, an influential friend, relative or acquaintance frequently becomes a means to material benefits for "getting around" or "getting on." Such influence, through a multitude of friendships and acquaintances, facilitates life in the city, making it easier, for example, to avoid red tape in dealing with a government office, to get a loan from a bank, to find a good job for one's children, to be promoted ahead of others or to have one's sons exempted from conscription.

The larger the number of people one knows personally, the greater is one's personal influence and prestige (Dore 1958: 259). While two friends may help each other because of personal ties in the name interpersonal solidarity, they are actually morally obligated to help each other precisely because of these ties. In the city, therefore, the personalist does not always seek close others merely for the pleasure of "being with them." Sociologists now recognize the economic implications of personal or affective networks as social capital (see, for example, Bourdieu 1986). When social capital involves luminaries, it also becomes "symbolic capital," as Pierre Bourdieu calls it, in that the connection bestows honour and unofficial social ranking, which gives one an advantage in pursuing political or economic ends (Bourdieu 1986).

In this book, we will explore the three major issues arising from the kŭndaehwa process in Korea: (1) How was the historical transformation made possible in the personalistic environment? (2) How personalistic is modern Korea? (3) How difficult is it to build an orderly public domain in the personalistic modern Korea, and how do Koreans respond to this dilemma of modernization?

This book consists of four major parts. Part one (Chapter 1) is an attempt to understand structural characteristics of Chosŏn Dynasty Korea before the opening of the hermit kingdom in 1876 to modernizing Japan and the West. Chosŏn Dynasty Korea was a largely Confucian, status-oriented hierarchical and predominantly rural agrarian society. In Chapter 1, two major points are to be underlined.

Chosŏn Dynasty Korea actually had twin concurrent projects of Confucian transformation – namely, that of the state system with a focus on building the state bureaucracy on the basis of individual merit regardless of status distinction and that of the family system based on the patrilineal lineage system and ancestor worship. The former represents the early pursuit of "modernity" in that its main goal was to promote the welfare of the people or the politics based on the people and to establish the government, which recruited its officials on the basis of merits, while the latter represents the counter efforts on the part of the yangban elites to protect their class privileges or to retain the status-oriented society. In the end, the latter prevailed, while the former remained merely as an ideal, not a firmly established moral and political tradition. The other point is that, in developmental terms, Chosŏn Dynasty Korean economy did not remain static as many Japanese pro-colonial government historians claimed, but experienced considerable changes in its institutions. But the changes do not signify the sprout of capitalism as nationalist Korean historians assert.

8 *Introduction*

The second part (Chapter 2) will cover the transition period from 1876 to the end of colonial period in 1945. In 1876, Chosŏn Dynasty Korea, which had confined its diplomatic and trade relations with China as a tributary state only, was forced by the Japanese to open its doors to Japan and Western nations; the event was called port opening. Korea signed unequal trade treaties with Japan, China and nine Western nations within the next years, letting into Korea their diplomats to open legations and traders to open commercial business enterprises and take over mines. At the same time, Korea became an independent kingdom known as Imperial Korea, free from Chinese influence, and began reforming efforts, replacing Confucian institutions adopted from China with those imported from the West via Japan and launching kŭndaehwa (modernization) efforts with a focus on expansion of new (Western) educational systems and industrial development to compete against alien traders and catch up with the West.

The kŭndaehwa efforts by Chosŏn Dynasty Korea came under control of Japan in 1905 when Korea became its protectorate and came to an end as Korea was colonized by Japan in 1910. During the colonial period (1910–1945), Korea went through limited modernization as a peripheral part of the Japanese empire in its scheme of building the Great Asia Sphere.

In the third part (Chapters 3, 4 and 5), an attempt will be made to investigate the modernization processes of South Korea after Liberation. As mentioned earlier, three historical kŭndaehwa projects – educational expansion, industrialization and democratization – were more or less completed by the end of the twentieth century. The first two were led by the two authoritarian states and the third initiated by citizens. Though not widely recognized, in all three projects, the personalist ethic served as a major driving force. This book, therefore, will stress the role of the personalist ethic in South Korean kŭndaehwa.

As much as the personalist ethic played a key role in the modernization process, the end product of that process is the emergence of a personalist – not individualistic – urban society. The fourth part (Chapter 6) will analyze the city as a network community where city residents constantly make efforts to build personal networks based on personal ties to the extent of forming the huge oligarchic society-wide elite cartel. One distinct consequence of widespread network building efforts is personalizing public roles or institutions for private gains at the expense of public interest, the practice known as corruption. The book will end with the observation that while Korea transformed itself as an urban market society, Koreans did not become individualistic with modernization or Westernization. In Korea, modernization is a historical process taking place mainly in the public space, not in the private and face-to-face interpersonal space. In terms of value orientations, Koreans are slow to or refuse to accommodate themselves to the modernization process, remaining largely as personalists. In other words, urban Koreans are prone to being guided by the personalist ethic, not impersonal rules and regulations, in social interaction in the public space.

Notes

1 http://anupamatc.blogspot.ca/2016/07/rise-of-south-korea-miracle.html
2 I have elsewhere (Chang unpublished) discussed the discourses on the rise of individualism in the West by classical sociologists.
3 I introduced this concept in my earlier paper (Chang 1991).

References

Amsden, Alice (1989) *Asia's Next Giant*, New York: Oxford University Press.
Bourdieu, Pierre (1986) "The Forms of Capital," pp. 241–258, in Richardson, John G. (ed.) *Handbook of Theory and Research for the Sociology of Education*, New York: Green Wood.
Chang, Yun-Shik (1991) "The Personalist Ethic and the Market in Korea." *Comparative Studies in Society and History*, vol. 33, no. 1 (January), pp. 106–129.
Change, Yun-Shik (unpublished). *On Individualism*.
Dore, Ronald P. (1958) *City Life in Japan*, Berkeley: University of California Press.
Dore, Ronald P. (1991) *Will the 21st Century Be the Age of Individualism*, Tokyo: The Simul Press Ideal.
Duus, Peter (1995) *The Abacus and the Sword*, Berkeley: University of California Press.
Dore, Ronald P. (1971) "Modern Cooperatives in Traditional Communities," pp. 43–60, in Worsley, Peter (ed.) *Two Blades of Grass: Rural Cooperatives in Agricultural Modernization*, Manchester: Manchester University Press.
Gibney, Frank (1992) *Korea's Quiet Revolution*, New York: Walker and Company.
Kim, Uchang (2006) "Confucianism, Democracy and the Individual in Korean Modernization," pp. 221–244 in Chang, Yun-Shik and Lee, Steven Hugh (eds.) *Transformations in Twentieth Century Korea*, London: Routledge.
Parsons, Talcott (1971) *The System of Modern Societies*, Englewood Cliffs: Prentice-Hall.
Putnam, Robert D. (2000) *Bowling Alone*, New York: Simon and Schuster.
Redfield, Robert (1947) "The Folk Society." *American Journal of Sociology*, vol. 52, no. 4 (January), pp. 293–308.
Riesman, David (1950) *The Lonely Crowd*, New Haven: Yale University Press.
Seth, Michael J. (2002) *Educational Fever*, Honolulu: University of Hawaii Press.
Wade, Robert (2002) "Creating Capitalisms: The Rise of East Asia and the Failure of Liberal Economics" (Manuscript).

1 Chosŏn Dynasty Korea

Kŭndaehwa is the process of primarily learning from or catching up with the West. It also signifies the end to learning from China or dismantling the social structure of the Chosŏn Dynasty society established through adopting Confucian and neo-Confucian moral teachings. It is an ongoing and selective process. How much has Korea changed after the port opening in 1876 or the Kaehwa (enlightenment) movement began, and what remains unchanged? To answer this question, it is necessary to explore – even if briefly – the structural characteristics of the pre-Kaehwa Korean society.

At the risk of oversimplification, I will portray pre-Kaehwa Korean society as a predominantly Confucian, hierarchical and agrarian society.

The Chosŏn Dynasty as a Confucian society

Chosŏn Dynasty Korea (1392–1910) is generally characterized as a Confucian society or a society even more Confucian than China, the birth place of Confucianism. This characterization, however, is inaccurate as well as misleading in that Chosŏn Korea actually carried out two Confucianization projects concurrently: first, the Confucianization of the state, the chief goal of which was to promote the welfare of the people in general, and second, the Confucianization of the family with a focus on establishing detailed kinship rules and rituals. Threatened by the onset of the status-free Confucianization of the state project, the gentry (yangban) class set in motion the Confucianization of the family as a countermovement in order to preserve status distinction by firmly establishing the elite culture, more specifically yangban prerogatives. During the period of five centuries, Confucian scholars and officials were largely preoccupied with Confucian transformation of the family system with little efforts to build the state according to the Confucian ideal. In the end, the latter project eventually prevailed over the former, becoming the dominant concern of the Chosŏn Dynasty politics.

Unfortunately, how these two concurrent projects were related and conflicted with each other has rarely been analyzed by historians. It is important to recognize the co-existence of and relationships between the two projects in order to understand the dynamic forces that played major roles in determining the historical trajectory of the Chosŏn Dynasty. I also think that the co-existence of the twin

Chosŏn Dynasty Korea 11

projects should conveniently serve as a strategic reference point against which the political history of post-Dynasty Korea could be measured and evaluated.

The Confucianization of the State Project – The Chosŏn Dynasty, upon founding, adopted Confucianism as the official ideology of governance. Their ultimate aim was to build a new kingdom patterned after the three ancient (Chinese) kingdoms of Hsia, Shang and Chou – considered to have achieved the "supreme form of governance" (samdae chich'i) – to replace the previous dynasty, Koryŏ, which had been deeply under the influence of Buddhism. Chosŏn Confucian scholars and politicians condemned Buddhist monks for amassing lands and slaves as temple property, constructing an excessive number of temples all over the country and engaging in commercial activities for profit. Confucian scholars also criticized Buddhism as a belief system that tended to neglect worldly affairs and social responsibilities in pursuit of individual salvation through contemplation and mystical enlightenment (Chung 1995: 18, see also Han Ugŭn 1993). Buddhist monks and temples were banished to remote mountains, and the lands and slaves they owned were confiscated by the government.

The plan to build a Confucian utopia was first outlined by the great Confucian scholar and statesman Chŏng Tojŏn (1342–1398), who masterminded the coup d'état of Yi Sŏnggye, the founder of the Chosŏn Dynasty in 1392, in his *Code of Administration* (Chosŏn kyŏnggukchŏn, 1394), which was subsequently consolidated in *The Great Code of Administration of 1498* (Kyŏngguk taejŏn). The essence of governance as described in the two books is, in modern parlance, to create a government for the people (Han Ugŭn 1974: 11–12). Chŏng Tojŏn and his followers also delineated the characteristics of the ideal king and minister on the basis of Confucian scriptures.

The ideal Confucian state envisaged by Korean utopian scholars and officials may be summarized as follows:

The king ruled his kingdom according to the "Mandate of Heaven." The people were the foundation of the country, and the king was their parent. As *the Doctrine of the Mean* states, the king should treat the people equally as his own children without distinguishing between the noble and base, those close to him or distant. Universal love or benevolence (Ch. *jen;* Kr. *in*) was a virtue he should cultivate. He should approach and solve all the problems from the perspective of the people. The king should like what people like; he should dislike what people dislike. He should win people's hearts by ensuring that they are not materially wanting (constant means of support, or *hangsan*) and helping people to cultivate their minds or the sense of personal shame and become self-regulating loyal subjects (constant hearts, or *hangsim*). If he lost people's hearts, he would lose the kingdom. Heaven monitored the administration of the kingdom to make sure that the people were well looked after. Should the people suffer from bad administration, the king would no longer be graced with the Mandate of Heaven. It was believed that the heavens used unusual celestial or natural phenomena such as eclipse, falling stars, droughts, floods and others means to express its anger at an inept king. Heaven's heart was the people's hearts (see Eberhard 1957). Thus if the king won people's hearts, he would win Heaven's heart.

12 Chosŏn Dynasty Korea

The king was not to rule people by force or coercive control of law, but by moral persuasion. He was expected to cultivate his mind by familiarizing himself with the Confucian canons and thus present himself as a model for the people to follow or to internalize a sense of propriety and shame, thereby fostering their inner capacity to regulate their social conduct. His education began early in childhood. As a prince, he regularly received lectures from noted scholars or sŏyŏn, or lectures for the Crown Prince, on Confucian classics to prepare for kingship. After ascending to the throne, lectures continued under a new title kyŏng'yŏn, or royal lectures. At the royal lectures, the king not only read Confucian classics with the lecturers but also discussed various administrative matters with them and formulated policies.

He was also assisted and advised in governing the kingdom by able ministers who were well versed in Confucian classics, had internalized the ideology of the Three (ancient Chinese) Kingdoms (samdae) and had passed the competitive civil service examinations. Recruitment of government officials was, in theory, based solely on merit – that is, passing the civil service examinations. Except for women and slaves, anybody was allowed to sit in the examinations. The Chosŏn Dynasty began with only the broad status distinction between good (commoners) and base people (slaves) without recognizing the existing elite group (yangban or sadaebu) – the status group differentiated from commoners (yangmin) – in the previous dynasty, Koryŏ.[1] The Great Code of Administration of 1498 and the Sequel to the Great Code (*Sok taechŏn*) of 1746 did not recognize the yangban class as an official category.

The king and ministers were "united by their common commitment to doing justice in governing the people" (Tu 1989: 49). Accordingly, the king should seek advice from his minister in formulating royal policies. He should be willing to listen to criticisms of his governance, even if they displeased him. If he preferred to hear only praises of his administration and was not willing to hear disapproval of it, good and wise ministers who could truly help him to govern the kingdom according to the King's Way (*chewang'ŭi to*), would leave him, and only those who were ready to go along with or appease him regardless of what he did would remain. The good and wise minister was the one who was not afraid of straight talk or disagreeing with the king on political matters and the potential negative consequences (the king's anger and/or punishment in the form of exile or even death) that may result. Chŏng Tojŏn, following Mencius's teachings, clearly stated that the king who failed to obey the Mandate of Heaven may be deposed (Han Yŏng'u 1999: 142–143). Later scholars significantly moderated Chŏng's insistence. The foremost Confucian thinker of the Chosŏn Dynasty, Yi Hwang (1502–1571) said, "If a minister felt he could not do his duty as a minister properly the only way left for him would be to leave" (Yi Hwang 1977: 400). Yi Hwang's view of an ideal minister appeared to have become the dominant one.[2] But the nineteenth-century scholar Chŏng Yag'yong reminded his contemporaries of Mencius's original view – which was often forgotten in Chŏng's time – that rulers are supposed rule on behalf of the ruled, and if they fail to do so, they need to be deposed (Baker 1997:26). In one of his essays, Chŏng likened the king to the

Chosŏn Dynasty Korea 13

leader of a dance troupe chosen by its members and demonstrated how when the leader failed to lead the troupe, he was replaced by another member:

> If he does a good job of setting the pace for the dancers, then the rest of the troupe calls him "our master of the dance." But if he turns out to be incapable of doing what is required of him, then the troupe removes him as head and tells him to rejoin the ranks of the other dancers. They then select one from their ranks and elevate him to the leadership position, calling him "our master of the dance." In this situation, the troupe as a whole decides who should be served as the leader, who should be elevated to that position and who should be unseated.
>
> (Baker 1997: 27)

He then goes on to ask, "So what grounds would there be for hurling a charge of rebellion from within the ranks at the person chosen to replace the previous leader?" (Ibid. 1997: 27). To Chŏng Yag'yong, such an act of leadership change would be perfectly legitimate.

Egalitarian and democratic – or modern – though this idea may appear, "the people" here did not mean everybody in the kingdom. Slaves (nobi) were explicitly excluded because they were considered undeserving of the king's grace and protection since they were criminals or children of criminals. Women were not allowed into the world of politics.

The Confucianization of the Family Project – Doing away with the elite status category in recruiting government bureaucrats was simply unacceptable to the yangban class whose elite status was established during the previous dynasty, Koryŏ (918–1392). Local yangban were quick to respond to this status-free policy of the new government. They organized themselves into an identifiable group by establishing the local yangban registry (hyang'an) system by way of differentiating themselves from commoners. The local yangban register established at the township (ŭp) level (usually the seat of the local magistrate office), listed members of the gentry status group residing in surrounding areas. To qualify for inclusion in the registry, one had to be born or married into a family that had produced a government official within three or four immediately previous generations. Those listed in the local registry then formed themselves into an organization called yuhyangso (local self-governing bodies) with the purpose of voluntarily assisting the local magistrate and overseeing the yamen clerks. This organization was later recognized as a semi- or pseudo-government organ (see Takawa Kōzō 1964).

As the size of the local yangban (or sajok) status group grew, they were dispersed into different regions. Each group that had the same surname and same birthplace (pon) as the founder of the same named group (sijo) established itself as an exclusive cluster or a lineage group, called munjung or chongjung. The lineage group became further divided into various segments (p'a) as some descendants decided to establish separate groups within it. This usually happened when direct descendants of an illustrious forebear (a meritorious courtier or eminent scholar) decided to honor him as the founder of a segment within a lineage group.

14 *Chosŏn Dynasty Korea*

The split of a lineage into segments may continue as the group produces more illustrious sons, although it is not always the case that descendants of an eminent ancestor would automatically form a new segment. But as Janelli and Janelli point out, the descendants of an outstanding ancestor were prone to form their own segment and thus "it is safe to assume that the expansion of a lineage group and its continuing division into different pas was closely related with the number of illustrious ancestors it produced" (Janelli and Janelli 1982: 138). Branching out into a new segment was a way of reasserting the gentry status of the lineage group by taking advantage of the eminence that members of a clan achieved – sometimes surpassing that of the founder. Lineage membership was almost essential for maintaining gentry standing (ibid. 1982:131).

Accordingly, remembering or revering ancestors became an important function of lineage groups. Ancestor reverence ritual, in theory, is an expression of the filial feeling of children to their ancestors – father, grandfather, great-grand father and so on. Such ritual also serves as a way of sustaining ties with one's ancestors as well as demonstrating their family lineage, thereby asserting and enhancing the relative status of their clans and hamlets. Status assertion, in fact, is an important corporate function of the lineage group. Each family was expected to produce sons that would write the civil examinations successfully and become government officials. If a man didn't pass even the lowest level of the civil service examination, he was at risk of losing the tax privileges of yangban status. Of course, he could keep that status by remaining a "Confucian student" into his 60s.[3] But it is the task of the lineage group to enumerate and advertise through ancestor reverence ceremonies and the compilation of family genealogy (chokpo) how many of its members achieved such eminence. Division of a lineage group into sub-lineage groups or segments was usually accompanied by the establishment of another hamlet under the same family name.[4] The families with the same name dispersed into different regions together constituted large lineage groups called p'munjung or chongmunjung. The p'amunjung consisted of all descendants of a segment (p'a) ancestor, whereas the chongmunjung were all descendants of the founding ancestor (chong).

This effort to have local yangban elites recognized as a distinct status group differentiated from commoners was followed by a further effort to establish the yangban way of life or culture in close accordance with Confucian teachings. They focused on establishing the firm Confucian foundation of the family system. As Deuchler puts, the most fundamental feature of the Confucianization of the family system was the development of the patrilineal lineage system based on the principles of primogeniture and ancestor worship (Deuchler 1992: 284). Unlike the Chinese lineage system, where the basic rule was equal fraternal inheritance, in Korea, "the singling out of the eldest son as the ideal and therefore preferred representative of his generation resulted from the greater emphasis on the continuation of the main line at the cost of collateral lines" (Ibid. 1992: 284). The ancestor reverence ritual clarified the lines of descent and marked kinship boundaries, and defined the ritual status and function of male descendants, together with their rights of inheritance and obligations of mourning (Ibid. 1992).

The ancestor reverence ceremony held at the eldest son's house was the occasion for geographically scattered agnates to gather together once a year, thereby reinforcing the consciousness of common descent and strengthening kin solidarity. "Ancestral rites," in the words of Deuchler, "thus introduced a kind of ideological corporateness that, detached from political and economic conditions, functioned as a prime mover in the formation of patrilineal descent groups in Chosŏn Korea" (1992: 285). As is apparent, my description of the Confucianization of the family system is adapted from Deuchler's *The Confucian Transformation of Korea: A Study of Society and Ideology* (1992) in which she rendered a detailed analysis of it. No further discussion of it will be attempted here since it will merely be redundant. At this point, I can only suggest that her book should be consulted for further details. The focus of the current study is on recognizing the existence of the other project, Confucianization of the state, and offering an explanation for why it did not work.

Failure of the Confucianization of the state project

The Confucianization of the state project that aimed at building a government for the people or pursuing the politics based on the people (*wimin chongch'i*) was not to be materialized, as it faced from the beginning stiff opposition of the majority of yangban elites who began the Confucianization of the family project as a countermovement. They were either reluctant or strictly opposed to supporting the government's intermittent reform efforts to reduce sufferings and plights of peasant commoners, slaves and yangban women – efforts that implied yangban giving up part of their status prerogatives. Their opposition to such reform efforts were so strong that the idea of the politics based on the people had little chance of becoming a political tradition of the Chosŏn Dynasty.

In explaining the failure of the Confucianization of the state project, however, we should first begin with the curious fact that from the beginning of the Chosŏn Dynasty, the public education on the Confucian ethic was not designed to produce the kind of minister loyal to the king whose prime concern was with taking care of the people or 'the politics based on the people' (*wimin* or *pomin chŏngchi*) but to produce one who was loyal to the king, the person, who appointed him.

Public Education on the Confucian Ethic – Model loyal ministers in the *Pictorial Books on Three Relations* (1432), the widely used text compiled by the government of the Confucian ethic, and the men entered as loyal subjects in the *Veritable History* and local geography books were not the kind of loyal subjects idealized in the Confucianization of the state project. The representative cases of model ministers were ones who were willing to give up their lives to protect the king at times of crisis (e.g., rebellion or foreign invasion), or to die fighting to the end against foreign invaders instead of surrendering or refusing to serve a king other than the one who appointed them and to whom they pledged their loyalty (that a minister should not serve two rulers was a widely held belief).

The ideal loyal minister envisaged by the advocates of Confucian transformation of the state was of a different type. His loyalty to the king was not loyalty to

16 Chosŏn Dynasty Korea

a particular king but to an abstract principled one, committed to creating a government for the people or protecting and promoting the material welfare of the ordinary people. No case of a minister who left the court because the king failed to live up to his expectation appears in the *Pictorial Book*.

The seventeenth-century scholar Kim Yuk (1580–1658) clearly realized that the public education on the Confucian ethics in Chosŏn Korea was not designed to produce the kind of minister loyal to the king devoted to the politics based on the people. In his view, scholar officials, men who were learned and ruled others, should be well aware that their prime duty was to make people's lives comfortable (*anmin* or *pomin*) and to cultivate the ability to perform that duty and always do their best, and they should be ready to give what belonged to them to others and extend this spirit of sharing to solving difficult problems of the people. As a learned statesman, Kim Yuk searched for exemplary officials who "loved people (in general) and were willing to help them." He actually compiled a book on such officials, *The New Book on Propagating Virtues* (*Chongtŏksinpyŏn*) in 1644, drawing examples from Chinese historical sources. Clearly, he intended for it to replace the *Pictorial Book on Three Bonds*. As a practising high official, he made it his life's task to implement the Uniform Land Tax Law (*Taedongpŏp*) countrywide (Kim Chunsŏk 2001).

I now turn to discussions of some major reform attempts that addressed the issue of poverty of peasant commoners and how they fared, and that were also part of creating a Confucian state, the goal of which was to make people live in comfort and peace.

The Equal Land System – At the beginning of the sixteenth century, some reformist officials brought to King Chungjong's attention on various occasions the "evil practices of the excessive possession of land" (Pak Siyŏng 1961: 161) by rich landowners and landlords. They recommended that the ancient Chinese equal land system or limiting landownership system be adopted to redress this issue. King Chungjong (r. 1506–1544) and conservative officials agreed that there was a serious problem with maldistribution of land, but they opposed "hastily enforcing" the equal land system. One opponent argued that adoption of the equal land system entails taking away land from the rich and giving it to the poor. The descendants of the rich will then become poor later. They will need more land, but it will be difficult to take back the land given away. King Chungjong himself said that taking away land from the rich will make them resentful, while the poor, even if they gained additional land, won't be able to cultivate it since they don't possess appropriate farm tools. Reformists held onto their position by arguing that since the equal land system was practiced in Tang China, there is no reason why it could not be done in Korea. One advocate of the equal land system defended his position on a moral ground. He said, "If the equal land system is introduced the rich will complain but it will be beneficial to the poor" (Pak Siyŏng 1961: 162). After some debate, the government in 1519 adopted the policy of limiting landownership at 10 kyol. This decision was a limited victory for the reformists, but the rich and powerful landowners loathed it.

Chosŏn Dynasty Korea 17

The land distribution problem was raised again after the outbreak of the Imjin War (1592–1598). Yu Hyŏngwŏn (1622–1673) was perhaps the most vocal and influential progressive reformist of the Chosŏn Dynasty who, along with other critiques, addressed the issues of maldistribution of land and wealth responsible for the plight of commoner peasants. He strongly criticized the large landlords for causing the pauperization of small peasants. Although Yu considered the well-field system of Ancient China as the model for rectifying the land system, he believed that it could not be adopted in his own time "unless private property were abolished and land tenure and distribution carried out in the context of public ownership" (Palais 1996: 351). The public ownership of land or a kongjon system, in his opinion, was necessary for land redistribution. He went on to argue that the state had every right to take over their land and redistribute it to poor peasants, as all land was public land or the king's land, and the landlord was really only borrowing the use of land from the king. Though he was reluctant to advocate use of force to confiscate land from the landlords, he admitted that he was willing to authorize its use if his plan of land redistribution confronted "the prospects of indefinite postponement" (Palais 1996: 351). His followers in the eighteenth century, mostly scholars of "practical learning" (sirhak), shared Yu's concerns with maldistribution of land and wealth, and his ideas about the need for land redistribution. But unlike Yu, they did not believe that anything like the well-field system could be restored. Instead, they agreed that some form of limited-land tenure would be the next best remedy (Palais 1996: 371). King Chŏngjo (r. 1776–1800) rejected the proposal of limited-landownership, as he found it impractical. He also lacked wide support. Court officials, who were mostly large landowners themselves, were never prepared to force landowners to adopt any reform measure weakening their prerogative (Palais 1996: 372).

Three Tax Reforms – Aside from the problems arising from land maldistribution, there was also an ill-functioning tax system that created significant burdens to peasant commoners. From the middle of the fifteenth century to the late eighteenth century, there were three major tax reform attempts – namely, enactment of the Land Tax Law, Uniform Tax Law and Equal Service Law.

Almost from the start of his rule, King Sejong (r. 1418–1450) discussed the ancient Chinese Land Tax Law (kongbŏp) with high officials with the intention that it replace the current tax law. Under the Land Tax Law system, the government collected the fixed amount of tax estimated on the basis of fertility and the loss of the crop. By fixing the amount of tax to be levied, the Land Tax Law eliminated the crop assessment each year, thereby preventing corrupt magistrates, clerks and runners from manipulating the amount of tax to be levied each year. Many officials, who were basically reluctant to change long-established social customs and laws, opposed it on the more or less a technical ground that the intended reform might or would cause unanticipated inconveniences and confusions. By way of countering the opposition and convincing himself of the positive results that the new law would bring, King Sejong asked those high officials who wrote the high-level civil service examination to express their views on the Land

18   *Choson Dynasty Korea*

Tax Law. He also conducted a survey of a large number of respondents on the desirability of enacting the law. With positive responses he received from these inquiries and further discussions with court officials, he introduced the law first in the Kyŏnggi Province. Over the next 48 years, the Land Tax Law was extended to the rest of the country.

In the late sixteenth century, some reform-minded politicians and scholars began to express their concerns about the negative impacts of another tax, the tribute tax, on the livelihood of the majority of peasants and proposed various reform measures to redress them. The tribute tax was a tax in-kind. The government collected the tribute tax in the form of products directly from producers for use by the government and royal houses. The direct payment of tribute was gradually replaced by indirect payment by tribute contractors. Tribute contractors negotiated with county magistrates to buy the tribute goods and delivered them to the government, and collected the price for the purchase and labour service from the magistrate later on. In the process, the price of tribute goods was vastly inflated, sometimes several times the market price. Consequently, taxpayers, the commoner peasants, ended up paying the tribute contractor a lot more than what it would cost them to produce or obtain the tribute good allocated. While tribute contracting was becoming a profitable business for the contractors and merchants, as well as a source of additional income for officials, it became a heavy burden on taxpayers or peasants. The tributary tax burden became so heavy that many peasants fled from their villages to avoid paying it, "only to have collection enforced upon their kinsmen or upon their neighbors" (Lee Ki-baik 1984: 203).

In 1594, Yi I, one of the two most prominent scholar officials of the Chosŏn Dynasty, discovered a solution to the problem of tribute while he was the magistrate of Haeju city in Hwanghae Province. He collected rice to provide funds for purchasing tribute items and paid it to the capital, thereby eliminating exploitation of the peasantry under the tribute contracting system. He then recommended that this measure of replacing tribute with a surtax on land be extended to the whole country to establish equitable tax rates and reduce unnecessary tribute requirements (Palais 1996: 774). But there was not enough support for this proposal to move King Sŏnjo to adopt it.

In 1608, shortly after the end the Imjin War, the conversion of tribute levies to a land tax finally became law when King Kwanghae enacted the Uniform Tax Law, and established the Tribute Bureau (sŏnhyech'ŏng) to administer it. The government collected rice from taxpayers in proportion to the size of land they owned in lieu of tribute goods. This method of payment not only simplified the tax levying process but also fundamentally changed the basis of assigning tax in-kind from household to landownership. This abrogated the rule of tax rates based on households applied equally to both small holders or landless tenants and large holders without differentiating the capacity to pay. In other words, under this law, poor peasants, in theory, no longer had to pay the same rate of tribute tax as rich landowners.

Chosŏn Dynasty Korea 19

This new tax system was, however, only enacted in Kyŏnggi Province as King Kwanghae was aware of wide opposition to the law and wanted to test the plan first. Many provincial governors, district magistrates, some high officials in the central government who enriched themselves by cooperating with the contractors in the business of tributary contracting and landlords who rebelled against the idea of a surtax on their landed property did not want change in the tribute tax system. Conservative officials who were themselves large landlords not only opposed the spread of the Uniform Land Tax Law beyond Kyŏnggi Province but also insisted that it be abolished altogether. While not denying the need of some kind of reform, they argued that the Uniform Land Tax Law was not the solution. Their reasons for opposing or abolishing it were varied: it would not be easy for rich landowners to find the amount of rice required to pay tributary taxes at once; a sudden change in the long lasting institution would create confusion, and the Taedong reform would and did not generate enough funds to increase government revenue. They also worried about the wreckage of ships transporting rice to the capital or the possibility of fires in granaries. Instead, they suggested updating the tribute ledgers and introducing household registers (*hopae*) to prevent tax evasion.

In an effort to counter the opposition, the Uniform Land Tax Law advocates first offered solutions to the technical problems of paying the new tax that the opponents raised: if it was difficult to come up with tax grains at once, payment could be done at different times instead of doing it at once, and the probable occurrence of shipwrecks transporting rice could be avoided by doing it during the seasons less vulnerable to bad weather – namely, spring and fall. Advocates of the Uniform Land Tax Law opposed its abolition on moral grounds. They pointed out that small holders or landless peasants paid more tribute tax than rich landowners. Some peasants did not have enough grain left from the crop harvest each year to feed their families after they paid high tenancy fees and taxes, while rich landowners accumulated many bushels of rice in their warehouses. They argued that this was not the way to govern the country. The "good" government should try to guarantee stable livelihood of the small people or poor peasants as they are equally the king's subject as rich landowners and landlords. For instance, Kim Yuk, the governor of Ch'ungch'ŏng Province, in urging the government to apply the Uniform Tax Law to his province, reasoned,

> The law is not enacted [here] because district magistrates opposed it even though the ordinary people all want it. I don't know how many millions the number of the people is in this province but I know that there are only 50 or so magistrates. How can you not enact it because 50 people do not want it while millions of them want it?
>
> (Quoted in Kim Yun'gon 1971: 144)

Though it took a century to extend it to the rest of the country, advocates of the Uniform Land Tax Law eventually prevailed over opponents by successfully

20 Chosŏn Dynasty Korea

persuading the three kings – Injo (r. 1623–1649), Hyojong (r. 1649–1659) and Hyŏnjong (r. 1659–1674) – to promulgate it in other provinces.

Peasants themselves largely welcomed the enactment of this law and played a role in preserving it. In 1612, when the government was about to abolish the Tax Bureau under pressure from high officials in the central government and rich local landowners who were highly critical of this law, a group of peasants in the province protested vehemently by distributing circulars and dispatching their representatives to the capital to deliver the circular to the government (Pak Siyŏng 1961: 225). The Tax Bureau was not abolished.

Remarkable as the enactment of the Uniform Land Tax Law might have been, it neither substantially reduced the plight of the peasantry nor augmented government revenues. The military cloth tax was another cause for these problems.

After the outbreak of the Imjin War (1592–1598), military service was converted into a cloth tax payment. This change was made necessary mainly because of the need to augment government revenue, which had been drastically reduced by the devastation of the war.

Yangban did not pay the military tax, as they were originally more or less exempted from mandatory military service. As the tax was the duty of commoners, slaves were also exempted since they owed the government labour service. Some peasants could afford to evade the tax through various means, such as by buying yangban titles, gaining exemption by bribing government officials or joining yangban households as labourers or slaves. Consequently, the number of military cloth taxpayers was substantially reduced, diminishing government revenue.

This fact more directly created the problem for magistrate offices of meeting their quota or gave them the excuses for resorting to illicit means of levying the military tax such as "registering boys as adults and levying the tax on them ('fledgling legerdemain,' hwanggu ch'ŏmjŏng) or keeping the names of dead men on the tax rosters ('skeleton levies' or paekkol chingp'o)" (Lee Ki-baik 1984: 226; Palais 1975: 89). Many peasants simply fled their villages to escape. Instead of writing off the escapees, the magistrate offices collected their unpaid taxes from their neighbors and kinsmen, which resulted in more peasants fleeing (Lee Ki-baik 1984: 226). Accordingly, the military cloth tax turned out to be even more burdensome to peasant commoners than other forms of taxes.

Many reform advocates felt that the problem could not be solved without requiring yangban to pay the cloth tax or perform the military duty or the Equal Service Law should be enacted. In support of this law, some reformists went as far as to insist that yangban should also pay tax like the peasants since they are all the children of the king. They basically argued that the poverty and plight of the majority of the peasantry was the result of excessive taxes, the yangban's refusal to pay taxes and the exploitation of corrupt central and local government officials and clerks. Thus, unlike those scholars and officials who supported the enactment of the Uniform Land Tax Law, some of them directly criticized yangban for not paying taxes and insisted that they did (Chŏng Manjo 1977).

But the majority of high officials were opposed to any suggestion that yangban pay the military tax. Various arguments were put forward by defenders of

Chosŏn Dynasty Korea   21

yangban's interests to counter the ones put forward by reform advocates. Unlike those who opposed the installment of the Uniform Land Tax Law mostly on technical grounds, the opponents of the military tax reform did so openly on the basis of status ideology. Their main argument goes like this:

Forcing the yangban to be enlisted as soldiers or pay support tax is tantamount to reducing yangban to the level of commoners and/or slaves. The king may collect more tax but will lose the "minds" of the yangban, the backbone of the kingdom. Discontent among yangban will rise. The social order based on the principle of status distinction will be threatened or destroyed. It is better to gain the "minds" of yangban than lose "minds" of commoners. If the king loses yangban's support and loyalty, then the kingdom will be likely to decline (Ibid. 1977).

King Yŏngjo (r. 1724–1776), though determined to reduce commoners' sufferings resulting from the military cloth tax, was not willing to take the risk of losing yangban's "minds." King Yŏngjo opted for a tax cut. In 1750, he decreed that the cloth tax be reduced from two *p'il* to one – the decree is known as the Equal Service Law. Two years later, he announced his decision to make up the lost revenue resulting from the tax cut by authorizing the newly established Bureau of Equal Service to manage taxes on fish traps, salt production and private fishing and trading vessels (the taxes that used to be levied by the royal households and other government bureaus), and by imposing a tax on idle *yangban* and surtax on land.

With the enactment of the Uniform Tax Law and the Equal Service Law, the early tax system that consisted of land tax, tributary tax and labour and military service was simplified to one of household land tax and military cloth tax.

These tax reforms might have reduced the peasantry's tax burden somewhat, but the reforms did not increase government revenue, as they failed to extend taxpaying duties to yangban, to collect tax on the unregistered land of yangban landowners and to eliminate the informal practice by government tax collectors of privatizing taxes levied. The government faced a revenue shortage problem. The financial crisis was serious, reaching a danger point toward the end of the eighteenth century. The government not only had to raise the rates of the land and military taxes, but also had to convert the public granary loan – begun as a poverty-relief system – into "an instrument of making usurious loans" (Lee Kibaik 1984: 249). It became necessary for the government "to utilize interest on state-sponsored grain loans as a means of supplementing its income, converting an institution devoted to the relief and welfare of the peasantry into one geared to the exploitation of the peasantry" (Palais 1975: 132).

The three taxes together became unbearable burdens[5] on peasants, causing much hardship. Moreover, the government was unable to even introduce major reforms such as the Uniform Land Tax Law and the Equal Service Law in the nineteenth century – a period where almost all the kings were under the control of the royal in-laws who almost completely dominated the political process, paying little attention to the problems concerning peasant plight.

As the above discussion shows, some reform efforts were made on behalf of peasants' interests and welfare during the century-long period of factional struggle among yangban scholars/politicians.

22 Chosŏn Dynasty Korea

In the nineteenth century, any debate on such reform attempt, however, was out of question. In an effort to avoid the high taxes, some peasants voluntarily became slaves to landlords. Those peasants who could afford it bought yangban titles. A growing number of peasants left farming to escape the high rent demanded by their landlords and the heavy burden of government taxes. Some went to the capital city or nearby towns to work as artisans, merchants or wage labourers. Others went to the mountains to become miners. But instead of abandoning farming, the majority of them chose to revolt to express their discontent and frustration. In addition to minor outbursts, the nineteenth century witnessed three large-scale peasant rebellions: the Hong Kyŏngnae Rebellion of 1812, the Imsul Rebellion of 1862 and the Tonghak Peasant Uprising of 1894.

Slave Liberation – There were also some limited attempts by reformist government and politicians to address the problems of slaves.

Basically, slaves were regarded as a kind of sub-human (Ibid. 1996: 235). More specifically, they were not regarded as legitimate subjects of the king in that they were criminals reduced to slave status or children of criminals. Slave status was hereditary in nature. Children of criminals or slaves became slaves. They were chattel property to their owners, bequeathed to their children, sold, given to others as gifts and exchanged for other property, including animals.

They were divided into two types: official (kwan nobi) and public slaves (kong nobi) owned by the government and public organizations, such as schools and temples, and private slaves (sanobi) belonging to individual masters.

Official slaves were further divided into those who owed labor service to the government and, working at the behest of government agencies for a certain portion of the year, called service slaves (ibyŏk nobi) and those who remained in their villages and simply remitted tribute payments to the government in lieu of labour service, called either tribute-paying slaves (napkong or sin'gong nobi) or "outside-resident slaves" (oekŏ nobi). Service slaves were recruited either from the capital or selected from local areas and sent up to the capital. The former were called "capital city slaves" (kyŏnggŏ nobi), while the latter were "select slaves" (sŏnsang nobi) (Lee Ki-baik 1984: 188).

The labour service rendered by male slaves consisted of miscellaneous kinds of office-related work. But some of them worked as artisans (more on this later). Female slaves did manual work including cooking, sewing and entertainment. They were required to work for the government as labour service duty (yŏk) and accordingly the labour was not compensated. For a living, male slaves did farming, cultivating the government land allocated to them, lived in independent households and managed their own household economies (Ibid. 1984: 186).

For official slaves, doing labour service for the government without pay meant losing time that could be spent earning an income. They also suffered while doing the service since they were not adequately provided with accommodation and daily meals, as they were expected to take care of themselves. Therefore, many official slaves paid other official slaves to stand in for them or negotiated with officials to pay tribute in lieu of the service.

Chosŏn Dynasty Korea 23

Those who did the service were expectedly inefficient workers, as they lacked motivation. Realizing these problems, the government eventually decided to collect tribute from them instead of mobilizing their labour. Tribute levying then became a heavy burden for official slaves and created the same problems that tax levying did for peasant commoners.

Private slaves were also divided into two types: resident slaves (solgŏ nobi) and outside-resident slaves (oegŏ nobi).

Resident slaves lived within the master's domicile performing miscellaneous tasks/duties and tilled the land adjacent to the master's house. In other words, they had to render labour service throughout the whole year without a break. In some cases, they were engaged in selling the master's farm produce and other commercial activities on his behalf. They were also subject to personal abuses by the masters from which they were not legally protected. Masters could even kill their slaves for their wrongdoings (Kim Sŏkhyŏng 1957: 66–70).

Outside-resident slaves lived separately from their masters in their own houses, cultivating their masters' lands located far away from their houses, sharing the crop with their masters' as tenants and paying personal tribute (sin'gong) annually in cloth or currency. They also provided labour service to their masters as requested. "Compared to the solgŏ nobi," Lee Ki-Baik says, "oegŏ nobi was relatively free" (1984: 188). Some outside-resident slaves refused to pay rent or personal tribute and even threatened to beat up the masters who went to their villages to collect them (Kim Sŏkhyong 1957: 84). Some of them became landowners and slave owners themselves. But they were still under the personal control of their masters.

The institution of slavery came under attack by a number of reformists in the seventeenth century. Their reform attempts were different from those discussed earlier, which were aimed at alleviating the plight of the peasantry. Instead of focusing on specific issues such as high tenancy rates or heavy tax burdens, they criticized the whole slave system as an inhumane institution and urged the government to do something about it. But reform efforts ended with the abolition of official slaves, not private ones.

The foremost critic of the slave system, Yu Hyŏngwŏn, refuted any classical justification of hereditary slavery and put forward a principle of human equality "nowhere to be found in the previous literature" (Palais 1996: 235). He argued,

> At the present time in our country we regard slaves as chattel. Now people are all the same (lit., people are of the same type or category). How could there be a principle by which one person regard another person as his property?
>
> (Quoted in Ibid. 1996: 235)

Yu Hyŏngwŏn urged that the slave system be abolished. But he did not suggest an immediate abolition, a gradual process of substituting hired labour for slave labour. He was hesitant about challenging the long-existing social custom and reluctant to risk the social disruption that would result from immediate abolition (Ibid. 1996: 252–263).

24   Chosŏn Dynasty Korea

Other reformist scholars such as Yi Ik (1681–1763) and Yu Suwŏn (1694–1755) later joined Yu Hyŏngwŏn in condemning hereditary slavery as an inhumane institution. But unlike Yu Hyŏngwŏn, they did not advocate the abolishment of slavery. Instead they more or less accepted that it could not be eliminated and proposed measures aimed at alleviating their sufferings including prohibiting the purchase and sale of slaves, limiting the number of slaves owned by slave masters and prohibiting the re-enslavement of freed or manumitted slaves (Palais 1996: 252–256).

King Yŏngjo (r. 1724–1776) responded by adopting in 1731 the matrilineal succession rule that limited the inheritance of slave status in the case of mixed commoner-slave marriages to the children of slave mothers. The new succession rule replaced the time-old practice of enslaving offspring if either parent was a slave (Ibid. 1996: 234). He then cut the tribute levied from both male and female slaves by half in 1755, and abolished tribute for official slaves attached to the capital bureau, post stations and shamans in 1774. But King Yŏngjo did not (or perhaps could not) go far enough to abolish public slaves, one of his earlier reform objectives, as his officials failed to respond to his wish.

It was King Sunjo (r. 1800–1834) who ordered the abolition of most official slaves, though not private slaves, in 1801. The records of 66,667 slaves attached to the Royal Treasury, palace estates of royal relatives and the capital bureaus of the regular bureaucracy were burned.[6] According to Sunjo's edict, his decision was motivated by the Zhu Xi's teachings that "the king should not distinguish between the noble and base since he is supposed treat his people as his own children." "How," the decree stated, "is it in conformity with the principle of regarding all as brothers (tongp'o) to label [some of the people] male or female slaves (nobi) and divide them up and separate them from the rest of the population." But, "at present," the decree concluded, "the grievances of the slaves reached to the heavens; the wind and rain had been put out of order and the ripening of the corps obstructed – all because slavery had not yet been abolished" (Ibid. 1996: 266–267).

Private slave owners did not share King Sunjo's sentiment expressed in the aforementioned decree and were not prepared to free their slaves under any circumstances. They held on to their logic of justifying slavery – namely, that the noble-base distinction of the people was a natural principle, that the abolition of slavery would result in weakening the long-established social order based on status distinction and that previous kings had upheld it and tried to keep the size of the slave population steady. Many slave owners continued the practice of enslaving commoners by force and through foreclosure of debt. Some commoners voluntarily commended themselves into slavery to powerful families to escape heavy tax burdens. The decision to abolish official slaves was not followed by abolition of private slaves until 1894 (Ibid. 1996: 247).

Women as Victims – The social exclusion of women from the yangban men's world and the restrictive codes of conduct of yangban women imposed by men hardly ever became a major political issue. There were, however, a few occasions for the court to discuss women's problems. In 1497, one local schoolteacher sent a

Chosŏn Dynasty Korea   25

petition to the king, bringing to his attention the "unnecessary hardships imposed upon women by the law of prohibiting them from remarrying." The petition reads,

> Prohibition of the remarriage of widows was intended as a means of enhancing morality, and to uphold honor. But sexual desire is a big human desire, therefore, a man wants to have a wife, a woman a husband. It cannot be suppressed since life originates from it and is an inherent part of human feelings. There is the principle of three followings for women, which prescribes that "a daughter follows her father, a wife (that is, when a daughter marries) follows her husband, and a mother (after her husband dies) follows her son. A woman, however, may become a widow three days after she gets wed or at the age of 20 or 30. Some women may keep their chastity to the end but it often happens that those women who did not have parents or brothers or sons lost it on the road or under the threat by strangers who broke into their houses at night. I therefore beg of you that the widows under age 30 and without sons be allowed to remarry and lead normal lives."
>
> (Quoted in Yi Nŭnghwa 1975: 171)

Recognizing the significance of the petition, the court discussed it in spite of the relatively low status of the petitioner. Officials sympathetic to its argument recommended that those young widows who could not possibly live alone while preserving chastity should be permitted to remarry and that their sons (if they are qualified) not be barred from appointments to any position in the government below the level of eminent post (hyŏnjik), thereby letting wise and able men enter the administration. They also argued that the Great Code of Administration of 1498 should have flexibility in certain situations. Against the humanist view that addressed the vulnerability of women, the conservative idealists were adamant in upholding the traditional Confucian moral standard. The following citation is representative of this opinion:

> In this country, it is of prime importance to teach ritual propriety (*ye*) and uphold morality. Widow remarriage is an evil custom left over from the previous Dynasty. But many yangban families let remarriage happen. Therefore, King Sŏngjong prohibited the recruitment of the offspring of remarried women to high government posts in order to establish proper customs. We cannot possibly go along with the recommendation that we change this beautiful law authored by our king.
>
> (Quoted in Ibid. 1975: 174)

The majority of court officials opted for the continuity of the past, protecting the sanctity of the law.

That a widow should never remarry was an act of fidelity to the man she married or preservation of chastity. Preserving chastity was considered the utmost virtue for women. Women were taught from early on that chastity should be defended at any cost. Some women killed themselves to avoid their bodies being "dirtied"

26   Choson Dynasty Korea

by alien invaders in times of foreign invasion. After wars, they were commended as women of fidelity (yŏllyŏ or chŏlbu). Many women, however, failed to do so and were captured, and most likely raped, by the invaders. Chinese soldiers, especially, made a point of capturing women for whom they would later claim ransom. From the point of view of the Confucian moralist, the mere fact that a married woman, especially one of noble family, was captured by a foreign invader was equivalent to her having lost chastity. Those yangban men who subscribed to this view naturally raised the question of whether they should bring back wives or daughters-in-law lost during the war by paying ransom. In fact, in 1638, one high official, Chang Yu, requested permission from the Ministry of Rites for his only son to divorce his wife who was released from captivity and returned from China. The reason for the request was that a captured woman lost chastity, and he could not possibly have a woman who had lost chastity conduct ancestor ceremonies and bear children. Officials in the Office of the Inspector-General (sahŏnbu) strongly recommended that the request be granted since the husband-wife relationship was the base of human morality, hence a woman who lost chastity should be divorced. But when the court debated Chang's request, one minister, Ch'oe Myŏnggil, took the opposite view and asserted that the request should not be granted. His counter-argument was that there were many yangban women who had been released from captivity and not all the women who got captured necessarily lost their chastity. If he were allowed to divorce his wife, those husbands who were yet unable to find release money would not try to bring their wives back. Then many women would become grieving ghosts in a strange country and thus one man's desire would cause resentment of hundreds of households. Caught between two opposite views, the offices of the Inspector-General and Rites came up with a compromise solution to allow either reunion or divorce of the returned wives according to their husband's wishes. King Injo expressed his preference for reunion as a solution.

The law of prohibiting widows to remarry remained unchanged, and the question of whether to bring back the captured wife or not was left to individual discretion. Ch'oe Myŏnggil, who advocated a change of law in a more humanistic direction, criticized the compromise solution by pointing out that the compromise itself recognized two different laws for the same issue. Ch'oe concluded that it was improper. The two ideas on the fidelity issue – the supremacy of fidelity which needed to be sustained even at the expense of a woman's own life and humanism which took into consideration crises over which the concerned parties did not have much control – survived through the compromise position that the court took. But later, historians disagreed with the advocates of change. In criticizing the argument forwarded by Ch'oe Myŏnggil, the *Veritable Records* of the Injo period (1628–1649) stated:

> A loyal subject does not serve two different masters, and a chaste woman does not take a second husband. That is the very basis of fidelity. This does not mean that we are not aware that some women have been taken captive by the enemy. It only means those who find themselves in such a pitiful situation

Chosŏn Dynasty Korea   27

cannot longer be called chaste, if they remain alive. Those who can no longer be called chaste must cut off all ties with their husband's family. If such a woman rejoins her husband, she will pollute his entire scholar-official household. Ch'oe Myŏnggil miscites precedents from the reigns of earlier kings to argue that we should allow separated husbands and wives to live like a married couple again. That is a big mistake! If we do as he suggests, we will throw into the trash the beautiful customs we have cultivated here in Korea for centuries and make Korea instead no better than a barbarian land.[7]

(Quoted in Pak Yong'ok 1976: 123)

In 1648, it was proposed that sons of captured wives be treated as sons of remarried women. (This section is adapted from Chang (1983)).

In spite of the grand beginning, the Confucianization of the state project was overwhelmed by the Confucianization of the family subsequently initiated by yangban. Ministerial loyalty to the king devoted to the politics based on the people was replaced by loyalty to the king who appointed them. The dominant belief was that a loyal subject did not serve two different kings. In other words, loyalty to the principle of the politics for the people was substituted by the loyalty to a particular person. Furthermore, the goal of politics based on the people or promoting the welfare of the people was largely pushed aside – though not completely forgotten – by the politics of filial piety and family rituals.

There were, however, some kings and reformist scholars and officials who were sympathetic to the underprivileged or victims of the status distinction – peasant commoners, slaves and women – and made humanistic attempts to alleviate their plight. But they were generally not strong enough to prevail over those conservative yangban forces who held on to the view that status distinction was the will of nature, the foundation of the social order, and could not be changed. They strongly objected to reformist claims that they pay taxes like commoners since both of them were equally the children of the king. They argued that if the government insisted that they should pay taxes, the king would eventually lose "the minds" of yangban, and that without their support, his regime might not last too long. Most of the kings were leery of doing away with the principle of status distinction for fear of losing yangban's support. Reformist officials never became the dominant force of the king's court.

It should also be noted that reformists themselves were never ready to directly challenge the status distinction principle, break down the system of status hierarchy and give up their privileges as yangban. Politics based on the people was not meant as the liberation of the underprivileged class from the domination of the yangban class. Even Yu Hyŏngwŏn was hesitant about abolishing the slave system immediately for the fear of undermining the welfare of yangban and disturbing the idea of social order (Palais 1996: 240, 243). Two sirhak scholars, Yi Ik and Chŏng Yag'yong, known as advocates of the politics based on people and as stern critics of the government for constantly failing to provide the means of livelihood to poor peasants, were at the same time strong adherents of the status

28 *Chosŏn Dynasty Korea*

distinction ideology (Pak Chongch'ŏn 2015). Thus, reform attempts had mostly limited results that left status distinction intact.

Consequently, the goal of building a government for the people or reviving the ultimate form of governance exemplified by Ancient China's Three Kingdoms was deluged by untiring efforts of the yangban class to build the family system in accordance with Zhu Xi's family ritual. The Confucianization of the family system prevailed over the Confucianization of the state project. In Confucian politics, the loyalty to the people could not effectively compete against the loyalty to the specific person, the king. The Chosŏn dynasty Korea remained as a person-oriented or personalist society.

The Chosŏn Dynasty as a predominantly hierarchical society

The Confucianization of the family project began as a countermovement against the Confucianization of the state project, which did not recognize the status distinction between yangban and commoners. Ultimately, an anti-egalitarian force represented by the former proved to be more powerful than the egalitarian force represented by the latter. In fact, status distinction became strengthened during the Chosŏn Dynasty period. Chosŏn Dynasty Korea remained a strictly hierarchical or status society.

Status Distinction – As discussed earlier, at the beginning of the Chosŏn Dynasty, there were officially only two status categories of people: "good people" (yangin) and "base people" (ch'ŏnin). The latter consisted exclusively of slaves (nobi).

Good people were legitimate subjects of the king and had the right to government protection for their livelihood and welfare. Adult male "good people" could become officials and bore the obligations of paying land and tributary taxes, as well as providing military and labour services. On the other hand, slaves, as mentioned above, were not legitimate subjects of the king, since they were either enslaved for being criminals or the children of criminals or the children born into slave families. They were not entitled to become officials nor were they liable to fulfill obligations of the king's subjects – namely, to pay taxes and perform military and labour service to the government. Instead, both male and female slaves were obliged to provide labour service or paid personal tributary taxes (sinkong) to their masters, the government or individual owners. The government granted only limited protection to slaves by restricting or prohibiting their individual owners from punishing (or even killing) them at will. Slaves were punished more severely than people of good status or commoners for the same crimes. Commoners who committed violations against slaves were punished less severely than if they had done so against other commoners (Palais 1996: 255). Individual slave owners also had "overwhelming power in commanding or disposing of the slave, the subjugation of the slave and his physical labour to the whim of the master, or the loss of basic humanity attendant upon enslavement" (Ibid. 1996: 212).

This broad status distinction between "good and base people" did not recognize the status prerogatives that the existing elite group (yangban) – the status

Chosŏn Dynasty Korea 29

group differentiated from commoners (yangmin) – was accorded in the previous dynasty, Koryŏ, in recruiting for the central and local government administrations.[8] The Great Code of Administration (Kyŏngguk taejŏn) of 1498 and the Sequel to the Great Code (Sok taejŏn) of 1746 did not recognize yangban as an official category.

As discussed earlier, the yangban of the Koryŏ Dynasty re-established in the Chosŏn Dynasty period their elite status by organizing themselves into exclusive status groups. The yangban thus lifted themselves out of the status category of "good people" (yangmin) and restored the old status distinction of three tiers: yangbans, commoners and slaves.

Occupational Hierarchy – A hierarchy similar to status distinction was also made on the basis of the work people did as an occupation or the labour duty assigned to status (yŏk). The hierarchy of work was based on two different criteria. The first one was derived from the Mencius dictum that society should be divided between the rulers and the ruled. The rulers were those who worked with their minds, whereas the ruled were those who worked with their hands. The basic assumption that underlies this notion was that the former are the men of virtue with superior moral quality to the latter and, hence, those who worked with their minds – namely, government officials and scholars – were distinguished as the rulers from the ruled who worked with their hands: production (agriculture and handicraft industry) and service (commerce) workers. The other criterion, applied to the latter category of people, was the time-old notion of agriculture as the root (bon) and the handicraft industry and commerce as the branch (mal) of the economy. Accordingly, those who were engaged in the root and branch economy were further differentiated into good (yang) and base (ch'ŏn) workers, respectively.

Thus the occupational systems of Chosŏn Korea basically consisted of four basic categories: government officials/scholars (sa), peasants (nong), artisans (kong) and merchants (sang).

i) Government Officials/Scholars (Sadaebu) – High-level government officials, whose job it was to govern people (ch'imin) or help the king to formulate policies, were made into a separate top occupational category, differentiating them from the rest of the government workers – middlemen, functionaries and runners.

Recruitment into the officialdom was done through competitive civil service examinations that tested candidates on their knowledge of Confucian classics. The king then appointed those who passed the examinations to government posts. As such, the government official was an achieved status.

Besides the examination, there was another way into the bureaucracy – namely, "recommendation" (munŭm), the system of directly recruiting sons of high-ranking government officials without resorting to the civil service examinations. The recommendation system enabled a yangban descendant to gain an official position below the seventh rank. As Yi Sŏngmu points out, the examination system was used to recruit talented persons from among the "good people," thereby creating a strong foundation in the bureaucracy, whereas the recommendation system contributed to the maintenance of a status society wherein lineage was the most important factor in entering government service (1980: 406).

30   Chosŏn Dynasty Korea

Upon appointment, these officials received a parcel of land (chikchŏn) and were paid prebends until their retirement. In the case of the three state councilors, prebends were paid even after they retired. Sons of the three state councilors were exempted from military service.

The scholar was strictly an achieved occupational rank. One became a recognized scholar through mastery of Confucian classics and creative writings. Scholarship was a career open to but a few with creative talents who devoted themselves to learning for themselves and for the improvement of the moral quality of society.

ii) Middle Men Strata (Chung'inch'Ŭng)[9] – Within the government bureaucracy, professional/technical workers and clerical workers doing actual administrative work were differentiated from the aforementioned group, forming a separate occupational category (Yi Sŏngmu 1980: 392–395).[10] This stratum consisted of two sub-groups: middlemen (chungin) and yamen attendants (ajŏn). The former referred to those who did the technical or professional work in the central government, including medical personnel (ŭi), translators (yŏk), accountants (sa), weathermen (kwansang), law enforcement officers (yul), relief workers (hyemin) and drawing men (tohwa). The latter were the workers who did actual administrative work, dealing directly with the public in the central and local government, including registrars (noksa), central government clerks (sŏri) and local government clerks (hyangni).

Unlike regular officials, both middlemen and yamen attendants did the office work as labour service duty (yŏk) and were not paid salaries or granted prebends. Their livelihood, therefore, depended upon the collection of fees, gratuities and bribes (Palais 1996: 33). They closely identified themselves with their jobs, which they bequeathed to their descendants, and lived closely to one another in a central district of the capital city, Hansŏng, forming their own community.

iii) Peasants – Peasants constituted the majority of the productive population that worked with their hands. Though one of the goals of the Confucianization of the state project was to give peasants the right to cultivate the land within the boundaries of the kingdom, which was in theory owned by the king, as a means to ensure their stable livelihood, it was unrealistic and never achieved. Land remained private property, and peasants were gradually turned into small holders, part owner-part tenant and landless tenants.

iv) Artisans – With the emphasis on the promotion of agriculture, the government made deliberate efforts not to lose peasants to other sectors. Thus it kept fixed the number of artisans (6,600)[11] and merchánts (unknown) with the monopoly right to conduct their business, prohibiting peasants from abandoning farming. The Great Code of Administration of 1498 specifically stipulated that only so many people were to be licensed as artisans. As a general rule, all artisans with special skills were enrolled on a separate roster as "government artisans" and were attached to various agencies of the central and local governments and the military garrison command.

Artisans either worked at government manufactories producing goods that the government and royal families needed and for various government projects such

Chosŏn Dynasty Korea 31

as constructing walls or as labour service duty for a limited period of time of the year – usually three months. Since they did handicraft work for the government as their status labour duty (yŏk), they did not get paid for their work. They earned their living while they were not doing the status labour duty. Those artisans attached to the central government agencies (kyŏnggongjang) "normally worked for themselves on orders from private clients" (Lee Ki-baek: 1984:186), whereas those attached to local government agencies (oegŏgongjang) would cultivate the land given to them by the government. Artisans were expected to pay taxes on their earnings to the government.

v) Merchants – As with artisans, the government also initially tried to keep the number of merchants fixed. There were three types of merchants: city shop merchants (sijŏn sangin),) itinerant peddlers (haengsang) and capital city river merchants (kyonggang sangin).

City shop merchants ran their businesses in shop spaces in the center of the capital city that they leased from the government. Each shop dealt with a single item. Their main job or duty was to deliver on demands of those items required by the government and royal houses, as well as to supply goods to some private buyers. In addition, they were responsible for selling those government goods left over from tributary goods the government collected annually. Unlike artisans, city shop merchants were engaged in merchandising not as labour duty but as their occupation. As the government granted merchants monopolistic privilege of dealing in designated items, they earned profits from their sales. In return, they were required to do municipal (siyŏk) or national (kukyŏk) duty. It included paying business tax, ch'aekp'yŏn, and miscellaneous labour services. The government levied business tax on each shop on the basis of the number of shop workers. Ch'aekp'yŏn consisted of three elements: the duty to provide those goods demanded by the government, the duty to provide items that were not collected through the tributary goods or royal tribute and the responsibility for welcoming visiting foreign diplomats and for disposing of the goods they brought. Labor services refer to such services rendered for constructing royal tomb, repairing government buildings, wall-papering and others (Pyŏn Kwangsŏk 2001: 70–71).

The itinerant peddlers consisted of pack (posang) and back (pusang) peddlers. They mostly dealt in luxury goods of finer craftsmanship such as brush and Chinese ink, and products of gold, silver and copper, while the latter sold mainly coarser necessities of life such as products of the farm and seas, and wood- and earthenware. River Capital city river merchants carried their merchandise – mainly marine products, grains and clothes – in boats, travelling long distances from one port to another. They mainly brought local products to the capital city to deliver them to the city shop operators.

The government issued certificates to itinerant peddlers and the river merchants to guarantee their monopoly rights to protect their businesses. In return, itinerant peddlers not only paid taxes but also provided the service for the government of disseminating news to local regions. These peddlers even organized themselves into a guild, the Pusangch'ŏng, which was formally sanctioned by the government.

32   Chosŏn Dynasty Korea

vi) Outcasts or the Lowly Born – Though not included in the four major categories of occupations – sa, nong, kong and sang – there was another category of occupation below that of commerce – namely, outcasts (paekchŏng) engaged in base jobs (ch'ŏnŏp). They included butchers, weavers, tanners, entertainers and shamans (both male and female). They formed a separate status group between slaves and commoners; kept their jobs to themselves, either living in an isolated community as in the case of butchers, tanners and weavers; or travelled, as in the case of entertainers and shamans.

Outcasts were not only looked down upon but also kept at a distance from the rest of the society as untouchables. According to the historian Kang Man'gil, they were originally foreigners, mostly nomadic hunters. They either migrated to Korea or came as part of the invading forces and stayed on after the war. Despite government efforts to facilitate adoption of farming, outcasts were apparently unable to adapt to the land-tilling, stable agrarian lifestyle (1984: 307–338).

Thus, in actuality, occupations in the Chosŏn Dynasty were not divided into four categories – government officials and scholars (sa), peasants (nong), artisans (kong) and merchants (sang) – but six categories with middlemen (chungin) and outcasts (ch'ŏnin).

The Relationship between Status and Occupational Hierarchy – How then were the two hierarchies interrelated? More specifically, how did members of each status group earn a living or become wealthy or impoverished? What restrictions were there in earning a living? One's status may restrict the kind of occupation one could have, but in a status-oriented society, one may also be restricted in utilizing his labour and disposing of what he produced. I will discuss what restrictions existed for each status group in earning a living or choosing an occupation and how the social tension created by those restrictions was managed.

Yangban – Yangban largely dominated officialdom and the scholarly world and brought other status groups under their control. Though commoners (p'yŏngmin or sang'in) were not legally barred from sitting the civil service examinations, government officials were largely recruited from among the male members of the yangban status group.[12] Besides, sons of yangban were given special considerations for their family backgrounds. Candidates with eminent ancestors – high government officials or famous scholars – in their family lineage had definite privileges in passing the examination and getting appointments to government posts. But some yangban members, such as nothoi, secondary sons, or sons of those women who remarried, were prohibited from sitting the civil service examination.

The number of government posts that yangban sought was small, slightly less than 2,300 (Yi Sŏngmu 1980: 135). In other words, only a small portion of yangban became bureaucrats with regular income. Most others were so-called book readers (toksŏin) studying Confucian classics either in preparation for the civil service examinations (there was no age limit to write the exam) or simply as scholars who did not pursue bureaucratic careers.

Whatever those non-bureaucrat yangbans did, they generally avoided doing work that did not require the application of knowledge of Confucian classics or

Chosŏn Dynasty Korea 33

productive work that required the use of technical knowledge, manual skill or labour.

What, then, did the majority of yangban families do for a living?

The yangban was basically a non-labouring (working with the mind) class whose livelihood depended on the land and slaves they owned. While old yangban re-established themselves as an elite status group, they also acquired land and slaves to sustain their mode of living. Owning as much land and as many slaves as possible thus became the means of fortifying the basis for the yangban as the ruling class. (For how yangban families acquire land slaves, see Yi Sŏngmu 1980: 342–353).

Middlemen (Chung'in) and Nothoi (sŏ) – At the beginning of the Chosŏn Dynasty period, the distinction between regular officials and technical and clerical personnel was not very clear. Middlemen did not constitute a separate occupational category, but as the former made a deliberate attempt to draw a line between the two, official posts eventually became closed to middlemen. They were consolidated into two separate strata by the mid-Chosŏn period. In other words, even though they were government office workers, middlemen were merely technical or clerical staff called on to assist the officials. Thus middlemen and yamen attendants came to constitute an independent status group, bequeathing their jobs to their descendants.

Middlemen did not have stable sources of income, living on fee gratuities and bribes. They were often accused of abusing their posts by appropriating public funds for personal ends. Local clerks (hyangni), in particular, were known generally for their exploitative practices, even though they were granted a parcel of land for their work – they were the only ones among the middlemen stratum to receive land grants. Local magistrates were officially cautioned to watch out for evil local clerks. Some of them accumulated wealth by engaging in commercial activities by utilizing their technical knowledge. Translators (yŏkkwan) who went to China with government delegations were said to have accumulated personal wealth by trading with locals on the road.

Nothois, or secondary sons of yangban men, were also a part of the middlemen stratum. From the beginning, yangban official scholars who were legitimate sons tried to prevent secondary sons from getting appointed to government posts. The Great Law of Administration of 1498 eventually had a provision of rank limitation (hanp'um-sŏyong), which stipulated that nothois may not be appointed to "eminent posts" (ch'ŏng/hyŏnchik), such as Office of the Inspector-General (Sahŏnbu), the Office of Advising and Monitoring (Saganwon) and the Office of Special Counselling (Hongmunkgwan), and they were barred from writing the higher civil service examinations (munkwa). They were only allowed to sit in for the technical examinations (chapkwa) and be appointed to technical posts supposedly for middlemen, such as document inspectors (komsŏkwan). The intention was to keep secondary sons in the category of middlemen.

Nothois themselves initiated the so-called Sŏŏlhŏtong undong or nothois status enhancement movement to elevate themselves officially to the rank of yangban with limited success. The distinction between secondary and legitimate sons was not formally abolished until the government undertook the Kabo Reform in 1894.

34   *Chosŏn Dynasty Korea*

Commoners – Commoners were not legally barred from becoming government officials. In fact, there is evidence that some commoners became government officials, bypassing the state examinations in the early Chosŏn period, but they were rare cases. Sons of peasants were vastly more disadvantaged in the state examination competition in comparison to their yangban counterparts. Most peasants could not afford to spare any of their sons for the preparation for the examination, which required a long period of study. According to the historian Song Jun-ho, it would take an average 25 to 30 years to prepare for the higher civil service examinations (munkwa) (1975, quoted in Yi Sŏngmu 1980: 59; see also Choe Young-ho 1974). Compared to the private academies established exclusively for the sons of yangban to prepare for the examination, the government schools, elementary schools (sŏdang) and local schools (hyanggyo), which admitted both yangban and commoner children, were not adequately equipped with facilities and teachers to prepare their students for the government examination.[13] Moreover, commoner examination takers were required to submit the record of family register and a letter of reference – requirements that were not applied to the sons of yangban families with ranking officials - within the four previous generations of their ancestors (Yi Sŏngmu 1980: 59–61). In theory, the door to officialdom was open to sons of commoners, but the government, which was dominated by yangban officials, made conditions considerably difficult for them to enter it. In practice, commoners becoming bureaucrats was rather an exception than a norm.

The majority of commoners were peasants. As mentioned earlier, a fixed proportion of commoners at the beginning of the Chosŏn Dynasty period were made into artisans and various kinds of merchants. Peasants were exhorted not to abandon farming. For that purpose, farming as an occupation was ranked higher than the handicraft industry and commerce, and categorized as a "good" occupation, while the latter were deemed "base" ones. However, while urging peasants to stay in farming, the government did little to make farming a stable source of income. It more or less failed to protect the livelihood of peasants by enabling them to keep their own land. Eventually the majority of them became full or partial tenants, tilling a minute parcel – about 0.5 kyŏl[14] – eking out a meagre living (Palais 1996: 359).

While the government had artisans produce artifacts for the use of the royal household and government, and permitted them to earn a living by selling their products to customers and city merchant stores, when they were off duty, it allowed merchants to fully engage in profit-earning activities.[15]

The Chosŏn Dynasty as a predominantly agrarian society

During the Chosŏn Dynasty, as mentioned earlier, agriculture was regarded as the root (bon) or foundation of the kingdom as opposed to the craft industry and commerce, which were regarded as the branch (mal) – that is to say, "if agriculture flourishes then the country prospers; if agriculture declines then the country is on the road to ruin" (Dore 1960: 71). In practical terms, agriculture was both the main means of people's livelihood and the chief source of tax revenue for

Chosŏn Dynasty Korea   35

the state. Accordingly, promoting agriculture and preventing peasants from abandoning the root or farming and chasing the branch (*ch'ukmal sabon*) were major policy concerns of the government from the king at the top down to the local magistrate (Kim Yongsŏp 1984; Pak P'yŏngsik 1999: 47).

Both yangban officials and scholars felt little need to search for alternative means of livelihood and sources of tax revenue. They were landlords whose wealth was based on accumulating farmland and slaves. Some merchants became rich, but they were small in number and did not challenge landlords to replace them as the hegemonic class. Instead of remaining as independent economic forces pursuing further wealth through commerce, they purchased yangban titles to become members of the yangban class. The status ideology and agrarian basism went together well until 1876 when foreign traders, Japanese and Westerners, came to Korea, taking over the economy and threatening national sovereignty.

Let us now review the economic structure of the Chosŏn Dynasty.

Agriculture – The central government set aside the model dry field (chokchŏn), which the king himself sometimes tilled by way of encouraging people to follow. It was also used for experimental purposes to grow new seeds. The queen too occasionally made public appearances sitting at the cotton weaving machine doing the actual weaving.

One of the seven main tasks of the local magistrate stipulated in the *Great Code of Administration of 1498* was promotion of agriculture. What the magistrate accomplished or failed to accomplish in agricultural promotion was one of the criteria for periodic evaluation of his administrative performance. For each township (myŏn), the magistrate selected an agricultural promotion agent (kwŏnnonggwan) from among the local elites and assigned him the task of ensuring that the tillers did the seeding in time, constructed and repaired dams to irrigate rice fields so as not to rely solely on the rain and built and managed silkworm-raising rooms.

The government also adopted policies to 1) to increase the volume of agricultural production through the improvement of farming methods and reclamation of waste lands for cultivation and 2) to compile and distribute books on agriculture for the purpose of teaching peasants about advanced farming methods.

Improvement of farming methods was to be achieved through 1) turning land that needed to be rested every other year into land that could be farmed every year and 2) sharing seeds and farming methods from the agriculturally developed areas with tillers in less developed areas.

Measures for the expansion of the size of farmland included giving tax exemptions to newly reclaimed farmland, awarding non-farmland to government officials as formal compensation in the hope that they would develop it into farmland and voluntary as well as forced migration of tillers, mostly commoners and slaves, from the agriculturally developed southern provinces where farmland was in short supply to the less agriculturally developed northern provinces where unused farmland was available.

As for agricultural education, the government at first distributed books on farming methods authored by Chinese scholars to local governments. Later, however, books compiled by Korean authors that more adequately took into account

36 Chosŏn Dynasty Korea

farming conditions in Korea replaced the ones imported from China. (This section was based on Kim Yongsŏp (1984)).

Agriculture grew, farming techniques developed, and in the seventeenth century, some peasants became what Kim Yongsŏp called the "rich entrepreneurial farmer" (kyŏngyŏnghyŏng bunong) who improved various farming methods to increase productivity and engaged in commercial farming – growing cotton, tobacco, vegetables and others for market with rented land and hired labour (1970). But, as discussed earlier, the majority of the peasant population became small holders or landless sharecroppers, cultivating land leased from absentee landlords and sharing half their annual crop with their landlords. Throughout the dynasty period, they remained impoverished at the subsistence level.

Commerce – While promoting agriculture, the government adopted the policy of suppressing the expansion of the non-agricultural sector or keeping the size of the agricultural population intact by preventing peasants from abandoning the "root" or farming to chase the "branch" or handicraft industry and commerce (*ch'ukmalsabon*) (Pak P'yŏngsik 1999: 47). Commerce was singled out as an activity that had the effect of corrupting the people's sense of morality since the merchant's pursuit of profits inevitably entailed the immoral act of cheating. But this policy was not to work as the government intended.

Soon after the opening of the aforementioned licensed shops and open markets known as hangsi or kyŏngsi in various places in the capital city where its residents purchased everyday necessities, peasants driven out of their villages by frequent natural disasters and heavy tax burdens went to the cities and earned a living as wage labourers or small unlicensed (illegal) traders. Some peasant migrants were actually not pushed out of the villages but pulled into the cities, as they came to realize that trading was more profitable than farming. They sold or leased their farmlands to neighbors and went to the cities to engage fully in commercial activities. The increasing number of peasants living adjacent to the cities took their surplus produce to open markets there to sell directly to buyers rather than selling them to the licensed stores as the law required.

Artisans, yangban, nothois and government functionaries also sold items in markets in addition to their primary occupation/status roles. (For more on this, see Yu Wŏndong 1977: 223–268).

Some slaves and secondary sons apparently became rich merchants.

Government functionaries also sold handicraft artifacts manufactured by those artisans attached to their offices. They did it regularly as a side job (Yu Wŏndong 1977: 268) and usually with the help of high-level officials with whom they shared the profits.

Perhaps, the strongest challenge to licensed merchants came from unlicensed private merchants living in the capital city – the people who did trading for a living. They were of three types, small merchants, big merchants and river merchants, known as the capital city river merchants (kyŏnggang sangin) (Pak P'yŏngsik 2006: 138–153).

The small merchants were engaged in selling daily commodities such as grains, clothes, foodstuffs and firewood. Though illegal, the government did not prohibit

Chosŏn Dynasty Korea   37

them from this practice, as this form of exchange was considered necessary for ordinary people, and those small traders didn't pose any real threat to the business of licensed shop merchants. Some of them grew big and rich and became serious competitors against licensed shop merchants.

There were also big merchants from the beginning. They were seasoned merchants who were either brought in or came on their own to the capital city Hanyang from Kaesong. They matched the licensed merchants in terms of wealth. In the early period, when agriculture was at a subsistence level and the market remained underdeveloped, they were actively involved in tribute contracting (pangnap). They not only did indirect payment but frequently prepared tribute goods before the tribute quota was assigned and got refunded by local magistrates later. Private merchants, however, were not alone in tribute contracting. They usually operated with the backing of the powerful families and the cooperation of the functionaries handling tributary goods. Without collusion with the powerful families, private merchants might not have been able to hold on to the tribute contracting rights too long. The powerful families not only protected the merchants but also put pressure on local magistrates to accept the merchants' indirect payment services. The lowly functionaries' job in this process was to make the local magistrate's office tribute clerks obtain tribute goods from the private merchants by making it difficult for tribute payers to get their tributary goods accepted. More often than not, they refused to accept the tributary goods delivered by the local tributary officers by making all sorts of excuses for not passing them.

As agriculture grew and the market expanded, private merchants came to engage more in commercial trading. They began selling items not carried by licensed city shop merchants. Subsequently, and inevitably, they expanded their business into the domain of licensed shop merchants by doing trading at places right outside of the borders of the capital where the monopoly right of the licensed merchants ended. They bought up the goods local producers and traders brought in and sold them to licensed city merchants or directly to small merchants and buyers. These unlicensed private merchants often went directly to the local producers, peasants as well as handicraftsmen, to buy their products rather than waiting for them or small traders to come to them. Sometimes, they paid the producers in advance to receive their products when actually produced. As their businesses grew in scale, they moved into the cities and opened unlicensed shops like those of licensed merchants and organized themselves into a kind of cooperative called kyebang to form a collective force to effectively compete against licensed merchants. Since these rich private merchants usually waited until the market prices of their goods went up, they reaped handsome profits and kept the general prices of commodities in the cities high.

Capital city river merchants (kyŏnggang sang'in) were relatively unaffected by government interference. They did transportation business on the Han River. Before the enactment of the Uniform Land Tax Law (taedongbŏp) in the early seventeenth century, river merchants were mainly engaged in transporting goods to the capital city from outlying areas. These included tribute goods from local areas to government warehouses in the capital city, grains – mainly rice – sent by

38   *Chosŏn Dynasty Korea*

tenants in the countryside as rent to their landlords living in the capital city and various goods produced in local areas to be sold to the residents of the capital city through the licensed city merchants. But river merchants did more than simply transporting goods. They often poured water over the tribute grains that they were carrying in their boats, thereby making them swell and become heavier, and kept the difference in weight of the grain. They removed a certain amount of grain before loading and sank the boat at the spot where the river was not too deep. When sinking accidents happened, the government would replace the rice recovered from the sinking in exchange for the new rice. Or they simply stole a portion of the tribute rice before loading.

After the tribute tax was converted into a land tax and landlords collected tenancy rent in currency, the river merchants turned to the method widely used by private merchants – namely, controlling the supply of goods to the market by buying them up from the producers or local traders and releasing them when their prices went up – a practice known as togo. With wealth thus accumulated, river merchants established shops at various ports along the riverside. Some extended their businesses to buying used navy ships from the government, repairing and reselling them to private transporters or building new ships for the same purpose (I relied mostly on Kang Man'gil 1973 here).

The government also came under pressure to grant permits to some groups to engage in commercial activities legally.

Those registered handicraftsmen in the capital city were allowed to manufacture artifacts while not on corvee duty and sell them to licensed shops. Once they started selling their products to the shops, they became greedier. They increasingly sold their products directly to buyers in the open markets. Some artisans even set up their own shops. Apparently, many of these shop-owner artisans had informal connections with high-level government officials who protected them from legal sanctions in return for a share of the profits (Yu Wŏndong 1977: 223).

During the Hyojong rein (r. 1649–1659), soldiers attached to various military units in the capital city were also granted the right to sell the artifacts they manufactured to the licensed shops. This measure was taken by the government after the Imjin War (1592–1598) as a way of increasing soldiers' pay because the government was unable to pay them adequately.

One of the most notable developments in commerce was the creation of a new type of merchant tribute middleman called kong'in when the government enacted the Uniform Land Tax Law. This law converted the tribute tax into a land tax and institutionalized tribute contracting by having tribute middlemen supply those goods previously levied as tribute tax. Tribute middlemen purchased tribute goods required by the government in the market, delivered them and charged for what they paid. Thus tribute contracting became a profitable business, and tribute middlemen did it as a regular job. Given the fact that tribute contracting was a countrywide practice, tribute middlemen became a merchant group comparable to licensed city merchants, even though their trading business was only with the government.

These developments, both legal and illegal, outside the domain where licensed city merchants operated inevitably posed a threat to them. The expansion of trade

Chosŏn Dynasty Korea 39

by unlicensed private merchants in particular was a direct challenge to the government policy of suppressing commerce and protecting government-sponsored merchants. The conflict between licensed shop merchants and unlicensed private merchants was inevitable from the beginning. Licensed merchants pleaded with the government to bar unlicensed merchants from invading their business domain, thereby infringing on licensed merchants' monopoly rights. The government responded by granting the licensed merchants the right to capture and interrogate those private merchants who opened shops or sold their merchandise in the city. The government also enacted a law prohibiting private merchants from buying up goods brought by local producers and traders at the border. The government felt oblige to protect the licensed shop merchants since they paid business taxes and rendered labour services which constituted an important source of city government revenue.

But the wisdom of such policy came under criticism in the early eighteenth century by some progressive high officials who defended unlicensed shop merchants' activities (Kim Yŏngho 1968: 46). After much debate, in 1791, the "joint-sales" decree, or Sinhaetonggong, was issued by King Yongjo, legally abolishing the right of licensed shops other than the Six Shops to prohibit unlicensed shops from opening and allowing unlicensed merchants to operate in the capital along the Six Shops (for more on this, see Kim Yŏngho 1968).

i) Changsi, Hyangsi or Changmun – Commercial activities also grew in the countryside. Like periodic markets in the capital city (hangsi or kyŏngsi), periodic markets began to appear in local towns (changsi or hyangsi or changmun) in Chŏlla province from the late fifteenth century onward.

The local periodic market is not a marketplace with shops, but an open space formed at a certain place at a certain time interval by peasants who exchanged with others goods they brought. Initially, it emerged spontaneously when those peasants attacked by severe famine went there to exchange whatever goods they had for grains. Once emerged, it gradually turned into a place where peasants traded their products for other products that other people brought that they did not have, or as Skinner put it, "What the peasant household produced but did not consume was normally sold there, and what it consumed but did not produce was normally bought there" (Skinner 1964: 6). As such, the open market came to be considered as "essential, both as a source of necessary goods and services unavailable in the village community and as an outlet for local production" (Skinner 1964: 6). Then the mere exchange of goods developed into an act of making money and profits – namely, buying a certain item cheaply and selling it at a higher price. As the local periodic market grew, some peasants even gave up farming to take up the commercial pursuit as their full-time occupation. It also drew in those peasants who were driven off from farming because of famine or who ran away from their villages to avoid paying heavy taxes.

Given the government policy of promoting agriculture and suppressing commerce, the development of local periodic markets naturally became a cause for concern of Confucian politicians and scholars. Unlike the licensed shop system in the cities, debates on the merits of the local periodic market took place as early

40   *Chosŏn Dynasty Korea*

as the fifteenth century during the Sŏngjong (r. 1469–1495) period and continued until the Myŏngjong (r. 1545–1567) period. Those officials who were concerned with the growth of local periodic markets argued that with the emergence of this type of market, peasants were increasingly leaving villages in order to engage in commercial activities in pursuit of profits instead of concentrating on farming; consequently, farmland remained wasted, and commercial activities undermined moral education (kyohwa) by making people cunning. They also pointed out that some peasants became bandits, making a living by selling stolen goods at the markets, implying that the markets promoted banditry. In order to protect farming from decline and to root out banditry, closing down local periodic markets, they reasoned, would be the only solution (Kim Taegil 2000: 15–16).

This moralistic anti-hyangsi argument was rebuffed by pragmatic hyangsi-defenders. They responded to the criticism of the local periodic market by pointing to the fact that it had the positive function of serving as a relief mechanism during years of poor harvest and had become so much a part of the daily life of the people that they came to rely on it to acquire goods they needed but did not have through exchange for ones they had (*yumusantong*).

When urged by the critics of hyangsi to shut them down, King Chungjong (r. 1506–1544) refused to do so, making points similar to the ones made by the defenders. He argued that the changsi was now so closely linked with commoners' livelihood that he was afraid that if periodic markets were banned, impoverished people might not find ways to survive and would worry and grieve (Ibid. 2000: 18–19).

It was not just the impoverished peasants who came to rely upon the local periodic market. District magistrate offices needed it to sell what their offices produced, such as salt, for the purpose of generating funds for military supplies including food, weapons and others.

Some rich landowners or landlords had their slave servants sell their surplus agricultural products, mainly rice, at the market to increase their monetary wealth.

Like their city counterparts, local handicraftsmen came to rely on the changsi to sell their artifacts and earn a living.

The government, therefore, decided to officially recognize changsi and let the magistrate's office collect taxes from those who traded there. This tax became an important source of the magistrate's office revenue. By the mid-sixteenth-century, local periodic markets had spread throughout the country, reaching about a thousand in number and remaining thereabout until the end of the Chosŏn Dynasty.

Initially, the periodic market opened twice a month or every 15 days. The growth of the market also saw an increase in its frequency to six times a month in the eighteenth century (Kim Taegil 2000: 45).

The growth of changsi also led to the development of special periodic markets dealing with unique local products such as the Ansong rice market and the Taegu herbal medicine material market.

Inevitably, then, shops began to appear in the open market places doing business every day, especially in port towns, making local town markets no longer of a periodic nature and people specializing in the business of brokerage, consignment

Chosŏn Dynasty Korea 41

selling, moneylending and lodging appeared. They were called kaekchu and yŏgaek.

However, there were other types of private merchants whose trading bases were outside of the capital city. They were like itinerant peddlers but their mode of trading was quite different in that they became more like the private merchants in the capital city. They competed against the licensed capital city shop merchants by controlling the supply of goods to the capital city. They either bought up the goods by itinerant peddlers or local producers right outside of the city borders or established a base in local towns or markets in order to buy directly from the producers – peasants or artisans – and then sold the goods thus acquired to the private city merchants. Some of them became rich, acquiring labels associated with the cities in which they were based: Songsang or Kaesong sangin (Kaesong merchants), Mansang or Ŭiju sangin (Ŭiju merchants), or Puksang or Pyŏngyang sangin (Pyongyang merchants).

Songsang or Kaesong sangin (Kaesong merchants), in particular, deserve further mention. Kaesong merchants distinguished themselves from other private merchants with their unusual relation with the government and unique business prowess. Kaesong was the capital of the previous dynasty, Koryŏ, and when Koryŏ fell, its government officials refused to be loyal to the king of the newly established Chosŏn Dynasty and to serve in his court. Following suit, many of those who were qualified to be government officials willingly chose the profession of merchants. In other words, the Kaesong merchants were more educated and intelligent, and therefore capable, than merchants elsewhere. Indeed, they grew to be big merchants. They established branch offices (songbang) of sorts in various towns in an effort to create a nationwide network to dominate local markets and to buy up local products from the producers or small traders directly. In other areas, they formed alliances with big merchants such as Ŭiju and Tongnae merchants. They developed their own accounting method (Kaesong puki). As will be discussed further next, they were also actively engaged in foreign trade. Kaesong merchants thus amassed sizable wealth.

Development of local periodic markets also affected licensed itinerant peddlers (haengsang or pobusang). Prior to the appearance and growth of changsi, itinerant peddlers went to rural villages to sell their merchandise directly to buyers – yangban aristocrats or peasants commoners. But when changsi opened they went to marketplaces to sell their merchandise instead of selling in the villages. Since changsi in a certain region opened on different days, they were able to trade every day by going to different changsi. By doing so, they not only connected one changsi to next, but also moved products from one area to the next. Unlike the licensed city shop merchants, itinerant peddlers were never given the monopoly right to deal with their merchandise or to prevent unlicensed peddlers from selling the same items that they were selling. Licensed peddlers differentiated themselves from unlicensed ones by organizing themselves into a guild-like organization and establishing the strict mode of social and business conduct. They also established close ties with the government by rendering various kinds of services. As will be discussed further, the licensed peddlers' organization played a significant role as

42   *Chosŏn Dynasty Korea*

political thugs in helping the government to suppress its critics. There is some evidence that some of these licensed peddlers grew into rich merchants.

Thus the expansion of commerce in various forms was inevitable and even some politicians and scholars realized that commercial activities had become part of the daily lives of both yangban and ordinary people, and that the idea and policy of promoting the root or agriculture and suppressing the branch or commerce and handicraft industry (ŏkmalmubon) was an unrealistic goal. Some Confucian thinkers and politicians began to entertain the idea of supplementing the "root" with the "branch" *pomakmubon* (Pak P'yongshik 1999). One sirhak scholar urged the government to promote commerce and went as far to say that yangban should take up commerce as a legitimate occupation (Kim Sŏnhi 2015: 129–130).

ii) International Trade – During the Chosŏn period (1392–1910), foreign trade was mainly limited to China and Japan, conducted in restricted forms, and strictly controlled by the government. Trade with China was largely carried out by diplomats from both sides. The Korean delegates did two forms of trade: official and unofficial. Officially, they were requested to purchase various items in China that the government needed. Unofficially, to supplement their funds and cover the expenses to be incurred during their stay in China, Korean delegates exchanged the goods they brought from Korea for other Chinese goods or money in the markets that the Ch'ing government established especially for them in several cities along the way to Beijing. The Chinese delegates also brought goods when they came to Korea for official visits for similar reasons. The Korean government usually purchased them for its own use or for the use by royal houses. When they were unable to afford the entire amount of goods that the Chinese delegates brought, licensed city merchants and unlicensed private merchants were asked to take over the remaining goods. Demand for such goods, which were usually high-quality and luxury items, was high, and market prices for them were much higher than purchase prices, yielding handsome profits (Kang Man'gil 1973: 113–114). Given the profit margins, those private merchants, especially Kaesong merchants, became more actively engaged in international trade. Instead of waiting for Chinese envoys to come, they informally or unofficially joined the delegations to China by bribing government officials and traded their goods on the way to Beijing. They, then, went a step further and went to China themselves, secretly and illegally, to trade with Chinese merchants, or they sent private merchants to Uiju, the city near the Korea-China border, to bring Chinese goods back (Ibid. 1973: 115). The main items they dealt with were ginseng, textiles, paper and leather goods. As their businesses grew, Kaesong merchants cultivated and processed ginseng into merchandise by themselves (Ibid. 1973:123–132).

Korea's trade with Japan, mainly Tsushima, took a different form. Officially, it was conducted at two levels: between governments and between private merchants at the Japanese living quarters called Oegwan (Japan House) established in select ports – Yŏmpo in Ulsan, Naeipo in Ungch'ŏn and Pusanp'o in Tongnae.[16]

At the government level, Japanese delegates met with Korean counterparts at the Japan House in one of the three ports and exchanged the goods they brought including copper, tin and sulphur, silver, medicines and spices with goods from the Korean side such as rice, cotton, hemp and ramie cloth, mother-of-pearl inlay, porcelain ware, floral design mats, the Buddhist Tripitaka, Confucian writings, histories, temple bells and Buddhist images (Lee Ki-baik 1984: 192).

Korean private merchants licensed by the government also met with Japanese counterparts at various Oekwan on designated days – five times a month – and traded similar items dealt with by the government. They were legally prohibited to trade with Japanese merchants elsewhere, and the number of goods they could trade was strictly limited.

Initially, the trade with Japan was largely carried out by the government with private merchants playing a minor role. However, later in the eighteenth century, private merchants, especially Tongnae and Kaesong ones who dominated the domestic market, became major traders. Apparently, there were a large number of unlicensed private merchants doing trading with the Japanese merchants secretly.

Certainly, international trade was a profitable business. But there is no evidence that both government officials and scholars seriously extended the idea of supplementing the "root" – agriculture – with the "branch" – commerce (*pomalmubon*) to international trade.

Handicraft Industry – The handicraft industry also went through a significant, but different, process of transformation. While collecting a variety of local products directly from producers in the form of a tribute tax and purchasing other items through licensed city merchants, the government also set up their own factories to manufacture a spate of handicraft objects.

The central government established some 30 workshops attached to 30 government bureaus to produce items such as weapons, cloths and mattresses for government use and the royal families' consumption. The government also established other manufactories unattached to particular bureaus, such as Punwŏn, the manufactory of ceramic goods.

Until the beginning of the sixteenth century, the state-run (public) handicraft industry was the predominant form of industry, while the private handicraft industry played an insignificant role, as the economy was largely agricultural and self-sufficient. The market for industrial artifacts was small since the majority of the population was composed of self-sufficient peasants.

Like those who did labour service duty, those artisans – commoners and public slaves – in the state-run industry suffered various forms of hardship. Although some were paid compensation, provided with two meals a day and even granted official ranks, the majority of them were not paid for their work, not fed, and not provided living accommodations. This service was particularly hard for those handicraftsmen who lived far from the capital city since they had to bring their own grains to feed themselves when they were called upon for duty. It was estimated that the grain they brought would last only about two months. Since they were required to perform the service for six months, they somehow had to find a way to survive after their grain ran out. Besides, government officials frequently required them to produce various artifacts for their private use.

Consequently, the flight of artisans from the workshops became a common phenomenon. The government tried constantly to find substitutes to fill the gaps left

44   Choson Dynasty Korea

by the runaways. Many entrepreneurial artisans chose to pay tribute with the artifacts they produced rather than doing the labour service. In fact, the government became more interested in collecting tribute of this kind, as it was always short of revenue. The government came to buy goods more and more from private artisans instead of manufacturing them by itself with corvee labour. Accordingly, the handicraft industry under the auspice of the government was sharply reduced, while the private counterpart grew. The growth of the private handicrafts industry gave rise to the birth of chŏmch'on, the village where handicraftsmen with similar skills lived together, built a joint workshop and manufactured special goods such as brassware, ceramics, ironware, silverware and copperware for the local markets.

The rise of the private handicrafts industry and chŏmch'on was followed by an increase in the household handicraft industry – that is, the growing number of peasant households engaging in producing various industrial goods, including cotton cloths, etc., to sell in the markets. Peasants tended to focus on producing industrial goods out of the ingredients that were abundantly available in the regions in which they lived. Thus various towns came to be identified with the handicrafts artifacts those peasant households produced.

Urban merchants saw an opportunity to make money by sponsoring peasant households to produce industrial goods. At first, they went to local areas to purchase those goods from peasant producers. Later, they made an arrangement of prepaying peasant households to produce certain goods for them. This practice was called sŏndae. (This section was largely based on Hong Hwayu (1989: 170–314).

Mining Industry – Like commerce and the handicraft industry, the mining industry at the beginning of the Chosŏn period was strictly controlled by the government. The government did not allow private individuals to own any mines, as it was worried about losing peasants to mining. Government mining operations were limited largely to extracting iron, sulfur and a few minerals – namely, gold, silver and copper. The government mining policy was to open mines in the districts where veins of ore (kwnagmaek) were found and to mobilize adult males in that district to mine them.

As happened with corvee labour used in other areas, labour required for mining posed hardship for the peasants. They were not paid for their labour. Furthermore, they were required to bring mining equipment with them. The work itself was also hard. When they worked in the cold river in the early spring and late autumn, they suffered from frostbite. Even though the government mobilized corvee labour during the slack seasons of spring and early autumn in an effort to avoid the planting and harvest periods, the government often failed to send workers home in time to keep up with the farming cycle.

Given these problems, district magistrate offices were reluctant to report to the central government when potential mines or veins of ore were discovered in their district. They even threatened anybody who intended to report it to the central government. The central government responded by issuing laws to punish those officials who failed to report and rewarded those who did with prizes, exemptions from other service including corvee labour duty (yoyŏk), and other rewards. This measure was only a partial solution and unable to save the industry.

Chosŏn Dynasty Korea 45

This method of operating mines also proved to be ineffective because, as was the case with the handicraft industry, many evaded doing this duty through various means, and many others fled the mines after they arrived, and the level of motivation of those who stayed and performed the duty was low.

The government was almost inevitably led to allowing private mining and collecting taxes from private mine owners. In the mid-seventeenth century, the government introduced the so-called boss (pyŏlchang) system to promote the mining industry. Under this system, the boss – a person usually selected from those who had informal or personal connections with the government, high-ranking government officers or influential families – was commissioned by the Ministry of Tax to run a government mine with a group of civilian miners. The boss assembled the group of no more than ten miners and collected a head tax from each one of them on behalf of the government. The boss kept two-thirds of what they unearthed, leaving the rest to be divided among the miners.

However, the new system turned out to be equally ineffective. While the number of mines increased, government revenue from mine taxes did not because of privatization of the mining output by bosses. Moreover, the boss system was sabotaged by the tripartite alliance of rich merchants, district magistrates and miners in the form of secret mining. Rich merchants secretly opened and operated mines, usually gold and silver, with wandering labourers, mostly those peasants driven off the farm by the high rental rate and tax burden. Thus rich merchants replaced the government as the financier (mulchu), and the boss became the mine operator and mine tax collector. But the financier had to have protection to continue with secret mining since it could not continue for any length of time without being detected by district or township offices. Thus the merchant financier negotiated with the district magistrate for approval of the secret mining for which he paid tax to his office.

While collecting the informal tax for secret mining, the district magistrate urged the central government to legalize the financier (mulchu) system of mining. In 1755, Chŏngjo (r. 1776–1800) agreed to do so despite his dislike of private mining. With the legalization of the financier system, the government-controlled mining system was completely privatized with merchant capital and free labour. The government now only levied mining tax without getting directly involved in mining. The financier (mulchu) system prospered; more and more peasants in the towns near mines abandoned farming to become miners. The mining industry not only grew but also became differentiated. The financier (mulchu) delegated the actual operation of mining to tŏkdae, or professional miners, who were more knowledgeable. Mining towns emerged with the growth of the privatized mining industry. (This section was largely based on Yu Sŭngju (1993)).

This review of changes in agriculture, commerce, handicraft and mining industries indicates that the Chosŏn Dynasty's economy clearly did not remain stagnant as some historians, especially those Japanese historians who supported the colonial policy, have claimed.

At the same time, it is difficult to say that these changes signify the "sprout of capitalism," or the beginning of the development of capitalist economy as many

46   *Chosŏn Dynasty Korea*

nationalist Koreans historians insist. The change might be in the direction of capitalism, but it is hard to be regarded as the beginning of capitalism.

In terms of scale, the growth of the non-agricultural sector, as indicated earlier, was minimal. Some economic historians spoke of the growth of commercial capital. But, as Palais points out, those rich merchants spent their wealth to purchase yangban titles and to live like yangban instead of reinvesting in their businesses to make more money (1996).

More importantly, the economic system of the Chosŏn Dynasty lacked two major requirements to make an industrial breakthrough – namely, technological development and the social values embodied in the capitalist economy, unlimited accumulation of wealth and maximization of efficiency, or what Weber termed the "spirit of capitalism."

The rise of capitalism entails more than changes in economic institutions. Capitalism refers to technological changes and "new social values called for a maximization of rationality, and prescribed unlimited gain as an end of economic behavior" (Birnbaum 1953: 127–129). David Landes defines industrial revolution primarily in terms of technological innovation which, "by substituting machines for human skills and inanimate power for human and animal force, brings about a shift from handicraft to manufacture and so doing, gives birth to a modern economy" (1969: 1).

Technological development or innovation during the Chosŏn Dynasty period was not considered by Confucian scholars as a part of civilization. Their primary concern was moral education with limited attention paid to the increase of agricultural production and productivity. Emphasis in the Confucian educational system was almost exclusively on learning Confucian classics. Matters concerning industrial technology and innovation were left to the two specific status groups: middlemen (chungin) and artisans. The relative lack of concern with invention and innovation was also related to the absence of the propensity to learn or import advanced technologies from foreign countries. Superior military technology, especially the development of firearms, which they learned from the West, partly explains the easy victory of Japan's invading army over the Korean Army, equipped with far less advanced arms during the Imjin War (1592–1598). In his book Pukhak'ui (*Treatise on Learning from the North* (Ch'ing China)), written after his visit to Ch'ing China in 1778, Pak Chiwŏn, the sirhak (practical learning) scholar, brutally criticized Koreans for looking down upon Ch'ing China as a barbarian kingdom and refusing to learn anything from her. Upon his visit, he realized that there were so many things, including wheels, bricks and others, from Ch'ing China that Korea could and should learn to use, but refused to do so.

Acquisition of unlimited gain through the most efficient or rational way was an idea very foreign to Confucian scholars/officials. Commerce was largely released from government control by the end of the eighteenth century. However, profit seeking still remained a desired goal of merchants who were looked down upon by the yangban aristocrats whose wealth was measured in terms of the size of land they owned and the amount of annual crop (or rice) they yielded from it. Any attempt to maximize individual wealth was regarded an act unfit to their social

Chosŏn Dynasty Korea 47

standing. Most yangbans remained poor, but refused to engage in the handicraft industry and commercial activities. Their first concern was to maintain yangban's dignity, to retain the yangban way of life and to read Confucian classics. Pursuing profit and searching for the most effective way of accumulating wealth was beneath their dignity. It is understandable that Korea fought vigorously against those foreigners who came ashore demanding trade relations with them. Doing trade with uncivilized barbarians was unthinkable to Confucian fundamentalists.

Capitalist development was not about to occur before Korea was forced by alien forces to open its ports to foreign traders. But there were changes nevertheless in the pre-Kaehwa period. If indeed the Chosŏn Dynasty economy did not remain stagnant, what does that signify? We can at least infer three implications.

First, it demonstrates that agriculture was a poor economic foundation for the kingdom. In essence, as Malthus pointed out a long time ago, given the basic limit to the expansion of agricultural land, it cannot adequately meet the demand of the ever-increasing size of the population. Furthermore, as long as agricultural land remains as the main source of personal wealth, the uneven distribution of wealth was unavoidable, resulting in the concentration of land in a small number of mostly yangban aristocrat landlords and the majority of peasants becoming landless sharecroppers and small holders. Agriculture failed to guarantee a steady means of support (hangsan) for the majority of peasants. They were continuously impoverished, left teetering at the subsistence level. The government, controlled by yangban aristocrats who were themselves landlords, did not or could not fathom the modern idea of returning the land to the tillers or sharing their wealth with them.

Second, the government policy to suppress the expansion of commerce was doomed to failure from the start. Commerce served to some extent as an exit for those peasants driven off farmland. However, more importantly, trading produces profit. Merchants were said to earn more in a month than what peasants did in a year. Though merchants were ranked lower than peasants socially, they were more likely to escape poverty and become rich. Private merchants rose. The early thinking of "suppress commerce, promote farming" gave way to the new thinking of "supplement farming with commerce."

Third, hired labour replaced labour mobilized without compensation as it proved to be inefficient. Accordingly, government-run industry was largely replaced by private industry and hired labour substituted corvee labour.

These changes, as mentioned earlier, cannot be taken as the sprout of capitalism, but they also cannot be dismissed as historical non-events. The changes were clearly in the direction of the capitalist economy. Thus they made the transition to capitalism easy when it became inevitable after the port opening in 1876.

Notes

1 Early Chosŏn Dynasty *Veritable Records* indicate that some commoners wrote and passed the examination, thereby becoming government officials (Choe Young-ho 1974: 611–631).

48 *Chosŏn Dynasty Korea*

2 Thus the contemporary Confucian scholar Kum Chang-tae characterizes a "true minister" in Chosŏn Dynasty Korea as "the one who did his best in assisting the king to promote the welfare of the people. When the king failed to take care of the people properly, it was the duty of the minister to remind him of the misrule. If the king did not listen and refused to follow his repeated remonstrations he should leave the court without any hesitation" (2000: 53).

3 I am indebted to Donald Baker for this point.

4 This does not mean that tongjokchon did not exist before the Chosŏn Dynasty period. Mention of *tongjokchon* is made in the *History of Three Kingdoms* (*Samguk sagi*) and elsewhere. But for the reasons mentioned earlier, the tendency for *yangban* elites to form *tongjokchon* became intensified in the Chosŏn Dynasty. According to Zenshō Eisuke (1933–35), who conducted numerous surveys on various aspects of the Korean social structure as the special adviser to the Japanese government-general of Korea, there were 15,000 *tongjokch'on* in 1930, accounting for one-third of the total number of hamlets.

5 The three taxes were regarded by the officials as the main cause of peasant rebellions in the late nineteenth century. Much has been written on the "three tax administrations in disarray" or *Samjŏng mullan*.

6 For reasons not given, those records of the Ministries of Works and War and offices of provincial governors and district magistrates, and the nationwide post-stations were not abolished.

7 This quote was translated by Donald Baker.

8 Recruitment was, in theory, based solely on merit – that is, passing the civil service examination. Any man, regardless of his status ascribed or achieved in the Koryo period, was allowed to write the examination. Early Chosŏn Dynasty Veritable Records indicate that some commoners wrote and passed the examination, thereby becoming government officials (Choe Young-ho 1974: 611–631).

9 Middle men strata is the concept coined by the contemporary historian Yi Sŏngmu (1981: 392–395).

10 There were two other categories of workers below the middlemen stratum, including workers of chapchik and ch'ŏngchik. These categories included messengers, guards, keepers of grazing lands and ferrymen, as well as tomb, forest and shrine guards. They did not, however, form independent occupational groups or strata like high officials or middlemen.

11 Twenty-eight hundred in 130 categories were employed in the capital, and 3,800 in 27 categories in the provinces.

12 Women were never even considered as candidates for government posts as their domain was confined to the domicile.

13 Yangban parents avoided sending their sons to these schools.

14 Kyŏl is a constant measure of crop yield produced by an area that varied from 2.2 to 9.0 acres depending on the fertility of the land.

15 I have already discussed how slaves fared in the world of work and status hierarchy.

16 Japanese merchants were allowed to establish residency in the three ports. The number of Japanese residents there was large enough to organize a rebellion in 1510 against the local administrations with the military support from the lord of Tsushima, protesting the mistreatment they received from them.

References

Baker, Donald (1997) "Chŏng Yagyong: 'The Roots of Royal Authority'," pp. 26–27, in Ch'oe, Young-h, Lee, Peter and de Bary, Wm. Theodore (eds.) *Sources of Korean Tradition, Volume 2: From the Sixteenth to the Twentieth Centuries*, New York: Columbia University Press.

Birnbaum, Norman (1953) "Conflicting Interpretations of the Rise of Capitalism: Marx and Weber." *British Journal of Sociology*, vol. 4, no. 2 (June), pp. 125–141.

Chosŏn Dynasty Korea 49

Chang, Yun-Shik (1983) "Women in a Confucian Society: The Case of Chosŏn Dynasty Korea (1392–1910)," pp. 67–96, in Yu, Eui-Young and Phillips, Earl (eds.) *Traditional Thoughts and Practices in Korea*, Los Angeles: Center for Korean-American and Korean Studies, California State University.

Choe, Young-ho (1974) "Commoners in Early Yi Dynasty Civil Examinations: An Aspect of Korean Social Structure, 1392–1600." *Journal of Asian Studies*, vol. 33. no. 4 (August), pp. 611–631.

Chŏng, Manjo (1977) "Chosŏn hugi'ŭi yangyŏk pyŏntongnon non'ui e taehan kŏmto: kyunyŏkbŏp sŏngnipŭi paekyŏng" (A Study of the Debate over Reform of the Common Service System in Late Chosŏn: Background to the Establishment of the Equal Service System). *Tongdae nonch'ong*, (April), pp. 15–29.

Chung, Chaisik (1995) *A Korean Confucian Encounter With the Modern World: Yi Hang-No and the West*, Berkeley: Institute of East Asian Studies, University of California, Center for Korean Studies.

Deuchler, Martina (1992) *The Confucian Transformation of Korea: A Study of Society and Ideology*, Cambridge, MA and London: Published by the Council on East Asian Studies, Harvard University and distributed by Harvard University Press.

Dore, Ronald P. (1960) "Agricultural Improvement in Japan, 1870–1900." *Economic Development and Cultural Change*, vol. 9, no. 1 (Part 2), pp. 69–91.

Eberhard, Wolfram (1957) "The Political Function of Astronomers in Han China," pp. 33–70, in Fairbank, John K. (ed.) *Chinese Thought and Institutions*, Chicago: The University of Chicago Press.

Han, Ugŭn (1974) "Kŭnse yugyo chŏngch'i ŭi sŏngkyŏk" (The Characteristics of Confucian Politics in the Chosŏn Period), pp. 1–33, in Liberal Arts College (ed.) *Mullidae kyoyang kangjwa* (The Liberal Arts College Lecture Series), Seoul: Liberal Arts College, Seoul National University.

Han, Ugŭn (1993) *Yugyo chŏngch'i wa pulkyo* (Confucian Politics vs. Buddhism), Seoul: Ilchogak.

Han, Yŏng'u (1999) *Wangjo ŭi sŏlgyeja Chŏng Tojŏn* (The Dynasty Designer Chong Tojon), Seoul: Chisik sanŏpsa.

Hong, Hwayu (1989) *Chosŏn Chungse sugongŏpsa yŏn'gu* (A Study of Handicraft Industry in the Middle Period Korea), Seoul: Chiyangsa.

Janelli, Roger L. and Janelli, Dawnhee Yim (1982) *Ancestor worship and Korean Society*, Stanford: Stanford University Press.

Kang, Man'gil (1984) *Chosŏn sidae sanggong'ŏpsa yŏn'gu* (A Study of the History of Commerce and Handicraft Industry of the Choson Period), Seoul: Han'gilsa.

Kang Man'gil (1973) *Chosŏn hugi sangŏp chabon ŭi paltal (The Development of Commercial Capital in the Late Choson Period)*, Seoul: Koryo taehakkyo ch'ulp'anbu.

Kim, Chunsŏk (2001) "Kim Yuk ŭi anmin kyŏngjeron kwa taedongbŏp" (Kim Yuk's Theory of the Economy for the People and the Great Equality Law). *Minchok munhwa* (National Culture), vol. 24, pp. 3–54.

Kim, Sŏkhyŏng (1957) *Chosŏn bonggŏn sidae nongmin ŭi kyegup kusŏng* (The Class Composition of the Peasant Population during the Chosŏn Feudal Period), Pyŏongyang: Kwahakwon ch'ulp'ansa.

Kim Sŏnhi (2015) "Kanan, pyŏng, chŭkum" (Poverty, Sickness and Death), pp. 110–154, Pak, Chongch'ŏn (ed.) *Chosŏn hugi sajok kwa yegyo chilsŏ* (The Gentry Class and the Ritual Social Order of Late Choson), Seoul: Somyŏng chu'lp'an.

Kim, Taegill (2000) *Sijang'ŭl yŏlji mot'hage hara* (Do Not Let Market Open), Seoul: Karam Kihoek.

50   Chosŏn Dynasty Korea

Kim, Yŏngho (1968) "Choson hugi e issŏsŏŭi tosisangŏp ŭi chŏn'gae" (New Development of Urban Commerce in the Late Chosŏn Period). *Han'guksa yon'gu* (The Study of Korean History), vol. 2, pp. 213–240.

Kim, Yongsŏp (1984) "Chosŏn ch'ogi ŭi kwŏnnong chŏngch'aek" (The Ploicy of Agricultural Promotion in the Early Chosŏn Period). *Tongbang hakchi*. (East-Asia Review) no. 42 (June), pp. 97–131.

Kim Yongsŏp (1970) *Chosŏn hugi nongŏpsa yon'gu: Nongch'on kyŏngje, sahoe pyŏndong* (Studies in the Agricultural History of Late Chŏson: The Village Economy and Social Change), Seoul Ilchogak.

Kim, Yun'gon (1971) "Taedongbŏp ŭi sihaeng ŭl tullŏssan ch'anban yangnon kwa kŭ paegyŏng" (The Pro and Con Debates Surrounding the Enactment of the Uniform Land Tax Law). *Taedongmunhwa yŏngu* (The Study of Pan-Asia), vol. 8, pp. 131–161.

Kŭm, Changt'ae (2000) Ŭ *Han'guk ŭi sŏnbi was sŏnbi chŏngsin* (Gentry and Gentry Spirit in Korea), Seoul, Seoul taehakkyo ch'ulp'anbu.

Landes, David (1969) *Unbound Prometheus*, Cambridge, MA: Harvard University Press.

Lee, Ki-baik (1984) *A New History of Korea*, Translated by Edward W. Wagner with Edward J. Shultz, Seoul: Ilchogak.

Pak, Chongch'ŏn (2015) *Chosŏn sidae yegyo munhwa ŭi kujo wa pyŏnhwa* (The Structure and Change of the Ritual Culture of the Chosŏn Period) (A Lecture delivered at the University of British Columbia 2015).

Pak, P'yŏngsik (1999) *Chosŏn chŏn'gi sangŏpsa yŏn'gu* (A Study of the History of Commerce in the Early Chŏsŏn Period), Seoul: Chisik sanŏpsa.

Pak, Siyŏng (1961) *Chosŏn t'oji chedosa* (Chung) (The History of Land System in Choson, (Middle)), P'yongyang: Kwahagwon ch'ulpansa.

Pak, Yong'ŏk (1976) *Yijo Chosŏn yŏsŏngsa* (The History of Women of the Yi Dynasty), Seoul: Han'guk Ilbosa.

Palais, James B. (1996) *Confucian Statecraft and Korean Institutions: Yu Hyŏngwŏn and the Late Choson Dynasty*, Seattle: University of Washington Press.

Palais, James B. (1975) *Politics and Policy in Traditional Korea*, Seattle: University of Washington Press.

Pyŏn, Kwangsŏk (2001) *Chosŏn hugi sijŏn sangin yŏn'gu* (A Study of Licensed Merchants in the Later Chosŏn Period), Seoul: Hyean.

Skinner, G. William (1964) "Marketing and Social Structure in Rural China." *Journal of Asian Studies*, vol. 24, no. 1 (November), pp. 3–41.

Takawa, Kōzō (1964) *Richō kōnōsei no kenkyū* (A Study of the Tribute System of the Yi Dynasty), Tokyo: Tōyō Bunkō.

Tu, Weiming (1989) *Confucianism in a Historical Perspective*, Singapore: Institute of East Asian Philosophies.

Yi, Hwang (1977) *Yi Hwang, Han'guk ŭi sasang taejŏnjip* (The Great Collection of Books on Ideology in Chosŏn Korea) Vol. 10, Seoul: Tonghwachulpansa.

Yi, Nŭnghwa (1975) *Chosŏn yŏsŏnggo* (A Study of Korean Women), Translated by Kim Sanghŏn, Seoul: Daeyangsŏjŏk.

Yi, Sŏngmu (1980) *Chosŏn ch'ogi yangban yŏn'gu* (A Study of the Yangban in the Early Choson Period), Seoul: Inchogak.

Yu, Sŭngju (1993) *Chosŏn sidae kwang'ŏpsa yŏn'gu* (A Study on the History of Mining Industry in the Chosŏn Period), Seoul: Koryŏ taehakkyo ch'ulp'anbu.

Yu, Wŏndong (1977) *Han'guk kundae kyŏngjesa yŏngu* (A Study of the Modern Korean History), Seoul: Inchisa.

Zenshō, Eisuke (1933–1935) *Chōsen no shūraku* (Villages in Korea), Keizō (Seoul): Chōsen sōtokufū.

2 Korea in transition 1876–1945

Kŭndaehwa efforts before liberation

After years of resistance to Westerners' repeated requests to establish trade relations, Korea became exposed to Western influences toward the end of the nineteenth century by recently Westernized Japan. In 1876, Japan sent delegates with naval fleets to forcefully demand the Korean government to sign a Friendship Treaty and Trade Agreement, also known as the Kanghwa Treaty. The signing took place on Kanghwa Island in a manner almost identical to what the American Commodore Mathew Perry did with Japan in 1868. While the Kanghwa Treaty recognized Korea as an autonomous (*chaju*) country, it one-sidedly granted Japan various political and economic privileges, such as the opening of three ports, Pusan, Inchon and Wonsan, to Japanese traders and diplomats; the freedom to engage in trade activities with extraterritorial rights; exemption of port authority tax for those ships owned by the Japanese government; several years of tariff exemptions for Japanese traders; and the use of Japanese currency by the Japanese to purchase Korean goods and by the Koreans to purchase Japanese goods. Korea also agreed to establish a Japanese legation in Korea's capital, Hansong, allowing Japanese diplomats and their companies to travel freely throughout Korea. These treaties were effective indefinitely and were then followed by equally unequal treaties with Qing China and nine Western nations.[1]

In this chapter, I will discuss in the first half reform efforts of self-strengthening by the government and "enlightened citizens" of the Chosŏn Dynasty with a focus on three kaehwa (enlightenment) campaigns – namely, the import of the new (Western) educational system, the shift in the government economic policies toward the promotion of commerce and industry and the attempts by enlightened civilian leaders to establish the legislative assembly and organize rallies and joint assemblies of ordinary citizens. In the second half, I will demonstrate how the self-strengthening kaehwa campaign was taken over and reduced to two limited expansion of education and economy by the Japanese authorities in the protective (1905–1910) and colonial period (1910–1945) during which Korea went through controlled developmental transformation as a peripheral part of Imperial Japan.

The Kaehwa (Enlightenment) period (1876–1905)

The opening of the three ports (kaehang) exposed Korea to wider external influences, effectively ending Korea's long seclusion policy and refusal to have any

52   *Korea in transition 1876–1945*

diplomatic or trade relations with "barbarian countries." It also ended Korea's cultural and political attachment to China, and its efforts to build an ideal Confucianist Kingdom, or a small middle kingdom (sojunghwa). While the three neighbouring countries, Japan, China and Russia, vied for political dominance and expansion of economic interests in Korea, the European countries that had treaties with Korea primarily sought economic concessions, showing little interest in getting involved in internal affairs.

Following wars with China (1894) and Russia (1904), Japan emerged as the dominant alien force in Korea, making Korea its protectorate in 1905. Subsequently, Korea became a colony of Japan in 1910.

Faced with the aggressive economic and political penetration by alien powers, Koreans were awakened to the fact that Korea was unprepared to defend itself against the penetration of the Western forces whose military strength was far superior to what Korea had ever had or that it was a backward country. It was widely felt by government officials and reform-minded elites that Korea had to learn from the West how to defend itself and to catch up with them.

Unlike his father, Taewŏn'gun (Yi Haŭng), who served as his regent from 1853 to 1863 and maintained a stern seclusion policy with the view that the West represented "barbarianism," King Kojong was favorably inclined to the idea of opening the country to the world beyond China and was eager to know more about the West and the then modernizing or Westernizing Japan and China. He sent delegates to Japan (1876, 1880 and 1881) and to China (1881) to inspect their modernization reform efforts known as the Meiji Restoration and the Self-Strengthening Movement, respectively, and to the United States of America and Europe (1883) to directly observe the modernized West. The delegates were impressed with what they witnessed first-hand in the countries they were visiting, including telecommunication systems, postal stations, factories, rural farms, trade centers, schools, military systems and government organizations, and submitted to the king detailed reports on what they observed with the recommendation that Korea should import them. The delegates also brought back concrete products of modern technologies, including farm appliances (thrashers, rice plant cutting machines) and advanced farming methods, scales and vaccines.

Orthodox Confucianists violently opposed the signing of treaties and tried to stall any attempt to learn from the West and Japan. They simply rejected anything Western or Japanese, which, they asserted, represented heterodox barbarian cultures (sa) as opposed to the orthodox Sinic-Confucian culture (chŏng). They were determined to "defend orthodoxy and reject heterodoxy (wijŏng ch'ŏksa)." Ch'oe Ikhyŏn, one of the noted wijŏng ch'ŏksa advocates, stated in his famous memorial to the king, "Signing treaties with them (the West and Japan) is an invitation to the Catholic religion to enter Korea and to Japan to attack Korea when the time is ripe" (Lee Ki-baik 1984: 272). They specifically criticized the open-door policy argument by Huang Zun Xian, the minister of Chinese embassy in Japan, set forth in his book *A Policy for Korea* (1880) – the book Vice-Minister Kim Hong who led the friendship promotion mission to Japan in 1880 received from Huang in Japan (Lee Ki-baik 1984: 270).

Korea in transition 1876–1945 53

Anti-reform conservative yangban forces, however, were no longer as strong to undermine reform efforts as they were before. The more direct pressure on the government to reform came from outside as well as from inside.

China was increasingly concerned with the mounting Japanese influence in Korea backed up by modern military might that considerably weakened its own and with possible Russian invasion for the purpose of establishing political control over Korea. Accordingly, China strongly advised or put pressure on Korea to sign treaties with Western nations, including the United States, Britain and Germany to stall the expansionist policy of Japan and Russia. The aforementioned book by Huang, which had considerable impact on the thinking of Korean scholars and politicians, stressed the need of Korea's extending international relations beyond China.[2] In 1882, China sent a force of 45,000 soldiers to Korea at the request of the Korean government to quell the mutiny of soldiers of pre-modern army units known as Imo Kullan (Imo Mutiny). China thus was able to restore its "position of supremacy in Korea that had been usurped by Japan" and to reassert itself as the suzerain power (Ibid. 1984: 273). Japanese troops in Korea were outnumbered by Chinese troops, and Japan was unable to remain in Korea as the dominant alien force. Chinese troops stayed on in Korea even after the mutiny was suppressed for ten years from 1884 to 1894, demanding various economic concessions and exercising direct control over Korea's foreign relations and economic matters.

Japan also had an opportunity to resume its dominant power position in Korea in 1894. In that year, a large-scale peasant rebellion, the Tonghak war, broke out, and the Korean government requested military support from China. China responded by sending 3,000 soldiers. The Japanese government quickly reacted by dispatching an army of 7,000 troops, backed up by seven warships, under the pretext of protecting its citizens in Korea. When direct confrontation between Japan and China appeared to be imminent, the Korean government decided to end the hostilities by accepting the demands of the rebelling peasant army leaders. After peace was re-established and peasant soldiers returned home, the government requested both China and Japan to withdraw their troops from Korea. But the Japanese government was not going to let an opportunity to establish itself as the dominant power in Korea and to squeeze more economic concessions from Korea go by (Duus 1995: 68). Instead of obliging the withdrawal request, the Japanese government proposed to the Chinese counterpart that Chinese and Japanese troops jointly put down the Tonghak rebels and then force Korea to launch an administrative reform; should China refuse to cooperate, Japan would try to do it alone (Ibid. 1995: 73). The Chinese government rejected the proposal and made a counterargument that since the rebellion was already put down, it was no longer necessary for both countries to do anything militarily, and administrative reform should be carried out by Koreans themselves since China had never intervened with Korea's internal affairs, and Japan had recognized Korea's autonomy (Yi Kwangnin 1981: 303). The Chinese position was fully supported by King Kojong and foreign powers. But Japan countered the Chinese counterproposal, insisting that "reform of Korea's internal administration was absolutely essential

54 *Korea in transition 1876–1945*

if internal unrest were not again to flare into open rebellion and the peace in East Asia depended on preventing such an occurrence" (Lee Ki-baik 1984: 289), and that the Koreans could not undertake such reform by themselves (Duus 1995: 73). Subsequently, Japan used its troops to occupy the Kyŏngbok palace and forced King Kojong to form a pro-Japanese cabinet with the moderate reformist King Hong-jip as the head and began a war in 1894, the Sino-Japanese War, attacking Chinese troops stationed in Korea. The war ended with a Japanese victory, and Japan replaced China as the main foreign power in Korea and continued to demand that the Korean government introduce administrative and other reforms. In 1894, under Japan's pressure, the Korean government instituted the large-scale reform known as Kabo Reform, which will be discussed next.

Demands for change also came from within, both reform-minded yangban and frustrated peasants themselves. Around the time of the port opening in the 1880s, a group of young progressive yangban under the influence of the reformist thinker Pak Kyusu, the grandson of the sirhak scholar Pak Chiwŏn (1737–1805) who was well informed of the Western civilization, formed a party called the Enlightenment Party (Kaehwadang) or Independence Party (Tongniptang). The party's primary goal was to establish Korea's political and cultural independence from China and to catch up with the advanced West through learning from Japan of its successful modernization attempt of the Meiji Restoration. Their reform efforts gained King Kojong's support and made some progress in modernizing the military system, sending students to Japan to learn about Western education, establishing a telecommunication system and postal station and publishing a newspaper. However, with China's active participation in the policy making of the Korean government after the 1882 military mutiny, their reform efforts became restrained. Furthermore, the pro-China Min clan (Queen Min's relatives) that dominated the court with the support of China was not friendly or even hostile to the progressive Kaehwadang member because of their pro-Japanese attitudes and willingness to collaborate with Japan in reform attempts. They deliberately blocked appointments of Kaehwadang members to pivotal government positions (Ibid. 1984: 276). Frustrated in their reform efforts, the Kaehwadang member officials decided to take action to remove the obstacle – namely, the Min-clan high officials in the government. When China was largely preoccupied with the Sino-French war in Indo-China the core members of the Kaehwadang, Kim Okkyun, Pak Yŏnghyo, Hong Yŏngsik, Sŏ Kwangbŏm and Sŏ Chaepil, with Japanese Minister Takezoe Shininchirō's promise of military help with the Japanese legation guards stationed in the capital, successfully staged a coup in 1884 – the event known as the Kapsin coup. The major pro-China faction was removed, a new cabinet with Kaehwadang members was formed and a reform program was quickly installed. The program consisted of 14 plans, including provisions such as ending the empty formalities of the tributary relationship with China, terminating the arbitrary exercise of the power of the throne and expanding the authority of ministerial deliberations by delegating the State Council (Ŭijŏngbu) to make important policy matters, abolishing ruling class (yangban) privileges, establishing the principle of equal rights in personnel appointment, namely, appointing

Korea in transition 1876–1945   55

officials to government posts on the basis of one's talent, ensuring the generation of sufficient revenues to meet government expenditures and alleviating the plight of the peasantry through revision of the land tax laws and rooting out the extortion practices of petty officials.

However, these reform efforts were short-lived. The Chinese troops quickly arrived in Korea at the request of the government to put down the coup. Some of the coup organizers fled the country together with the retreating Japanese troops and others were arrested and executed. The newly established government fell after three days.

The more notable demand for reform after the port opening came from peasants themselves in the form of rebellion. The aforementioned Tonghak peasant war in 1894 was a case in point. Previous reform efforts directed at the plight of peasants were initiated by reform-minded scholars or officials and remained as yangban elite campaigns for the peasantry without involving peasants. It began as a revolt led by the parish leader of Tonghak religion Chŏn Pongjun against the tyrannical magistrate of the Kobu county in the Chŏlla province who illegally collected a large amount of tax (in grain) to erect a covering structure over his father's tombstone, force tax on the irrigation water from a public reservoir, mobilize their labour for construction of a new reservoir and then charge them for the use of the water. The peasant rebels occupied the county office, seized weapons and distributed the illegally collected tax rice to the poor, and they destroyed the reservoir. Instead of looking into their demands, the government charged the Tonghak with responsibility for the uprising and arrested and executed some Tonghak leaders. Angered by the government's actions, more peasants in surrounding areas rallied under the leadership of Chŏn Pongjun and other Tonghak leaders. Thus the rebellion that began as a protest against the tyranny of a county magistrate expanded further into a large-scale war against the government.

The major aim of the collective protest by the alliance of peasants and the Tonghak leaders was clearly stated in their proclamation:

> The people are the root of the nation. If the root withers, the nation will be enfeebled. Heedless of their responsibility for sustaining the state and providing for the people, the officials build lavish residences in the countryside, scheming to ensure their own well-being at the expense of the resources of the nation. How can this be viewed as proper? We are wretched village people far from the capital, yet we feed and clothe ourselves with the bounty from the sovereign's land. We cannot sit by and watch our nation perish. The whole nation is as one, its multitudes united in their determination to raise the righteous standard of revolt, and to pledge their lives to sustain the state and provide for the livelihood of the people. However, startling the action we take today may seem, you must not be troubled by it. For as we felicitously live out the tranquil years ahead, each man secure in his occupation – when all the people and enjoy the blessings of benevolent kingly rule, how immeasurably joyful will we be.
>
> (Quoted in Ibid. 1984: 284)

56   *Korea in transition 1876–1945*

Here Chŏn Pongjun clearly reminded, or urged, the government to bring back the aborted Confucianization project – the main aim of which was to build a government for the people. The highly motivated peasant rebels, though not well armed, defeated the government forces in two major battles and subsequently occupied much of the Chŏlla province and eventually its capital, Chŏnju. I have already discussed how the panicked government then brought the Chinese troops by request and the Japanese troops, inadvertently, into Korea, thereby creating an unanticipated crisis situation of war between the two alien forces and quickly ended the peasant uprising by accepting reform demands by the rebel leaders in an attempt to preempt an unwanted military conflict.

When the peace was restored, the governor of the Chŏlla province asked Chon Pongjun and other leaders to stay and help him to re-establish an order in the region. Chon accepted the invitation, as he thought it would be a good opportunity to carry out needed reform in the direction of the Confucianization of the state project. He swiftly reorganized the administrative organization by extending Tonghak's network organization into the area. Civil congregations called chipkangso (local directorate) were established in 53 counties of the Chŏlla province. And as the head of taedongso (directorate headquarters) in Chonju, Chon introduced various administrative reform plans which were focused mainly on eliminating the causes of sufferings of the peasantry and other underprivileged people. They included punishment of corrupt officials and men of wealth who owed their fortunes to high-handed extortionate practices; appointment of government officials on the basis of talent, not on a regional or class basis; burning of all documents pertaining to slaves; rectifying the treatment of those engaged in "despised occupations" and freeing the outcasts (paekchŏng); banning collection of all arbitrary and irregular taxes; cancelling all outstanding debts, whether owed to government agencies or to private individuals; distributing land equally for cultivation by owner-farmers; and permitting the remarriage of young widows (Ibid. 1984: 286–287).

Like the Kaehwadang's attempts in 1884, Chŏn's reform attempt was also short-lived. When Japan refused to oblige the government request to withdraw its troops after the truce with the Tonghak rebels, Chŏn Pongjun decided to deploy the peasant armies to drive the Japanese from Korea, but they were no match for the modern army of Japan, and the government also sided with the Japanese to defeat them. Chŏn Pongjun was captured by the Japanese army and put on trial. He was executed in 1895. The administrative reform, together with independence of Korea from China's control, was Japan's excuse for staying on in Korea, and Japan was even willing to go to war against China for it. In the same year (1894) that Chŏn Pongjun was introducing his reform program in the Chŏlla Province, Japan aggressively put pressure on the Korean government to undertake a reform plan. Inoue Kaoru, the Japanese minister in Korea, advised King Kojong early that year that internal reform was necessary for Korea to fortify the foundation for independence and to declare that ties with China were severed. Subsequently, as mentioned earlier, under Inoue's pressure, the government implemented numerous, wide-ranging reform measures in the form of edicts, decrees, laws, orders, acts and announcements. It implemented these reforms times over the period of 2.5 years, the first in July–November 1894, the second in November 1894–May 1895 and the third in August 1895–February 1896.

They may be grouped into six major categories of changes: (1) political or administrative changes – the declaration of Korea as Imperial Korea with King Kojong crowned as the emperor and severing Korea's tributary ties with China, the separation of government administration from that of the royal palace, the establishment of a cabinet system presided by the prime minister (not directly by king), independence of the judiciary branch and establishment of law courts and abolition of the civil service examinations; (2) status hierarchy – abolition of status distinction in the government personnel appointment system, abolition of rank distinction between civilian and military officials, abolition of the guilt by association system, abolition of both public and private slaves, prohibition of early marriage and permission of remarriage of young widows; (3) economic institutions – unification of fiscal administration, adoption of the silver standard (with nickel, copper, bronze and brass coins made subsidiary units of exchange), payment of taxes in cash instead of in-kind, introduction of the banking system and privatization of mines; (4) educational institutions – replacement of the existing Confucian educational system (for males only, and based exclusively on learning Confucian classics) with the Western-style public school system (for everybody irrespective of status, age and sex with the new curriculum including subjects such as arithmetic, science, history, geography); (5) military institutions – establishment of the modern army; and (6) others – replacement of lunar calendar with solar calendar and enactment of vaccine law, top-notch cutting and opening of the modern postal stations. These reform efforts came to be known as the Kabo Reform (Lee Ki-baik 1984: 290–292).

It appears that in putting pressure on the Korean government to launch reform programs, Japan was keen on institutional reforms – reforms that facilitated "the further penetration into Korea of Japan's developing capitalist economy" (Lee Ki-baik 1984: 293), but not with alleviation of the plight of the peasantry and strengthening of the national power. As Lee Ki-baik points out, "The reforms, then, did nothing to ensure adequate military manpower resources or the provision of new weaponry, both of which are essential to the security of a modern state" (1984: 293).

Still, national self-strengthening was a major concern widely shared by the Korean government and civilians. However, for reasons that are as yet to be explained fully, Korea endeavored to achieve this goal through expansion of the new education and the non-agricultural sector – commerce, industry and mining and democratization. The government initiated the first two projects, while civilian leaders initiated the third.

Thus began the historical kŭndaehwa (modernization) projects as part of the self-strengthening efforts under less than ideal conditions – without national security guaranteed. Next, I will discuss them in some detail.

New Education Campaign – The "save the nation through education" movement began in the 1880s. A series of government ordinances modeled after Japanese educational laws were enacted, providing guidelines for establishing a new

58 *Korea in transition 1876–1945*

(Western) educational system. It included types of schools to be built, school ages, budgets, curriculum, entrance requirements and entrance examinations.

The government began building new schools in the 1880s to meet the needs arising from foreign residents speaking foreign languages. In 1886, Yukyŏngwŏn (Royal English School) was established with the aim of training English interpreters. Several language schools followed: Japanese (1891), English (1892), French (1895), Russian (1896), Chinese (1897) and German (1898).

The government also built professional and vocational schools: a "normal" school (1894), a medical school (1899), a school of commerce and engineering (1899) and a school of agriculture, engineering and commerce (1904).

Building public schools for general academic education came in 1895 after the issuance of the imperial edict, Building Educational Korea, which stated, "Citizens in those wealthy, strong and independent countries are well educated. Acquiring knowledge is the utmost goal of education and education is the basis for preserving the nation" (Son Insu 1971: 28). In the same year, the government founded 4 elementary schools (financed by the central government) in the capital city and 38 schools (financed by local governments) in newly established administrative districts, *si* (city) and *kun* (county). Children aged 8 to 15 were selected from those who applied. The school curriculum consisted of topics such as arithmetic, the Korean language, composition and science. No tuition fee was charged, and the government loaned textbooks and provided stationery free of charge.

In 1899, the government built its first middle school in the capital city, Seoul. Males aged 17 to 25 were qualified to write entrance examinations testing their basic knowledge of Korean and Chinese. Like elementary schools, schooling at this level was free of charge, with the government providing textbooks and stationery.

Reform-oriented (kaehwa [enlightened]) civic leaders – former government officials, military officers and landlords (see Oh Chŏnsŏk 1964) – also eagerly participated in the public education expansion campaign. In fact, the first Western-style primary school was built in 1883 by a group of civilian leaders in Wonsan (Sin Yongha 1974) and was followed by numerous others elsewhere (Furukawa 2004: 179). These civilian leaders also built middle schools. The first school at this level appeared in Pusan in 1896.

By 1911, there were 43 private schools with 2,960 students and 6 vocational (sirŏp) schools with 249 students (Ōno 1936: 8). Courses taught at these schools included Japanese, English, geography, Korean and world history, physics, chemistry, jurisprudence, economics and international law.[3] Civilian leaders aimed at making students more patriotic through learning about their own history and culture, and raising awareness of the danger of foreigners taking over the country.

Christian missionaries, however, played the most important role in introducing the Western-style education. A small number of American Presbyterian ministers who came to Korea in 1884 began missionary work by building schools and propagating Western education. They obtained permission from King Kojong to build the first boys' school, Baejae Haktang (in 1885), the first girls' school, Ehwa

Korea in transition 1876–1945 59

Haktang (1886) and the first medical school, Kwanghyewŏn (in 1885). They then introduced the educational system of primary, secondary and tertiary schools, and taught subjects that had been unfamiliar to Korean students, such as arithmetic or mathematics, science, geography, history and physical education. By the time the residency general of Japan was installed in 1905, Christian missionaries had built 796 schools of various kinds (Son Insu 1971: 86).

Growth of Commerce and Industry – After the opening of Korea's ports and the economic take-over by the treaty countries, it was clearly demonstrated to Koreans, from the government officials down to the peasants, that the superiority of the industrial nations posed a considerable challenge to Confucianist Korea, which had historically maintained the idea of agricultural basism. The Korean government deliberately did not promote the growth of non-agricultural industry out of fear that it would lure away agricultural producers. As such, commerce and industry had long been held in low esteem. The transition to commerce and manufacturing industries became urgent, however, as Korea was forced to defend its economy against further penetration of foreign traders and eventually to compete against them.

In 1883, the government established the Bureau of Commerce (Hyesangkuk) specifically for the purpose of protecting licensed merchants with monopoly rights for wholesale and retail from unlicensed domestic[4] and foreign traders. In the case of peddlers, the bureau helped them to organize a nationwide cooperative. In the same year, the government also created various bureaus to be responsible for the development of manufacturing industries, including weaponry, weaving, paper mills, tobacco and distilleries. Model factory building was the first task these bureaus undertook by way of encouraging civilians to follow. The Bureau of Weapon Manufacturing built a weapon manufacturing factory in Seoul with the help of technicians invited from China. The Bureau of Weaving built a weaving factory equipped with machines imported from Japan and had Chinese weaving technicians train Korean workers. The Bureau of Mining established in 1889 invited three American mining technicians to conduct an exploratory survey on Korean mines and purchased mining equipment from the United States. This bureau also encouraged civilians to start mining companies and to adopt Western mining methods.

As was the case with the new education campaign, many civilians followed the government's lead in their efforts to develop new economies. Influx of foreign traders changed the economic landscape of Korea. It was widely felt among civilians that further penetration of foreign (especially, Japanese) traders into the Korean economy should be stalled before it was taken over by them. Need for creating native entrepreneurs rose sharply. At the same time, some Koreans with wealth and industrial skills learned from the foreign traders a new way of making money, and became entrepreneurs or businessmen, a new name for merchants and manufacturers. Economic historian O Miil (2002) grouped them into three categories: (1) incumbent and retired high ranking government bureaucrats who became wealthy through informal management of their offices (e.g., extortion and

60   *Korea in transition 1876–1945*

bribery), or became big landlords through management of farm lands they owned; (2) rich merchants, licensed city shop merchants, the capital city river merchants and kaekchu; and (3) enterprising artisans. High-ranking bureaucrats first established corporate-type business enterprises, supplying goods to the government, and subcontracting government projects on land development, commercial railway construction and other projects. Their close ties with the government gave them the advantage of easily procuring sub-contract works from the government. They later expanded their business into banking, marine and land transportation, warehousing, life insurance, some manufacturing (textile) enterprises, and mining. Rich merchants became corporate businessmen doing what they used to do, namely supplying goods to the government. In this connection they established warehousing companies, marine transportation companies, promissory note cooperatives, and agricultural and industrial banks. Some rich artisans also turned into entrepreneurs. Since the newly developing commodity market was inundated with foreign goods brought in by foreign traders they built factories (mostly small scale) to manufacture traditional (or indigenous) commodities such as brassware, ironware, paper and paper products, cotton and silk products, ceramics, and liquors. A few skilled artisans acquired advanced industrial skills – some went to Japan to get enrolled in technical schools for advanced training – to enter into new industries such dyeing, weaving, making matches, and soap production. Most of them, however, did not possess large capital to produce modern goods that would match against the imported goods in terms of quality and price, so they turned to rich merchants to have them as sponsors in order to become modern entrepreneurial manufacturers (O Miil 2002).

Three decades (1876–1905) after the port-opening, as discussed above, marked the turning point in the economic history of Korea where the traditional anti-mercantilism ended and the making of modern enterprise or capitalism began.

Democracy Campaign – The government more or less concentrated on the earlier two projects as means of strengthening the national power. However, one newly formed civilian group, the Independence Club (IC) (Tongniphyŏphoe), held the view that in order for the nation to be independent and strong, the people that constitute it should each become a self-reliant individuals, should actively participate in the government (political) process and, ultimately, should form a strong united force of the government and the people.

The IC was one of the first civilian groups formed in 1896 by Sŏ Chaepil with a number of progressive reformists after he returned from the United States where he had lived in exile for 14 years and studied medicine. It may be recalled that he was one of the core members who staged the Kapsin chŏngbyŏn in 1884.

IC had as its main objective to strengthen people's power to solve problems that the nation faced in time of crisis by themselves and to defend the independence of the nation. Until they were dissolved by the government in 1898, the IC carried out various reform campaigns including building the Independence Gate, the Independence Park, the Independence Hall to replace the Yŏng'ŭnmun or the gate at which Chinese delegates were received in the past and the Mohwakwan or the

Korea in transition 1876–1945 61

quarter where visiting Chinese delegates stayed, organizing debating groups and public meetings for ordinary people, forming collective forces of people to campaign against the invasion of foreign capitalists, criticizing corrupt bureaucrats, introducing Western ideas of citizenship and establishing the legislative assembly (Sin Yongha 1976: 250–275).

Here I will only discuss the club's attempt to democratize the government process, an important historical episode, in some detail.

IC members felt strongly that the most urgent reform required for national self-strengthening was to enhance and protect the rights of the people, and to change the monarch from an absolute to a constitutional system by establishing the people's assembly (ŭihoe) to advise and monitor the king's court.

Viewed from the historical perspective, the democracy campaign by the IC was a progressive reform effort to build the government for the people. This campaign, however, was different from similar attempts made previously by reform-minded Confucian scholar officials in that they adopted the Western concept of the people. They directly challenged the yangban ideology of status distinction. Instead of regarding all the people as being children of the king as the Confucian reformists did, the IC members argued that the people were born free and equal with a series of inviolable individual rights – to have their life (body) and property protected, to labour to accumulate wealth, to express their opinions, to assemble, to associate with others – which, they maintained, were what Heaven endowed. They criticized the remnants of the status distinction between yangban and commoners, of the slavery system and of the discrimination against women. They further refuted the time-old idea of the distinction between the rulers and the ruled. They asserted that the rulers and the ruled are the same, they are the people who are the master of the nation and sovereignty of the nation is derived from the people and urged people to participate in the government (political) process.

The democracy campaign began with the movement to establish the popular assembly in the spring of 1898. The first step the IC took was to enlighten people about the necessity of having such an organ. The then president of the IC, Yun Ch'iho, distributed to IC members copies of a shortened version the Robert's Rule of Order, which he himself translated and published, and put on sale for the public. The IC also began providing training to the public on meeting procedures in the assembly. The government reacted to this movement by conveying their view to the IC that as an organ monitoring the court administration, an advisory organ would be more appropriate, as it is too early to have the "thoroughly representative government" as suggested by Sŏ Chaep'il and Yun Ch'iho. The IC upheld their position and argued that in Eastern thoughts, people's opinions are sought after when the government recruit personnel, and in European countries, even under the absolutist political system, communications channels (ŏllo) are wide open through the establishment of the upper and lower house, and doing so is the universal rule. The IC made the appeal that the government should gather people's opinions as widely as possible. They then made a concrete suggestion to reorganize the Office of Ministers without Portfolio, an advisory office affiliated with the court established at the time of Kabo Reform (1894–1896), into the people's assembly.

62   *Korea in transition 1876–1945*

Subsequently, at the IC's request, the representatives of the government and the IC met to discuss and negotiate the proposal. After further discussions, the government finally agreed to create the assembly consisting of 25 members of the IC; 25 members of another civilian group, Imperial Nation Council; and 20 members to be selected through popular election. This plan was, however, aborted because while waiting for the election to take place, the conservative opponents persuaded the king that this movement to establish the popular assembly was a move on the part of the IC to replace the monarch with the assembly. King Kojong became furious and had 17 members of the IC arrested and ordered the dissolution of the IC.

IC's efforts to encourage people to participate actively in the political process was more successful. By way of achieving this goal, the IC first organized the joint assembly of all people (manmin kongdonghoe) and the joint assembly of government officials and ordinary people (kwanmin kongdonghoe) for public dialogues.

In March 1898, the rally of the joint assembly of all people was held under the auspice of the IC to which about 10,000 civilians attended. The main purpose of the rally was to denounce Imperial Russia's expansion policy. They elected a rice merchant as the chairman of the assembly. At the rally, a number of speakers, including IC members and students, delivered speeches, urging people to unite to protect the independence of the nation against foreign invasion. This rally was followed by another one two days later, which was organized not by the IC but civilian themselves for the same purpose, and more people attended it. According to the sociologist Sin Yongha the two successful gatherings of a large crowd of civilians in protest had the effect of Russia withdrawing the demand for coal storage in the Chŏlhyŏng Island, the closing of Korea-Russia Bank and the removal of the Russian finance adviser and the military instructor (1976: 398).

Encouraged by the success of mobilizing a large crowd for political protest and in their attempt to have the aforementioned public meeting for debates with the representatives of the government, the IC proceeded with their plan to organize similar meetings between government officials and ordinary civilians. One hundred and fifty letters of invitation were mailed to discussants selected from all walks of life. Meetings were held six days from October 28 to November 2. The government representatives attended all meetings except the first one. A large crowd, estimated to be several tens of thousands including students, city licensed shop merchants, butchers, blind men and women, Buddhist monks and nuns, bureaucrats and "gentlemen" were gathered there. Invited discussants delivered speeches discussing and criticizing the government misrules and other social issues. A butcher spoke of his patriotism and urged that all the people, including bureaucrats and ordinary civilians, should unite in support of the emperor and the prosperity of the country. On the second day, the assembly adopted a resolution consisting of six articles called Hŏnuiyukcho:

1   That both officials and people shall determine not to rely on any foreign aid but to do their best to strengthen and uphold the Imperial prerogatives;
2   That all documents pertaining to foreign loans, the hiring of foreign soldiers, the grant of concession, etc. – in short, every document drawn up between

the Korean government and foreigner shall be signed and stamped by all the Ministers of the State and the President of the Privy Council;

3   That no important offender shall be punished until after he has been given a public trial and an ample opportunity to defend himself either by himself or by a counsel;

4   That to His Majesty shall belong to the power of appointing his ministers, but that in case the majority of the cabinet disapproves a man, he shall not be appointed;

5   That all sources of revenue and methods of raising taxes shall be placed under the control of the finance department, no other department or office, or private corporation being allowed to interfere there with and that annual estimates and balance shall be made public;

6   That existing laws and regulations shall be faithfully enforced (translation by The Independent Vol. No. 128, November 1, 1898).

(Sin Yongha 1976: 388)

What is so unusual about IC's success in mobilizing such a huge crowd for political purpose is that people so readily responded to the call of the IC. The rising sense of national crisis or nationalistic consciousness in the wake of the invasion of foreign forces and traders may be one factor accounting for this phenomenon.

The IC also took it upon themselves to defend the rights of the ordinary people guaranteed by the law. When these rights were violated unlawfully the IC took direct action to restore them through various means (for more on this, see Sin Yongha 1976: 311–315).

Although the IC prevailed over the government in their defense of commoners' rights in various cases (Sin Yongha 1976: 311–315). It appears that the government felt uncomfortable about being subject to IC's frequent attacks. In October, King Kojong issued an order that the IC confine its public discussions to non-political matters and to hold discussions only in the Independence Hall in the IC office building. In the order, King Kojong also stated that the convention in foreign countries (meaning the West, not China) is that the National Assembly is a public organ making policy decisions about the interest of the state and people, whereas the civilian association is a private organ whose function is no more than merely assisting the National Assembly, and in our country, civilian private associations also began to play a role in the process of enlightenment and progress. But it is not the role of the civilian association to criticize government ordinance (chŏngryŏng) and to demand the firing of ministers or to intimidate high officials. The IC defied the order, which in fact was prohibiting their discussions and criticisms of politics and government policies or restricting the freedom of expression and assembly, and held a public protest meeting in the street and then marched to the police headquarters, demanding that they be granted the freedom of expression and assembly or be arrested for violating the emperor's order. The IC further stressed that (a) people's discussion of political problems is necessary because of injustice and corruption of the government, (b) the freedom of the press cannot under any circumstances be sacrificed and (c) the way to make bureaucrats to do

64   *Korea in transition 1876–1945*

their duty for the emperor and the state is to allow people to express their opinions freely (Sin Yongha 1976: 356).

The IC members made it clear that they would not end their rally until their demand was granted. In the end, King Kojong relented and admitted, "As it is the duty of subject to exercise the privileges of expressing his opinion when certain evils are to be rectified" (translation by the Independent, the IC's newspaper). (The above discussion of the IC is largely based on Sin Yongha (1976)).

Such national self-strengthening efforts by both the government and civilians, expansion of new education, development of commerce and industry and democracy campaign, however, were not sufficient to prevent imperialist expansion into Korea. Enterprising civilians could not effectively compete in the market against foreign traders in terms of capital, business skills and industrial technology. Furthermore, the Korean government was unable to build up their military might strong enough to renegotiate the unequal treaties it signed recently and drive out imperialist powers from the peninsula. Alien forces, especially Japanese, continued to demand further economic concessions, and Japan made an all-out effort to become the dominant force over Korea instead of China and Russia. Korea could not prevent the country turning into a battleground for the duration of two wars (1894–1905). It was even forced to rely on both China and Japan to suppress internal rebellions. Korea eventually was forced to give up its sovereignty and became Japan's protectorate in 1905 and its colony five years later.

Reform efforts under the auspice of the government and enlightened citizens or bourgeoisie accordingly came to an abrupt end and were placed under Japan's control. The education campaign was turned into a policy effort to weaken the rising anti-Japanese sentiment among Koreans by the Protectorate government, and a imperialization project (kōminka seisaku) by the colonial government and the economic plan was focused on the increase of rice production in the first two decades and industrial development as a part of the larger scheme of wartime expansion of the Japan's economy after 1930. Any attempt to democratize the nation had to wait until Korea was liberated.

The protectorate period (1905–1910)

In 1904, before the Russo-Japanese War ended, Japan coerced the Korean government to appoint Japanese politicians to all key posts in government ministries as advisers, thereby establishing the so-called advisory administrative system. As Korea formally became Japan's protectorate in the following year, the Japanese resident-general was to guide the Korean government in its administration and the Korean government was required to seek the resident-general's approval on all decisions regarding legislative and administrative matters prior to the king making them public with his seal. Government policies were formulated largely on the basis of what Japanese officials[5] thought would be good or bad for the Koreans. Accordingly, Korea's kaehwa project came under the close supervision and control of the Japanese resident-general.

Korea in transition 1876–1945   65

Educational Transformation – Regulating what appeared to be the "disorderly building of private schools" by civic leaders and the "de-politicizing of the education system" was one of the immediate aims of the government under Japanese control. Accordingly, the purpose of education was redefined and the structure of the school system was revised.

In 1906, Ordinance No. 40 was enacted, regulating the establishment of schools by the Ministry of Education (kwallip hakkyo, mostly in the capital city, Hansŏng) and public schools (kongnip hakkyo, mostly in local cities).

The primary school system established in 1895 was replaced by the common school system in 1906, reducing the number of school years from six to four. The rationale behind this decision was that considering the new (Western) school system was just introduced and the overall educational level of Koreans was low, what Korea needed most was elementary common school education with a shorter school year, not primary school education with six long school years that prepared students for secondary and eventually tertiary education (as intended by the Korean government before 1905).

In the same year, high schools and vocational schools substituted the middle school system. They consisted of various types of schools, including academic high school, normal, foreign language (English, Japanese, German, French, Russian and Chinese), technical (or vocational) and the Women's Upper Level School. High school was considered the final stage of education, and government authorities argued that under present conditions, it was unnecessary to establish tertiary level schools (colleges and universities) (O Ch'ŏnsŏk 1964: 158).

Upon being appointed as the resident-general, Ito Hirobumi borrowed five million Yen from the Bank of Japan to finance the so-called Administration Reform and allocated half a million Yen for the educational expansion program. This fund for educational expansion, however, was mostly (82.1 percent) expended on expansion of common schools.

In 1910, there were 101 common schools with an enrollment of 16,946 students: one government school (263 students), 59 public schools (12,469 students) and 41 supplementary schools (4,214 students). In the same year, at the secondary level, there were two boys' high schools (366 students), one girls' high school (224 students), one normal school (302 students), 12 vocational schools (546 students)[6] and one foreign language school (538 students) (O Ch'ŏnsŏk 1964: 158).

Japanese advisers also pressed the government to regulate educational content. The government established guidelines for compiling textbooks aimed at standardizing educational content, eliminating anti-Japanese and nationalistic elements and fostering pro-Japan sentiment. They undertook the task of replacing existing textbooks authored by private individuals, which varied widely in content and quality (Son Insu 1971: 65–66). Private schools were encouraged to adopt the textbooks compiled by the government. In the instances where there were no adequate official textbooks or private schools preferred to use non-official textbooks, those books adopted were required to be inspected by the Ministry of Education. A system of inspection was introduced, which authorized the government to

66   *Korea in transition 1876–1945*

approve or disapprove textbooks written by private individuals. In order to monitor what the private schools taught their students, Japanese teachers were brought in from Japan and placed in private schools. Teaching the Japanese language was particularly emphasized. Each government-sponsored common school (kwallip bot'ong hakkyo) was required to teach Japanese for six hours a week.

Such government policies on public school education were not well received by Koreans. Korean civic leaders found that the education provided by government schools was not doing an adequate job of "enriching and strengthening" the nation. Local Confucian elites pointed out that the number of hours allocated to teaching Chinese characters was not sufficient. Many Koreans suspected that making the Japanese language mandatory was an effort to replace the Korean language and culture with Japanese, and they expressed their worries over the increasing presence of Japanese teachers at schools. Most importantly, they were concerned that students were discouraged from expressing their patriotic ideas at school. Consequently, there was widespread distrust in the schools established by the government, central or local. Many Korean leaders came to consider private school as the only alternative. The campaign to build private schools for school-age children and night schools for illiterate adults spread rapidly through the nation as civic leaders actively promoted building new schools, more so than the government was able to with limited funds. In 1908, there was an estimated 4,000 private schools.

Japanese advisers were not eager to see private school education spread, as they were mindful of the "negative" effects arousing nationalistic and anti-Japanese sentiments could have. In 1908, the Private School Act was promulgated with the primary aim of reducing the number, role and influence of private schools in the country's educational system. The act stipulated the budget, the size of the land site and the number of teachers as conditions for building a private school; ruled that a private school could not use a textbook that was not compiled or approved by the Government Education Bureau; granted the government the right to close a private school if and when it was considered to be seriously disturbing "peace and order"; and made it mandatory for a private school to submit a list of the school staff, courses taught, the number of students enrolled and attended by grade, the titles of the textbooks used and a report of the annual budget at the end of the academic year.

The act imposed conditions on private schools that were not easy for Korean civilians or Western missionaries to meet and many of the private schools were closed. By 1910, the number of private schools (established by both Korean civilians and Christian missionaries) was reduced to 2,250 (1,449 Korean schools and 801 missionary schools) (Son Insu 1971: 86).

As it became difficult to open and run private schools, nationalist Koreans opted for the expansion of night school education, including school-age children who were not regulated by the Private School Act. Between 1906 and 1910, 1,000 night schools were founded. The overwhelming majority remained as unofficial "miscellaneous" or "religious" schools (Son Insu 1971: 86–87).

Economic Transformation – As was the case with the educational system, shortly after the war against Russia was declared in 1904, the Japanese government

Korea in transition 1876–1945 67

formulated a clear plan as to what to do with Korea's economy in anticipation of eventual control of Korea after the war. The plan had three objectives:

> (1) The establishment of Japanese supervision over Korean government finances, providing Korea with a financial adviser to supervise the reform of tax collection, to change and rationalize the currency system, and eventually to put actual control of financial affairs directly in Japanese hands; (2) The acquisition of Japanese control over the Korean railway, telegraph, telephone, and mail systems; and (3) The promotion of Korean economic development with the Japanese playing a key role in the development of the primary sector of the Korean economy.
>
> (Duus 1995: 184–186)

Between 1906 and 1908, the resident-general had the Korean government abolish the policy prohibiting foreigners from owning land and then issued a series of ordinances on landownership to make it possible for foreigners to freely purchase or own real estate. In a similar manner, the Korean government was pressured to allow foreigners to own mines and to freely transfer and mortgage those mines.

In 1906, the Korean government signed with the Japanese government the Agreement on Cooperation in Management of Tumen and Yalu River Area Forestry. With this agreement, Japan acquired almost exclusive rights to cut trees in this area despite the agreement in principle that Korea and Japan were supposed to cooperate in doing so (Ch'oe Yun'gyu 1988: 157–168).

The Korean-Japanese Fishing Industry Agreement followed in 1908, allowing Japanese fishermen to freely catch fish in all coastal areas, rivers, streams and lakes in Korea. Japanese fishermen were then encouraged to migrate to Korea.

In order to control the Korean financial system, the Japanese government took a more direct approach. In 1906, Megata Chūtarō, chief of the Taxation Bureau of the Ministry of Finance of the Japanese government, was sent as a special financial adviser to the Korean government to undertake necessary reform. Megata introduced two major reform measures: tax and currency reform (Ibid. 1988: 169–170).

The tax reform was designed to centralize and rationalize the existing "disorderly tax system," thereby increasing government revenue. Megata demanded the Korean government to revise the existing land and mining tax, and introduced various taxes for household, liquor, tobacco, salt, ginseng, boats, fisheries and pawnshops, as well as a stamp duty (Ibid. 1988: 170). In 1909, following his advice, the Korean government also enacted a regional tax law which allowed the regional government to receive a portion of the tax levied by the central government and to collect additional taxes such as market tax, merchant (yŏkaek) tax and flower (brothel) tax (Ibid. 1988: 172).

The currency reform consisted of the adoption of the Japanese currency system, the use of Japanese currency as a means of operating government finance, the abolition of the Korean Government Bureau of Mint and authorization of the Japanese

68 *Korea in transition 1876–1945*

Government Bureau of Mint to mint new Korean currency and the exchange of current coins, white copper coins and copper coins, with new currency.

Then the banking system was brought under Japanese control. The Japanese resident-general advised the Korean government to issue the joint-stock company Daiichi Bank ordinance, which assigned the Japanese Daiichi Bank the task of dealing with matters related to currency reform, national treasury funds, and issuance of new bank notes, and made it the central bank managing 13 regional branches established in cities across the peninsula.

Thus the Daiichi Bank came to manage not only the circulation of currency but also banking business in Korea (Ibid. 1988: 173–174). It also assisted other Japanese banks in Korea, such as the Fifty-Eighth Bank, the Eighteenth Bank and the Shūbo Bank, to expand their business by establishing branches in different cities, merging with other banks or increasing capital assets and helping Japanese businessmen to open new banks in Korea.

While bringing the banking system under Japanese control, the resident-general also advised the Korean government to create more bank-related organizations, including credit cooperatives, joint warehouse companies, agricultural and industrial banks, regional banking cooperatives and the Oriental Development Company to facilitate circulation of new currencies, thereby making them more widely available. These organizations were established with funds raised either jointly by Koreans and Japanese or Koreans alone, but the actual operation was conducted by the Japanese under close scrutiny of the government (for more on them, see Ibid. 1988: 173–177, and O Miil 2002: 45–49).

The Japanese control of Korea's transportation and communication systems was achieved by forcing the Korean government to sign various agreements, which entrusted the Japanese government to construct major railways and highways and to manage telegraph, telephone and mail systems.

Japan had already acquired control over the major railways prior to the outbreak of the Russo-Japanese War. Construction of the Seoul and Ŭiju lines, which began during the Russo-Japanese War, was completed in 1906. Two additional railways, the Pyongyang Coalmine Railway and P'yŏngnam Rail, were built with funds provided by the Korean government and came under the control of the Japanese government before 1910.

Four highways connecting Pyongyang to Wonsan, Kwangju to Mokpo, Taegu to Kyŏngju and Yŏng'il and Chinju to Kunsan were then built in 1907 to connect railways to ports (Ibid. 1988: 149–150). In 1909, the Residency General Bureau of Railway was abolished, and the management of Korean railways was handed over to the Japanese government.

Establishment and expansion of the communication system of Korea also came under Japan's control. In 1909, the number of post offices and telecommunication centers under the management of the Japanese government reached 484 (Ibid. 1988: 152).

The third objective – namely, "the promotion of Korean economic development with the Japanese playing a key role in the development of the primary sector of the Korean economy" (Duus 1995) – did not, however, proceed as planned.

Korea in transition 1876–1945 69

In 1908, the Japanese government created the Oriental Development Company as a "colonization company" (Duus 1995: 381) to serve "as a prime mover in the improvement and modernization of Korean agriculture" and to settle "large numbers of Japanese farmers in Korea" (Moskowitz 1974: 75). But the company was unable to find as much uncultivated and unclaimed land as expected (Moskowitz 1974: 86). The plan to bring over settlers from Japan had to be abandoned. Instead, the company opted to become the largest landlord, purchasing land under cultivation and collecting rent from Korean tenants.

Land owning had been one of the most favourable methods for Japanese investors in Japan and settlers in Korea to accumulate wealth quickly after migrating. Arable land in Korea was considerably cheaper than in Japan, and it was "just as profitable to cultivate" (Duus 1995: 365). They made money by buying land and leasing it out to Korean tenants. By 1910, the proportion of the total arable land under Japanese control, including holdings individually owned, the land owned by the Oriental Development Company Japanese and public land under the control of the government-general, was 7 to 8 percent (Ibid. 1995: 377).

Japanese capitalists saw other possibilities of doing profitable business in Korea and became active investors. The establishment of the Protectorate Regime put Japan in a superior position relative to other treaty countries in acquiring the rights to open new mines. Japanese investors outdid both foreign and Korean counterparts in obtaining licenses to open mines, and between 1906 and 1909, the number of mines and alluvial gold mines owned by Japanese increased from 16 and 12 to 297 and 100, respectively, whereas those owned by Koreans, increased from 1 and 3 to 10 and 38, respectively (Choe Yun'gyu 1988: 151–153).

The fishing industry fell under Japan's control long before Korea became a protectorate. Japanese fisherman came to Korea in large numbers after the signing of the Korean-Japanese Fishing Industry Convention in 1883. Unlike Korean fishermen, they used petroleum propelled fishing boats and modern fishing equipment such as diving apparatuses to catch fish. In 1899, there were reportedly about 8,000 Japanese fishermen living in Pusan during the busy fishing season. *Kokumin sinbun*, a Japanese newspaper declared that Korean coastal waters were practically 'our colony' (Ibid. 1988: 59). The 1908 Korean-Japanese Fishing Industry Agreement further strengthened Japanese fishermen's position in Korea.

The Japanese money, mainly that of settlers, found its way into various industries such as the agricultural products processing (rice polishing), cotton ginning, brewing, tobacco, construction materials (bricks, roof-tiles, and earthen pipes), ironware (weeding hoes, rakes, sickles and other), gas and electricity and printing. Japanese businessmen had decisive advantages over their Korean counterparts. They now had full support from the government and banking organizations in opening and running new businesses. Much of the Korean market for industrial products had been inundated with goods mostly imported from Japan. A market for their products was already established. They built factories equipped with power driven machines and steam engines, and hired a large number of workers, with some factories having more than 100 workers earning a low wage. It was estimated that 5 percent of the output of the processing industry in

70 *Korea in transition 1876–1945*

1911 (one year after the annexation) was attributed to Japanese manufacturers (Ibid. 1988: 167).

In short, the Japanese in Korea during this period found other ways of making money than playing an important role in the primary sector of the Korean economy.

The institutional transition of the Korean economy to a capitalist one was almost completed during the protectorate period. At the same time, Japan was now firmly in control of the Korean economy. Moreover, Japanese capitalists emerged as the dominant force in the budding industrial sector of the Korean economy under the protection of the Japanese resident-general.

The Korean government under the "protection" of the Japanese resident general was no longer in a position to initiate any government projects for the purpose of development, nor was it able to provide protection for Korean economic actors in competition against or aggression from foreign, mainly Japanese, traders and capitalists. Koreans were forced to adapt to the new capitalist economic system dominated by the Japanese.

Major Korean investors, retired high government officials, wealthy landlords and merchants, invested their wealth in various ways, such as banking, agricultural businesses (land reclamation, raising silk worm and tussah, growing vegetables and fruits, mining, fishing, wholesale and retail business and some manufacturing industries (ceramics and dyeing brick, leaven, brewery and tobacco)). In doing so, they appeared to be more profit seekers than patriotic entrepreneurs devoted to the nationalist cause of saving the Korean economy from take-over by foreigners.

Korean investors founded banks, cooperatives and factories in the form of joint-stock companies, and it was not unusual for them to form partnerships with Japanese capitalists. In some instances, the initiative of forming a company came from Japanese businessmen. Collaboration with the Japanese was becoming an accepted business practice. In the banking business, Korean investors received assistance from Chief of the Taxation Bureau Megata Chūtarō. With the help of Megata, the previous owners (royal families and other aristocrats) of two Korean banks, Ch'ŏnil Bank (established in 1895) and Hansŏng Bank (established in 1897), which were closed in the wake of the currency crisis caused by the 1905 currency reform, were able to reopen for business with a Japanese bank loan (Y22.5 thousand) arranged by Megata. Megata also persuaded a group of rich Korean merchants to reopen the Hanil Bank.

Moneymaking through non-agricultural activities became a legitimate practice for former *yangban* elites, yet there was indication that many of them did so more as investors than as active participants in the business of commerce and industry. For example, a group of former high government bureaucrats invested a large amount of capital in building 16 factories jointly with Japanese capitalists in 1906 to 1910, but they remained as stockholders content with collecting annual dividends and relied on their Japanese partners for actual management (O Miil 2002: 6).

Korea in transition 1876–1945 71

The colonial period (1910–1945)

Educational Transformation – In 1910, the Japanese governor-general of Korea officially replaced King Kojong as the head of the state and Japanese advisers in the protective government became government administrators. The majority of Koreans holding senior government positions were removed. Korea as a colony was now required to fulfill its function as defined in terms of the interest of the Japanese empire.

In formulating policies to educate Koreans, the colonial administrators' foremost concern was to halt Korean nationalist "campaigns to save Korea through new education" to redirect their loyalty from their fatherland to Japan (as the colonial administrators were aware of widespread anti-Japanese sentiment) and provide necessary training for carrying out government plans.

Under the colonial government, the Korean educational system went through major modifications under four separate educational ordinances.

The First Korean Educational Ordinance promulgated in 1911 unified the school system into three sequential levels of education, four yearlong (shortened from six years) common schools at the elementary level, four yearlong high common and vocational schools at the middle level and four yearlong college schools at the tertiary level. Normal school was replaced by a one yearlong teacher-training program placed within the high common schools for those who wished to become common schoolteachers.

This Ordinance, however, only applied to Koreans. Japanese residents in Korea were covered by the regulations set out in Japan's Educational Ordinance. Therefore, unlike Korean students, Japanese students went through six years of primary school, six years of middle school and four years of university.

In 1922, the Second Korean Educational Ordinance was enacted, the chief aim of which was "to remove ethnic inequalities in the current educational system" by integrating the school system of Korea with that of Japan. This change was a response to the shift in the colonial policy from one of militant oppression to one of reconciliation. Accordingly, the course of study was expanded from four to six years in common school, from four to five years in high common school and women's high common school, thereby extending regular education to 15 or 16 years (instead of 11 or 12 years) as in Japan. Additional changes that occurred under this ordinance were the reintroduction of normal school in response to the expansion of common school enrollment, which made it harder to meet the demand of teachers with the teacher training programs attached to high common school and the establishment of the first university, the Keijō Imperial University, in 1924.

In 1938, the Third Korean Educational Ordinance was issued in anticipation of the launch of the National Mobilization Plan (to begin in 1941), created in connection with Japan's expansion into the Asian continent – a scheme abolishing the separation of the educational system for Korean and Japanese students. In theory, Koreans came to be regarded as subjects of the Japanese empire as the Japanese

72   Korea in transition 1876–1945

were. The primary-middle-college-university system replaced the old common school-high-common/vocational school-college system.

After the Pacific War broke out in 1941, the Fourth Korean Education Ordinance was promulgated in the same year, outlining the government's plan to mobilize middle and college students for the war effort and strengthen science and engineering education. These policies were closely reflected in changes to and the expansion of Korea's education system.

Initially, the purpose of a common school was to provide "common" practical education in the Japanese language, in topics deemed necessary to make virtuous subjects out of the Koreans to the Japanese emperor. The colonial government began with a plan of having one common school in one province. In 1922, it was amended to be one common school in three myŏn (sub-county) under the First Primary School Expansion Plan, and then in 1936, it was changed to one common school in one myŏn. In 1937, the goal was revised again under the Second Primary School Expansion Policy to double the 36 percent enrollment rate within five years. In 1944, the plan to make primary school education compulsory by 1946 was made.

As the Japanese governor-general was preoccupied with making loyal subjects out of Koreans through common school education, there was little concern with the expansion of high common school education until the middle of the 1930s when Japan adopted a policy of territorial expansion into the Asian continent and Korea was called on to participate in the project by developing a defense industry. In 1936, the colonial government introduced a plan to expand secondary education, replacing the existing policy of one secondary school (high common school and vocational school) in one province with two schools in one province. In 1937, yet another plan, the Six-Year Plan of Middle School Education Expansion, was launched to build 75 schools with 420 classrooms, adding 280 classrooms to an existing 62 schools.

At the beginning, colonial authorities maintained that Koreans were not ready for higher education. Even after primary and secondary education expanded and demand for more university and college increased, the government was not eager to expand tertiary education. For practical purposes, with Japanese residents holding the senior positions in the colony (administrators, managers, educators), the colonial authorities did not feel they needed many Koreans with a higher education. For mid-level jobs (technicians, clerks, and primary school teachers), and low- to medium-level jobs (mail deliverymen, locomotive engineers, telephone operators and nurses), the colonial government considered secondary academic and vocational school education sufficient to produce them.

Throughout the entire colonial period, the colonial government built 1 public university, Keijō University; 9 government and public colleges; and elevated 11 private schools to the rank of college when they met standards specified in the Private College Regulations,

In 1943, the total number of students enrolled in public colleges was 2,702 students, of which 1,711 students (or 70.7 percent) were Japanese. In the same year, there were 4,025 students, mostly Koreans, enrolled in private colleges. Private

Korea in transition 1876–1945 73

colleges founded by Koreans thus largely provided tertiary education for Korean students.

Over three decades between 1910 and 1940 (for which official statistics are available) the number of public common schools[7] increased from 128 schools (8,960 students) to 2,851 schools (343,642 students), whereas the number of private common schools increased from 43 schools (2,960 students) to 136 schools (57,878 students). During the same period, public secondary schools increased from 26 (1,105 students) to 311 (50,100 students) and private secondary schools increased from seven (526 students) to 39 schools (18,191 students).

What then was the overall impact of colonial education on the Korean population?

In 1940, 60 percent of children aged 6 to 12 attended primary schools, 2.4 percent of adolescents aged 13 to 18 attended middle schools and 0.2 percent of youth aged 19 to 24 attended colleges or universities (Chang 1975: 44). By 1944, of the total population (22,793,768), 0.12 percent (0.23 percent males, 0.01 percent females) had university or college degrees, 1.1 percent (1.8 percent males, 0.4 percent females) had secondary education or more (middle school and high common school) and 10.9 percent (13.4 percent males, 8.6 percent females) had primary school or more. Those who attended temporary school and those who never received any form of school education accounted for 4.3 percent (7.9 percent males, 1.0 percent females) (Chōsen sōtokufu 1945: 142–143).

The colonial educational policies imposed a huge dilemma on nationalist Koreans who viewed school education as a means to instill nationalist spirit. At the schools founded by the colonial government, Korean students were being taught to become loyal subjects to the Japanese emperor, not to become patriots.

The colonial government also restricted the number of private schools being built and rigorously controlled their educational content with the aim of eliminating nationalist elements and Christian teachings. Many of these schools were closed because they were either unable to meet the standards set by the government or unwilling to abide by them for ideological or religious reasons. Those private schools that met government requirements were incorporated into the colonial government's educational system and taught more or less the same curricula as the government or public schools did.

Korean parents were left with the choice of either refusing and denying their children the new Western style of education or sending them to sŏdang, where they would remain nearly illiterate (Kim Hyŏngmok 2003: 48).

The newly educated became "modern" men and women with a new (Western) way of life, liberating them from old traditional Confucian customs and ethics. The Western education provided by the public school system offered various forms of knowledge hitherto unavailable to students. Aside from teaching those courses – the Japanese language, Japanese history and culture and moral education – designed to make Japanese out of Koreans, the new educational system also taught students arithmetic, science, technical education, foreign language (mainly Western), geography, history and philosophy. It gave students access to Western civilization, but, more importantly, education provided students with a diploma, which became necessary for landing prestigious occupations and

74 *Korea in transition 1876–1945*

professions such as government administrators, judges, prosecutors, teachers, doctors, engineers and scientists.

Nationalist Koreans, at least in the 1920s, refused to accept this choice and demanded that the colonial government build more schools for Korean school-age children and provide more Korean content. Such demands were a direct challenge to the Japanese assimilation policy and had little chance of eliciting a positive response from the colonial government. Nationalist Koreans were left with little choice but to continue the education campaign, demanding that the colonial government build more public schools for Korean children and raise funds for government projects to build schools (see Pak Chindong 1998; O Sŏngchŏl 1999).

The campaign to increase the number of higher education institutions for Koreans made little progress. The governor-general recognized 11 private colleges but no private universities during the three-and-a-half decades of his rule.

Competition for admission to post-secondary schools intensified among Koreans, and there were increasingly more applicants to schools at the post-primary level than existing facilities could accommodate (see Chu Ikchong 1998). Those parents who could afford to send their children overseas for higher education, mainly to Japan. In 1939, there were 12,500 Koreans in Japan attending middle schools (7,500) and colleges and universities (5,000) (Chu Ikchong 1998: 107–108). The number of Korean college and university students in Japan remained higher than that in Korea until the end of the colonial period.[8]

Economic Transformation – The incorporating the Korean economy into that of Imperial Japan began with a nationwide land survey which the colonial government conducted from 1910 to 1918 with the objective of estimating the existing taxable land. It located the land, which hitherto had remained unregistered, thereby increasing the amount of taxable land from 995,000 kyŏl in 1909 to 1,072,000 kyŏl in 1918 (Miyajima 1991: 504).

The land survey was followed by various institutional reforms. A new land tax system was installed to calculate land tax on the basis of the market price of the land tract rather than the anticipated amount of potential grain produced by the land tract, as it was done during the Chosŏn Dynasty period to collect it in cash.

The more important part of the reform plan was the reorganization of the banking system. The Bank of Korea was placed under the direct control of the Japanese government, which was to appoint a director to supervise and control the management of the bank.

Moving forward with the plan of establishing infrastructure, four major railway lines, P'yŏngnam, Kyŏngwŏn, Honam and Hamkyŏng were built to connect major ports, factories, industrial towns, towns of agricultural product assemblage and other cities with political importance. The highway was also expanded 17,000 km in 1910–1914 and 2,600 km in 1911–1917.

In 1912, the colonial government also initiated a project to build the Korean Packet Ship Company (Chōsen yūsen kabushiki kaisha) with a capital investment from marine transportation companies owned by Japanese residents in Korea (47.2 percent), the Japan Packet Ship Company (Nihon yunsen kabushiki

Korea in transition 1876–1945   75

kaisha) and the Osaka Merchant Ship Company (Osaka shōsen kabushiki kaisha) (45.8 percent).

The extension of the communications network then ensued. From 1910 to 1921, the telecommunications network expanded from 5,454 km to 8,030 km in length. During the same period, the telephone line increased from 486 km to 7,056 km. Together with the extension of the communications network, the number of postal offices grew from 506 in 1910 to 683 in 1920 (Ch'oe Yun'gyu 1988: 245).

i) The Agricultural Development Plan – In the late 1920s, the role of the colonial economy changed when Japan faced a food shortage. Agricultural output in Japan was no longer keeping pace with the growth of its population and the price of rice rose sharply. As part of an Agricultural Development Plan, the colonial government considered their Rice Increase Plan to be the answer. Launched in 1926 and pushed forward until 1934, the plan had two major objectives: increase of productivity per unit of land and enlarge farmland.

Financing for the plan came primarily from the colonial government and quasi-state development banks. The former provided subsidies, while the latter was largely responsible for supplying needed funds in the form of loans. The government also supplied new seeds and chemical fertilizers, introduced new methods of cultivation, established modern irrigation systems for the reclamation of wasteland and underwater land and turned dry land into paddy fields.

As the plan went ahead, landlords, Japanese as well as Korean, were called on to play leading roles. Landlords eagerly responded to government initiatives, enforcing their tenants to adopt new methods of rice cultivation recommended by the government. They also collected high rates on tenanted land in-kind, most of which was sold in the Japanese market.

The outcome of the plan was remarkable. Over two decades, from 1915–1919 to 1935–1939, the five-year average value of total agricultural output (at the constant price) more than doubled. Rice production during the same period increased by 50 percent, and the average rice yield per acre increased by 26 percent. Although land under cultivation increased by 5 percent, the increased production was a result of improved farming methods and use of fertilizer and superior seeds.

Agricultural exports grew 3.8 times faster than the increase of production. At the beginning of the plan, 96.1 percent of exported rice went to Japan. At the end of the plan, the percentage increased to 99.8 percent. The growth of rice exports thus met the increased Japanese demand and kept the retail price of rice "almost parallel to the general price movement" (Ohkawa and Rosovsky 1960: 56). By 1930, this brought Japanese farmers into opposition to the plan, and it was dropped in 1934 (Chang 1971: 172–175).

The Rice Increase Plan resolved the grain shortage problem in Japan. As an incorporated part of the larger Japanese economy, the Korean economy performed its role as a supplier of grain, dutifully meeting Japan's needs.

What impact, then, did the plan have on Korea? How did Koreans respond or adapt to the plan forced upon them?

Unlike Korean landlords who were able to collect more rents from the increased productivity of their land rented out to tenant, farmers benefitted little from the

76   *Korea in transition 1876–1945*

plan. As mentioned earlier, rice exported to Japan exceeded the increase of rice growth in Korea, which indicates that their consumption of home-grown rice was reduced. Cheaper, coarser grains were imported from Manchuria as a substitute for the rice exported to Japan. The import of these grains, however, did not offset the reduced per capita consumption of rice. The per capita consumption of grains gradually declined over the colonial period. "The large exports," in the words of Bruce Johnston, "seem to have involved not only a qualitative sacrifice in substituting coarse grains for rice, the preferred cereal, but also a quantitative sacrifice of the level of consumption"(1953: 56). These so-called forced or starvation exports had less to do with farmers voluntarily selling more rice for the extra income but more to do with landlords turning rents in-kind (rice) collected from their tenants into commodities in the export market. By the middle of the colonial period, four out of five Korean farm households were tenants or semi-tenants, and on average, one-half or more of their crops went to the landlords as rent. And most of the rice collected as rent moved into the export trade, and 60 percent of Korea's exports of rice came from the landlords (Johnston 1953: 50). It is true that the Rice Increase Plan by the colonial government made the rice exports of such magnitude possible. But equally significant is the role landlords, both Koreans and Japanese in Korea, played in the export trade market in pursuit of profits.

The extensive commercialization of rice under the colonial authorities also radically altered the relationship between Korean landlords and tenants. Korean landlords' concept of the farmland they owned and attitudes toward their tenants significantly changed. Unlike former yangban landlords during the Chosŏn period, they became active in forcing their tenants to increase productivity through new methods promoted by the government. They enforced the adoption of superior seedlings, new methods of creating seedling beds, deep seedling planting and the application of chemical fertilizers. It was customary during the Chosŏn Dynasty period that tenants could continue leasing the land indefinitely as long as they did not neglect to pay rent or did not have other faults. When a landowner leased a plot of land, they assumed that the tenant-landlord relationship would last at least 20 to 30 years in the southern region and 10 to 20 years in the northern region. Tenants were also allowed to sublease their tenancy to other tenants. Under the colonial authorities and with the growth of agricultural market, Korean landlords became much more profit oriented. They shortened tenancy period and did not automatically renew leases with the current tenant, instead giving the land to someone else at a higher rate. Tenants were no longer allowed to lease or sell their tenancy to other tenants, losing their right to claim occupancy of the leased land (Hori 1983: 363). Landlords also came to impose rent on what the tenants had been allowed to grow in the land free of charge after harvesting rice. They also demanded the tenant pay rent of unpolished rice even for dry fields they leased. If the rice they received as rent from tenants was of poor quality, the landlords would collect an additional amount of rice or cancel the tenancy. Furthermore, they held the tenant responsible for paying expenses incurred in managing or repairing the leased land, new irrigation cooperative fees and transporting the rent rice to the landlord's house, often located at a distance from the rice field. More importantly,

Korea in transition 1876–1945 77

they became less willing to negotiate the rent rate with the tenant in a year of bad harvest (Hori 1983: 363).

Strained relationships between landlords and tenants led the latter to find a more advanced (or modern) way of negotiating with the former about the conditions of tenancy. Tenants formed – with the help of urban intellectuals of Marxist orientation – various types of local cooperatives and subsequently became members of the national labour federation in the early 1920s, thereby confronting landlords as a collective body. The tenancy union as a part of the labour federation played an important role in resolving tenancy disputes in the early 1920s, until the tenancy union was outlawed by the colonial government in 1930. (This section was adapted from Chang (1971: 171–175).)

ii) The Industrial Development Plan – When Japan planned its territorial expansion into China, and eventually started a war against China in the early 1930s as a step towards building an empire in East Asia under Japanese sovereignty called the East Asia Co-prosperity Area, Korea came to be viewed as a base for advancement into the continent (Suzuki 1942: 296-301). With the outbreak of the Sino-Japanese War in 1936, the colonial government established an industrialization plan to develop war-related industries and mining.

Accordingly, Korea (together with Taiwan) was forced to develop nonagricultural sectors of its economy in conjunction with Japan's efforts to militarize its economy (Barclay 1954). At the time, however, colonial Korea did not have sufficient funds or technologies to carry out a large-scale industrial development program. Inevitably, the colonial government turned to giant Japanese enterprises (zaibatsu) for the supply of the two major ingredients, capital and technology, and made the transfer process easy and ensured a profitable venture by offering numerous incentives.

To generate enough power for the new industries, the colonial government sponsored the development of electric power, exercising overall control and offering various subsidies to all generating stations. In 1935, with the establishment of a hydroelectric power station based on the Yalu and Tumen rivers, the potential capacity for electric power was estimated at some four million kilowatts, far more than was required. Resource surveys were also conducted in the same year, and it was estimated that some 200 minerals and ores had been found – the majority of which were useful for these new industries.

Restrictions on the establishment of new factories were then minimized by the government, and land prices were controlled to help provide suitable land for new industrial plants and to reduce the cost of new projects.

In 1939, the government also introduced the Temporary Wage Control Act to keep labour wages low. Trade union laws, labour laws and the Factory Law, promulgated in Japan in 1916, giving legal protection to labourers had yet to be enacted in Korea (Ōjima 1938: 35). (The above two paragraphs were adapted from Chang (1971: 75–77).)

Furthermore, the government offered subsidies and generous tax rates, and expanded limits on company bond issues to encourage private investment (Eckert 2001: 67).

78 *Korea in transition 1876–1945*

Lured by these incentives, many giant Japanese enterprises such as Mitsui Mitsubishi, Sumitomo, Nitchitsu, Tōtaku, Kanebō, Tōyōbo and Nittetsu quickly opened branch offices or built independent factories in Korea. The governor-general encouraged Japanese businessmen in Korea to actively participate; expanded the factories affiliated with and run by the bureaus of railway, transportation, telecommunications and monopoly; and built new factories to manufacture and repair weapons (Ch'oe Yun'gyu 1988: 339).

In 1939, the colonial government also established chartered companies such as the Korean Magnesium Exploitation Company (with Mitsui), the Korean Mining Development Company, the Gold Production Promotion Company, the Korean Gold Production Development Company and the Korean Mica Development company, specifically for the purpose of mining resources (Ibid. 1988: 339).

As of 1942, the government's capital investment in Korean industrial installations accounted for 74 percent, 24 percent from companies owned by Japanese capitalists in Korea, with the remaining 1.5 percent from Korean capital or nationalist capital (minjok chabon). However, since this data does not include state-run railway, transportation and telecommunications companies; their affiliates; and military industry companies, the Japanese economist Kobayashi points out the actual share of Korean capital would be even smaller (Ibid. 1988: 502).[9]

Colonial Korea provided cheap labour. When Japan began the "militarization of its economy," the colonial government established job guidance centers in various cities to provide job information to the public and supply and recruit labour for the industry in accordance with the government's development aims.

One source indicates that the number of factory workers, mining workers and engineering and construction workers increased almost three times between 1933 and 1938 from 247,105 to 689,720 (Ibid. 1988: 390). However, the existing labour market alone was not enough to supply the workforce required by expanding war industries in Korea and Japan.[10] The Tokyo government promulgated three labour mobilization acts – the National General Mobilization Ordinance in 1938, the Patriotic Labour Service Ordinance in 1941 and the Female Voluntary Service in 1944 – to enable the colonial government to fully and forcibly mobilize the workforce to meet the rising wartime labour demand.

The aim of the National General Mobilization Law was to control and make use of all the resources of the nation, including "the regular workforce" most effectively during war times or the times of crisis equivalent to war.

The aforementioned ordinance was supplemented by the Patriotic Labour Service Act to enable the government to mobilize a "non-regular workforce" including students, women and rural labour.

The Women's Voluntary Service Corps Ordinance was specifically designed to mobilize single or unmarried women (12–40) for essential war industries such as filature and the textile industry. The institution of this ordinance was primarily aimed at solving the labour shortage problem created by conscription of the majority of Japanese youth (males) for military service.

Korea in transition 1876–1945 79

With these acts, the colonial government came to be deeply involved in forceful labour mobilization. It began with helping employers to recruit by urging unwilling workers to volunteer and transporting them to workplaces and later drafting workers by itself. Drafted labour was sent to munitions factory, coals and other mines, as well as construction and engineering workplaces in northern Korea and Japan.

Altogether, some 5 to 6 million workers were said to be mobilized during the war period, and 700,000 to 1 million of them were sent overseas to Japan, Sakhalin and Pacific Islands (Kim Hokyong et al (2010).

One distinct aspect of the labour mobilization scheme by the Japanese and colonial government was to mobilize young single and unmarried women, Koreans, Japanese, Chinese, Philippinos and Indonesians, to provide sexual service to soldiers at so-called comfort stations established near the places where the soldiers were stationed. The government did not openly draft young women for the purpose of providing sexual service, but it is now well known that women in the Women's Voluntary Service Corps were sometimes "diverted into prostitution" and the corps "became so identified with it that women who actually did work in factories have been reluctant to acknowledge their membership of Corps" (Hicks 1994: 52). How many Korean women ended up in comfort stations is not – will never be – known. However, there are claims that there were some 150,000–200,000 comfort women and 80 or 85 percent of them were Koreans.

Drafted Korean workers in Korea and overseas worked under poor working conditions. Wages they received did not guarantee the minimum living expenses. Japanese employers in Japan paid one-eighth or one-tenth of the monthly wages they promised at the time of hiring and kept a portion – one-fourth or one-third – of their pay in the name of saving in an effort to prevent them from escaping. They worked long hours ranging from 10 to 12 hours. Employers paid little attention to protecting their employees from work injuries. Numerous deaths of draft workers have been reported. On the average, one-third of conscript workers escaped from their workplaces.

The impact of the industrialization plan focused on the growth of the wartime industry on the Korean economy has not been fully analyzed by scholars due mainly to paucity of data.

But with available statistical information limited largely to pre-1940 period, one may still be able to draw the overall picture of economic transformation of Korea under Japanese rule. The per capita gross output of goods grew at the annual rate of 3.7 percent. The proportion of this increased production exported increased from 6 percent to 27 percent between 1910–1914 to 1935–1940. But for most of the colonial period, production for export was largely accounted for by agricultural products and raw materials which were mainly oriented to the markets in Japan. Korea imported manufactured products mostly from Japan.

Change in emphasis in the government's economic policy after 1930 is clearly shown in the increase of the value of products of both mining and manufacturing industries between 1930–1934 and 1935–1939. During the period, mining production increased by more than four times, from Y28 thousand to Y97.8 thousand,

80 *Korea in transition 1876–1945*

while the production of manufacturing industry increased about three times, from Y234.1 thousand to Y527.7 thousand. In the period from 1935 to 1939, mining and manufacturing accounted for 40 percent of the total gross output of goods, compared to 27 percent for the previous five years. More than 40 percent of the total gross output of goods in 1940 was still agricultural and more than 60 percent of the total population found their means of livelihood in agriculture. Although this rapidly increasing amount of manufactured industrial products came from new factories,[11] Korean industry still retained many traditional elements. Household industry accounted for 40.1 percent of the total gross value of industrial products in 1933. Although this decreased after 1936, the share of household industry still was responsible for 22 percent as late as 1939. (This paragraph was drawn from Chang (1971): 178–180).

How then did Koreans per se fare in this process of industrial development?

Unlike Korean landlords in the Rice Increase Plan, they were not invited by the colonial authorities to participate as active players. Their contribution to capital formation was minimal (1.5 percent) relative to their Japanese counterparts, and they were mostly small- and medium-sized enterprise operators (92 percent of factories owned by Koreans were hiring less than 50 workers). However, Korean capitalists appeared to have learned to adapt to the slowly expanding capitalist market dominated by the Japanese (Ho Suyol (1990).

The data on factory ownership indicates that during the period of 1930 to 1939, the number of factories in all size categories owned by Koreans grew. The number of factories hiring 5 to 49 workers increased from 2,168 to 3,693, those hiring 50 to 99 workers increased from 43 to 150, those hiring 100 to 199, increased from 12 to 54 and those hiring 200 and more increased from 10 to 19 (Ibid. 1990: 38).

Minimal though it may be, this growth reflected Korean entrepreneurs' efforts to grow and survive. The early nationalistic push for industry as a means to build national strength became the promotion of industrial production movement (mulsan changryŏ undong) after Korea became a colony. The movement officially began in 1920, when a group of Korean civil leaders in Pyongyang founded the Society to Promote Industrial Production by Koreans (mulsanchangnyŏhoe) and began a nationwide campaign – the main goal of which was to "produce what we (Koreans) need by ourselves (chajokchagŭp)." Koreans were urged not to buy foreign products and consume only goods produced by the hands of Koreans (Pak Chansŭng 1992: 262–267). This campaign, however, revealed its own internal dilemma in that in the capitalist economic system controlled by Japanese authorities and dominated by Japanese capitalists, cooperation with them was unavoidable for the Korean's success and/or survival as entrepreneurs. While the Korean civil leaders appealed to the nationalist sentiments of Korean consumers in selling their products, they became more like profit-seeking capitalists, learning the skills to survive or succeed in the hostile competitive market from their Japanese counterpart. A handful of Korean businessmen made the rank of conglomerate (zaibatsu or chaebŏl) by successfully establishing personal ties with high-ranking government bureaucrats and Japanese businessmen, especially bankers. They also proved to be tough employers for their Korean workers (Eckert 1991: 96–110).

Korea in transition 1876–1945 81

In contrast to the limited growth of Korean investors/capitalists, the size of the industrial workforce grew substantially. In 1937, there were about 200,000 Korean factory workers (Kim Kyŏngil 2004: 54) working under poor conditions – low wages, long hours, little to no protection from work injuries, and ethnic discrimination.[12] Like tenant sharecroppers in the 1920s, they began to organize themselves into unions at various levels – factory, sub-county, county or city, province and nationwide, with the help of progressive intellectuals. They collectively negotiated, sometimes successfully, with employers for wage increases and improvement of working conditions. Labour disputes or strikes became a negotiating technique for labourers. In the early 1930s, the fear of labour unions growing into an anti-government political force caused the colonial authorities to strictly prohibit organizing labour unions (Kim Kyŏngil 2004: 266).

We should also note the rise of the middle class. The middle class consisted of two occupational categories, independent small business owners including small factory owners, and office workers commonly known as white-collar workers or organization men who were employed by large organizations (e.g., government and large business enterprises, including banks and large factories), such as professionals, technicians and clerics, and live on salaries and work for institutions, not for persons. The emergence of this occupational category, typically an urban phenomenon, has historical significance in that artisans and merchants were no longer considered men engaged in base work and even ranked higher on the modern occupational scale, and similarly white-collar jobs were not the ones persons with education avoided. In fact, they competed against government and scholarly jobs in attracting people with school education as a career choice by generally paying higher salaries. In short, the traditional concept of work changed.

Notes

1 Korea-America Trade Treaty (1882), Korea-England Trade Treaty (1882), Korea-Germany Trade Treaty (1882), Korea-China Trade Agreement (1882), Korea-Russia Trade Treaty (1884), Korea-France Trade Treaty (1886), Italy-Korea Treaty (1884), Austria-Korea Treaty (1892), Belgium-Korea Treaty (1902) and Denmark-Korea Treaty (1902).
2 Huang, however, was mainly concerned with Russia's policy of territorial extension over Far East, especially Korea. He, in fact, said in the book that Korea should be friendly with China, have ties with Japan and establish connections with America.
3 No information on the exact number of primary and middle schools established by civilian leaders is available.
4 There were five types of merchants during the Chosŏn Dynasty period, city merchants (sijŏn sangin), wholesalers and brokers (kaekchu and yŏgak) and boat merchants (sŏnsang).
5 In 1909, 466 Japanese high-ranking officials (kotŭnggwan), 1604 bureau chiefs (pan'inimkwan) and 1,548 police officers were affiliated with the Korean government.
6 The number of students enrolled in five vocational schools (mostly in small cities) is unknown (O Chŏnsŏk 1964: 158). Since the number of students attending a vocational school in a small town at the time was less than 50 on the average, the missing number would not be more than 100.
7 Including two government common schools.

82 *Korea in transition 1876–1945*

8 Christian church organizations sponsored a small number of students to go the United States.
9 If we measure the total value of Korean capital invested in establishing joint stock companies in all areas including trade and banking, the Korean share of the total value of paid-up capital would be 6 percent (Hŏ Suyŏl 1990: 28).
10 Japanese capitalists in Japan also went after the cheap Korean labour force.
11 The number of factories employing 5 or more workers increased from 442 in 1910–1914 to 6,287 in 1935–1939.
12 The Factory Act, designed to reduce the maximum working day from 12 hours to 11 hours and to prohibit child labour in mines and night work by girls under 16, was promulgated in Japan in 1926, whereas no such move was made in Korea.

References

Barclay, George W. (1954) *Colonial Development and Population in Taiwan*, Princeton: Princeton University Press.
Chang, Yun-Shik (1975) "Growth of Education in Korea 1910–1945," *Bulletin of the Population and Development Studies Center*, vol.4, pp. 40–53.
Chang, Yun-Shik (1971) "Colonization as Planned Change: The Korean Case." *Modern Asian Studies*, vol. 5, no. 2, pp. 161–186.
Ch'oe, Yun'gyu (1988) *Kŭnhyŏndae Chosŏn Kyŏngjesa* (The History of Recent and Contemporary Korean Economy), Seoul: Kalmuj.
Chōsen, sōtokufu (1945) *Jinkō chōsa kekka hōkoku* (Population Census Report), Keijō[Seoul]: Chōsen sōtokufu.
Chu, Ikchong (1998) "1930nyŏndae chungyŏp ihu Chosŏn'indŭl ŭi chungdunghakkyo'ui hwakch'ung" (Expansion of Middle School Education of Koreans After the Mid-1930s), *Kyŏngjesahak* (The Study of Economic History). vol. 24, pp. 97–137.
Duus, Peter (1995) *The Abacus and the Sword*, Berkeley: University of California Press.
Eckert, Carter J. (1991) *Offspring of Empire*, Seattle: University of Washington Press.
Furukawa, Noriko (2004) "Tŏksan School in Taegu in the 1920s: Contradiction in Educational Administration in Colonial Korea" (Unpublished).
Hicks, George (1994) *The Comfort Women*, New York: Norton.
Hŏ, Suyŏl (1990) "Chosŏnin chabon ŭi chonjehyŏngt'ae" (On Types of Capital Owned by Koreans), *Kyŏngje nonjip* (Economic Journal), vol. 4 (December), pp. 73–110.
Hori, Washō (1983) "Chosŏn'e issōsŏ'ŭi sikminji chŏngch'aek" (The Colonial Policy in Korea), pp. 331–374, in Kajimura, Hiteki and Others (eds.) *Han'guk kŭndae kyŏngjesa yŏn'gu* (A Study of the History of Recent Korean Economy), Seoul: Sakyejŏl.
Johnston, Bruce F. (1953) *Japanese Food Management in the World War II*, Stanford: Stanford University Press.
Kim, Hyŏngmok (2003) "Ilche kangjŏmki sasŏl ch'odŭnggyoyuk kigwan ŭi yŏkhwal – hanmal 1920nyŏndae'rŭl chungsim'ŭro " (The Role of Private Primary Educational Organizations Under Imperial Japan's Occupation – With a Focus on the Period from the End of Choson Dynasty to 1920s), *Proceedings of the 2003 Annual Academic Symposium of the Korean Association of Primary Education*, pp. 145–171.
Kim, Hokyŏng et al (2010) *Ilche kangje tongwŏn, kŬ allyŏjiji anhun yŏksa* (The Forced Labour Mobilization, the Unknown History), Seoul: Tolbege.
Kim, Kyŏngil (2004) *Han'guk nodong undongsa* (The History of Korean Labor Movement), Seoul: Chisik Madang.

Korea in transition 1876–1945 83

Lee, Ki-baik (1984) *A New History of Korea*, Translated by Edward W. Wagner with Edward J. Shultz, Seoul: Ilchogak.

Moskowitz, Karl (1974) "The Creation of the Oriental Development Company: Japanese Illusions Meet Korean Reality," *Occasional Papers on Korea*, no. 2 (March), pp. 73–121.

O Chŏnsŏk (1964) *Sin kyoyuksa* (The History of New Education), Seoul: Hyŏndae kyoyuk ch'ongsŏ ch'ulpansa.

O Miil (2002) *Han'guk kŭndae chabon'ga yŏn'gu* (A Study of Recent Korean Capitalists), Seoul: Hanul akademi.

O Sŏngch'ŏl (1999) "Sikminji ch'odŭnggyoyuk p'aengch'ang ŭi sahoesa" (The Social History of the Expansion of Colonial Primary Education), *Ch'odŭng kyoyuk yŏn'gu* (The Study of Primary Education), vol. 13, no. 1, pp. 5–29.

Ohkawa, Kazushi and Henry Rosovsky (1960) "The Role of Agriculture in Modern Japanese Economic Development," *Economic Development and Cultural Change*, vol. 9, no. 1 (Part II), pp. 43–67.

Ōjima, Seiichi (1938) *Sen, Man, Chi shinkō keizai* (New Industries in Korea, Manchuria and China), Tokyo: Miraisha.

Ōno, Ken'ich'I (1936) *Chōsen kyōiku mondai kanken (Survey of Problems in Korean Education)*, Keijo: Chōsen Kyoikukai.

Pak, Chansŭng (1992) *Han'guk kŭndae chŏngch'i sasangsa yŏn'gu* (A Study on Modern Political Thoughts in Korea), Seoul: Yŏksa bipyŏngsa.

Pak, Chindong (2007) "Ilche kangjŏmha (1920nyondae) bot'onghakkyo 6 nyŏnje sŭngkyŏk undong ŭi chŏngae wa kwigyŏl" (Development and Consequences of the Movement to Upgrade Six-Year Common School Education Under Imperial Japan's Occupation [1920s]). *Yŏksa kyoyuk* (History Education), vol. 102, pp. 97–126.

Sin, Yongha (1976) *Tngnip hyŏphoe yŏn'gu* (A Study of the Independence Club), Seoul: Ilchogak.

Sin, Yongha (1974), "Uri nara ch'oech'o ŭi kŭndae hakkyo sŏllip e taehayŏ (On Establishing the First Modern School in Korea), *Han'guksa yŏn'gu*, no. 10, pp. 191–204.

Son, Insu (1971) *Han'guk kŭndae kyoyuksa* (The History of Recent Korean Education), Seoul: Yŏnsei daehakkyo ch'ulp'anbu.

Suzuki, Takeo (1942) *Chōsen no keizai* (The Korean Economy), Tokyo: Nihon hyōronsha.

Yi, Kwangnin (1981) *Kaehwap'a wa kaehwa sasangyon'gu* (A Study of the Enlightenment Party and Enlightenment Thought), Seoul: Ilchogak.

3 Growth of new (Western) education

Korea became liberated in 1945, and the two allied forces, the United States and the USSR, divided the peninsula into two and occupied, respectively, the southern and northern parts. In 1948, the south became the Republic of Korea and the north the People's Republic of Korea. The two republics revived the kŭndaehwa project after the occupation forces left, adopting two radically different strategies: guided market approach in the south and socialist approach in the north. Taking separate paths to the kŭndaehwa project reflects that the two sides have chosen to go different ways in nation building – namely, democratization in the south and socialization in the north. Establishing a new political system became a new modernization project in the independent Koreas. Owing to the lack of space and adequate information on North Korea, I will only discuss post-Liberation kŭndaehwa process in South Korea.

This chapter will discuss the expansion of education. In doing so, I will underscore the role played by the personalist ethic, focusing on parental roles in paying for children's education, formal as well as informal, and parental involvement in children's education. They are so deeply involved in their children's education to the extent that they should be responsible for making informal education as a regular part of the formal school education process.

Growth of education

In the Republic of Korea, established in 1948, formal education was viewed as a constitutional right. Article 16 of its new constitution states, "It is the right of every citizen to receive education; and at least elementary education should be provided free of charge."

Primary Education – In 1949, the new government announced a six-year plan for compulsory primary education with the proclamation of the Compulsory Education Act. But the Korean War, which broke out in the following year, derailed the plan. The same plan was revived in 1953 with the revised goal of achieving an enrollment rate of 96 percent of primary school-age children by 1959. Citizen response to the plan was overwhelming, and the government made noteworthy efforts to build more schools and to train teachers.[1] In 1959, the enrollment rate of primary school-age children reached 95.2 percent; the enrollment rate increased

Growth of new (Western) education 85

much faster than the rate at which schools were constructed and teachers were trained. The policy the government adopted was to meet the rising demand for schooling with minimum expense (Kim Yŏnghwa 2004: 69). Consequently, classrooms became crowded – the number of students per class and teacher reached 60 to 70, and double- or triple-shift systems had to be introduced. The Park Chung Hee government (1960–1979) implemented three five-year plans – in conjunction with the five-year economic development plans – to expand compulsory education and educational facilities by creating new schools, constructing new classrooms and repairing old classrooms.[2] As a result, the number of students per class was reduced to 52.2 in 1979 from 61.1 in 1970, and the number of students per teacher fell to 48.1 from 56.9.

Given the difficulties in building new schools and additional classrooms to adequately accommodate the rising demand, in 1955, the Rhee government decided to involve private schools in the compulsory primary education scheme. Under this scheme, private schools would take pupils allocated by the government, thereby alleviating government expenditure on public primary education. The Park government maintained this policy. The number of private primary schools increased from 22 in 1962 to 94 in 1966. A small number of private primary schools with more qualified teachers and better facilities soon became "aristocratic schools" coveted largely by wealthy families. In an effort to stall this trend, the Park government adopted the policy of allowing private schools to admit only those children from the school district in which they were located through lottery, and in 1966, stopped licensing the building of private primary schools altogether.

Secondary Education – Completion of compulsory primary education created enormous pressure on middle schools to expand. The increasing proportion of primary school graduates advancing to middle school further accelerated expansion. While in 1950, 48.5 percent of primary school graduates advanced to secondary school, by 1980, the great majority of them (96.8 percent) did so.

As middle school education became widely accessible, competition to enter selected prestigious schools became fierce, and pressure to prepare for the entrance examination mounted. After the Korean War, some schools began to offer special classes in the evenings or on weekends for additional fees. Soon the practices of extracurricular preparation became widespread, and primary school teachers "often saw their role as preparing students for the exams" (Seth 2002: 142). Formal education oriented to preparation for the examinations came under heavy criticism, for it was thought likely to undermine creativity. In 1955, President Rhee ordered that all schools close the extra classes. But that did not stop after-school study sessions (Ibid. 2002: 142).

In 1968, the Park administration took the drastic measure of abolishing middle school entrance examinations and introduced a lottery system to replace it. Under this system, primary school graduates were allotted to middle schools through a lottery, both public and private, within the district in which they resided. This no-entrance examination system meant that any primary school graduate who wanted to go to secondary school could do so; very few opted not to. In 1950, the enrollment rate of middle school-age children was 27.0 percent. It reached 95.1 percent

86 Growth of new (Western) education

in 1985 – the same year the government decided to make three-year middle school education compulsory.

With the decision to make middle school education compulsory, the government restricted creation of new private secondary schools and expansion of existing ones. In 1965, the proportion of students enrolled in private middle schools was 44.4 percent, falling to 20.0 percent in 2000.

Expansion of middle school education inevitably resulted in expansion of high schools. As Table 3.1 shows, the number of high schools and students increased sharply. With the government educational fund mostly spent on primary and middle school education, the government was unable to expand public high schools to adequately accommodate the increasing number of middle school graduates. The burden of expanding high school education had to be shared with private schools. During the same period, private high schools accommodated about one-half of total high school students – 50.7 percent in 1965 and 49.3 percent in 2005. The government did, however, provide limited financial assistance to private high schools for participating in the government plan.

The abolition of middle school entrance examinations did not, however, resolve the problem of severe competition for entrance into elite schools. Middle school graduates came to be engaged in similar competition for elite high schools that produced proportionately more graduates entering elite universities. Middle school education came to center on preparation for the high school entrance

Table 3.1 Growth of School Education 1945–2015

Year	Elementary School Student*		Junior High School Student*		Senior High School Student*		Higher Education School Student*	
1945	3,037	1,373	97	10	–	–	–	–
1950	3,942	2,658	395	381	–	–	–	–
1955	4,205	2,947	949	226	578	268	44	79
1960	4,496	3,621	1,053	529	645	273	52	93
1965	5,125	4,941	1,208	751	701	427	118	129
1970	5,961	5,749	1,608	1,319	899	590	136	180
1975	6,367	5,599	1,967	2,027	1,152	1,123	173	272
1980	6.487	5,658	2,100	2,472	1,353	1,697	213	568
1985	6,517	4,857	2,371	2,782	1,602	2,153	220	1,174
1990	6,335	4,869	2,454	2,276	1,683	2,284	224	1,364
1995	5,772	3,905	2,683	2,482	1,830	2,158	376	1,758
2000	5,267	4,020	2,731	1,861	1,957	2,051	319	2,578
2005	5,646	4,023	2,935	2,011	2,095	1,763	331	2,740
2010	5,854	3,299	3,130	1,975	2,253	1,962	341	2,806
2015	5,978	2,715	3,204	1,586	2,344	1,893	359	2,778

* The number of students in thousands.

Sources: Han'guk kyoyuk *Kaebalwŏn* 2005 for 1945–2005 and Han'guk kyoyuk kaebalwŏn 2015, for 2010–2015

examination. The informal after-school preparation for exams became a normal practice. In 1974, the government abolished high school entrance examinations under the High School Equalization Plan in the hopes of eliminating these problems (Seth 2002: 156). Consequently, what happened to high school enrollment after the abolition of the middle school entrance examination was repeated at the high school level. At the end of the 1990s, high school enrollment became almost universal, even though it was not compulsory.

The rapid growth of post-Liberation secondary education had another distinct feature – namely, dominance of academic schools at the expense of decline of vocational schools. Reconstruction of the economy devastated by the Korean War and the undertaking of a series of five-year economic development plans made the vocational training at secondary schools all the more necessary to produce skilled workers required for these projects. Successive administrations promoted various policies to attract students to vocational high schools, but they did not succeed. With educational opportunities wide open, high school education came increasingly to be perceived by students and their parents as the intermediate stage between the primary and tertiary academic education. As will be discussed further, most Korean parents desire to send their children to university. In 1965, vocational schools recruited 44.5 percent of the total number of high school students, whereas in 2000, it did only 28.5 percent.

Tertiary Education – The post-secondary education was not equalized in the same way as public primary and secondary education but grew at an accelerated rate under the mounting pressure created by universal primary and secondary school education.

Continuing with the laissez-faire policy adopted by the US military regime, the new republican government made higher education accessible to the wider public. While encouraging civilian organizations to create new higher education institutions, the government built more universities, upgraded private colleges to universities, increased the quota of existing colleges and universities and established junior colleges. Such expansionist policies continued until Park came into power and began to control what he deemed runaway university expansion.

Park's administration first enacted the Private School Ordinance in 1963, which enabled the Ministry of Education to increase its control over private universities through the exercise of the authority to approve appointments of the directors and members of private educational foundations. It was followed by the University Student Quota Ordinance in 1965, which introduced ceilings on enrollment and the number of registrants for university degree programs. These two ordinances aimed at eliminating illicit admittance and issuance of graduation certificates to those who were ready to pay a high tuition fee but not prepared to attend classes, practices that were reportedly rampant at private colleges and universities whose owners invested their wealth into the institution mainly for profitable gains (Kim Yŏnghwa 2004: 128). During the Park period, the government policy was to control the further growth of university education except in those areas required for the implementation of development plans. Government control was not strictly enforced, however, and university enrollment tripled during Park's stay in power.

88   *Growth of new (Western) education*

University enrollment spiked when the Chun Doo Hwan government initiated an educational reform, known as the July 30 (1981) Educational Reform. One important feature of this reform was the introduction of the graduation quota system. Under this system, universities could admit up to 30 percent more students than their quota allowed, but they could graduate only their allotted quota – that is, fail the same percentage of the students admitted over the four-year period. The manifest aim of this change was to improve the quality of higher education by forcing students to devote more time to their studies. Prior to the quota system, once admitted, graduation was almost automatic. But many suspected that the more expedient reason behind introducing this measure was to prevent student activists from demonstrating against the regime. In any event, these reform measures did not produce intended results. The number of students attending colleges and universities more than doubled during the Chun administration – from 402,979 in 1980 to 971,127 in 1986 (Kang Sŏnguk et al., 2005: 190). Universities, especially private ones, were "reluctant to fail students for fear of losing tuition, for fear of protest and campus disturbances that would cause the government to intervene, and for fear of the wrath of parents" (Seth 2002: 152). University officials petitioned the Ministry of Education to lift the requirement of failing 30 percent of students admitted. In 1987, the graduation quota system was repealed.

Consequently, university enrollment grew at an accelerated rate. In 1948, when the First Republic was born, there were only about 30 higher education institutions – colleges and universities combined – with 45,000 students. In 2005, the corresponding figures were 173 with 1,886,639 (Han'guk Kyoyuk Kaebalwŏn 2005: 68–69). At the end of the colonial period, the proportion of the population aged 19 to 24 receiving tertiary education was 0.2 percent; in 2005, it was 80.0 percent. Higher education has not become universal, but it is safe to say only a few high school graduates fail to enter universities.

Such a broad access to higher education has been largely attributed to the rapid expansion of private universities. From 1965 to 2005, the period for which reliable statistics are available, the number of private higher education institutions increased from 56 with 79,679 students to 147 with 1,485,971 students. Private institutions thus accounted for 80.0 percent of the total number of higher education institutions and 75.4 percent of the total number of students enrolled in 1980, and 85.0 percent and 78.8 percent, respectively, in 2005 (Han'guk Kyoyuk Kaebalwŏn 2005: 68–69).

Adult Education – While making formal education accessible to the wider public, the government also made efforts to reach out to those adults who could not attend school when they were of school age. A nationwide campaign was launched in 1946 under the auspice of the US provisional government to "wipe out" illiteracy by building civic schools. This project continued into the early 1960s, by which time the literacy rate rose to 80 percent from 30 percent in 1946. The civic school system was also used as a means to provide basic education for adolescents between 13 and 16 years of age who did not receive a primary school education. The civic school had a three-year course with a curriculum equivalent to that of primary school. Civic high schools providing middle school–level instruction were also created to service youth and adult graduates of primary or civic schools. The civic high school, in particular, played an important role briefly after the Korean War. But with most school-age children entering primary and secondary schools, the need for this institution has declined. In 1947, there were 15,400 civic schools. In 1985, only three such schools remained with 195 students. It should be noted that while civic schools are mostly run by the government, civic high schools are mostly under private auspices (McGinn et al., 1980: 9).

Equal opportunity to receive school education proved to be perhaps the most coveted and realized goal. Elites in the post-kaehwa period considered the school education as the means to strengthen the nation and catch up with the developed West and Westernized Japan. Korea now ranks high in educational achievement among OECD countries. More importantly, with the abolition of the status distinction that more or less denied commoners the opportunity to receive education, individual parents saw the opportunity to help children to move up the ladder of society by sending them to school without restriction. The school education is also widely open to women who were denied to enter public schools. Liberated Korea made public school education accessible to every citizen. Equal opportunity to receive school education, which King Kojong declared as a goal to be achieved in kaehwa Korea, is no longer a remote ideal but a reality. Primary school education now, as Dore points out, is a prerequisite for being a citizen (1980: 295). Korean parents, rich as well as poor, came to accept that it is their parental duty to provide as much education as they can and help children to do well in competition at middle school and above (Chang 1989). It was sons' education they were primarily concerned with, at first. Daughters of poor families often sought employment to help their brothers go to colleges. Now women are catching up with men in entering high educational institutions and sometimes excel men in competition in school performances and professional races.

Financing education

The underlying cause of this remarkable transformation was primarily the governments' commitment to the national project of expansion of formal education as an integral part of political development. As was the case with economic development (to be discussed in the next chapter), the massive expansion of new education was a state-led project – the origin of which goes back to the transition period after the port opening in 1876. But one should not lose sight of the fact that ordinary citizens, especially parents of students, actively participated in the educational project, just as they did before Liberation. The project was costly, and the government educational budget was limited. Parents had to and were willing to bear the financial burden of their children's school education.

Major sources of education funds were drawn from those portions of the national budget allocated for education, culture and science, as well as from the educational taxes and other types of funds raised by local governments. These two sources, however, did not and do not cover all educational expenditures adequately. Student fees and other forms of direct payment by parents and private

90 *Growth of new (Western) education*

revenue constituted an important additional fund for the school system. This mode of financing education was established during the period that followed Liberation, and it has remained unchanged. Over the years, the central government has consigned an increasing proportion of the national budget to the Ministry of Education. Nevertheless, that figure has never exceeded 10 percent and was largely expended for the cost of the government compulsory education program. In other words, the majority of government funding is taken up by primary education. Private schools assumed much of the education above the level of primary school in 1953, at which time the proportion of students in private institutions was 31 percent for middle school, 26 percent for high school and 50 percent for colleges. In 1999, corresponding figures were 33 percent, 60 percent and 77.2 percent.

Private education foundations established schools, but the main source of their finances was student fees. During the period from 1966 to 1978, student tuition, according to one survey, constituted 83.7 percent of the total annual income of private colleges, while private donations accounted for only 13 percent (Han Chunsang 1983: 313). In 2007, the financial burden of students decreased only slightly, still constituting 80.0 percent. Other sources of funding are the monies transferred from the university endowment (8.8 percent), private donations (8 percent) and the government supplementary fund (1.2 percent) (Kong Ŭnbae 2007: 30). Private tertiary education has proven to be a lucrative enterprise. It is now a well-known fact that private education foundations, mostly established by giant corporations, are eager to build and operate colleges primarily as profit-seeking ventures. Parents have been and are paying for their children's school fees. The education market in the south, until recently, was a seller's market; as long as students receive their diplomas, their parents are willing to pay for their children's education.[3]

Westernization of education

As shown earlier, at the end of the twentieth-century kŭndaehwa, or Westernization of the Korean educational system, was more or less complete. Confucian learning, focused on metaphysics and ethics, and limited to the *yangban* elite class male has been entirely replaced by Western learning primarily oriented to empirical knowledge.

De-Confucianization of the educational system is also de-sinicization or nationalization of education. Chosŏn Dynasty Korea adopted neo-Confucianism as the state principle and considered itself a small middle kingdom. China represented to Korea the only advanced civilization from which it could learn, and Korean scholars eagerly studied the Chinese characters, history, literature and, above all, Confucian canons which constituted the elements of the Confucian gentleman. After the port opening in 1876, Koreans reacted strongly against this "serve the powerful" (sadae) element in the old educational system and tried to strengthen Korean content. The Chinese characters which served as the official language have now disappeared in the public media. Chinese history and literature have been relegated to a subject that a small minority studies.

Growth of new (Western) education 91

The Japanese elements introduced into the educational content by Japanese colonialists in order to transform Koreans into loyal subjects of the Japanese emperor have also been completely eliminated. The Japanese language, history, geography and literature have all disappeared from the school curriculum at all levels. Only recently have attempts slowly been made to learn about Japan. The Japanese language is becoming a popular foreign language as a result of increasing economic, academic and other cultural exchange between the two countries. The number of university departments specializing in Japanese studies is increasing, and Japan specialists are growing in number. More university graduates are also going to Japan for advanced degrees.

De-Confucianing the educational system as well as eliminating Japanese elements from it was a necessary step for the government to take priority in promoting new ideals for liberated Korea through formal education.

The democratic basis of education was clearly outlined in the education law promulgated in 1949. This law stated that the school system, educational facilities, textbooks and curriculum should all be designed in such a way that individuality was respected, thereby enabling the student to fully utilize his or her ability. Individuality – in terms of character, ability, taste, interest and experience – was emphasized because the new educational model conceived of human beings as ends in themselves, not as means to achieve desired goals as perceived by the Japanese colonial authorities. The educational system, it was said, should not aim at a uniform product applying a narrowly defined, fixed idea. That an individual is free to differ from others to the extent that the law permits is a right guaranteed by the constitution. The ultimate purpose of the newly conceived program was to train citizens with the ability to express themselves to the fullest according to their own capacities, while respecting other people's rights.

The ideal of equal educational opportunity was an integral part of the new scheme of building a free society. The effort to put these ideas into practice in the formal education system came to be known as the "new education movement." Dewey's philosophy of education was adopted as the main thrust of this movement. His ideas were introduced in the hope of providing guidance in carrying out this new task.[4] Dewey's books, such as *Democracy and Education, School and Society* and *Experience and Society*, together with others in the same school of philosophy following Dewey, were translated into Korean in the late 1940s. A series of seminars and conferences were held among educators to exchange opinions on education and democracy. Numerous lecture series on democratic education were organized for schoolteachers during their vacation period (Oh Ch'ŏnsŏk 1964: 412).

While accepting the democratic framework of a new educational system, political leaders and educators expressed other concerns which were not always in line with the democratic idea of education. The first minister of education in the newly established republic proposed that the ideas of Hong'ik in'gan be adopted as the ideal standard of education. The notion of Hong'ik in'gan that the good man is he who endeavors to work for the good of others while minimizing his own interest is said to have originated from Tan'gun, the founding father of the nation, regarding

92   *Growth of new (Western) education*

the historical origins of Korea in two sources, *Samguk yusa* (*The History of the Three Kingdoms*) and *Chewang Un'gi* (*The Royal History of Korea*). A national system of education founded on the idea of Hong'ik in'gan would be oriented primarily to the cultivation of the personality in the direction of altruism and for molding a "perfect (total)-man," fully equipped with the traditional virtues of knowledge, human dignity, physical training and human feeling. Hong'ik in'gan ideas were adopted by the 1948 education law as the goal of the new school education system. With an emphasis on helping others and discouraging self-interest, this new system was expected to produce patriots devoted to national welfare. In this sense, the Hong'ik in'gan would eventually become a democratic citizen.

It is apparent that from the beginning there was a structural factor militating against the development of a democratic school system based on the individualistic ideology implicit in the American theories of democratic education. Koreanization of the democratic principles of education thus began very early.

The Hong'ik in'gan model put primacy on personality development. However, the second minister of education, An Ho Sang, educated in Germany, was of the opinion that school education should be geared toward producing a person who is fully aware of his or her national identity and who is completely loyal to the nation; thus, he proposed his own "Nation First" theory. Education based on this principle was to be primarily concerned with the development of the nation, with only secondary emphasis on the individual's interest. During his tenure, the minister took great pains to explain the idea and to translate it into practice through the organization of the Student Patriotic Association. Since then, it has become customary for each minister to redefine the goal of education in the hope that school principals (as they were mostly aimed at high school and below), and teachers would reflect it in their teaching. Whatever idea each minister had, they failed to provide any clear guidelines for concrete educational plans. Even if the goal was clearly conceived by the incumbent minister, he did not stay in office long enough to see the tangible results of his own plan. Each minister's average length of service was one-and-a-half years. A new minister was usually not keen on continuing the project initiated by his predecessor. None of the ministers of education who have served in the last 60 years have been able to come up with a philosophy of education that would absorb all the concerns of the previous ministers. Besides, as indicated earlier, the Ministry of Education has been too busy with more practical and administrative issues, such as entrance examinations at various levels, imposing a ceiling on school enrollment, controlling the number of students who graduate college each year, the expansion of vocational schooling and so on (Cho Kanghwan 1985).

During the Park regime, the authoritarian president tried to formulate some unifying notion of a national school education system. He commissioned a group of scholars to formulate a set of statements that was supposed to give the education program a clearly stipulated meaning and direction. The result was the National Charter of Education (Kukmin kyoyuk hŏnjang) (see Yu Hyŏngjin 1969). Efforts were made to formulate concrete educational policies on the basis of the Charter. Both primary and secondary school textbooks were revised in accordance with the

Growth of new (Western) education 93

ideas delineated in the Charter. The Charter, with presidential signature, appeared on the cover or back page of every textbook and government publication. It is difficult to measure what impact the Charter had on students. Park's concerns with formulating an educational philosophy and carrying out educational reforms were not nearly as strong as his concern over the modernization of the national economy. The initial zeal with which the Charter was created waned slowly. Eventually, the presidential signature disappeared from the Charter.

The government's effort to indoctrinate students politically meant a shift in the focus of education toward anti-communism. Given the perceived threat of military invasion from the communist north after the Korean War, the Ministry of Education endeavored to instill anti-communist (or anti-North Korea) sentiments in students at the primary and secondary levels. During the Park period, new school subjects known as "Democratic Life" and "Anti-Communism" were introduced at the secondary level for the purpose of "arming the students with a heightened political and ideological consciousness." At the college level, however, the government adopted an indirect method of denying students access to the literature on communism and North Korea – although occasionally it made an attempt to "help college students mold their ideology into the right direction" by introducing a course like "Citizen's Ethics" at the freshman level.

One may safely conclude that the authoritarian government's efforts to indoctrinate students with anti-communism through the enforcement of the Anti-Communism Law (later the National Security Law) has had the effect of making communism into a strictly taboo subject and North Korea into an archenemy. But these measures failed to produce the intended results, at least, in one regard. Many university students, known as "movement-circle" students, emerged as an anti-government or pro-democracy force, adopting a labour-friendly, anti-capitalist perspective with socialist orientation (for more on this point, see Chapter 5).

Meritocracy and diploma disease

Apart from whatever role it plays in national politics, education also serves as a means of social mobility for individuals. The education market is closely tied with the job market. Formal education has traditionally been a primary means of testing qualifications for recruitment into the government bureaucracy. As discussed earlier, during the Chosŏn Dynasty period, sons of yangban elites studied the Confucian classics at school or at home mainly in the hope of passing the civil service examination. Since sons of yangban elites did not become bureaucrats automatically, and since the number of applicants far exceeded available posts, examinations were highly competitive, and the competition intensified over time.

Under the Japanese authorities, secondary and tertiary school education served similar purposes. The government looked for recruits mainly among graduates of high schools and colleges, who were established largely for the purpose of training civil servants. Vocational high schools and professional schools at colleges produced the skilled manpower that the small modern sector of the economy required. New legal and medical institutions were imported from the West that

94 *Growth of new (Western) education*

trained lawyers and doctors. The Japanese colonial government limited the expansion of this modern sector to which educated youths aspired in order to maintain a balance between increasing demand and limited supply.

Educational Level and the Job Market – After Liberation, the modern sector of the economy expanded, reducing the agricultural sector to a negligible minority. As is the case with most developing countries, educational expansion preceded the growth of the labour market, providing educated human resources to employers. Education now is closely linked with the labour market, as Table 3.2 attests, serving as a major determinant of job allocation and the level of salary or wage.

During the period between 1985 and 2010 (see Table 3.2), the level of education attained by gainfully occupied workers rose substantially. One should first

Table 3.2 Employed Labour Force by Occupation and the Level of Education 1985–2010

	1985	*1990*	*1995*	*2000*	*2005*	*2010*
Total						
Total	100.0	100.0	100.0	100.0	100.0	100.0
Middle	58.9	48.6	36.8	40.8	24.8	20.7
High	30.9	48.7	43.9	44.1	42.8	40.4
College	2.0	3.4	5.3	7.5	10.0	12.2
Univ.	8.3	10.3	14.0	17.2	22.4	26.7
Professionals						
Middle	8.8	6.0	3.0	1.9	1.1	0.9
High	27.5	24.9	21.4	25.0	18.1	15.9
College	14.0	15.4	14.6	15.5	17.4	17.6
Univ.	49.8	53.7	53.9	57.6	63.4	65.6
Managerial Work						
Middle	13.3	10.1	8.4	6.2	4.2	2.3
High	34.4	35.5	38.3	35.5	29.7	23.7
College	0.9	3.0	5.1	6.7	6.0	9.8
Univ.	51.8	5.2	48.4	51.4	60.1	64.1
Clerical Work						
Middle	6.9	5.0	4.5	4.3	2.0	1.7
High	65.2	61.4	62.2	50.2	39.1	32.8
College	4.1	28.7	9.8	16.4	19.3	20.4
Univ.	23.7	25.7	23.5	29.2	39.7	45.1
Sales/Service						
Middle	59.0	49.9	39.8	33.3	24.7	20.2
High	34.5	41.5	50.1	53.6	54.4	54.8
College	1.3	2.5	3.8	7.0	8.3	11.1
Univ.	5.3	6.3	6.4	7.6	12.6	14.00
Skilled Work						
Middle	73.4	63.6	43.5	37.9	28.6	25.9
High	23.6	33.3	50.8	53.7	57.3	53.5
College	0.8	1.3	3.4	5.3	8.0	12.2
Univ.	1.7	1.8	2.3	3.2	6.2	8.4

Growth of new (Western) education   95

	1985	1990	1995	2000	2005	2010
Semi-Skilled Work						
Middle	44.6	40.6	33.1	27.8	24.0	20.8
High	38.4	55.0	62.5	64.8	64.4	44.5
College	1.1	2.9	2.4	4.1	6.9	10.1
Univ.	1.0	1.6	2.0	3.2	4.8	7.0
Labour Work						
Middle	68.5	57.8	62.6	58.4	51.5	48.3
High	30.1	39.7	33.8	37.9	41.3	43.2
College	0.6	1.3	1.4	1.9	3.3	4.2
Univ.	0.9	1.1	2.2	1.8	3.9	4.2
Agriculture, Forestry and Fishing Jobs						
Middle	89.0	88.4	84.2	80.4	78.7	72.3
High	10.0	10.5	13.8	16.9	17.4	21.1
College	0.4	0.4	0.6	0.7	1.6	2.2
Univ.	0.5	0.7	1.4	1.9	2.2	4.1

Source: Han'guk nodong munje yŏn'guwŏn

note that the proportion of those workers with primary school education is so negligible that the Korea Labor Institute included them in the category of middle school education and less. The overall trend is the increase of the proportion of the total number of employed people who completed university and college education (from 10.3 percent to 38.9 percent), and the decrease of that with high and middle school education (from 89.8 percent to 61.1 percent). Put differently, one out of ten employed workers had tertiary education in 1985, whereas the rate was four out of ten in 2010.

While the average level of workers' formal education was rising, the industrial category of work became more selective to the educational level of workers.

As of 2010, the three categories, managerial, professional and clerical jobs were largely occupied by graduates of higher institutions. Clerical jobs entered this category after 2005. Up until 1993, high school graduates constituted the majority of this category (65.2 percent), but the percentage was reduced to 34.5 percent in 2010. It appears that college and university graduates began to consider clerical jobs as an acceptable career path after 2000.

In contrast, service and retail work are largely shared by middle and high school graduates (75.0 percent). At the beginning of this period, this category was largely taken up by middle school graduates (59.0 percent against 34.5 percent high school graduates). From 1995, there were more high school graduates (50.1 percent) than middle school graduates (20.2 percent) in this category.

The similar trend occurred in the educational level of skilled and mechanical workers.

Though the proportion of high school graduates of those workers engaged in farming, forestry and fishery increased from 10.0 percent in 1985 to 21.1 percent,

96 *Growth of new (Western) education*

jobs in this category were largely occupied by those with middle school education (72.3 percent).

Clearly, the university degree has become a necessary requirement for reaching the upper echelon of society. A high school diploma no longer gives the kind of advantages in the job market it did during the colonial period.

Government offices nowadays recruit almost exclusively those applicants with university degrees. In 1980, the majority (83.4 percent) of those who were hired by the government for positions above Class 9 were high school graduates. In 1999, none of the applicants without higher education were hired. Most of the hired applicants, it should be noted, were university graduates; only a negligible proportion of recruits were college graduates (Yi Chonggyu and Hong Yongnan 2002: 104).[5]

Within large corporate organizations, it is generally the case that a university graduate will be promoted much faster than a high school graduate. In most corporate organizations, there is a limit to how high a high school graduate can reach. In fact, with the abundant supply of university graduates, top business firms do not even hire high school graduates these days. The job posting usually specifies that only university graduates may apply.

Since more prestigious jobs normally come with higher wages, there is a close correlation between the level of educational attainment and that of job holder compensation. The overall trend during the two decades from 1982 to 2002, as Table 3.3 indicates, is that wage differences by educational Level (in 1,000 Won) gradually decreased. In 1982, wages of high school graduates were slightly higher than a half (54.4 percent) of those of university graduates whereas in 2002 the percentage figure increased to 70 percent. (Chŏng Chinho, Yi Kyuyong and Choe Kangsik 2004: 65).

A university degree not only entitles one to a prestigious job but also becomes a status symbol. A man with a university degree is almost automatically regarded as superior in social standing to a man without one or with only a high school degree, regardless of what he is capable of doing.[6] In a survey conducted by the Hyundai union in 1995, 57.6 percent of a sample (the number unknown) of Hyundai automobile workers said that they suffered inferiority complexes because of their low educational background (Kang Chunman 1996: 238).

Table 3.3 Wages by Educational Attainment (in thousand Won)

	Total	Middle School	High School	College	University
1982	740 (100.0)	539 (72.8)	707 (95.5)	846 (114.3)	1,299 (175.0)
1985	817 (100.0)	586 (71.7)	783 (95.8)	882 (108.0)	1,463 (179.1)
1990	1,139 (100.0)	854 (75.0)	1,091 (95.8)	1,179 (103.5)	1,731 (152.0)
1995	1,590 (100.0)	1,239 (77.9)	1,522 (95.7)	1,564 (98.4)	2,069 (130.1)
2000	1,823 (100.0)	1,378 (75.5)	1,646 (90.2)	1,717 (94.1)	2,392 (131.2)
2002	1,961 (100.0)	1,438 (73.3)	1,738 (88.6)	1,806 (92.1)	2,495 (127.2)

Source: Chŏng Chinho, Yi Kyuyong, and Choe Kangsik (2004: 65)

Growth of new (Western) education 97

Some men of "success" – corporate executives, National Assembly members, high-level government officials, military generals, writers and actors – often confess to having endured suffering because they did not have a university degree. The stigma attached to not having a university degree is such that many celebrities try to acquire it by attending regular or short-term night universities in order to join the ranks of university graduates or falsely claim to have a university degree. Recently, media exposed a number of men and women of note whose degrees turned out to be fakes. The philosopher Kim Sang-bong points out that "all the problem surrounding Korean universities is that you have to go to a university – any university – if you do not want become a low-born" (2004: 304). The title of a book recently published is *Academic Clique in Korea – Is It Another Caste?* (Kim Tonghun 2001). Acquiring a university degree, in fact, is widely perceived as attaining a new social status. "Your University Diploma Goes with You to the Grave " is the headline of an article in a weekly (Hankyoreh 21, November 1, 2000). One scholar urged that the current practice of issuing university graduation certificates be eliminated. Another scholar went even further by demanding abolition of the university system altogether (Kang Chunman 1996:135).

Such criticisms notwithstanding, diploma disease continues to prevail. Indeed, the majority of high school students aspire to go to university. Ninety percent of a sample of high school students surveyed by the Korean Education Development Institute said they would like to go to a university (Hyŏn Ju 2003: 125).

What we need to understand, however, is that behind those students, there are parents who are eager to see their children get a university education. Thus the responses to the survey question might reflect their parents' desire for their education more than their own. This same survey asked children's parents how much education their children should receive, and 92.3 percent of them said university education and more. Moreover, the parents appeared to be prepared to make their desire for children's education to be that of their children; 80.4 percent of them said that they would either try to persuade their children to change their minds (64.0 percent) or to make them change their minds (16.4 percent) if their children did not wish to go to university. Also to be noted is that more than half the parents thought that their children should go to university even if they could find a satisfactory job without a university degree (52.1 percent), or could get a job and receive a salary or promotion according to their ability with only a high school education (58.9 percent) (Hyŏn Ju 2003: 125–138).

With such education fever and easy access to university education, even a university degree no longer guarantees a "respectable" job. The number of university graduates grew faster than the job market could adequately accommodate them. Already in the late 1950s, there were severe job shortages for university graduates. A large number of university graduates were competing for a small number of administrative and professional career-oriented work posts such as civil servants, lawyers, judges, company executives, bankers and newspaper reporters.

Since "respectable" or "prestigious" jobs that university graduates seek are largely offered by the government and a small number of large corporate groups, they were given the privilege of selecting the best crop of university graduates

98 *Growth of new (Western) education*

each year. In doing so, they tended to give preference to top university graduates under the assumption that if someone was good enough to enter a top university, he or she should make a good employee. Top university graduates have also performed better than graduates of other universities at whatever written tests job applicants had to take.

Consequently, the graduates of a few select top universities dominated elite positions. According to Kim Sangbong's enumeration, graduates of three top universities (SKY or Seoul National, Yŏnsei and Koryŏ) occupied the majority of the high-level government posts of the recent Roh Moo Hyun administration (2003–2008): 72.4 percent of the cabinet members (ministers and vice-ministers) (Seoul National 62.3 percent, Koryŏ 5.8 percent, Yŏnsei 4.3 percent) and 44.4 percent of high government officials (Class I–III) (Seoul National 30.5 percent, Koryŏ7.9 percent, Yŏnsei 6.5 percent) (2004: 62, 69).[7]

The legal profession, which recruits its incumbents through the national judicial examinations, has long been dominated by graduates of top universities. Of the 5,067 who completed internships at the Judicial Training Center (from the first to twenty-sixth term), 72.5 percent were from the aforementioned three universities (Seoul National 53.1 Percent, Koryŏ 14.2 percent, Yŏnsei 5.3 percent) (Kang Chunman 1996: 21–22).

The three universities' graduates also were favorites of voters and tend to occupy the majority of National Assembly seats. In the fifteenth National Assembly (1996), 53.8 percent of the total 299 National Assembly members graduated from the three universities (Seoul National 37.5 percent, Koryŏ 14.3 percent, Yŏnsei 4.3 percent) (Ibid. 1996: 23).

Prominence of these graduates extends beyond the government domain. For example, 70.4 percent of the executive directors of 100 business firms in 2003 were graduates of the aforementioned three universities (Seoul National 43.7 percent, Koryŏ 13.4 percent, Yŏnsei 13.4 percent) (Kim Sangbong 2004: 72).

The majority of opinion leaders in the media world are also graduates of these three universities. In 1992, 67 out of 71 managing staff above the rank of director of major daily newspapers graduated from them (Seoul National 66.0 percent, Koryŏ 19.7 percent, Yŏnsei 14.2 percent (Ibid. 1996: 23).

The elite world, which is largely dominated by the graduates of top or "the first-rate" universities, is becoming even less accessible to those graduates of other universities. According to a survey conducted by *Hankyoreh 21* in 2000, 63.4 percent of the 700 respondents agreed with the statement, "Even if one has excellent ability, it is difficult to succeed without a degree from a prestigious university" (Anonymous 2000). The majority of them said there is a discrimination against those who did not go to a first-rate university for employment opportunities (83.5 percent) and promotion within the workplace (79.4 percent) (*Hankyoreh 21* 10–27–28). There is a widespread psychological restraint among those who did not go to a first-rate university. One well-known politician told Kang Chunman, a mass-communication professor at Chŏnbuk University, "Since I did not graduate from a prestigious university I could not help thinking that my future was all but uncertain" (1996: 216). A character in a popular TV drama tells his son, "If you

Growth of new (Western) education 99

were thinking of going to a local university you might as well forget about going to university" (Kang Chunman 1996: 215). The tendency of high school students is to aim for the first-rate university, or at least a university in Seoul. These days, lesser local universities do not even have enough applicants to fill their quota. Local universities are doing their best to attract good students. With the declining fertility rate, this trend will likely intensify.

As the above statistical figures (cited to illustrate the dominance of the three top universities of the elite world) indicate, Seoul National University graduates far excel those of the other two universities in advancing to the elite world.[8]

Seoul National University is in a privileged position in yet another way. The government allocates a disproportionate amount of the budget for higher education aid to Seoul National University. A big chunk of the special grant, called BK (Brain Korea) 21 – a six-year project from 1999 to 2005 designed to promote graduate school and local universities – went to that institution. Furthermore, it is customary for big business firms to donate money first to Seoul National University and then think about others next.

Some local government bureaus of education rank high schools in their district in terms of the number of students admitted to Seoul National University and provide financial support on the basis of that ranking. Kang Chunman reports of high school teachers telling their students that if "you do not enter Seoul National University, you won't be treated as a decent human being," other teachers refusing to sign a student's application if he is one of better students and wants to go a university other than Seoul National University, and a high school principal instructing third-year homeroom teachers to persuade their better students to apply for a less prestigious department at Seoul National University rather than for a more prestigious department of a lesser university (1996: 43–44). When the Ministry of Education instructed high schools not to force students to apply to Seoul National University against their will, many schools had parents of those students who had a good chance of acceptance sign agreements at the beginning of the year that they would apply only to Seoul National University. When a bright student tells his teacher that he is not very confident about being accepted to Seoul National University, the teacher persuades him to change his mind by offering to pay the expenses to repeat the entrance examination. Some schools reward teachers who succeeded in sending many students to Seoul National University with all-expense-paid overseas trips. Hagwŏn (cram schools) advertise widely about how many of their students have been admitted to Seoul National University.

If one gets admitted to both Seoul National and Yŏnsei at the same time, he or she is bound to choose the former. Many universities do their best not to lose "superior" entrants to Seoul National University by offering numerous lures such as tuition exemption, overseas language training during summer vacations, exchanges to a foreign university, scholarships to study overseas and priority in hiring for a faculty position upon completion of a doctoral degree. When the top entrant of Koryŏ University was known to have also been accepted to Seoul National University, the president of Korea University himself tried to persuade him – without success – to choose his university. Some students who are admitted to Korea

100 *Growth of new (Western) education*

University or Yŏnsei University but do not make Seoul National University apply again the following year. Kim Tonggil, a history professor at Yŏnsei University, was quoted as saying, "One hundred out of one hundred Yŏnsei students have the Seoul National University complex. The majority of Yŏnsei students became Yŏnsei students because they failed to enter Seoul National University" (Ibid. 1996: 127). Commenting on the phenomenon of Seoul National University taking in the crème de la crème high school graduates, Han Wansang, the minister of education from 2001 to 2002 and himself a Seoul National graduate, said, "It is very difficult to stabilize the public education when one specific university takes all the students with the highest sunŭnggosi (state-run ability test) marks to the 5,000th" (Ibid. 1996: 127).

Before 1994, when the sunŭnggosi was first introduced, top-ten universities were able to share bright students since each one of them drafted their own entrance examinations, and examinations were held on the same day. Under the new system, all university applicants write the sunŭnggosi at the same time and are ranked on a uni-dimensional scale. This system allows each student to apply to more than one university. Accordingly, all high school students determine which universities to apply to according to their test scores. Such a monolithic method of determining which student goes to which university has come increasingly under criticism recently. More universities are now supplementing the sunŭnggosi scores with naesin (school records), reports by the teachers based on their evaluation of a pupil's achievement and character (Seth 2002: 141).

Supplementary Education – Given the fierce competition to enter the prestigious universities, Korean students begin their preparation by seeking outside help as early as kindergarten.

How to prepare for the sunŭnggosi has become the primary concern of the students, their parents and teachers. Consequently, school education, especially high school education, is largely oriented to preparing students for it.

University entrance, however, is not the only reason schoolchildren get outside help. Many students do so in order to enter special schools at levels below university, admission to which is based on competitive entrance examinations.

This trend began in 1983 with the establishment of the Science High School (Kwahak kotung hakkyo), which was an attempt by the government to produce first-class scientists by providing a small number of gifted children with scientific training at an early age. Later, the Kim Young Sam administration broadened this program by creating the Special Purpose High School system (T'ŭksu mokchŏk kodŭnghakkyo), introducing the Self-governing Private High School (Chayul saripko) and the System of Schools for Education of Gifted Children (Yŏngjae kyoyuk chedo).

This reform effort by the Kim Young Sam government – known as the 5–31 Reform – was implemented in the hope of introducing a new educational system that puts an emphasis on excellence and competition, thereby enhancing the nation's competitiveness in the global world. The new system, the government reasoned, would supplement the existing one based on the ideas of equal educational opportunities and uniform quality of education that does not recognize the

Growth of new (Western) education   101

innate differences in abilities of children. The special purpose high school aims at training specialists at an early stage in various areas such as science, engineering, agriculture, marine science, foreign languages, art, sports and international relations. The Self-governing Private High School is to allow private educational foundations to establish schools for gifted children, recruit students and teachers on a competitive basis, organize the curriculum, select textbooks and determine student tuition and fees. The school for gifted children is designed to provide special training for gifted children at the primary and middle school levels. As of 2005, there were 115 special purpose high schools, two self-governing private high schools and 3,342 gifted children schools.

Unlike other regular schools, these two special schools recruit a small number of gifted children through their own entrance examinations. The average number of students per teacher in these schools is five to ten, much smaller than that of regular schools. The quality of teaching at these schools is thought to be decisively better, and the academic environment is more conducive to hard and excellent work than at regular schools. Given these advantages, graduates of special high schools are bound to do better in advancing to "first-rate" universities. Unavoidably, these special schools became coveted places for students with high grades.[9]

One of the two existing special purpose private high schools, the Korean Minjok Leadership Academy, is known for getting a large proportion of its graduates admitted to the top-three universities and also for sending a substantial number of their graduates to Ivy League schools in the United States. There is an emerging trend among high schools graduates to go to select American universities. The number of high school graduates advancing to prestigious American universities, such as Harvard, Yale and Princeton, is increasing. More students and parents think that entrance to American schools is attainable. Going to these American universities is also more desirable than attending the top-rated domestic universities. Consequently, competition for admission to these special schools is getting tougher.[10]

In order to compete successfully in university and special schools entrance examinations the majority of students seek outside help. Outside help is provided by either hagwŏn (cram school) or individual tutors. There are two types of hagwŏn: supplementary hagwŏn and university entrance hagwŏn. The former offers various courses to help elementary, middle and high school students supplement their school education. Courses offered might include the national (Korean) language, English, mathematics, Chinese characters, essay writing, art, athletics, artistic ability, etc. One can sit in a combination class that covers multiple subjects such as the national language and mathematics, or a class for a single subject. The university entrance hagwŏn prepares students for all the subjects covered by sunŭnggosi. A student may sit in a class or receives lessons on an individual basis. A hagwŏn may specialize in a single subject, such as music and drawing. A few of hagwŏn that have grown into big enterprises[11] dispatch their tutors to clients' houses upon request.

Many hagwŏn provide a special program for a small (but increasing) number of middle school students with good grades preparing for entrance examination for

102   *Growth of new (Western) education*

special purpose high schools. Unlike regular schools, hagwŏn operate on the market principle in that they are competing against one another in attracting students and that students may choose to go to another hagwŏn if they are not satisfied with the one they attend. Therefore, they make special efforts to being student friendly. They organize classes on the basis of each student's learning ability. The class size is small – usually around 20 – and what progress each student makes is closely monitored by instructors. In addition to classroom sessions, some large-scale hagwŏn offer online instruction and publish *haksŭpchi* (book of model examination questions) for independent study after school. They also organize so-called English camps or science camps during the summer vacation, offering single-subject tutoring. Individual consultations on matters regarding advancing to university for students and their parents are provided; hagwŏn may even establish an "advancement to university module" on the basis of individual learning ability and aptitude to help them to decide on which university to apply to (Kim Yangbun and Kim Misuk 2002: 17–21).

With the exception of a small number of private tutors who have built the reputation for successfully helping students enter first-rate universities, preparation for entrance examinations for students in their final year at high school or repeaters preparation for sunŭnggosi is largely done by hagwŏn.

How widespread is supplementary education (private and hagwŏn tutoring) among students and what does it consist of? The Korea National Statistical Office (Tonggyech'ong) published a report in 2008 on the basis of a sample survey of 2,078 students from 62 primary, middle and high schools; 2,658 parents of students; and 1,090 teachers from 60 schools. As of August 2002, 77.0 percent of student respondents were currently receiving various types of supplementary education: 47.2 percent hagwŏn lessons, 9.6 percent individual private tutoring, 11.8 percent group private tutoring, 25.2 percent haksŭpchi exercise under the supervision of an instructor, 3.2 percent Internet or media learning and 37.0 percent lessons in athletic and artistic ability for personal interest. Of those students who received supplementary education, 58.6 percent did so in the math class, 55.6 percent in the English class, 39.3 percent in the national Korean language, 25.6 percent in social studies and science and 37 percent in athletic and artistic ability.

If we look at them separately by school level, 88.8 percent of primary school students, 74.6 percent of middle school students and 55.0 percent of high school students – 62.0 percent of general high school students and 33.7 percent of professional high school (chŏnmun'go) students – were receiving out-of-school education.

The spread of outside help is such that it is no longer of a supplementary nature. Many students and their parents in urban areas tend to think that out-of-school education is more important than the education provided at school. Schoolteachers often complain about their students doing hagwŏn homework at school, dozing off in the classroom and failing to pay attention to classroom lessons. On the other hand, some schoolteachers ask their students who do not perform well in the class to go to a hagwŏn or to find a private tutor.

Growth of new (Western) education 103

To be sure, one cannot think of school education without taking hagwŏn tutoring into account. A government report on a survey of a sample of 34 thousand parents of schoolchildren (primary, middle and high) from 272 schools indicates that 77 percent of Korean parents were providing their children with hagwŏn tutoring. The total cost of hagwŏn tutoring estimated on the basis of this survey was 20 trillion won in 2007, which is equivalent to more than half of the government educational budget and constitutes 2.8 percent of the annual GDP (Korean National Statistical Office 2008).

Most parents appear to feel that they should provide their children with as much hagwŏn education as possible. But a family with a high income can naturally do much more than a family with a lower income could. Table 3.4 shows that as the level of family income goes up, the percentage of children receiving private tutoring and the amount of money spent on it increases. This finding was more or less expected. But what is so unusual about this table is that with the exception of the families at the bottom level, the majority of families – rich as well as poor – are providing private tutoring for their children (Korean National Statistical Office 2008: 6).

As such, private and hagwŏn tutoring creates a considerable burden on the family budget of the majority of households. In a 1995 survey conducted by the Ewha Women's University research team (Han Insuk and Pak Ch'unho 1996: 67), 62.3 percent of respondents said that it did. When there is a child in the family preparing for a university entrance examination, other members of the family usually forego expenses on cultural or leisure-time activities such as eating out, vacationing, travelling or going to see movies so as not to affect the budget for educational expenses. In some cases, fathers have taken out bank loans to pay for their children's private tutoring. It has been reported that many middle-class fathers incur debt to pay for their children's after-school lessons. Many wives with ordinary family incomes work in order to earn additional income for their children's private tutoring (Kang Chunman 1996: 29 and Han Insuk and Pak Ch'unho 1996: 66). For example, some mothers have taken on jobs as insurance company

Table 3.4 Private and Hagwŏn Tutoring Expense and Attendance Rate by Monthly Income

Income	Private and Hagwŏn Tutoring Expense	Attendance Rate
	(10,000 Won)	*(%)*
Total	22.2	77.7
Less than 100	5.3	36.9
100–199	10.7	59.7
200–299	17.7	77.7
300–399	24.1	84.4
400–499	30.3	89.2
500–599	34.4	90.5
600–699	38.8	92.7
700 and more	46.8	93.5

Source: Korean National Statistical Office (2008: 6)

104 *Growth of new (Western) education*

saleswomen, dispatch cleaning maids, haksŭpchi deliverers or toy assemblers. Their attitude is that they do not mind suffering the mental or physical stress caused by such income-generating activities by themselves because it is much more painful not to be able to afford their children's private tutoring for financial reasons (Han Insuk and Pak Ch'unho 1996: 67).

As an effort to bring education back into public schools, the Ministry of Education recently introduced after-school tutoring for an additional expense (much smaller than what hagwŏn or private tutors charge) and an "independent study" (chayulhaksŭp) period of two to three hours in the evening in the school library. The idea is to help students in order to reduce the cost of education and to redirect money spent on private education toward public schools. This move, however, has had an unintended consequence of deepening class barriers since only parents who can afford the additional cost can have their children take the after-school tutoring. As a way out of this dilemma, the Ministry of Education instituted Educational Broadcasting System (EBS) for sunŭnggosi – Internet lectures designed to prepare students for sunŭnggosi at a low cost for every child who has access to TV – and guaranteed that sunŭnggosi questions would be constructed on the basis of the EBS lectures (Yi Huiu 2007).

There is, however, little evidence that these remedial measures are bringing students back to school from cram schools or private tutors. The obvious consequence is that students are required to spend more time on study or exam preparation. Those students who receive hagwŏn tutoring, including those children from poor families, now also take advantage of what the school and EBS are providing instead of letting it replace private tutoring.

In short, supplementary or out-of-school education is becoming an integral part of the educational process of children. Students study longer hours and pay added expenses. Education is no longer confined to what lessons the public educational system provides. Students used to go to school from nine o'clock in the morning to two o'clock in the afternoon for eight months a year and were released for four months of vacation to do whatever they wanted. With supplementary education becoming a necessity, study hours are longer and vacation is also used for extra studying.

As noted previously, modernization in the Korean context is a project of establishing non-personalist Western-style institutions. The educational expansion can be considered as a depersonalization process: elementary and middle school education has become universal, high school and university education is open to anybody who is prepared to pass the entrance examination and students compete among themselves on the basis of individual capacity to excel. Nevertheless, the educational system remains considerably personalistic. Students have not become independent, tending to rely on their parents. For their part, parents are deeply involved in their children's schooling with a strong desire for their children to get as much education as possible and a willingness to pay money to give their children an edge by providing private tutoring.

Parental support for their children's education played a decisive role in the educational modernization of Korea. They actively fundraised for the government

Growth of new (Western) education 105

for the construction of more schools for their children. They have been willing to pay for children's educational expenses.

Furthermore, parents do not leave their children to compete against other children by themselves. There appears to be a consensus among Korean parents – rich or poor – that it is the father's responsibility to finance children's educational expenses, while it is the mother's responsibility to help them perform well at school. Even working and professional mothers would not disagree with this generalization. They often confess that they feel guilty about not being able to spend more time with their children who are preparing for exams. One research report indicates that 64.3 percent of the respondents (mothers) replied positively to the statement, "Children's school grades depend on how parents (meaning mothers) help them prepare," and 67.3 percent thought it would be necessary even to "force children to some extent to study even if they do not want to" (Hyŏn Ju 2003: 112).

Many parents believe that they should help their children to get good grades in any way possible whether that means doing homework together, hiring private tutors, sending their children to cram schools, visiting the homeroom teacher frequently, getting involved in parent and teacher activities or making cash donations to the school. Many mothers think that maintaining a friendly relationship with homeroom teachers is important for their children. The mother of a child who is doing well, a classroom leader, or a member of the class student committee is likely to be involved in class or school activities more actively than other mothers, thereby regularly in touch with the homeroom teacher. Mothers make donations to school on special occasions such as a picnic, a class day or school building expansion project. Expressing gratitude with an envelope containing cash – known as chonji (small token of goodwill) – on teacher's day or other occasions is a widely practiced custom. Such a gift is supposed to be a voluntary act on the part of mother. But expectation has been so well established that some teachers demand such ch'onji when parents fail to offer it. In many cases, ch'onji received by a homeroom teacher is known to be shared with the principal, who does not have direct contact with students' parents.

There is a long-standing custom among the parents with children of high school ages of moving into the school district in which a school with the reputation of successfully sending their graduates to top universities is located. The presence of such a famed school is said to contribute to the increase in the price of houses in the district and allows only rich families to move in (Im Taeho and Cho Chaekŏl 2006). It is customary for real estate companies to indicate in their advertisement the school district in which the house for sale is located (ibid). Parents who cannot afford to buy a house in such a district create a false certificate for residence in the district to help their children to be able to enter the famed high school.

Collecting information on the ever-changing university entrance procedures is also an important task for mothers with a child preparing for exams. They regularly drop by their children's hagwŏn for any news related to sunŭnggosi or attend a meeting organized by a major hagwŏn on how various universities will admit new students.

106 *Growth of new (Western) education*

Mothers also collect whatever information is made available through newspapers, the Internet or personal networks on upcoming university entrance examinations to guide their children's exam preparation. They also consult with hagwŏn teachers about their children's progress, which universities to apply for and what kind of help they should provide to their children.

At home, mothers spend much of their time creating an environment conducive to studying and exam preparation. The aforementioned survey by the Ehwa University team in 1996 asked respondents how they help their child prepare for exams: 79.5 said that the entire family is cooperative in helping the child with entrance examination preparation, 57.2 percent of them said that their family restrains TV watching, 54.5 percent said that they try not to invite guests, 56.2 percent said they sleep less than usual and 40.0 percent said they refrain from sexual activities (Han Insuk and Pak Ch'unho 1996: 68). Many mothers also pay special attention to their children's health by managing the intake of nutrients and giving them herbal medicine traditionally known to invigorate one's health. It is also worth noting that special care is taken not to hurt the child's feelings. Some mothers even try to modify their children's genetic factors. For example, many mothers use certain traditional herbal medicines advertised as having the effects of improving brain functions. Others use a machine that controls brain waves, which was, according to an ad, invented by a German research team. There are some ten brands of such machines which cost from 200,000 to 1 million won, and it was reported that about 10 percent of high school students are using or have used such a machine (Kang Chunman 1996: 55–56).

Many mothers also turn to supernatural forces as a last resort for augmenting their children's chances of success. Michael Seth reports on such efforts by mothers:

> Shamans were consulted. One shaman reported that an average of twenty students and parents came to her per day to find out about their exam prospects. Buddhist temples saw an influx of mothers and grandmothers, some praying hours each day for one hundred days. Some temples reported that the donations given for exam success were their largest single source of revenue. Some hopefuls buried personal items on the campus of the school they sought to enter, and girls wore silver rings given to them by their parents during the admission season. Hundred won coins with the lucky dates of 1984 and 1994 were valued as talismans and owners of Hyundai Sonatas reported the "S" in "Sonata" was stolen as the S also stood for student success. Pigs, a traditional symbol of good fortune and the character for fortune on underwear; socks with the characters for "passing"; forks to select the right answers; mirrors to see better; and the compasses for the right direction – all were put to use by anxious students and their families.

(2002: 170–171)

In some universities, a classroom is set aside on the examination day for parents to pray. Sunŭnggosi is considered by many as a national event. It is not rare that a

Growth of new (Western) education 107

taxi driver will drive an exam taker to her school free of charge. They also do not honk near the school where examinations are taking place.

In short, the mother who is devoted to her children is their planner, supporter, mentor and manager (Yi Tuhyu et al. 2007: 87). One mother told Yi Tuhyu, "I think there is a kind of certificate for mother's quality (ŏmma chagyŏkchŭng)" (2007: 173).

Many agree that Korean education is in crisis and that the educational issue is increasingly becoming an object of ideological debate. The progressive teacher association, the National Union of Teachers, advocates reforming the educational system that, in their view, rewards children from rich families. Then there are the Korean Federation of Teachers' Association members who counter the National Union of Teachers' argument by pushing forward the neoliberal market principle which emphasizes rewards for individual efforts without government interference. The results of these ideological debates remain to be seen.

Some parents complain or are critical of the educational system and its primary focus on diploma seeking, which makes supplemental education necessary. Other parents lament that the educational system is too cruel to children, as it forces them to work so hard. A group of concerned parents formed the Federation of Real Education. Their goal is to overcome exam-oriented education and to bring back more human-oriented education. But these individual criticisms do not lead to collective actions to reform the system. Moreover, it is not likely that these ideological debates will persuade parents to change their minds about their preoccupation with their children's success in school and in the job market. Even those parents who are critical of the system quickly realize that there is no viable alternative to participating in competition for diplomas (Yi Tuhyu et al. 2007).

Notes

1 Most of the statistical information on school education in this paper is derived from two main sources, *Statistical Yearbook of Education* and population censuses.
2 During the three plans period, 913 new schools were built, 120,925 classrooms were constructed and 102,510 class rooms repaired.
3 But tuition and other fees constitute only half the educational expenditures incurred by those parents who send their children to kindergarten, primary school, secondary school and universities. As will be shown later, they also pay huge sums of money for private lessons.
4 For example, Oh Chŏnsŏk wrote a book entitled *Minju kyoyuk ŭl chihyang hayŏ* (Toward a Democratic Education) in 1960 as an introduction to Dewey's ideas on education.
5 It should also be noted that the university degree became an important factor in voters' minds in electing a national assemblyman. In the first National Assembly election in 1948, slightly more than 30 percent of those elected (161) had a high school education and less. In 2001, that figure was reduced 4.0 percent (Yi Chonggyu and Hong Yŏngnan 2002: 298).
6 Former president Roh Moo Hyun, who, with only a high school education, passed the higher civil service examinations, become a human rights lawyer and, finally, was elected the president, is an exceptional case. He has not become a model for those youths aspiring to be politicians with only a high school education.

108 *Growth of new (Western) education*

7 President Roh Moo Hyun himself did not go to university and expressed his negative views on the "excessive weight ascribed to university degrees" during the campaign.
8 Defenders of the privileged status of the top-three universities, and Seoul National University in particular, point out that since they attract the best students, their graduates are likely to do better than others in the elite job market. Critics, however, argue that there is no significant difference in the state examination scores among students entering the top-ten universities. They further argue that the continuing monopoly of the top-three universities has a lot to do with the fact that graduates of these schools who occupy elite posts tend to help the new graduates of their alma mater to succeed them (Kang Chunman 1996). No attempt has been made to assess how much of the linkage between top university graduates and top jobs depends on the general level of ability versus nepotism among the alumni of the graduates of certain universities. But there is no question that graduates of the same universities, especially top universities, help their alumni in promoting each other's career.
9 Not all special purpose high schools, however, enjoy such a reputation. Only two types do: science and foreign language schools are sought after, and they have come to represent special purpose high schools.
10 In this connection, it should also be mentioned that a small but increasing number of parents at the top end of the income scale, such as corporate executives, high-ranking government officials, news media personnel, university professors and others, are sending their young children to English-speaking countries such as the United States, Canada, Australia, New Zealand, Hong Kong, Malaysia and the Philippines during summer vacations to learn English or to attend schools (primary or high) there. When these children go abroad for an extended period of time, as in the latter case, their mothers often accompany them, leaving their fathers alone at home. These fathers are referred to as "wild-geese papas" as they visit their wives and children during seasonal holidays.
11 Private tutoring has become a mammoth industry. Even foreign capitalists play a part in this expansion drama. Fifty percent of the assets of the giant hagwŏn, Megastudy, are foreign capital.

References

Anonymous (2000) "Mudom kaji kanda, tangsin ui hakpŏl" (Your University Diploma Goes with You to the Grave), *Hankyoreh* vol. 21, n. 332 (November 1).

Chang, Yun-Shik (1989) "From Filial Piety to the Love of Children," in The Korean Christian Academy (ed.) *The World Community in Post-Industrial Society 1: Changing Families in the World Perspective*, Seoul: Wooseok Publishing.

Cho, Kanghwan (1985) *Paeknyŏn taekye* (A Hundred-Year Plan), Seoul: Ho'am Chulpansa.

Chŏng, Chinho, Yi, Kyuyong and Choe, Kangsik (2004) *Hangyokkan imgŭmgyokch'a ŭi pyŏnhwa wa yoinbunsŏk* (Analysis of Changes and Causes of Wage Differences by Educational Achievement), Seoul: Han'guk nodong yŏn'guwŏn.

Dore, Ronald P. (1980) "South Korean Development in Wider Perspective," pp. 289–305, in Chang Yun-Shik (ed.) *Korea: A Decade of Development*, Seoul: Seoul National University Press.

Han, Chunsang (1983) *Han'guk taehak kyoyuk ŭi hŭisaeng* (Sacrifices of University Education in Korea), Seoul: Munŭmsa.

Han, Insuk and Ch'unho Pak (1996) "Suhŏmsaeng chanyŏrul tun ŏmŏni ŭi noryŏk kwa han'gye" ("Efforts of Mothers with Children Preparing for University Entrance Examinations and Their Limits"), pp. 59–90, in Yi, Dongwŏn et al. (eds.) *Taehak ips iwa Han'guk kajok* (University Entrance Examinations and the Korean Family), Seoul: Tasan ch'ulpa'nsa.

Growth of new (Western) education 109

Han'guk Kyoyuk, Kaebalwŏn (2015) *2015 kanch'urin kyoyuk t'onggye* (Brief Statistics on Korean Education 2015), Seoul: Han'guk kyoyuk kaebalwŏn.

Han'guk Kyoyuk, Kaebalwŏn (2005) *Han'guk kyoyuk 60nyŏn songjang e taehan kyoyukchip'yo bunsŏk* (Index Analysis of the 60 Year Growth of Korean Education), Seoul: Han'guk kyoyuk kaebalwŏn.

Hyŏn, Ju (2003) *Han'guk hakpumo ŭi kyoyukyŏl bunsŏk yŏngu* (An Analysis of Education Fever of Korean Students' Parents), Seoul: Han'guk kyoyukkaebalwon.

Im, Taeho and Chaekŏl Cho (2006) *Kangnam apatŭ* (Kangnam Apartment), Seoul: Ilchiibuk.

Kang, Chunman (1996) *Sŏuldae'ŭi nara* (Korea, Seoul National University's Country), Seoul: Kaemakowŏn.

Kang, Sŏngku and Others (2005) *Han'guk kyoyuk yuk simnyŏn sŏngjang e taehan kyoyukchip'yo punsŏk* (Analysis of Educational Indicators on the 60 Years' Growth of Korean Education), Seoul: Han'guk kyoyuk kaebalwon.

Kim, Sangbong (2004) *Hakpŏlsahoe* (The Society of Academic Sectarianism), Seoul: Hangilsa.

Kim, Tonghun (2001) *Han'guk' ŭi hakbŏl, tto hana ŭi kasŭtŭ in'ga* (Korea's Academic Clique – Is It Another Caste?), Seoul: Chaeksesang.

Kim, Yangbun and Kim, Misuk (2002) *Ipsi hagwon ŭi kyoyuk siltae punsŏk* (An Analysis of the Conditions of Cram School Education), Seoul: Han'guk kyoyuk kaebalwŏn.

Kim, Yŏnghwa (2004) *Han'gukŭi kyoyuk'kwa kyŏngje balchŏn: 1945–1995* (Education and Economic Development in Korea: 1945–1995), Seoul: Han'guk Haksul Chŏngbo.

Kong, Ŭnbae (2007) *Han'guk kyoyuk chaejŏng* (Finance of Korean Education), Seoul: Han'guk koyuk kaebalwon.

Korean National Statistical Office (2008) *2007 nyŏn Sakyoyukpi siltae chosa* (A Survey on Private Education in 2007), Seoul: Korea National Statistical Office.

McGinn, Noel F. et al. (1980) *Education and Development*, Cambridge: Council on East Asian Studies, Harvard University.

Oh Ch'onsŏk (1964) *Sin kyoyuksa* (The History of New Education), Seoul: Hyŏndae Kyoyuk Ch'ongsŏ Ch'ulp'ansa.

Seth, Michael J. (2002) *Education Fever: Society, Politics, and Pursuit of Schooling in South Korea*, Honolulu: University of Hawaii Press and Center for Korean Studies, University of Hawaii.

Yi, Chonggyu and Hong Yŏngnan (2002) *Han'guk sahoe eso'ŭi hangnyŏk ŭi kach'i pyŏnhwa yŏn'gu* (A Study of Change in the Values of Educational Achievement in Korean Society), Seoul: Han'guk kyoyuk kaebalwŏn.

Yi, Huiu (2007) "Nonnch'on haksaeng ŭi alch'an men'to EBS pangsong" (The EBS Broadcasting System, a True Friend to Rural Students). http://home.ebs.co.kr/click/board/9/500500/popupPrnt.

Yi, Tuhyu et al. (2007) *Hakpumo munhwa yŏn'gu* (A Study of the Culture of Students' Parents), Seoul: Han'guk kyoyuk kaebal yŏn'guwŏn.

Yu, Hyŏngjin (ed.) (1969) *Kungmin kyoyuk hŏnjang ŭi iron kwa silche* (The Theory and Practices of the National Charter of Education), Seoul: Paeyŏngsa.

4   Industrialization

The kŭndaehwa project to transform the predominantly agricultural economy to an industrial capitalist market economy, like the expansion of the new education project, is more or less complete now. This chapter will make an attempt to explain how this transformation, commonly known as the "miracle on the side of the Han River" was accomplished. Here again, I will underline the role the personalist ethic played in the process, the role that hardly ever received scholarly attention.

Economic reconstruction under the American military government

When the Pacific War was over, Japanese entrepreneurs who controlled more than 90 percent of the invested capital and Japanese technicians who accounted for more than 90 percent of the manufacturing industry's technical and professional manpower returned to Japan. As a result, 40 percent of factories were shut down, and industrial workforces were reduced by 30 percent. The American Provisional Military Government (APMG 1945–1948) that replaced the colonial government had no resources available to continue with industrial facilities left by the Japanese. The manufacturing industrial productivity was reduced by 83 percent (An Ch'unsik 1982: 132).

The partition of the peninsula into north and south created an additional problem. Heavy (metal and chemical) industries and electric power stations developed during the colonial period were mostly located in the north, while light industries (textile, machine, etc.) were located in the south. Trade between the north and south came to an end in 1948 when the supply of electric power from the north was also shut off. An influx of about one million refugees from the north and another million expatriates from Japan and Manchuria further aggravated the situation (Kwon Taihwan 1977: 163).

Immediate problems that the US military government had to tackle were (1) the shortage of food grains and most types of consumer goods and (2) inflation. The military government initially abolished the existing rice rationing system and introduced the liberal market system, allowing free exchange of agricultural products. But rice produced at the time could hardly meet the increased demand. Rice retailers saw the opportunity to make profits by buying up rice from farmers cheap and selling it at a higher price to consumers. The price of rice went up sharply. In an effort to control the supply of rice, the government decided to purchase rice directly from farmers and sell it to consumer. This rice collection system did not, however, enable the government to collect enough rice to meet demand. There were no funds available domestically to resolve these problems. Moreover, the rise of the price of rice led to inflation. The wholesale price index was estimated to have increased fortyfold fold between June and August 1945, and quadrupled again from then to the end of 1946 (Ban, Moon and Perkins 1980: 239).

Relief for the economic crisis came from the United States. South Korea received more than US$400 million from the United States under the relief program called GARIOA (Government Appropriations for Relief in Occupied Areas). Major objectives of the American aid program to South Korea were (1) prevention of starvation and disease, (2) the massive provision of imported commodities and (3) economic rehabilitation, more specifically, the raising of agricultural output (Cole 1980: 3). Ninety percent of the grant was in the form of food, fertilizers, clothing, fuel and other commodities while only 10 percent was allocated for rehabilitation efforts (Cole 1980: 3). According to Cole, "America had no real stake in a costly and taxing program that would aim for economic development of a South Korea which might shortly be reunited with its northern half" (1980: 4).

While concentrating on relief efforts, the military government did, however, make some attempt at economic reconstruction. Industrial plants left vacant by the Japanese owners were sold off to Korean entrepreneurs. The government also began implementation of land reform. In October 1945, the APMG enacted Ordinance No. 9, which restricted the amount of rent to the maximum one-third of the land product. The following year, at the advice of the State Department, it began selling the farmland previously owned by Japanese landlords to former tenant farmers on the basis of "the farmland to the tiller principle." By the end of the military governorship, most of the Japanese-owned lands had been disposed of (Chosŏn Ŭnhaeng 1948: 1–38).

Industrialization efforts by the First Republic

In 1948, the American Military Government (AMG) was succeeded by the newly established government of the Republic of Korea. But the United States continued to provide aid under GARIOA, and several AMG officials remained as economic advisers to the Korean government. Further progress was made in land reform and the sale of the vested properties left by the Japanese. The Agricultural Land Reform Law was finally passed by the National Assembly. In December 1948, the Korean government and the American government signed the ROK-US Agreement on Aid. The pact required the Korean government to follow certain stable economic policies aimed at strengthening the economy, including balancing the budget, regulating foreign exchange and effectively disposing of the formerly Japanese-owned properties.

112   *Industrialization*

Later the Economic Cooperation Administration (ECA) took over responsibility from GARIOA for the American aid program in Korea. It proposed a recovery program explicitly aimed at development focusing on three basic areas of capital investment necessary to attain a viable Korea: the development of coal, expansion of thermal power-generating facilities and construction of fertilizer plants (Cole 1980: 5). Following the ECA proposal, the Korean government established the Five-Year Industrial Reconstruction Plan in 1949. Although the program was never completed, the South Koreans were, "by June 1950, beginning to create some order out of the economic chaos that had existed in 1945 and to plan the future of the economy" (Lyons 1961:12).

But the Korean War (1950–1953) devastated the reconstructed economy of South Korea. It was estimated that over one million lives were lost, about one-quarter of the fixed capital destroyed and the average unweighted production index of major commodities (excluding tungsten) fell from 250 in 1949 to 124 in 1951 (Mason et al. 1980: 178).

American economic assistance continued during the war, mostly in the form of relief supplies. Still, when the war ended, "the output of agricultural and manufacturing production had returned to the admittedly low level of 1949" (Mason et al. 1980: 180).

Altogether, South Korea received nearly US$1.2 billion from the United States in economic assistance over the eight-year period from the time of Liberation to the year internal hostility ended (1953). American economic assistance helped the South Korea economy to reorganize itself into an independent unit and kept it in existence during the trying years (Mason et al. 1980: 180).

The United States continued to provide economic assistance after the war, until the early 1960s. It played a crucial role in the rehabilitation of the war-torn Korean economy and its subsequent development since there was little domestic capital and foreign private investors were hesitant to enter developing countries at the time (Mason et al.1980: 85 and Reeve 1963: 117). The United Nations and other international organizations also sent a considerable amount of funds for the reconstruction of various non-economic institutions.

The armistice was signed in July 1953, and one month later, President Eisenhower obtained the approval of US Congress for $200 million in economic aid as a first installment of a billion dollar aid program. The administration of American economic aid to Korea was put under the Foreign Operations Administration (FOA) in 1955, later re-designated as the International Cooperation Administration (ICA), a semi-autonomous agency of the Department of State with a resident mission established in Seoul (Reeve 1963: 112).

Over the period 1953 to1961, the United States provided 4.14 billion dollars – 2.57 billion dollars for economic assistance and 1.56 billion dollars for military assistance. Virtually all aid during this period was on a grant basis and in the form of material goods and equipment (Cole 1980: 2; Reeve 1963: 117).

Military assistance was primarily aimed at strengthening the Korean defense force, thereby relieving the government budget of a major part of military expenditures. The paucity of information available on management of military assistance

Industrialization 113

makes it difficult to gauge the extent to which it contributed to the development of the Korean economy (Cole 1980: 182). But Mason et al. enumerate some of the possible contributions the military assistance would have made. First, organization, management and technical skills acquired by military personnel during their training must have been useful in finding jobs after leaving the military service in industrial or service occupations and managerial positions in private or public firms. More directly, "military units have undertaken the construction of roads, bridges, and other infrastructure." The construction of roads, bridges, and other installations built for military use involved to a significant extent private firms which marked "the beginning of what has become a very large and efficient construction industry" (Mason et al. 1980: 180–184).[1]

Economic assistance consisted of two types, project aid and program aid. Project aid comprised "commodities and technical assistance directed toward specific projects" (Mason et al. 1980: 190). Commodities brought in were mostly construction materials in the area of transportation, manufacturing, electric power and housing (see Yi Taegŭn 2002: 316–318, 325–333).[2] Technical assistance was used for sending Korean technicians – broadly defined to include government officials and schoolteachers – abroad for advanced technology training and for covering personal and other expenses incurred by foreign technicians working in Korea. Technical assistance accounted for 1.4 percent of the total aid.

Program aid, which constituted over 80 percent of the total aid (Mason et al. 1980: 190), financed specific categories of imports, mainly raw materials and semi-finished products. They included fertilizer, cotton, petroleum products, silk, wheat and barley (Yi Taegŭn 2002: 327).

In addition to the FOA aid, the United States provided a grant under the PL 480 program. Between 1955 and1960, Korea received US$156 million worth of PL 480 commodities such as raw cotton, wheat and other surplus food (Mason et al. 1980: 93).

Korea also received economic aid from various international organizations such as the United Nations Korea Reconstruction (UNKRA), Civil Relief in Korea (formerly the United Nations Civil Assistance Command Korea), the United Nations Educational and Scientific and Cultural Organization, the United Nations' Children's Fund and the Food and Agriculture Organization. Numerous international voluntary agencies from various countries contributed aid or did charitable and relief work for the poor, orphans, the homeless, war victims and widows; they also provided related help by training relief and social workers.[3]

Rehabilitation Plans[4] – With the new aid fund made available, reconstruction of Korea entered a new stage. But the donors and the receivers could not readily or easily reach agreement on how the aid money should be spent.

UNKRA commissioned the Nathan Associates, an American firm, to draft a comprehensive plan for rehabilitation and development of the post-war Korean economy. But the Nathan Plan "was never formally adopted or even recognized by the Korean government, mainly for political reasons" (Cole and Nam 1969: 11).

The FOA also came up with a similar plan, known as the Tasca Plan, as a blue print that they hoped the Rhee government would follow in undertaking

114 *Industrialization*

rehabilitation projects. The Rhee government did not adopt it but drafted its own, known as the Overall Three-Year Plan of Reconstruction and Development of Korean Economy, on the basis of the FOA plan. The Korean program put more emphasis on economic growth rather than economic stabilization which was the main objective of the FOA plan. The FOA found the Korean government version unacceptable and demanded revision. The disagreements between the two parties reflected different concerns they had in approaching the Korean rehabilitation issue. While the Korean government aimed at the long-term development of the Korean economy through rehabilitation, the US government had the short-term objectives of stabilization of the economy and building up the Korean Army. Agreement on an overall plan was not reached until 1958 when the Korean government came up with a revised seven-year plan which the US aid agency accepted.

While negotiations were ongoing, without an overall plan and centralized planning, various rehabilitation projects were undertaken by separate ministries of the government in response to immediate needs. They included plans to (1) reduce reliance on imported production materials through construction of large-scale factories to produce fertilizer, cement and pan-glass; (2) develop electric power and other energy sources such as oil, briquette and coal; (3) upgrade manufacturing, agricultural and marine industry production; (4) promote export in an effort to free the Korean economy from foreign aid; and (5) foster medium- and small-sized enterprises (for more on these plans, see Yi Taegŭn 2002: 364–386).

The government then took various measures to facilitate the implementation of these plans.

First, it issued a national bonds law in order to raise funds for industrial rehabilitation and created special accounts for managing these funds. In 1955, the Office of Planning was promoted to the Ministry of Rehabilitation and created a "rehabilitation committee" consisting of five ministers responsible for rehabilitation, finance, agriculture, commerce and industry and defense that were to evaluate and decide major economic policies.

The government also created the Korean Industrial Reconstruction Bank (December 1952) and later the Agricultural Bank and Agricultural Cooperatives (February 1957) as state banks responsible for long-range development banking. A plan was also made to establish a state-run medium and small enterprise bank. These banking organizations were designed primarily for creating funds for economic rehabilitation and subsequently made bank loans, foreign loans and subsidies available to domestic firms at cheap rates.

"Vested properties" – including industrial plants – left by the Japanese (or "enemies") were also sold to private business firms at a low cost, even lower than the current market price. Since payment for the properties was to be made over an extended period of time, the high inflation rate at the time considerably reduced the actual value of money owed to the government. Furthermore, many purchasers received preferential loans from the government with which they paid off what they owed the government. Those privileged businessmen – usually with good "connections" with the government – more or less received the vested properties free of charge.

More directly, the government created conditions for them to do profitable business.

A system of tariff exemptions[5] on both aid and non-aid financed imports was installed to help channel imports at reduced cost to selected domestic industries and to reduce undesired competition from imports and overvalued exchange rates (Hong 1979: 45–49).

Tax law reforms in 1954 and 1956 helped businessmen in capital formation and accumulation. The Korean government adopted a tax system heavily centered on indirect tax rather than on direct tax. In other words, while those in the business of making money paid the same rate of commodity taxes, their income tax did not increase progressively with increasing income. Furthermore, the government introduced a temporary land tax system mainly aimed at farmers during the Korean War to increase tax revenue. In short, the tax system was designed to reduce the tax burden of high income and corporate groups. The government also reduced or completely exempted private firms, designated by the president and engaging in industrial production, from paying income tax, corporate profits dividend tax, business tax and corporate tax. Thus industrial firms selected by the government had the usual advantages of doing profitable business, but they also used them to evade taxes. It is difficult to measure the extent to which this occurred but the consensus is that "tax evasion was rampant and was one major reason why the entrepreneurs who made bids under the Rhee government were put on trial by Park's military government for illicit accumulation of wealth" (Hamilton 1986: 41; Kim Taehwan 1981: 191).

Growth – Such state-directed rehabilitation efforts carried out with the help of foreign aid and in cooperation with foreign aid agencies not only brought stabilization to the South Korean economy but also helped it to grow. Between 1953 and 1959, the annual increase rate of wholesale commodity prices decreased from 25.7 percent to 7.1 percent and that of retail commodity price from 52.5 percent to 4.2 percent, while the annual increase rate of the total amount of currency in circulation also decreased from 111.6 percent to 9.0 percent. During the same period, the GNP grew at the annual rate of 5.5 percent with the total industrial production index increasing at the rate of 15.4 percent. The overall trend of the South Korean economy during the 1950s (after the signing of the armistice) is, as one economist concluded, that reconstruction was completed by 1956 and stable growth began in 1957 (Yi Taegŭn 2002: 420).

i) Manufacturing – Rehabilitation efforts were focused mainly on manufacturing, which grew sharply from 1955 to 1957, then began slowing down from 1958 with the reduction of US foreign aid. The growth rate of the manufacturing industry between 1955 and 1959 averaged 16.0 percent per annum. The immediate concern of both foreign aid agencies and the Korean government in promoting the manufacturing industry was import, as many consumer goods or basic necessities to be imported.[6]

116 *Industrialization*

Thus industrial growth during this period was largely dominated by production of consumer goods which accounted for more than 80 percent of the total production value added from the manufacturing industry (Im Chongch'ŏl 1975: 11 and Kim Taehwan 1981: 209).

ii) Agriculture – The progress made in the manufacturing industry was starkly contrasted by slow or stagnant growth in agriculture. While the productivity index for the manufacturing industry increased from 74.7 to 317.7 percent from 1950 to 1960, for agriculture it increased only from 91.5 to 116.1 percent during the same period. The various plans designed to promote self-sufficiency in the supply of grains fell far short of reaching the intended targets (Yi Taegŭn 2002: 425). Two factors may account for this. In May 1955, as mentioned earlier, Korea signed the Agreement to Import US Surplus Agricultural Produces in accordance with PL 480. Consequently, in 1956, massive amounts of grain including rice, barley, flour and beans began to flow into Korea. These US aid grains amounted to 14.1 percent of Korea's total grain supply. This generous aid had two negative effects on agricultural development. The price of grain fell sharply, and other products, such as cotton, silk worms, ramie fabric and wheat destined for market, lost competitiveness to imported goods of lower prices and better quality.

Domestic cotton production fared even less well. In 1950, imported cotton constituted 75 percent of what domestic cotton textile manufacturers used and entirely replaced the domestically produced cotton. At the same time, the Korean government, preoccupied with the development of the manufacturing industry, maintained the so-called low grain policy as a means of keeping the commodity price and industrial workers' wages low. Consequently, the average farm household's spending exceeded its income, and the negative balance between the two continued to grow in the 1950s. The government low grain price reduced incentives of farmers (Yi Taegŭn 2002: 427).

iii) Trade – The emphasis given in the 1950s to assist growth of manufacturing industries and reduce commercial imports succeeded by dropping imports by 50 percent between 1953 and 1959. Expanded production of select goods such as textiles, sugar, cotton wood products and paper replaced potential imports. But there was still an increase in import (foreign aid) dependence in many manufacturing sectors during the 1950s, including processed food, clothing, printing, and almost all heavy, chemical, and machinery sectors. The total value of imports continued to grow until 1957 when it reached the peak and began to decline in 1958. In 1959, foreign aid accounted for 72.2 percent of the total value of imports, which was almost 15 time that of exports (see Han'guk ŭnhaeng chosabu 1960: 174).

Import substitution effort did lead to a drive of exports. Toward the end of the 1950s, select commodities – cotton textile products, sugar and cement – were produced in excess of domestic demand, and exploration of foreign markets became necessary for surplus products. In 1957, the trade law directed toward free trade was enacted, and the Korea-US Treaty of Friendly Trade and Navigation was signed. In 1957, US$855,000 worth of textile products were exported to Hong Kong. Encouraged by this experience, the government came up with the Cotton

Product Export Five-Year Plan in 1959 in an effort to find foreign markets for cotton yarns and cotton textile fabrics, and created a fund for promoting export (Yi Taegŭn 2002: 412). Even rice was exported for the first time since Liberation – $775,000 worth to Ryukyu Island (Yi Taegŭn 2002: 417). But this was only the beginning. Exports during this period did little to reduce the amount of imports. In fact, the total value of exports decreased from US$39.6 million in 1953 to US$19.2 million in 1959 (Han'guk ŭnhaeng chosabu 1960: 174).

iv) Growth of Private Enterprise – Planning and implementation of the rehabilitation program during the post-war period, as we have seen, was guided by the state and foreign aid agencies with the government being an active producer. But from the beginning, under the aid donor's influence, the government's aim was to build a market economy and vigorously foster private enterprise. The government took responsibility for large-scale projects that required a kind of capital revenue that a private enterprise could not raise at the time, such as development of rural and fishery sectors or the construction of highways, ports and sewage systems. Meanwhile, other projects were relegated to private enterprises. Private entrepreneurs took full advantage of the incentives offered by the government and expanded their businesses rapidly.

They began with what came to be known as "junk trade" with China. Chinese and Korean traders swapped various goods that the Japanese military or private business firms left behind. Chinese traders were interested in acquiring military supplies, while Korean traders wanted consumer goods. Since foreign trade was strictly restricted by the AMG, it was Chinese traders who smuggled goods into Korea in their "junk boats." The junk trade lasted about six months and was replaced by the so-called Macao trade. Chinese traders based in Macao brought in consumer goods and took back Korean grains, soap, leather, tungsten and livestock (see Yi Chongjae 1993: 51; Yi Taegŭn 2002: 126).

As the economic reconstruction began after the war, Korean entrepreneurs shifted from trade to manufacturing for the domestic market. Foreign aid organizations had provided raw materials such as cotton, sugar and flour free of charge in an effort to encourage the Korean government and entrepreneurs to produce them directly instead of importing them. The government sold the aid materials cheaply to private enterprises. Since there were shortages of these basic necessities, demand was high, and private firms seized the opportunity; sales of flour, sugar and cement, in particular, began to grow rapidly (see Yi Chongjae 1993).

Another lucrative business was supplying what the UN army stationed in Korea needed. Hyundai Construction, for example,

> began repairing bridges, paving roads, and building army barracks, simple dams, and reservoirs in 1947. With the start of the Korean War and in its aftermath, however, construction projects became the more lucrative. Between 1963 and 1966, for example, military projects accounted for 26 percent of Hyundai's total construction revenue but for almost 77 percent of its total profits.

> (Amsden 1989: 266)

118   *Industrialization*

Table 4.1 Growth of Enterprises by Size 1955 and 1960

	Small*	Medium	Large	Total
1955	7,871 (89.3)	694 (7.9)	244 (2.8)	8,809 (100.0)
1960	14,027 (92.3)	832 (5.5)	361 (2.4)	15,220 (100.0)

* Small enterprise employing less than 49 workers, Medium-sized enterprise employing 50–99 workers; large enterprise employing more than 100 workers (*Kwangkongŏp census* 1955 and 1960 quoted in Yi Taegŭn 2002: 439)

From 1955 to 1960, the total number of private enterprises increased from 8,809 to 15,220. The largest increase was in the category of small-sized firms, which more than doubled. In 1960, large enterprises even decreased proportionally. On the surface, it appears that the late 1950s was the most rapid period of growth for smaller entrepreneurs. What we should take notice of, however, is the fact that while large enterprises constituted only 2.4 percent of the total number of enterprises, they accounted for 39.8 percent of the total value added.

Some large firms had survived from the Japanese period, but most of them began as smaller business enterprises with "bare hands (maenjuŏk)" after Liberation. It should be noted that they owed much to the government for their rapid growth as "the government was more eager to foster the large enterprise than small ones and the large one took a lion's share of government subsidies" (Hamilton 1986: 40). This small number of large business enterprises continued to play an important role during the Park period (Kim Taehwan 1981).

It is apparent that rehabilitation efforts after the armistice resulted in stabilization and modest growth, returning to the pre-war level of the South Korean economy. The aggregate value of domestic production increased at an average rate of 5.2 percent, or about 2.5 percent per capita between 1953 and 1959 (Reeve 1963: 123). But the South Korean economy at the end of the 1950s on the whole remained underdeveloped. Whatever effect economic growth had, it was largely offset by the rapid population growth. The Korean population – mostly residing in the rural areas – was growing at the rate of 3 percent annually. The agricultural sector released a surplus population, which went to cities in large numbers but was unable to find jobs. Manufacturing, mining and construction together employed not much more than 20 percent of the labour force in 1960. The average per capita income in the same year was only US$60 (Reeve 1963: 125–126).

The Korean economy during this period was, in the words of Hamilton, "a derivative one; industry and agriculture were dependent on imports for survival. Imports mainly were in the form of aid of basic necessities" (1986: 41). The total value of imports, as mentioned earlier, was 15 times that of exports, and "only US aid kept the economy afloat" (Hong 1979: 46). The significance of this was brought home by the cuts in aid in 1958–1960, which were accompanied by falling growth rates. Given the grim prospect that US aid would not last many years, South Korea had to find a way to survive the anticipated crisis. With hindsight, perhaps, promotion of exports was the only alternative left for the Korean government. Park

Chung Hee did that exactly when he seized power in the 1960 coup after over-throwing the Chang Myŏn Regime that briefly (July 1960 – May 1961) succeeded Rhee's.

Park Chung Hee and the "Economic Miracle" (1961–1979)

Economic development plans

The Developmental State – Park Chung Hee's "revolution promise" (*hyŏkmyŏng kongyak*) made at the time he launched the coup was "uplifting the nation from chronic poverty by building a strong self-standing (*charip*) national economy." Park stated in one speech, "If there is one strong wish, it is that we also live as well as other advanced rich countries." In another speech, he stressed,

> Only when people are fully employed and don't feel hungry can you expect them to be disciplined in their social (or moral) behavior. . . . Achievement of a self-standing national economy is a way of enhancing the nation that does not rely on sympathy or aid of foreign countries, but is capable of helping others.
>
> (Chŏng Chaegyŏng 1991)

It should also be noted that he was fully aware of the fact that North Korea at the time was economically well ahead of South Korea. In the 1960s, the per capita GDP (US$137) of the former was 1.5 or 3 times that of the latter (US$94). Measured in terms of various indices of economic production – coal, chemical fertilizer, cement, fish catch, food and war industry – the North Korean econ-omy was performing far better than the South Korean economy. The North-South War ended in a truce. But it appeared that the socialist economy in the north was defeating the capitalist economy in the south.

Park Chung Hee felt compelled to declare a war against poverty and the social-ist economy. He was firmly convinced that that economic development was the key to the problems that Korea faced and the success of his new job as a civilian president. Thus "maximum possible growth or growth at any cost" became an urgent task for the military government (Song 1990: 83).[7]

Such an approach to economic development necessitated that the government play an active role in modernizing the economy. Park and his assistants argued,

> The time when the state functioned as a night-watchman has passed. The modern state should have the characteristics of a protectionist state that actively protects people and guarantees their decent living. Capitalist produc-tion cannot be left to the mechanism of natural adjustment.
>
> (Chŏng Chaegyŏng 1991: 166)

Indeed, planning the future path of the nation's economy was not a choice but a necessity. While reduction of foreign aid made planning more difficult,

120   *Industrialization*

the Korean government became free of foreign policy intervention and planned development projects as it saw fit to the Korean situation. A year after the coup, the junta government announced the first five-year economic development plan, hurriedly drafted by the newly established Economic Planning Board based on the five-year plan established by the Chang Myŏn government. This plan was then followed by three more. They set forth major goals for economic growth. The First Five-year Plan (1962–1966) aimed at building "an industrial base principally through increased energy production" and developing import substitution industries. The Second Five-Year Plan (1967–1971) attempted to "to promote modernization of the industrial structure and to build the foundation for a self-supporting economy." The Third Five-Year Plan (1972–1977) shifted its emphasis from economic growth to a balanced economy by "expanding regional development," "improving life in rural areas" and "improving the quality of life of workers." As Paul Kuznets points out,

> Each plan has also included a list of major projects, grouped by sector. Later plans provide more information and reflect the increasing sophistication gained from experience with earlier plans, but the main features of all the plans are essentially the same.
>
> (1977: 196)[8]

i) Economic Bureaucracy – Park's was not a popular government by any means, but its commitment to economic modernization had wide appeal, with many Koreans willing to join the government in its undertaking to modernize the fatherland (choguk kŭndaehwa).

To establish itself as the leading agent in charge of development, the Park government created a new super-ministry, the Economic Planning Board (EPB), almost exclusively responsible for planning economic development. It also reorganized the Ministries of Commerce and Industry (MCI) and Finance (MF) to design specific projects and fund them in coordination with the EPB. Park recruited the best economists, scientists and engineers and posted them as ministers, members of the presidential secretariats or at the level of bureau chief, and had them in charge of implementing specific plans.

As a first step toward undertaking development, the government nationalized commercial banks and assumed the responsibility of mobilizing and allocating financial resources – domestic savings, foreign funds, aid and loans – thereby establishing itself as a senior partner to private businesses. In executing its duties, the state bureaucracy was given sufficient scope to take initiative and operate effectively as it was under protection of the executive office, which brought under its control any political or social forces which would challenge the presidential authority, including the legislature, the judiciary branch, the government party, labour unions and the mass media. (More on this subject see Chapter 5). Park's government came to be regarded by its critics as a 'developmental autocracy' (*kaebal tokchae*).

ii) Export-led Industrialization – Economic development thus conceived was to be achieved through industrialization. The Park government continued

Industrialization 121

the development effort started earlier – namely, pushing import substitution. As mentioned earlier, formulating and implementing specific measures to achieve the goals set by the EPB's plan fell to the MCI. MCI first identified and chose the industries to be developed and then drafted plans for specific projects to be carried out. Some large-scale plans, such as constructing a steel plant that private enterprises were not ready to undertake, were made into government projects for public enterprises. Smaller-scale projects were delegated to private enterprises. In its relationship with private enterprises, the government also made effective and selective use of its licensing and approval authority. The government power to audit taxes was also used as a powerful mechanism in persuading corporate firms to comply with government guidance.

The dominant goal of development planning in the first plan period was to reduce Korea's dependence on foreign aid. This meant import substitution and vigorous export promotion. Korea began with import substitution. The prime concern at the beginning was to build industrial plants to produce necessary basic goods such as textiles, fertilizers, petroleum, cement and electricity, which were in short supply and had to be imported. Accordingly, the government constructed an industrial site, provided all the facilities that such a base requires, and invited private firms to move in and build factories according to the government plans.[9]

The military government also promoted select heavy industries. In May 1962, for example, it introduced a law designed to promote and protect the domestic automobile industry and established the Sae Na Ra Auto Company, which in 1964 merged with Sinjin and assembled passenger automobiles.

Two years into the first five-year economic plan, the government realized that there were not enough funds to complete projects conceived in 1962. The government had used up much of its foreign currency in reserve, and in 1963, the remaining amount was less than US$100 million. This was Korea's first foreign currency crisis and development plans had to be revised. Most of the heavy industry plans were put on hold, and those plans with poor results were dropped. The twenty-second minister of Commerce and Industry, Pak Ch'unghun, strongly advised Park Chung Hee to switch policy emphasis from import substitution to export of manufacturing goods.[10] Park Chung Hee agreed and declared in his 1965 "State of the Nation Message," "In a country that depends heavily on imported raw materials for its industries, export is the economic life line" (quoted in Amsden 1989: 69).

Development plan policy shifted to promoting the export of what Korea could readily produce with the cheap labour force abundantly available. The new motto adopted was "export first," and a new export promotion system was introduced. The new goal, established in 1964, was to build up substantial productive and export capacities by utilizing cheap low-skilled labour – teenaged female workers – in relatively labour-intensive light industries, such as textiles, rubber footwear, toys, food stuffs, wood products and furniture (Stern et al., 1995; Enos and Park 1988: 34). The aim was to export US$100 million worth of products within a year and increase this progressively year by year. In 1964, export increased by 40 percent, with its total value reaching US$102 million, exceeding the targeted amount. In 1967, exports broke "the wall of 300 million dollars," which both

122   *Industrialization*

scholars and exporters thought was impossible to surpass under the current conditions. Encouraged by this achievement, Park insisted that exports be increased to US$700 million by 1969 and US$1 billion by 1970 (O Wŏnch'ŏl [7] 1999: 39).

It became apparent, however, that exporting cheap light industry (consumer) products would not achieve the export goal in time. The Korean government requested that the US, its main trade partner, increase its import quota, but the US declined. With the U.S. import quota unchanged, Korea diversified export goods and improved quality. By 1971, the number of types of goods exported to the United States increased from less than 50 in 1960, which consisted of low-skilled textiles, to 983 in 1971, which included high-skilled, labour-intensive products such as appliances, ceramic and chemical products and electronics (Choi and Lee 1990: 55). At the same time, the government urged export good producers to improve the quality of products by technological innovations – including better packaging and design – thereby making them more competitive in the international market and increasing unit value. The goal of exporting US$1 billion was accomplished in 1970.

Encouraged by export results, the government became more ambitious and set a new target for US$10 billion of exports. At the same time, the government realized that exporting light industry commodities had a limited capacity to earn foreign currency and the country's interest might be better served by developing a heavy industry sector. Development of heavy and chemical industries also became necessary because light industry required heavy industry products such as petroleum and steel that Korea imported from the United States and Japan at a high cost.

In 1972, at the beginning of the Third Five-Year Plan, the government decided to make the capital-intensive heavy and chemical industries – electronics, shipbuilding, petrochemical, steel, machine and non-iron-metal – the strategic industries for the next ten years. In 1973, "the HCI (Heavy and Chemical Industry) Declaration" was issued and the new motto adopted was "turn the entire manufacturing industry into an export-oriented one" (chŏnsanŏp ŭi such'ulhwa). According to Stern and colleagues,

> The years 1973 through 1978 involved an across-the board effort to develop a heavy industry sector. During the third five-year plan period, 60.4 percent of all investment funds going to industry – a total of 1,693 billion won (US$3.8 billion) – went into this project.
>
> (Stern et al., 1995: 29)

The HCI Declaration was soon followed by another important decision – the promotion of defense industry. The defense industry drive was not primarily motivated by economic concerns, but more by national security concerns and the fall of South Vietnam to communist rule. Earlier in 1970, the Nixon doctrine indicated the possibility of withdrawal of the US troops from Korea. US troop withdrawal remained a possibility into the Carter administration. The push for the defense industry also came from yet another direction. In spite of the July Fourth

Industrialization 123

North-South Peace Pact signed in 1972, tension between the north and the south continued to rise.[11] Military self-reliance thus became a policy issue as important as battling against poverty. Most advanced high-powered weapons would be purchased, but others needed to be produced domestically.

As a first step toward implementing the new industrial policy, the government selected industrial parks to house HCIs and provided the infrastructure they required. In order to support construction of these parks, the Industrial Site Development Promotion Law was enacted in 1973. Under this law the government established the Industrial Sites Development Corporation and the Water Resources Development Corporation, which, in turn, built several industrial complexes (Enos and Park 1988: 35–36; Kim, Shim, and Kim 1995: 188–189).

The government then created guidelines for aspiring firms (mostly chaebŏls): first, suppliers of technology and foreign loans would be selected in a competitive manner, second, projects funded by foreign loans should be internationally competitive in scale, since the domestic market was too small for the large factories to be built in the industrial park, and prices of their products must be in the neighborhood of international prices (Kim Chŏngnyom 1990: 133–134). Those firms selected for the HCI projects, as will be discussed next, received various subsidies from the government intended to guarantee profits from the new ventures.

The results were remarkable. Between 1964 and 1970, many heavy industries experienced increases in excess of 200 percent.[12] It took only 15 years for the ratio of value added in light industries over HCI (known as the Hoffman coefficient) to fall from four to one in Korea, whereas the same shift took 25 years in Japan and 50 years in the USA (Kim 1988: 125). By the end of the1970s, manufactured products accounted for 60 percent of the total volume of South Korea's exports, and it exported one-third of its manufactured products. Exports came to account for 60 percent of the country's GDP. The total value of exports increased from US$ 121 million in 1964 to US$1 billion in 1970 and to US $10 billion in 1977 (O Wŏnch'ŏl 2006: 81).

"Korea, along with Taiwan," Amsden declared, "are the first nations to penetrate the world market dominated by advanced industrial nations with little comparative advantage other than cheap abundant labour" (Amsden 1989: 143). Korean industrialization thus came to be known as export-led industrialization.

How Exporting Was Promoted – When the government shifted policy emphasis from import substitution to export private enterprises were slow to respond to the export drive the MCI had to encourage (or urge) them to participate in the new plan. It made every effort to help them to produce for export and to become competitive in international market by providing various incentives.[13]

While subsidies encouraged exports, they also changed the "process whereby relative prices are determined" (Ibid.1989: 144). Even if it was more profitable to sell their products in the domestic market, producers were obliged to trade them in the international market at a lower cost in order to meet export quotas. They were then "compensated for having to export by being allowed to sell in the domestic market at inflated prices" (Ibid. 1989: 144).[14]

124   *Industrialization*

Other protective measures included import restrictions on foreign goods manufactured in Korea, bans on consumption of foreign luxury items and the introduction of reserve funds created from taxable income to develop new foreign markets.

The government also applied this wide variety of other promotional instruments.[15] In other words, the Korean government deliberately intervened in the market to give corporate firms an edge in international market competition. In economist's terms, the government "set the price right" (Johnson 1982) or "set the price wrong" (Amsden 1989) as it became necessary to protect the exporters. The Korean government has never believed in the economist's "invisible hand."

While providing incentives and protections, the government expected good results from the participating private firms. Government bureaucrats constantly exerted pressure on corporate leaders to sell more abroad and meet ambitious export targets the government set. Only good performers were assured of continuing government support and allowed to enter new industries, thereby further expanding and diversifying their businesses. Corporate investors were also subject to control of capital by restriction of speculation and remittance of liquid capital overseas. This combination of incentives and disciplinary measures together created and sustained what Akyuz and others called "a dynamic profit investment nexus" in Korea (1998: 9). There is no doubt that Koreans won the export war through their hard work.

But one should not forget about a favourable external factor: the international environment was in Korea's favour. There was unusually rapid growth of external demand as world exports more than doubled during the decade after 1963. Initially, in the 1960s, the United States and Japan were the destination of more than two-thirds of Korea's exports. But later in the 1970s, their share was reduced to about 50 percent, with the European and Third World markets accounting for the other 50 percent (Westphal, Rhee and Pursell 1979: 385).

Factors of Korean economic development

In marketing manufactured exports, it should be noted that Korea's exports have not been dependent upon close foreign participation, as less-developed countries' exports more generally have been, and initial contacts leading into new markets for Korean exports were made through Korean initiatives (Westphal, Kim and Pursell 1979: 383–384). What then are the factors responsible for the success of this independent export-led industrialization project?

i) Technology – Export activities forced and fostered acquisition of foreign technologies as South Korea's strategy turned to the development of new industries in which Korea did not have technological capability (Westphal et al., 1984: 907). "The rapid growth and increasing diversification of exports of all kinds," write Westphal and his associates, "give the most compelling evidence of the country's acquisition of technological capability over time" (1985: 196). Korea acquired technological capability through various means, including technology transfer, human resource development and promotion of scientific research.

Industrialization 125

Technology Transfer – Technology transfer occurred extensively during the colonial period. As shown previously, Japanese technologies were brought in after the abolition of the Company Act in 1920 for the industrial growth planned by the colonial government in connection with the Japan's territorial expansion into the Asian continent. Korean workers and engineers acquired some imported technologies from Japanese engineers and scientists. It is difficult to estimate how much this contributed to the economic development of South Korea in the 1960s. But the basic production technology for non-synthetic textile yarn and fabric, and for plywood are obvious cases of the inheritance from the colonial past (Westphal, Kim and Dahlman 1985: 194).[16] To this should be added technical assistance received from the United States and others after Liberation, especially during the rehabilitation period after the Korean War.

Inherited technology, however, was hardly sufficient for successful implementation of the development plans that focused on export-oriented industrialization. Foreign technologies had to be imported. At the early stages when exports were concentrated on the relatively simple products of light industries that did not require high levels of technology, Korea used technologies that could be easily assimilated. Koreans then assimilated technology through both informal and formal learning. In the late 1960s, Korean firms and engineers relied on simply copying – reversed learning – from technologies imported through capital goods, foreign-finished products or equipment and/or consulting with foreign trade magazines, technical journals and other industrial literature. This mode of technology transfer was relied on more frequently by innovative small firms than by large ones engaged in light industries (Kim 1988), but it was also used – though to a lesser extent – in heavy industries. O Wŏnch'ŏl relates in his memoir how, in 1971, the Agency for Defense Development successfully manufactured various weapons simply by copying those items the United States provided Korea during the Korean War. Such efforts were prompted by the simple idea that "almost any weapon could be dismantled into pieces. Then reproduce each piece separately and assemble all the parts thus produced into a finished weapon" (O Wŏnch'ŏl 1999: 388).[17]

Formal learning was primarily used in heavy industries when the government decided to redirect the export drive to the development of heavy and chemical industries, especially after the HCI Declaration in the 1970s. The kind of technology required for this purpose had to be learned formally from foreign countries at cost. Formal learning occurred primarily by two means: Direct Foreign Investment (DFI) and licensing.

One may learn new technology by working in firms in Korea owned by foreign investors and operated by foreign engineers and/or in firms overseas. This mode of technology transfer, Direct Foreign Investment, is what most developing countries rely upon (Kim 1984: 78). But DFI was largely limited to heavy industries such as chemicals, basic metals and machinery (Westphal, Kim and Dahlman 1985: 186).[18] While the Korean government was eager to acquire foreign technologies that it lacked, it again tried to minimize foreign ownership (Enos and Park 1988: 39). Even though some equity participation was allowed, Korean

126 *Industrialization*

firms were expected to maintain their management independent from foreign multinationals (Kim 1988: 125). As Westphal and Pursell point out: "Government policy was biased in favour of foreign capital goods as a way of strengthening international competitiveness of the capital goods user industries" as modern capital goods came with the know-how to operate them (Enos and Park 1988: 39). According to Kim Linsu,

> DFI's contribution to the growth of GNP in Korea in the 1972–1980 period amounted only to 1.3 percent while its contribution to total and manufacturing value added was only 1.1 percent and 4.8 percent respectively in 1971, and 4.5 percent and 14.2 percent respectively, in 1980.
>
> (1988: 125)

Another means by which Korea acquired advanced foreign technologies, which minimized reliance on DFI, was through technical licensing or international subcontracting (Westphal, Kim and Dahlman 1985: 186). When foreign companies established turnkey plants or operated licensed technologies, local engineers were usually dispatched abroad to be trained. Additionally, Korean firms also sent their qualified engineers to foreign firms to learn other production technologies, mostly through on-the-job experience (Lee 2000: 176). Such apprenticeships involved large investment afforded only by large firms. Those technologies thus acquired were quickly adapted and then modified or innovated to meet changing internal requirements. Once assimilated, these imported technologies were passed onto other domestic firms. They were either sold or diffused through "transfer of labour and management among domestic firms" (Westphal, Rhee and Pursell 1979: 385). There is ample evidence that "a quantum leap in technological capability in small firms is commonly associated with the arrival of technical personnel recruited from other firms" (Kim 1988: 134). Technology diffusion through inter-firm movement in the early stage was almost inevitable since the sudden increase of entries of new firms in the wake of the export drive resulted in competition for a limited number of experienced personnel, with new firms luring them away from old firms.

Large state-owned chemical and machinery companies in the 1950s and 1960s were primarily built on a turnkey basis by foreign firms with foreign technologies. Many industries, including cement and synthetic fibers (specifically, nylon and polyester), either are known or appear to have followed this mode of apprentice learning (Westphal, Kim and Dahlman 1985: 97). Those companies which acquired technology through turnkey plant construction were sometimes required to pay royalties to the licensing company.

Licensing remained modest until the mid-1970s and grew sharply thereafter. The average number of licenses approved was about seven per year during the 1962–1966 period. It increased to 57 during the 1967–1971 period, 87 during the 1972–1970 period, and then to 244 during the 1977–1980 period. The total number of licenses approved by the government during the whole period (1962–1980) was 1,726. These paid licensed technological enterprises came mostly from Japan and the United States, together accounting for 81.4 percent of the total royalty payments (Kim and Lee 1990: 93).

There has been more diffusion from domestic sources rather than repeated transfer from abroad (Westphal, Rhee and Pursell 1979: 385). According to Westphal, Kim and Dahlman, "The transfer of labor among firms was more important than contacts with suppliers alone or with buyers alone" (1985: 192). Such diffusion of imported technologies eventually extended to exporting them to foreign countries. The rapid increase of exports of capital goods and related services "comprises all flows that involve the transmission of technological knowledge and the performance of activities that reflect its application in establishing and operating productive system" (Westphal, Kim and Dahlman 1985: 202).[19] In other words, what Korea did in the early days was repeated elsewhere.

The government facilitated foreign technology transfer by offering various inducements to producers of capital goods, including creation of hospitable environments for development of selected industries, loans at less than market rates for the purchase of plants and equipment, tax privileges – exemption or reduction of income and corporate taxes, acquisition taxes and property taxes on enterprises with foreign capital and creation of hospitable environment for selected industries (Enos and Park 1988: 35).

While promoting and supporting foreign technology imports, the Korean government closely monitored the transfer process to ensure that only the most modern techniques, those representing the current "state of the art" in the developed countries and meeting the following standards were to be chosen (Enos and Park 1988: 34–35): (1) technology with high potential to expand export markets, (2) technology for manufacturing components and developing new processes for the capital goods industry, (3) technology which would be costly in time and expenses to develop domestically and (4) technology whose spill-over had the potential for cost reductions and productivity increases. The government also "took part in any negotiations involving large expenditures and it vetted all agreements for lesser sums" as it thought that Korean firms lacked "accumulated experience in screening the proposals of prospective suppliers and conducting negotiations with them" (Enos and Park 1988: 35).[20]

Successful technology transfer, evidenced by the sharp increase of import or growth of capital products, was due in part to the hospitable external environment. Korea followed the Japanese development route, taking advantage of production technologies Japan made available to Korea as Japan moved to another level. As Enos and Park point out, in the 1960s, Korea attracted "Japan's fading industries such as metal castings, bicycles, sewing machines, ceramics, leather products and the like" (1988: 34). The Korean government's decision to enter the heavy and chemical industries also coincided with the Japan's announcement of "a new policy which was to reorient the economy, away from 'pollution-prone' and 'natural-resource-consuming' heavy and chemical industries to 'clean' and 'brain-intensive' industries" (Enos and Park 1988: 34). Changing focuses of five-year economic development plans, as pointed out earlier, were made primarily in response to internal need, not Japan's industrial policy changes. But it cannot be

128 *Industrialization*

denied that they made it easier for Korea to procure technologies relevant to its development plans.

Human Resources Development – According to Amsden, the basis of late industrialization is neither invention – as it was the case with the First Industrial Revolution (England) – nor innovation as with the Second Industrial Revolution (Germany and the United States) but learning which involves borrowing, adapting and improving on foreign designs (1989: 140–141). South Korea, being a late developer, indeed did a lot of learning foreign technological knowledge in undertaking industrialization. But learning technology from foreign countries has a limit. Advanced industrial countries are "reluctant to sell their high technology to less developed countries" (Wade 1996: 253) as it would undermine their comparative edge in the international market. Korea, on its part, was resolute in minimizing reliance on foreign technology and in diffusing the acquired technology as fast as possible among Koreans and developing its own capacity for technological innovation. Thus import of foreign technology was accompanied by training of domestic skilled workers and engineers. Such training became urgently necessary since Korea's policy on technology transfer was to import only technological knowledge, not foreign technicians. The Park government made a series of attempt to transform the educational system to be directed toward economic development. Shifting emphasis from academic education to vocational, engineering and scientific education and more directly to training and procuring engineers and scientists in order to meet immediate economic needs arising in the nation's industrialization drive.

With the launching of the Vocational Education Promotion Policy as part of the First-Five-Year Educational Development in 1963, the Ministry of Education attempted to convert academic schools to vocational institutions. The plan was to change the five to three ratio of academic to vocational enrollment in secondary school to a three to seven ratio by 1966 (Seth 2002: 120). But the plan was not successfully carried out because, as Seth points out,

> Vocational and technical schools were unpopular; and in practice officials conceded to pressure by not carrying out plans to convert academic schools to vocational ones. Nor were they enthusiastic about constructing new non-academic schools, allowing them to increase their enrollments; in some cases enrollment guidelines were simply ignored.

> (Seth 2002: 21)

Nevertheless, major changes took place after the HCI plan was launched. In 1973, the government enacted the Industrial Education Promotion Law.[21] The next four years (1974–1978) were devoted to promotion of vocational school specialization. Eighty-two vocational schools were selected for specialization in areas matching the skills demanded by targeted industries. The proportion of the government budget allocated for vocational secondary education doubled between 1970 and 1979 (Seth 2002: 126).

Technical education was also extended to industrial workers. The Ministry of Education encouraged vocational high schools to establish night schools and set up a special curriculum for those industrial workers who were not otherwise able to attend school thereby enabling them to earn a middle school or high school degree.

Further attempts were made to solicit cooperation from industries in promoting vocational education. The government strongly advised both public and private companies to establish vocational secondary schools. Major public and private enterprises, such as the Pohang Steel (public) and the Daelim Industry (private), each set up a vocational high school. In those regions without vocational high schools, on-the-job training centers were built by the government. It also set up numerous training institutes in HCI development areas such as Ch'angwŏn, Ulsan and Taejon, which were supplemented by private firms' sending their workers (see O Wŏnch'ŏl 1996 [2]: 92–93; Seth 2002: 126–127). As a result, the number of in-plant vocational trainees drastically increased in 1976, reaching an annual level of almost 100,000. Large numbers of workers continued to be trained from 1977 to 1980, averaging about 70,000 annually (O Wŏnch'ŏl 1996[2]: 93).

The government also encouraged the growth of junior vocational and technical colleges, and the Ministry of Education (MOE) ordered the conversion of vocational high schools and various junior colleges into junior (two-year) vocational colleges (see Kim Yŏngh-wa 2004: 130–133; Seth 2002: 126–127). The establishment of junior vocational colleges aimed at producing intermediate level technical workers (technicians) between vocational high school graduates (craftsmen) and technological college graduates (technologists) (Kim Yŏngh-wa 2004: 133). During the period from 1965 to 1980, the total number of vocational high schools almost doubled – from 314 in 1965 to 605 in 1980 – and students increased 4.5 times – from 172,436 to 764,187 (Kim Yŏng-hwa 2004: 110). Vocational education received more attention from the government than before and consequently there was a sharp growth.[22]

Promotion of Scientific Research – Promotion of vocational education was coupled with government support for scientific research that facilitates technological development. In the wake of the industrial drive – especially the HCI and defense industries – there was urgency in promoting scientific research as the existing universities were not actively engaged in research activities directly linked with industrial development. In 1967, the Ministry of Science and Technology (MST) was established with the aim of enhancing scientific development to meet rising industrial technological needs or more directly to resolve the issue of the shortage of highly trained scientists.[23] In 1968, the MST established the Korean Institute of Science and Technology (KIST) in 1968[24] with the help of the United States. It was primarily involved in industry-oriented research covering a wide range of areas – chemicals, machinery, electronics, ocean science, standardization, nuclear energy, bio-technology, system engineering and aerospace – for the purpose of serving the growing needs of the private sector.

The initial aim of establishing KIST was to attract those Korean technical and scientific specialists who had not returned after receiving graduate training abroad.

130   Industrialization

According to one informal survey conducted by the MST around 1969, "Some 1,200 Koreans had received PhDs in the natural sciences in the United States and Europe, but only a few dozen of those scientists were working in Korea" (Stern et al., 1995: 25–26).

In 1971, the MST also founded the Korean Development Institute to bring back Korean economists overseas. It successfully persuaded "a dozen economists with PhDs to return, thereby roughly tripling the number of economists with this degree in Korea" (Stern et al., 1995: 25).

While actively advancing research activities by opening new institutes, the government turned to private corporations, encouraging them to rationalize resource allocation for technology development by increasing R&D (Research and Development) activities. As it did with the export promotion drive the government also offered private enterprises various incentives – including tax incentives, preferential financing, direct R&D equipment and venture capital creation – to expand R&D programs (Kim and Dahlman 1992: 449–450). Response to this request was again prompt. The number of corporate R&D laboratories increased from 1 in 1971 to 122 in 1983. The total R&D investment increased from W3.4 billion in 1971 to W171.4 billion in 1981, raising its share in the nation's total R&D expenditure from 32 percent to 58 percent over the period. In 1976, R&D expenditures in the manufacturing sector, as a percentage of total sales, were 0.36 percent. Five years later, it increased to 0.67 percent (Kim and Dahlman 1992: 449).

Active generation of new knowledge through knowledge conversion and creation by research marked the beginning of a new era. Korean scientists and engineers were no longer mere learners, but became innovators. The number of patents granted to Korean user firms for machine tools was seven during the 1975–1979 period to 42 in 1980–1984, and to 408 in 1990–1995 (Lee 2000: 185).

ii) Financing – When Park came to power in 1960, there were no domestic savings to speak of. What domestic saving there was constituted about 1.7 percent of GNP (Im Chongch'ŏl 1975: 7). South Korea could no longer rely on US foreign aid for undertaking development plans.

The military government had to take initiatives in finding funds to finance the development plans.

First, the military government attempted to have those entrepreneurs assumed to have accumulated wealth illicitly during the Rhee period return their wealth. The total amount the government was able to collect was 4 billion won, hardly a substantial amount for undertaking a national development plan. Second, currency reform was instituted in the hope that it would "bring out the hoarded currency for developmental purposes, limit currency speculation, and end inflation" (Kuznets 1977: 203). This measure, however, only resulted in creating economic chaos and conditions for inflation. Third, an attempt was made to stimulate the recently established stock market. But those military officers in charge of managing it were more interested in creating political funds by manipulating it than convincing people that buying stock would be a profitable investment. The last effort was to control bank interest rates on the assumption that this move would make people think that saving money in the bank would be profitable. It turned out,

Industrialization 131

however, that there was not enough money in people's possession to be deposited in banks (see O Wŏnch'ŏl 1995 [1]: 52–54).

Foreign Loans – Having failed to raise funds domestically, the government sought foreign capital (i.e., loans). At that time, the ability of Korean entrepreneurs to attract foreign capital was very limited due to the low creditworthiness of domestic firms. The government, therefore, tried to make a loan arrangement directly with the US government. However, the US government, not favourably inclined to the military regime, refused to give loans on the ground that South Korea was a recipient of aid-in-grant. The Japanese government took the position that in the absence of diplomatic relations formal loan agreement (ch'agwan hyŏpchŏng) was impossible.[25]

In 1964, Park himself went to Germany and met with the then German chancellor Erhard. Park requested a loan with a plea, "Please, lend us money to feed our people. Half of them are starving. We do not lie. The money lent will be returned without fail." West Germany offered to lend 13.5 million US dollars as a financial loan and 26.25 million US dollar as a commercial loan. Park's visit also resulted in an arrangement with West Germany to send Koreans to work in mines and hospitals, and an agreement for future cooperation for industrialization of Korea (see O Wŏnch'ŏl [1]1995: 111). Between 1963 and 1977, 7,396 men and women went to West Germany as miners and nurses. Together, they remitted US$10.153 to their families in Korea (*Kyŏnghyang.com*, April 21, 2009).

In 1965, South Korea, against stiff opposition from many groups, signed a normalization of diplomatic relation with Japan. After much negotiation, the Japanese government agreed to provide US $300 million in grants, $200 million in government loans and 300 million in commercial credit. The total figure (US$800 million) was substantially lower than that sought by previous regimes, but was no small sum for a country whose entire exports in 1964 amounted to US $200 million (Woo 1991: 87). The normalization of diplomatic relations was also the beginning of direct Japanese involvement in Korea, which "within a few years Japanese direct investment outstripped the American total" (Cumings 1985: 78).[26]

Overseas Adventures – The Vietnam War also played an important role in financing the development project. In 1964, Korea readily responded the President Lyndon Johnson's request to American allies to send troops to join US troops fighting north Vietnamese forces.

Over a seven-year period from 1966 to 1973, the Korean government dispatched 300,000 troops to Vietnam. Of them, 5,099 died, 10,962 were injured, and 89,708 suffered after returning to Korea from the aftereffect of the weed killer, Defoliage, which was widely sprayed in Vietnam by the American military.

On the other hand, there were some handsome economic gains. Korea received $ 2.2 billion as military assistance in 1968–1972, almost three times the amount ($800 million) received in previous four years (1961–1965).

As stated in the so-called the 1966 Brown Memorandum, which laid out arrangements for American utilization of Korean forces, the United States provided $150 million aid loans in addition to the same amount already committed to support economic development of Korea.

132   *Industrialization*

Korean troops in Vietnam sent home a total of $1.95 billion, 82.8 percent of what the US government paid them for their service in 1965–1973.

The war helped civilian corporate enterprises to extend their business to Vietnam. Big enterprises such as the Hyundai Construction, the Hanjin Trading Company, the Dae Woo Industry and the SK Electronics were engaged in the business of providing military supplies and various services including transportation of military supplies for the US troops. Cho Chunghun, the chair of the Hanjin Group, boasted in his memoir of earning $150 million in five years during his stay in Vietnam from 1965 to 1971 (Cho Chunghun 1996: 79).

Korea also sold its industrial goods to Vietnam. Although the values of commercial exports were modest, the Vietnam market served as an outlet for new industrial products such as steel, transportation equipment and non-electric machinery. Until then, Korea mainly exported to America and Japan labour intensive goods such as textile and plastic goods, and wigs (Woo 1991: 95–96).[27]

Just as they discovered Vietnam as a potential market, the Korean government also discovered the Middle East. After the oil crisis in 1973, Korea established South Arabia and South Korea Economic Cooperation, and private businessmen busily turned to the construction industry which was booming in the Middle East (Deyo 1987: 76).

DFI – Legislation allowing non-grant capital inflow was promulgated in 1960, with an array of incentives including tax concessions and guarantees of principal and profit repatriation.

The first case of DFI after the launching of the economic development plan occurred in 1962. By 1978, some 900 foreign investments – mainly by Japanese and Americans – had been approved by the Korean government. But as Westphal et al. point out, "Most of these involved either 50–50 joint ventures or minority foreign participation, in line with the government's policy to encourage these forms. As a rule, investments by foreigners were individually rather small" (1979: 368). During the ten years from 1962 through 1971, DFI contributed only 4 percent of the total net inflow of the foreign capital excluding assistance. It contributed 11 percent of the total during the following five years, 1972–1976. Westphal et al. concluded, "While it is true that foreign capital has financed a high, though steadily decreasing, percentage of investment activity in Korea, only a small proportion of the inflow has been in the form of DFI" (369; see also Akyuz, Chang and Kozul-Wright 1998: 15).

Domestic Resources Mobilization – Efforts were also made to increase domestic savings through tax collection and raising interest rate. With the help (or under the pressure) of the United States, the Park government implemented both tax and interest reform. In 1965, the Monetary Board of Korea raised the maximum interest rate on time deposits from 15 to 30 percent per annum and the interest rate on bank loans from 16 to 26 percent. In 1966, the Office of National Tax Administration was created with the centralized authority to collect taxes and to investigate tax fraud. A year later, it was followed by "a tax reform that raised assessments on the wealthiest individuals and corporations" (Brazinsky 2007: 143). Reform results were remarkable. Adjusted household savings increased from less than

Industrialization 133

one percent of disposable income in 1965 to 4.1 percent in 1966 and remained higher than 3.4 percent for the remainder of the decade, and gross domestic investment as a percentage of GNP rose from 15 percent in 1965 to 29 percent by 1969. More striking was the increase of tax revenue. It surged from 29.2 billion won in 1964 to 156.4 billion won by 1968 (Brazinsky 2007: 144). American advisers fondly called the tax reform the "quiet revolution in tax administration." (Brazinsky 2007: 143). Thus domestic savings "enabled growth to proceed without hitting balance of payment constraints" (Dornbush et al., 1987: 413). According to Dornbush and others,

> During the 1960–69 period, the total amount of national (domestic) – business and personal – saving was 8.9 percent of GNP whereas that of foreign saving was 9.1. But it was reversed in the next decade 1970–1979: the former 20.5 whereas the latter 6.8.
>
> (1987: 413)

Private Loans (sach'ae) – It is widely known that both large and small business firms often use informal private loans. Yet little is known about the extent to which this competes with banks and other financial organizations. That private loans played a significant role in corporate finance, however, became evident in 1972 when the Federation of Korean Industries chair appealed directly to President Park in a desperate effort to save many private firms from going into bankruptcy because of their inability to pay back private loans. Facing an historical crisis of Korean enterprise, Park's government accordingly took the extreme measure of freezing private loans under a presidential emergency decree. This measure came to be known as the P'alsam choch'I (August the Third Settlement). Private firms reported 40,677 private loans, which had a total value of 34.6 billion won, equivalent to 34 percent of currency in circulation (Kim Chŏngnyŏm 1990: 275). The Korean financial market has changed considerably since then but there is no evidence that the private loan market has disappeared.

The Stock Market – The P'alsam choch'i was soon followed by the enactment of the law (January 5, 1973) expediting the opening of enterprise to the public The aim of this law was twofold: (1) to reform the corporate financial structure by inducing corporations to switch from financing through bank and/or informal private loans to stock issuing and (2) to help promote healthy development of the national economy through public participation in corporate enterprises. By opening the stock market to the public, the government expected to (1) help corporate firms reduce their financial deficits by issuing company bonds and stocks, (2) separate capital from management and leave management to professional managers, thereby advancing socialization of corporate enterprises and (3) help redistribute income, thereby promoting social stability. Opening stock to the public, the government argued, "is to compensate those middle class – not professional – informal private lenders for their sacrifice incurred in saving the large corporate firms" (Kim Chŏngnyŏm 1990: 275). In an effort to expedite public participation, the government selected those firms thought to be in need of assistance and

134 *Industrialization*

offered them various benefits, including reduction of corporate and income tax, reassessment of corporate assets and the like. Firms that refused to accept government advice suffered numerous disadvantages, such as a 20 percent corporate tax increase, increase of the tax on stockholder dividends, withdrawal of business loss allowance and reductions of the extent of tax exemption for donation or public relation expenses. More importantly, the Minister of Finance was authorized to request banking organizations to restrict loans to them.

Though they were grateful for what the country did to save them from bankruptcy, corporate response to stock opening was lukewarm. With the P'alsam choch'i, their financial burden was considerably lessened. The lowering of the interest rate of bank and informal private loans also reduced production costs and thus increased corporate income. Incensed by the slow response, Park issued a warning to corporate owners and made clear his resolution to push the policy of strengthening tax management on enterprises and big stockholders, and opening participation through the stock market. Coming from Park, the warning was not ignored. The stock market began to change. While in 1972 there were only 66 firms listed in the stock market, by 1979, the number increased to 355, including 309 large firms. Similarly, whereas in 1971, company bonds were not even issued in the stock market, by 1975, company bonds on the order of 300 billion won were issued. In 1980, the volume reached 1 trillion won. Still the majority of firms did not enter the stock market. Korea had to wait two more decades for full participation of domestic firms and ordinary citizens in the stock market and its opening to the outside world. (This section is largely based on Kim Chongnyon (1990)).

iii) The Role of Private and Public Enterprises – Whilst emphasizing the role of the government in economic development that goes beyond that of old nightwatchman, Park also declared his belief in the principle of a liberal market economy. "The wholesale command economy," Park said, "would destroy freedom. The kind of society we hope to build is the one based on the principle of free market where competition is an effective norm." He further stated that the role of the state in such a society is "to establish a necessary mechanism that would prevent the market from falling under the control of an individual or a group so as to ensure economic freedom". The principle here is combining broad possible competition with minimum necessary planning (Park Chung Hee 1962: 235–236, quoted in Chŏng Chaekyŏng 1992: 167).

Thus private business enterprises were encouraged (or pressured) to participate in the development projects led by the state as active players. Although the government never stopped emphasizing the importance of small- and medium-sized enterprise in economic development, subsidies and protective measures it provided to private firms to become exporter-industrialists, as mentioned earlier, mostly went to those large firms that closely collaborated with it. Rapid growth of selected large enterprises, relative to medium and smaller enterprises, became clear. Between 1966 and 1971, the value added share of firms with 200 or more employees rose from 58 percent to 72 percent (Pack and Westphal 1986).

It is clear that chaebŏl became big with the help of the government, but little is known about how they helped themselves grow so rapidly and so big. They made

Industrialization 135

the best use of government subsidies. In fact, the idea of private entrepreneurs becoming partners to the government in the modernization project came from the side of entrepreneurs. They took initiatives and often led the government in development projects. "In Korea," remarked Jones and SaKong, "despite the pervasive activity of the government's visible hand, the bulk of decisions leading to production are taken in the private sector" (Jones and SaKong 1980: 167). They borrowed money from foreign banks, negotiated with foreign companies for joint projects, went abroad to persuade countries to buy Korean products, even those countries with which Korea did not have a diplomatic relationship. They broke into the international markets dominated by the advanced industrial countries. Forced, encouraged and assisted by the government to become exporters, they quickly outgrew the small domestic market, going to every corner of the world. They became expansionists and built their empires.

The government actively subsidized those firms with good track records, but even so, those firms had to compete against each other in receiving special "favours" from the government, such as loans, grants, licenses, etc. The process of allocating such "favours" was accompanied by a good deal of informal personal negotiation between businessmen and government bureaucrats through personal ties (kinship, school, regional ties) or other lobbyist channels.

Once a favour had been received, it needed to be properly appreciated in the form of monetary or material payment. As such practices were repeated, it became customary for corporate enterprises and government officials to routinely exchange favours and donations (or contributions) in order to maintain mutually helpful relationship. The former needed the latter's favour for their business's interest and protection while the latter needed the former's donations for informal office and personal expenses, and party political funds. This may be a cynical view or theory of corporate success, but there is no denying that good performance measured in terms of profit alone does not account for being selected for government assistance – although this tends to be ignored by economists. Maintaining good relationship with government is very important, and there is ample evidence that those firms with good connections with the government, but without good track records, received special favours from the government and failed to produce good results. (This issue will be discussed in detail in the last section of this chapter.)

Despite the government's commitment to a market economy and effort to foster private enterprise, private agents have not been exclusively relied upon in implementing key undertakings in Korea's industrial evolution. The Park government invested in and operated a wide range of public sector enterprises. Public corporations have been important in some key industries such as steel, fertilizer, petrochemicals, refined petroleum products and infrastructure project[28] (Amsden 1989: 92). According to Amsden, "The initiative to enter new manufacturing branches has come primarily from the public sphere and. . . . every major shift in industrial diversification in the decades of the 1960s and 1970s was instigated by the state" (1989: 80). Decisions by the government to take the initiative were made on several pragmatic grounds, including the absence of private enterprises qualified to or

136 *Industrialization*

willing to undertake the venture, and the need to produce non-tradables or import substitution rather than exports. Furthermore, the government had

> the desire to exercise direct control over the start-up and operation of an industry with multiple linkages to other industries and the expectation that a public agent could achieve a far more favorable outcome in negotiations with foreign suppliers of capital and technology.
>
> (Westphal 1990: 49. See Rodrik, Grossman and Norman 1995: 90–91)

There were also other reasons for creating public enterprises. As Westphal explains,

> Some of them came into being as a transitional phase in government actions to regenerate moribund firms. In a number of these cases . . . bankruptcy has led to public sector ownership as a consequence of government debt-repayment guarantees. Typically, the firms have been quickly restructured and then sold to private interest, so the set of such enterprises has undergone continual change.
>
> (Westphal 1990: 49)

Like their private counterparts, public enterprises received favorable credit terms. They also received direct allocations from the government budget. They have been managed as autonomous profit-seeking entities and many of them acquired international competitiveness quickly and contributed materially to government revenues. Not only did public enterprises account for a large share of manufacturing output and investment, the importance actually increased during the critical take-off years of the 1960s.[29]

Three reasons account for the significant role played by the public sector. First, Korea inherited an economy from the colonial authority in which 95 percent of the major facilities were owned and operated by the government. The government officially stated that it would continue to own and operate those industrial plants for "strategic reasons" because of the nature of the industries. However, Leroy Jones points out that the public sector could have been divested after Liberation. Indeed, while a portion of it was divested, a large proportion was retained, and in fact, the public sector grew substantially during the Park's era. Jones again offers a convincing argument that the retention and expansion of the public sector was due to Park's concern with the growth of the private sector which might challenge the government authority. The government decided to retain a portion of industry under its control as a way of countervailing the runaway expansion of the private sector (Jones 1975).

Second, public enterprises partly served as a connector between the government and private economic sector through which a functional division of labour between the two sectors inevitably established reciprocal relationship. Public enterprises were geared to developmental goals whereas private enterprises sought profit maximization (Amsden 1989: 68).

Third, public enterprise also played an important non-economic role. According to O Wŏnch'ŏl, during the Park period almost all directors' positions in state enterprises were occupied by retired army generals (1996 [3]: 208). Park maintained a friendly relationship by rewarding military leaders, especially those who remained personally loyal to him, with such appointments after their retirement.

iv) Industrial Workers – The unity of government and business in this era was sharply contrasted by the relationship between government and labour. When Park Chung Hee came to power, he disbanded the Korean Federation of Trade Unions (KFTU), along with many other political organizations. Park was not prepared to see the development of a large-scale organization such as KFTU as a political entity with a fair degree of autonomy which might challenge his power and control of labour. As we have seen, the cheap, schooled, energetic labour was the only internal asset South Korea had. Taming labour to maintain comparative advantage in the world market became absolutely necessary. Labour was a key factor to economic growth.

Consequently, the government became very sensitive to any movement among industrial workers to organize themselves into collective forces and was determined to establish an industrial community free of disputes. Accordingly, it did its best to discourage workers from forming unions.

In 1971, the government promulgated the Special Law on Labour in Foreign Invested Firms, which stipulated that those who intend to organize a union or to launch a labour protest should get permission from the Office of Labour Administration. Under this law it became difficult, if not impossible, for those workers employed by foreign firms to organize a labour unions or labour protests as the government's intention of instituting this law was to discourage them from taking such action. This law was soon followed by the Special Law on National Security which extended the same stipulation on collective labour action to domestic enterprises.

The government further revised it in 1973 to confine collective labour action to company unions only, eliminating the national and industrial union from the process.

The aim of the new regulations was to make it difficult for industrial workers to actively engage in collective bargaining and protest, without undermining their right to form union.

In addition to changes in labour laws, the government promulgated a series of laws outside the framework of labour law for the purpose of restraining collective labour action, providing the government with a broader basis to deal with labour protest (Choi 1989: 97).[30] Under these laws, union action could be easily interpreted as unlawful civil disorder and criminal acts rather than as lawful acts of demanding correctives for inadequate labour conditions (Choi 1989: 97). These moves were prompted by concern with inviting foreign capital to invest in Korea.

They also reflected Park Chung Hee's views on the labour union. Park found the labour unions "conflictual, unproductive, and disruptive in the context of economic growth" (Choi 1989: 177). Park's own image of labour management relationships was one of cooperation, mutual care and harmony, rather than conflict

138 *Industrialization*

and dispute (Park 1992: 89–93). He felt rather strongly about developing a new model for labour management relations. In the late 1960s, all industrial firms with 100 or more employees were required to establish a labour management council. In implementing the council system, the government hoped workers would join management in its efforts to improve productivity, avoid disputes through the development of mutual concerns and care for each other's interests. At first, the council functioned as a nominal substitute for a labour union – all workers' demands for wage negotiation, improvements in working conditions, and other grievances could be channelled only through the council. This stipulation was revised in 1973 to return what was considered a union job to the union (Bae Kyuhan 1987: 78). The 1973 revision of the labour law also gave the president the authority to make rules necessary for the operation of the labour management council – i.e., establishment and registration of the labour management council, its modus operandi and frequency of regular meetings. In other words, with these regulations imposed by the government, the labour management council was no longer an arrangement struck by workers and owners on a voluntary basis. The revised law also ruled that government officials should be present at council meetings, expressing their opinions and policy concerns (Han'guk kidokkyo hyŏpŭihoe 1987: 2281). When government officials did not attend, the minutes of council meetings were required to be sent over to the Office of Labour Administrations (Choi 1989: 198).

With such legal restrictions and control on labour rights of industrial workers, corporate employers did little to improve working conditions for their employees. On average, workers worked more than ten hours a day throughout the entire development decade of the 1960s, even though the standard working day according to the labour law was eight hours. Each year, the EPB set the ceiling for the wage level, which no firm was allowed to exceed although it could pay less. The pay average workers received was called a "starvation wage" as it did not even cover minimum living expenses. In the 1970s, South Korea was ranked highest in industrial accidents, measured in term of the frequency of accidents over the total hours worked per year. Workers were also not properly protected from occupational disease. Workers also suffered from the condescending attitudes of managerial and clerical employees. It was also normal practice for supervisors and management staff to use disrespectful language in addressing workers (Hanguk kidokkyo sahoemunje yŏn'guwŏn 1987).

Despite such oppressive and poor working conditions, industrial workers worked hard. Labour productivity continued to increase during the Park period. Economic bureaucrats and corporate employers were pressured to work hard with various incentives. Such incentives were not offered to industrial workers. Since their cheap labour was Korea's cutting edge in the industrialization drive, their wages had to be kept low to maintain Korea's competitiveness in the world market.

The question then is, as Choi Jang Jip asks, how was such a workforce was created – with its habits of "punctuality, discipline, regulation, hard work, conformity and obedience to the instructions of superiors" (Choi 1989: 175). Former

MCI minister Pak Ch'unghun, in reminiscing the period during which export values reached US$100 million (in 1972) and US$300 million in 1976, attributed this success to the monthly export promotion and expansion meeting at the Blue House, the devoted efforts of the MCI staff and "the noble sacrifice of textile and rubber shoes factory girls who endured difficulties with the sincere belief that 'export is patriotism'" (O Wŏnch'ŏl 1996[1]: 320). O Wŏnch'ŏl echoes Pak Ch'unghun in saying that factory girls worked diligently because they took pride in the fact that what they produced was exported to foreign countries and made the country rich.

Amsden stresses the role of peer pressure and governmental promotion of workers' education for creating a hardworking workforce (1989: 178). Choi Jang Jip, by contrast, puts emphasis on the disciplinary side:

> While inherited traditions may have played some role and the fact that workers were educated was of considerable consequence, the fact is that a deliberate, coercive effort of enormous proportions was deployed and redeployed continually to produce a "disciplined" work force that would work hard for low wages.
>
> (1989: 176)

It is difficult to refute the above explanations. What each author emphasizes is an aspect of workers work habits with which they were impressed with. There is no question that there was patriotism, mutual regulation and encouragement, coercion and discipline in the factory. But there was another factor. Industrial workers, young female and male, mostly came from rural villages. Going to the factory was not their first choice. They would rather have continued with their school education. But their parents could not afford to give their children further education. Most of them were driven into the factory by poverty. When they left their rural villages they did not intend to return. Their plan was to find a job in the city, to become financially self-sufficient and to send a part of their wage to parents back home. They worked hard to keep the job; they worked extra hours to earn more money, as the wage was low. They endured hard working conditions and demanded wage increase. Some of them eventually decided to form their own unions, calling them "democracy unions" (see Chapter 5 on this subject). They were united in fostering collective action to be able to negotiate with the employers and claim their rights stipulated in the labour law. They did not opt for "exit"; instead, they chose "voice."

v) Economic Nationalism – Like most latecomers, South Korea as an independent nation successfully carried out the economic development project by taking advantage of what advanced industrial countries could offer – be it capital, technology, markets, development models or advice.

Japan was eager to establish economic ties with South Korea after the normalization of diplomatic relations (1965) (Chang 1985). But Park and his government were fully aware of the danger of relying too heavily on certain other countries for the nation's economic development. "Without a self-standing economy (*charip*

140   *Industrialization*

kyŏngje)," he said in a 1965 speech, "there won't be political sovereignty." To Park, a self-reliant economy meant an economy open to the outside world, but one managed almost exclusively by Korean nationals, not by foreigners. Park's idea was to borrow what Korea needed – capital and technology – for its industrial growth but not to let foreign capitalists, scientists and engineers to come in and be in charge of projects and eventually run the Korean economy. "Korea's export-led industrialization," remark Westphal, Rhee and Pursell, "has been overwhelmingly and in fundamental respects directed and controlled by nationals" (1979: 385). Koreans furthered the national interest, as John Enos points out, "by construction of a modern industrial economy, involving the adoption of the best foreign technologies and institutions, and employing all the talents and industry of its citizens" (1984: 28). "Nationalism," says Harry G. Johnson, "attaches value to having property owned by nations and having economic functions performed by nationals. Further, nationalism attaches particular value to property and functions which are considered important to the identity and the power of the nations" (Johnson 1967: 127).

Until quite recently, that is after the *segyehwa* (globalization) drive began, the real estate and stock market have been closed to foreigners by law. The majority of Chinese businessmen in Korea found Park's Korea a difficult place to do profitable business and left for foreign countries without being adequately compensated for the real estate they owned. Administrative and executive positions of economic organizations – public or private, home-based or overseas – have rarely been occupied by foreigners. Enterprises such as steel, electricity and banking, considered "important to the identity and power of the nation," have been nationalized until recently.

There was also a strong urge to be independent of foreign aid. Vital though it might have been in rehabilitating the South Korean economy crippled by the division and devastated by the war, foreign assistance did restrict the autonomy of the nation in making decisions regarding Korean affairs. The United States exercised its hegemonic power through the threat of withdrawal of aid, which had direct bearing on economic welfare and national security. Foreign aid ceased shortly after Park seized power. The value of military aid continued to decline. South Korea was forced to be independent.

Economic nationalism is not merely an expression of negative attitudes toward foreign direct investment and foreign enterprises. As Johnson further points out, nationalism is more positively concerned with "establishing the self-respect of members of the nation in comparison with members of other nations and with creating a distinctive national identity" (1967: 126). As a latecomer fully conscious of its economic backwardness, an independent South Korea had a lot of catching up to do. Attention now turned to the relative standing of Korea in an international community dominated by the Western nations. Catching up with the "advanced" West or establishing an "advanced fatherland" (*sŏnjin choguk*) became a new goal solidly uniting Koreans with a deep-rooted collective sense of cultural gulf. Western education, as discussed in the previous chapter, was accepted as a path to modernization and future independence by many Koreans. Economic development

Industrialization 141

and building up a strong army came to be considered as means to compete against other nations, thereby upgrading Korea's status in the international arena and defending national sovereignty. South Koreans take enormous pride in becoming a member of OECD and more recently one of the G-20 nations.

More specifically, South Koreans prodded themselves to catch up with Japan, which had deprived Koreans of the right to modernize by themselves for four decades. The rationale the Japanese provided was that Koreans were not themselves capable of doing so. Koreans were continuously reminded during the colonial period how stagnant Chosŏn Dynasty Korea was and how developed Korea became after the Japanese arrived. Despite the much-publicized economic transformation under Japanese authorities, the standard of living of Koreans remained low. Koreans after Liberation were continuously reminded of the "dark and painful" *(ŏdupko koeroun)* colonial period of "oppression and sorrow" *(appak kwa sŏrŭm)*, an experience which should not be repeated. Anti-Japanese sentiment was and is still strong among Koreans, and it helped Koreans to unite in whatever competition or conflict between the two countries. The effort to transform South Korean into an industrial nation was, in some ways, an effort to prove to themselves that they could do it on their own. It was a strong nationalist reaction against the colonial past. South Korea continued to rely on Japanese loans and technology, but guarded the sovereignty of the economy, and the one specific aim in industrialization has been to catch up with and eventually surpass Japan.

South Koreans were also united in the competition against the other Korea, the People's Republic of Korea. The two Koreas fought a war and remain in a state of truce with continuing threats of invasion by the other side. North Korea's recovery from the devastation of war was faster than that of South Korea, which began industrialization a decade after the north (O Wŏnch'ol 1999[7]: 348). North-South competition is a competition between the socialist and capitalist systems, and the north boasted of the superiority of its system. The North-South gap was a growing concern among South Korean leaders. After the Park government successfully implemented the first and second five-year economic development plans, Park challenged the north to a goodwill competition to see which system was better. Park put this proposal to the north's Kim Il-sung on August 15, 1970, the twenty-fifth anniversary of regaining independence. "A talisman double digit GDP growth figure," in the words of Woo, "was the Korean score in the race to catch up with Japan and also to surpass the DPRK economic performance" (1991: 98).[31]

vi) The Park Chung Hee Factor – a Personalist Leader – The South Korean developmental experience, along with that of Japan, is frequently cited by political economists as a case of state-led development. Broadly speaking, high-speed economic development in both countries was led by the state. But there are important differences between the two which should not be overlooked. In the case of Japan, it was led by the Ministry of International Trade and Industry (MITI), whereas in the case of Korea it was led by Park Chung Hee himself through the EPB, MCI and MF.

The implication of this difference is that while the MITI as an institution was capable of leading the development project on its own, both the EPB and MCI did

142   *Industrialization*

so under Park's command. As mentioned earlier, Pak Ch'unghun, the Minister of Commerce and Industry, asked Park Chung Hee to become the commander in the export war in 1964. When Park Chung Hee appointed Tae Wan-Son as the minister of EPB, he did not think that Park was asking him to play a leading role in the development project. He told O Wŏnch'ŏl, the then special economic adviser to the president, "My job is to follow President's Park's will and manage or adjust various ministries' differing views on economic policy" (Segye Ilbo 1996: 05–04). Park made it very clear to all the economic bureaucrats and his cabinet that he was in charge of implementing the development plans and involved himself deeply in every step of it. The EPB prepared five-year economic development plans. But Park approved of every industrial project plan prepared by the Ministry of Commerce and Industry, often setting or changing the project target by himself. I have already mentioned that Park had instructed the MCI to achieve the export goal of US$100 million in 1972. He carefully selected qualified persons to be in charge of planning and undertaking specific projects, and kept able bureaucrats long in the same position or transferred them to other positions for related roles.[32] When the government initiated plans or projects which private enterprises found unwise to commit a large sum of funds to, or felt they lacked adequate technological competence to undertake them, Park talked directly – and persuasively and forcefully – to the directors of those private firms he chose to projects he initiated. Chung Chuyoung, the chair of the Hyundai Group, decided to go to the Middle East to earn oil dollars through construction projects and build shipping yards at Park's request. "Without the personal involvement and encouragement of President Park," state Rodrik and colleagues, "Hyundai would not have embarked and completed what eventually became one of the world's best shipyards" (1995: 86). Park thought of young Kim Ujung as one of the most promising businessman and his business to grow develop and frequently asked him to take over insolvent companies (see Clifford 1998: 118–123). Appealing to businessmen on a personal basis with handsome rewards and occasional threats won Park many dedicated corporate followers.

Whatever major industrial plans the government created – the plan to foster the electronic industry, the long-term export plan, the plan to supply electricity to rural fishery areas, the petro-chemicals and steel mills construction plan, the automobile industry promotion plan – Park was involved in the planning stages and made the final decision regarding them. He then established a temporary position within the presidential office to be in charge of undertaking them. He often made unannounced visit to work sites to check progresses and encouraged the workers and supervisors (O Wŏnchŏl 2006: 26). When a project was completed, he attended the closing ceremony and commended select workers, and sometimes left a hwiho (brush handwriting) to be hung on the wall of the plant. According to O Wŏnch'ŏl Park had never missed the "export expansion meeting" held at the MCI and the "monthly economic progress briefing meeting" held at the EPB. The aim of these monthly meetings, which representatives of each ministry, business leaders and academicians attended, was not only to check on the current state of exporting in particular, and economic progress in general, but also to discuss and solve problems arising from the implementation of specific plans. The two

Industrialization 143

meetings were held monthly from 1965 to 1979. Park's determination shown in pushing economic development was such that he appeared to his subordinates to be a man possessed (O Wŏnch'ŏl 2006: 43).

Such personal participation and encouragement from the most powerful man in the nation worked as an effective driving force. Economists and political economists tend to focus on material incentives the government provided in explaining the growth of export and industry in the 1960s and 1970s, rarely mentioning human relationship as a source of work incentive. The famous Hawthorn Study by Elton Mayo and R. J. Roethlisberger, for example, reminded economists and others as early as the 1950s that "between the vitality of incentives to production and the vitality of the worker's informal social relationships in the work room of the factory, there is crucial relationship" (Nisbet 1953: 231). Nisbet thus concluded, "The intensity of personal incentives tend to fluctuate with the intensity of meaningful social relationships" (1953: 231).

Economic development, more generally known as choguk kŭndaehwa (modernization of fatherland), was Park's personal project. Many critics point out that Park must have thought that he alone was capable of undertaking such a historical task. Already in his "Revolution Promise" issued shortly after the coup in 1960, he stated that he took the "revolutionary act to save the country on the verge of economic bankruptcy and political collapse under the inept previous regime" (see Park Chung Hee 1997: 39–67).

In 1972, when the development policy switched its focus to the development of heavy and chemical industry, he dissolved the National Assembly, declared an emergency decree and amended the constitution, removing, among other things, the provision of the four-year presidential term. The October 17 Presidential Special Announcement said, "Disorder and inefficiency are rampant, political parties – ruling as well as opposition – are irresponsible, devoid of the sense of national duty and politics are mired in factional struggle and conflict of political maneuvering" (cited in O Wŏnch'ŏl [7] 1997: 496). This decision came to be known as the "October Restoration" (siwŏlyusin). O Wŏnch'ŏl, who worked closely with Park, speculates on why Park took such a drastic action. He said,

> President Park must have thought that 'Since my term ends in July 1976 the time remaining is only three years. In this situation I cannot launch a heavy and chemical development plan. Without heavy and chemical industry it is impossible to accomplish the goal of 100 billion dollar exports and 1,000 dollar per capita income. Therefore, I have to stay in power until construction of heavy and chemical industry is completed. I have therefore no choice but to revise the constitution so that I can remain in power'.
>
> (O Wŏnch'ŏl 1999[7]: 500)

O Wŏnch'ŏl's speculation also seems to indicate that Park's decision was inevitable under the circumstance. He himself expressed worry about Park stepping down in 1976, without completing the heavy and chemical industry project (1999: 500). It would be difficult to believe that Park's loyal subordinates involved in

144 *Industrialization*

the development project and those business leaders who benefited from government subsidies and protection, would have objected Park's decision to amend the constitution.

As O Wŏnch'ŏl puts it, the so-called the developmental state operated as an efficient military unit under Park's leadership (1999[7]: 500). He personally appealed to able bureaucrats, technocrats and corporate leaders to join him in carrying out the development project in the name of the nation. Park commanded unquestioned loyalty and devotion from his administrative staff in charge of development plans and corporate leaders. They had almost unconditional trust in him, believing he was a leader who would steer the nation toward a prosperous future and consider it a privilege and honour to be in his personal favour and work for him at a close distance.

Personalism indeed played a crucial role in the rise of modern industry. There was, in the words of Dore, "a sense of group solidarity breeding the kind of loyalty that makes members willing to make some immediate personal sacrifices in the interest of the ultimate common good" (1971: 58).

vii) Personalist Corporate Leaders – The Park Chung Hee style leadership was replicated at the corporate level, and the two corporate chairs mentioned earlier, Chŏng Chuyŏng and Pak Taejun, are typical examples. In 1965 Park Chung Hee personally assigned Pak Taejun, a junior officer in his military munition basis command in Pusan, and the secretary in the post- coup Supreme Council for National Reconstruction, the task of building the first ever large-scale steel company in Korea.

At the time, many critiques in and out of Korea opposed to undertaking of such a large-scale costly project on the ground that Korea did not have enough fund and appropriate technology to carry it out and the chance of making it into a profitable business in the international market was very slim.

But two Parks agreed that the only way for Korea to break into the development path and catching up with advanced industrial countries was to enter into heavy (or steel) industry. The International Bank of Reconstruction and Development's refusal based on the advices of the Korea International Steel Associates[33] to finance the project did not deter Park Taejun's determination He persuaded both Japanese and Korean government to use the compensation money which Japan paid Korea after signing the normalization treaty for the project and open the headquarter (small warehouse) of the Pohang Steel Company (POSCO) in the construction site.

He also arranged with two Japanese steel companies for technical assistance, dispatched some 600 workers to Japan, Australia and West Germany for technical training, and negotiated with two Australian companies for guaranteed supply of ingredients.

In his first speech (which became famous) delivered to an assembly of company workers he said that "we are building a steel company with ancestors" "blood tax" (money paid by the Japanese government in compensation for the occupation of Korea for 35 years) and therefore it would be a grave offence to "our ancestors if we failed; if we failed we should all turn to the right and throw ourselves in

Industrialization 145

to the Yŏngil Bay sea to die." He lived with the workers at the construction site throughout the entire construction period (three years). When the construction work was delayed for three months for some unavoidable reasons, the Japanese field manager recommended that the project deadline be extended. Pak Taejun refused to go along with it. He declared a "construction emergency" and reorganized workers into several groups so that they could work 24 hours a day by taking turns. According to one of his biographers, he slept only about three hours a day during that period, often in his office without removing his boots. He acted like a military platoon commander. With a command baton in his hand, he closely monitored the work process. Solidarity was built between the boss and workers and the construction work was completed two months ahead of the deadline (Yi Taegwan 2004: 338). Even subcontractors were

> so moved by Pak Taejun's conviction, workers' genuine sense of mission, and the spirit of responsibility and capacity for united action that they began to participate in the project not just for making money but doing something for the country.
>
> (Yi Wansang 1993 in Yi Taegwan 2004: 339)

Chung Chuyoung was a self-made businessman who began as a small enterprise owner and eventually made himself the chair of the second largest conglomerate in Korea. In 1967, Chung was personally requested by President Park Chung Hee to participate in the Soul-Pusan highway construction project which was one of his election promises. Like the POSCO project, it also met with strong oppositions.

But the two leaders were determined to go ahead with it. The government budget allocated for the project on the basis of his estimate of the construction cost was rather low. As Chung Chuyoung said himself in his autobiography, "It is a kind of risky venture to construct the 428 km long highway with the budget of 43 billion won in three years" (1991: 109). "The entrepreneur's job," he said, "is to generate profits, thereby creating incomes and jobs for the people, not to become a philanthropist who pour money into the state or society. . . . Under any circumstances the entrepreneur has to make profits" (1991: 109). He concluded that the only way to make profit from a low budget project is to shorten the construction period without breaking the law or doing a sloppy job. When the highway work started, he was at the work site almost every day, making himself visible to the workers and sometimes doing the work himself, mixing cements and breaking rocks with an excavator. He often slept in a small jeep parked in the work field. He later reminisced,

> I once sat with President Park in his office, briefing about the work progress. Without knowing it, I dozed off momentarily. It was the time when I did not change my socks for six days. I spent many days and nights at the work site and slept without removing the work boots. My toes, like everyone else's there, were all swollen up. When I woke up President Park said, "I am sorry, Chairman Chung, I should have let you sleep a little more, you must be very

146 *Industrialization*

tired." Since then I used that experience as a guide for dealing with my workers. While making rounds for checking work progress I sometimes came across workers falling asleep at work because of fatigue. I then look the other way and went to other places and return later to wake him. He became panicy when he realized that it was the work site tiger who woke him up. I then simply say, "I am sorry." Frightened though he was I knew he was moved by my act as I was before.

(Pak Chong'ung 2015: 13)

Doing the work fast or finishing, the contract work prior to the deadline had another meaning than simply making profits. In his reminiscence of the history of building the shipbuilding company, he said,

We are well behind in technology and experience (industrial development). So if we spent the same amount of time (one year) to finish something as which workers in the advanced country did there is no way to catch up with them. We need the will and effort to finish it faster, say, in ten or eight months. If we finish our contract project before the deadline we would generate more profits, improve our capacity and will receive more orders since our shipbuilding company will gain the reputation of making good ships fast at low costs. If we think that everything is possible (*mansanŭn toendago saengkakhamyŏn*) we will be able to see the way which we did not see before but if we think otherwise we won't even be able to see the way that already exists.

(Pak Chong'ung 2015: 33)

He was not afraid of undertaking a new project which appeared to others as something impossible to complete. When some members of his work team expressed doubts about the feasibility of some project, his usual reply was, "Hey you, have you ever tried (Iboa, hae boatsŏ)?" He succeeded not only in introducing the shipbuilding and automobile manufacturing industries into Korea but also in making them profitable businesses. He fondly reminisced in his autobiography how some people tried to persuade him to change his mind when he was contemplating about entering into these hitherto un-trodden areas. One cabinet member said "if he succeeds with his venture with the ship building enterprise, I will make soybean sauce with my fingers" (*son'ŭro jang'ul chijigetta*) (a Korean folk expression, meaning an usual act one promises to do when he is sure of winning a bet). The American Ambassador Brown paid personal visit to his office to tell Chung that starting a car manufacturing business has no future at the time. The better thing for him to do is to concentrate on producing parts for the existing major automobile companies.

Pak Taejun and Chung Chuyoung are only two representative cases of successful entrepreneurs. There are many others like them. Many Korean entrepreneurs at the beginning stage of industrial development were dare devil adventurers, not afraid of entering into the area that no one has gone into before.

Industrialization 147

Park stayed in power for 18 years and his military government undertook three consecutive five-year economic development plans, which transformed South Korea into an industrial nation. Park died in 1979 and Chun Doo Hwan succeeded him through yet another coup and prolonged the authoritarian era another seven years. His coup comrade, Roh Tae Woo, brought an end to military government rule and became the president through popular election in 1988. Return to democracy was completed with the election of Kim Young Sam. The South Korea economy continued to grow until 1997 when Korea was hit by the liquidity crisis. The value of exports reached the US$100 billion target in 1995, and six years later reached US$150 billion. GDP accordingly grew fast – 9 percent per annum between 1960 and 1990. This growth increased real per capita GDP fivefold after 1970 and ten-fold since 1953. Measured in terms of GDP, the South Korean economy is ranked fourteenth in the world. The output growth, combined with declining rates of population growth, raised incomes so that the average annual income reached US$10,000 in 1995 and $20,000 in 2011 from US$60 in 1960. The percentage of the labour force engaged in agriculture decreased from 63 percent in 1953 to 11.6 percent in 2000. The World Bank and the IMF recognized Korea as "developed" or "high income," and in 2009, the Financial Times Stock Exchange granted "developed status" to South Korea. In 1996, Korea joined the club of rich countries in the OECD and is now competing against other capitalist countries in the global market.

Personalism and Korea's economic miracle

As was the case with kŭndaehwa of educational system, industrialization has had depersonalizing effects. The impersonal market, both international as well as domestic, has been fully utilized, and whole economic development processes have been rationally planned. Government officials involved in undertaking the development plans have been kept in the government for a long time, promoted and decorated on the basis of their achievement. Participating corporate firms are all large, formal, bureaucratically structured organizations run by professional managers. Over 80 percent of standard workers of giant firms or chaebŏl are unionized. The union-management relationship is largely characterized as contractual.

The depersonalizing tendency did not, however, result in the development of impersonal capitalist economy. In order to understand this point, one needs to look at the corporate structure of the chaebŏl firm, the major partner to the state in the national development project and the representative agent at the forefront of capitalist economy. It remains to be a largely person-oriented formal organization.

Chaebŏl groups are largely family controlled. Owners manage their entire business group through the office of secretaries or more widely known as the Office of Planning located at the principal firm and staffed with professional managers hired (usually hand-picked by the owners) for their expertise. Owner-managers tend to view the firm "our business." Family members with varying degrees of managerial capacity are involved in running the business together with hired

148   *Industrialization*

professional managers To keep the group enterprise as a family business, those offspring of the owner-managers appear to have potentiality for and willingness to become top managers are sent graduate business schools (if possible, overseas) for MBAs and the owner will select one – usually a son –and groomed for group directorship. This practice will continue as a family tradition of the owner family, and the separation of ownership and management is not likely to occur in the near future.

Although the corporate employment system is widely characterized by many scholars as one of life-time employment (e.g., An Ch'unsik 1982; Hong Yongbok 1979) not everybody hired at the entry level stays with the same employer until he/she retires. Inter-firm mobility rate is not negligible. But there is a general consensus or convention that the employer does not fire his employees before they reach retirement ages (Hong Yongbok 1979). The labour law prohibits the corporate employer firing his employers without reason. In other words, employees are not continuously in the job market looking for better job opportunities. Staying on the first job until retirement is a norm held by both employees and employers. And the enterprise offers a variety of incentives to get their employees to stay with it until their retirement and rewards employees for continuous service.

Each employee gets promoted automatically on the work grade scale. In other words, promotion is more person related than job related. But promotion to higher administrative positions from ordinary staff to bureau chief is not automatic since the number of those positions gets smaller as the rank goes up. Job performance and loyalty to the company play an important role in the selection process. The seniority dimension is still not completely ignored. It is customary for the enterprise not to promote someone ahead of a person who joined the company before he did.

Wages and salaries are based on seniority, or the length of continued service, not the rate for the job. Employees' pay goes up automatically each year on an incremental scale of some 30 grades without review. The incremental pay scale and the rate of increase, however, vary according to age, sex, marital status and type of work.

In addition to the basic wages or salaries (kibon'gŭp), there are various allowances: family allowance, living expense allowance, commodity price allowance, overtime allowance, continuous service allowance, encouragement (*changryŏ*) allowance and so on. Basic wages plus allowances are generally considered employee remuneration. One source identified some 60 different allowances being offered by corporate enterprise. Allowances account for 25.7 percent of the regular pay in 1982 (An Ch'unsik 1982: 244).

Employees are also paid bonuses, usually twice a year: the August Full Moon and the New Year.[34]

Corporate employers pay retirement gratuity to supplement what was considered to be a low salary and wage, and as insurance for post-retirement living for continuously serving members. The Basic Labour Law made it a duty of large business group employing more than 500 workers to pay retirement gratuities to

Industrialization 149

employees. Article 28 of the Basic Labour Law says, "The employer should pay the employee 30 days per year wages times the number of years continuously served." Bur many companies use the progressive, not the fixed legal, rate in calculating the amount of retirement gratuities, hence paying more than the legal entitlement.

They extend their care to the living conditions of employees beyond the workplace and retirement by creating numerous welfare provisions. Some of them, however, are made obligatory by the law.

There are also numerous workers' insurance programs for workers which were more or less forced on large business enterprises by the government as it made it mandatory that enterprises assume payment for them when it introduced them. They include industrial injury insurance, medical insurance, unemployment insurance, the national pension and others. Regardless of how those welfare provisions came about, big business firms see the positive effects of motivating their workers to work harder and to love the company, and, consequently, stay longer.

Besides the welfare provisions, there are other provisions for housing, meals, commuter transportation, scholarship of the children of employees, recreational activities, sports activities and others. In the past, employers themselves provided a variety of welfare provisions which they thought their employees would need. The new trend is to let employees choose what programs they need in accordance with their personal needs, preferences and tastes.

Members of a firm form numerous informal personal cliques, factions and clubs on the basis of school, regional or other ties within the organization may be identified. While promoting the solidarity of the group as a whole, members also help one another on whatever personal problems they encounter within and without the formal organization. Social networking goes beyond the organizational boundary of the firms.

Aside from the aforementioned personalistic dimensions of the formal structure of organization, one should also take notice of informal social networking building with those who would prove to be useful to their business. Much of scholarly analysis of the growth of chaebŏls failed to discuss how important informal networking is for chaebŏl to grow or stay alive.

Most business firm deliberately make efforts to create informal (personal) connections with high-ranking government officers – retired and currently practising – and other chaebŏl families through intermarriage of the children of group chair.

Chaebŏl groups are also eager to hire retiring high officials. Between 2004 and 2007, Samsung Group hired 41 retiring senior public officials, while Hyundai Group, Uri Kumyung Group and Tusan Group hired 29, 25, and 15, respectively (*SisaInLive Mobile* 2013–03–19). Since these chaebŏl groups are engaged in multiple lines of business, they hire a wide range of retiring high officials, including cabinet ministers, judges, prosecutors, taxation and finance officials, banking and trade officers, high-ranking police officers and military generals.

Those business firms doing a single line of business usually approach those offices directly related to their business. Firms supplying or manufacturing goods

150 *Industrialization*

to military companies customarily hire retired military generals, especially those who worked at the Defense Acquisition Program Administration. Law firms go after Supreme Court justices, judge and prosecutors. But if a law firm grows large and deals with court cases involving conglomerates, it also seeks to hire influential retirees from other public offices such as retirees from the Blue House, National Tax Service, Financial Supervisory Service and Fair Trade Commission.

They hire retired high-ranking officials for two reasons. Those who are hired by big corporate firms could provide useful advice on how to do business with the offices where they worked previously. Their employers usually argue that the main reason for hiring them is to make use of the expert knowledge they accumulated as public officials for management of non-governmental organizations.

But as critics of this practice point out, high-ranking officials may use their knowledge accumulated and personal ties with former colleagues, mostly their subordinates to promote the interests of their new employers. Former high officials have the privileges of making use of the *chŏngwanye'u* practice – the practice of government officers treating former – recently retired – superior officers with reverence, which means, in practical terms, that the former cannot easily ignore the latter's personal (private) request to personalize his or her public role or bent whatever the rule that he or she is supposed to abide by as a public officer. The chŏnkwanye'u practice makes retired high-ranking government officials good lobbyists for corporate employers. As one critic wryly commented, "A former public official who was an expert on tax collection becomes an expert on tax evasion" (*Ohmynews* 2007–01–01). There is also an additional advantage of hiring retired high-ranking public officials: their previous high social standing enhances the reputation and image of the firm. (For more on Chon'gwanye'u , see pp. 224–6.)

For their service, former high officials usually get paid huge salaries by their new corporate employers. They make in a month what they previously earned in a year. A retired chief Supreme Court justice, for instance, almost doubled his personal wealth in two years as a corporate lawyer.[35] It should be apparent now that offering jobs to retiring government officials is a way that public and private companies network or establish informal ties with the government. High ranking government officials also try to maintain friendly relations with chaebol firms in the hope of receiving job offers from them when they retire.

But their network making is not limited to retirees or former titleholders only. They actually try to penetrate into the government organizations by establishing informal ties with government officials currently occupying high posts who could help promote or protect their business directly. Creating personal ties with targeted public officials requires a more subtle and arduous approach. One corporate group executive explained to Ham Yŏngjun anonymously how it is done:

> Public officials (senior) in general need to spend a lot of money to promote their careers and to maintain dignities that befit their posts but their monthly salaries are not sufficient to cover the necessary expenses, and are always short of pocket money. But elite bureaucrats would not extend their hands to request (for monetary help) nor easily get involved in corruption. They

may, however, accept ritualistic ch'onji (token expression of goodwill in the form of cash) from you once you get to know them and if the amount of cash gift is not too large to make them feel burdened. The gift is a way of saying, "I would like to get to know you" or "I have a good feeling toward you."

(Ham Yŏng'jun 1990: 159)

As such, cash is usually offered or made to look as a "gift with no string attached," or a gift not accompanied by a request for a favor. Such a gift is an offer that cannot be easily refused or not accepting it might even make the public official appear inhuman.

This initial cash offering is followed by more regular gift–giving. It is usually made on holidays – New Years' Eves, the August Full Moon Days – or on special occasions – weddings, births or deaths in public officials' families. The amount of money in the regular envelope varies according to the position, rank, and personal disposition of the official, but it is roughly between 500,000 and 2 million won (in the late 1980s) (Ham Yŏngjun 1990: 160). Besides gift-giving, they are often treated to fancy dinners, games of golf and other forms of entertainment.

Once such an informal "human relationship" is established through the combination of close feelings and money, it is not very difficult to ask for small formal (official) favours. If the gift-giver anticipates an occasion in the future to ask for a really big favour, or decides to make a real ally out of "our man," he increases the amount of the gift by several times. At this stage, the gift, even if it is unusually large, is not likely to be declined. One senior staff of the H group told Ham Yŏngjun,

> In my experiences of gift-giving, such offers of a large amount of money was never refused. If he (the public official) is a sensible man he already knows what he is expected of when he receives the money. As you know, do businessmen spend money for nothing?
>
> (Ham Yŏngjun 1990: 160)

Eventually, what began as a friendly relationship with a public official evolves into a close tie or union. They feel obligated to help the firm and function as "lobbyists" or "troubleshooters" (haegyŏlsa). Therefore, it is common knowledge among businessmen and bureaucrats that a certain corporate enterprise has a certain lawmaker, a cabinet minister, and a superintendent public prosecutor as its 'man' (Ham Yŏngjun 1990: 160).

The "making 'our man'" effort is supplemented with widening the network to include many selected "VIPs." VIPs not only include high-ranking, top-level government officials, but also well-known media personalities, academics and even those public figures who are considered to have the potential to become influential figures in the future. (Ham Yŏngjun 1990: 160). The goal is to form informal alliances with men of power and influence and to cultivate favourable public images in their eyes (Ham Yŏngjun 1990: 159). The method of creating friendly relations with VIPs is different from that of making "our men."

152 *Industrialization*

One executive member of the L group told Ham Yŏngjun that any large corporate firm usually sends an envelope of money or a wreath to a man of high social position on happy or sad occasions, even if he is not closely related to the firm (1990: 159). Sending a gift to a well-known person on such occasions is a common practice in Korea. Gift is a way of recognizing the eminence of the receiver and beginning an informal relationship with him. Similar practice also takes place when a public figure, like a well-known lawmaker an eminent media person holds a party in celebration of the publication of his book. A high public official will receive cash gifts when he goes on an overseas trip. Sometimes, gifts are almost forced upon public officials.

Pharmaceutical companies usually invite lawmakers and their aides to attend conferences on new products with all expenses paid. Some staff members of the Korean Stock Trade Center drop by lawmakers' offices and leave portable cell phone chargers as gifts on their desks (*dongA.com* 2008–12–22). "One of the most difficult things to refuse," says one lawmaker "is contribution money (kibugŭm)." An aide to another lawmaker said, "When he refused to meet for dinner in spite of repeated requests, one businessman established a credit at a nearby restaurant for him to use whenever he dines there" (*dongA.com* 2009–12–22). Gift-giving is not always a one-way transaction. Request for donations often comes from members of the elite group.

Unlike big corporate firms, small business firms usually try to cultivate friendly relations with only those public offices they are directly related to their business.

Small business owners – especially those businesses which are under regular official surveillance and are likely to be engaged in shady business, such as drinking places, massage parlor and gambling places – regularly offer small tokens of goodwill (ch'onji), "rice-cake money" (ttŏkkap – money to buy small things) or entertainment (hyang'ŭng – treating to sumptuous meals at fancy restaurants) to that have the power and authority to affect and help their businesses. For example, members of their district's police station, fire station, taxation office, local office of prosecution and the like. These gifts are given on a regular basis – usually once a month, or on special occasions such as their going on official oversea trips.

In network building with government officials and other elites chaebol firms utilize whatever personal ties their employees have beyond their organizations. They normally keep the personal background files of employees, which include what personal ties they have with high government officials, and make use of employees' networks if necessary. They also keep close contacts with former employees who have been appointed to high-level government posts. Furthermore, it is customary these days for large firms to ask job applicants about any personal connections they might have with influential or eminent people. Those who do are likely to have a considerable advantage in getting hired over others who do not. "Good personal connections" has become an important job requirement.

In this regard, we should also take note of the practice of regionalistic recruitment, namely, the tendency to hire natives of the region that the incumbent president is from. We have previously shown that each president usually filled a large number of government positions with persons from his home province.

Industrialization 153

When Yŏngnam native presidents (Park Chung Hee, Chun Doo Hwan, Roh Tae Woo and Kim Young Sam) successively ruled the nation, the majority of government officials – central as well as local – were natives of Yŏngnam (*ch'ulsin*). Corporate firms accordingly hired people from that region proportionally more than people from other provinces. When Kim Dae Jung became the president, he recruited Chŏlla natives into the government. Private business firms – including some which were known for their anti-Honam attitudes in recruiting new members – eagerly hired Honam natives.

Chaebŏls also establish close inform ties with other elites, including media persons, academicians, men of letters, and others.

Corporate gift-giving is a costly business. It is common knowledge that chaebŏl firms are creating huge secret funds (pijakum) or dark money (kŏmŭndon), to cover the expenses incurred in the gift-giving process. According to Kim Yongch'ŏl's estimate, Samsung's secret fund established within the country (not counting the overseas funds) would be over 10 trillion won (Kim Yongch'ŏl 2010: 37). Estimates of secret funds of other large firms made public by the Public Prosecutors Office vary from several billion won to several hundred billion won – e.g. 900 billion won for Hanbo Steel, 100 billion won for Hyundai Group, 200–400 billion won for Tusan Group, and 107.7 billion won for Korean Explosives.[36]

If *chaebŏl* groups keep a huge secret fund (pijakŭm) in cash ready all the time to create a goodwill towards the government and other influential people, they are also under pressure to make such donations. They constantly receive requests for donations by individual VIPs and/or government offices. But in some cases, gift-takers resort to informal corporate gifts for office purposes. Most notably, corporate gifts, as will be discussed later, constitute a main source of so-called political fund (chŏngch'i jakŭm) for the president to run his office and finance election campaign costs for his political party's candidates.

Chaebŏls also establish personal ties with other chaebŏls through intermarriage. Children of chaebŏls marry each other. An arranged marriage between two families in need of each other – for whatever reason – is an age-old practice used for forging new ties in the upper stratum of the society. Although young people these days tend to marry someone they love, arranged marriage continues to be prevalent among members of elite groups; elite groups get linked with each other through their children's marriage. For example, the sixth son of Chung Chuyoung, the chair of the Hyundai Group, is married to the daughter of Kim Tong-jo, the former minister of foreign affairs; the third son of Koo In-hoe, the chair of LG group, is married to the second daughter of Yi Byongchŏl, the late chair of the Samsung Group; the daughter of the former president Roh Tae Woo is married to the first son of Choe Chonghyŏn, the chair of the SK Group; and so on. Since this practice is so widespread, such marriages are increasingly mediated by a professional broker, known as Madame T'u (O Kyŏng-hwan 1995: 185–194). Two families become in-laws with the clearly calculated expectation that each side could count on help from the other side when the help is necessary. Families with power and influence are naturally drawn to one another and establish a close tie through marriage.

154   *Industrialization*

But such marriages often end up in divorce these days. Some children refuse to maintain a marriage without love for the sake of their parents or families. Thus, children of elite families are finding a way out of the dilemma posed by arranged marriage. They form exclusive clubs where the solidarity of the elite class is reproduced, and they meet and choose someone they like and may possibly marry later. Some private bankers managing the financial assets of wealthy people arrange meetings of their clients' children as a part of client service or run a social club, members of which are largely drawn from children of wealthy parents (Kim Sŭng-yong 2008: 102).

Notes

1 Such developmental effects of military assistance are not confined to the 1953–1960 period since the US government continued to provide it, even after economic aid was terminated (Mason et al. 1980: 183–184).
2 Mason et al. further point out, "Agriculture, education, health, and other social services," received relatively minor allocations, generally amounting in each case to less than 5 percent of the total project assistance" (Mason et al. 1980: 193).
3 These agencies included Quakers, the Roman Catholic Church, Salvation Army, Northern Presbyterian Mission, YMCA, the National Catholic Welfare Conference, Methodist Mission, Maryknoll Sisters of American origin, Australian Presbyterian Mission, British Red Cross Society and United Church of Canada Mission.
4 Information used in this section is largely drawn from Yi Taegŭn (2002).
5 Tariff rates rose in accordance with the degree of competitiveness of the imports with domestic production (but with very heavy rates levied on luxury goods) and were low on necessary imports of raw materials and capital goods.
6 Rapid progress was made in production of such commodities as sugar, cement, and cotton textiles, achieving the goal of self-sufficiency or completing import substitution before the end of the 1950s.
7 Growth as the priorities of Park's regime replaced those of the previous regime, namely, democracy and reunification. Park did not dismiss democracy as a major concern. He frequently mentioned democracy as an important goal in his public speeches and candidly admitted that without economic development democracy is an abstract goal that cannot be achieved. He also emphasized the fact that Korea is a democratic country but that the democracy that existed was a Korean-style one. Reunification, the rising concern among student activists who brought down the Rhee regime, quickly gave way to anti-communism. Building a nation that strongly opposed communism was another "revolutionary" promise, one he kept judiciously. Also of note was the absence of the mention of welfare as a goal to be achieved by his planned economic development. The word welfare does not appear until the third economic development plan (1972–1976). Like democracy, Park reasoned that the government cannot pay much attention to welfare until the economy grew to the level of an advanced industrial country. The slogan adopted by the government was "growth first, distribution later."
8 Kuznets then summarizes what these plans entailed: "They reveal the priorities attached to different goals, how problems are perceived, and, to a lesser extent, the means chosen to cope with them. Annual GNP levels and growth rates are included as are private and public consumption targets. The saving (domestic and foreign) and investment (government and private) needed to meet these goals are also specified. Export, import, and balance-of-payments targets are provided. Population projections are given and the increase in per capita income and consumption is derived. Changes

Industrialization 155

in economic structure can be seen in the estimates of income originating in each sector and in the sectoral distribution of employment and investment" (1977: 196).

9 It became the Ulsan Industrial Park, which was mainly petrochemical companies. The idea of creating an industrial park came from Van Fleet, the former commander of the Eighth Army who, as a private businessman, went to the United States in search of loans after promulgation of the first five-year plan. This industrial complex served as a model for future promotion of specific industry and many such complexes were to be built throughout the country.

10 The minister told Park, "Export is the only way to survive. Export-first-ism must be adopted as the supreme policy of the state and the entire nation should strive toward it. And I beg your Excellency to lead the nation as the supreme commander, giving encouragement and solving difficult problems for us" (O Wŏnch'ŏl 1995[I]: 229).

11 In fact, when Yi Hurak, the representative of the South, returned from the meeting in Pyongyang, he told Park Chung Hee that the north was preparing for a war.

12 Chemical industries increased by 443 percent, textile industry by 436 percent, wood and wooden products by 362 percent, cement and non-metal mineral products by 361 percent, machine by 300 percent, metal by 297 percent, food by 250 percent and paper products by 240 percent (O Wŏnch'ŏl [3] 1996: 186).

13 They included subsidized short- and long-term credits for purchase of inputs and financing of fixed investments; unrestricted access to imported inputs; tariff exemption; tariff exemptions on imported raw materials and intermediate and capital goods for export production; the reduction of direct taxes on profits earned through export activities; wastage allowances on imported duty-free raw materials over and above the requirements of actual export production; exemptions from indirect taxes for intermediate inputs and export sales, direct tax preferences, relaxed tax surveillance; creation of an accelerated depreciation allowance for fixed capital used directly in export production.

14 More often than not, the same product sold in the domestic market was of poorer quality than that sold in the foreign market.

15 These included quarterly export targets for individual firms by commodity market; daily contact with major exporters; monitoring potential shortfalls; interceding in the event of possible difficulties in meeting targets; reviewing monthly the current export performance with export associations; establishing academic and business representatives in the presence of the president to identify problems and, where possible, resolve them on the spot; honoring the most successful exporters with the national medal of honor or public presidential commendations; installation of Export Day (November 30) (see, among others, Westphal 1978; Kuznets 1977; Rhee, Ross-Larson and Pursell 1984; Ryu Sin-kei 1983).

16 Westphal, Kim and Dahlman write, "Among today's leading textile exporters are several that were established before independence, and some senior managers and technicians who gained their initial experience during the colonial period were still active in the 1970s . . . the first plant (plywood) was constructed in 1975" (1985: 94).

17 Korean engineers had the skill to cut those parts accurately and they were able to produce first, carbines, grenades, anti-tank rocket guns, landmines and trench mortars, and later 90mm and 106 anti-reaction gun (mubandongch'ong) and 105 mm howitzers. (O Wŏnch'ŏl [7] 1999: 385–422).

18 There was no DFI between 1945 and 1960, when the first legislation controlling non-grant inflows of foreign capital was promulgated. The first instance of DFI in the period after World War II was in 1962. By the end of 1981, the government had approved 693 instance (or cases) of DFI in manufacturing. The cumulative gross inflow amounted to roughly US$1.25 billion. This figure may be compared with cumulative total investment in manufacturing over the same period, US$22.7 billion, to show the relative magnitude of DFI.

156   *Industrialization*

19 Information on technology transfer is generally limited. But even more limited is information on transfer of social technology.

20 Four laws – the Foreign Capital Inducement Law, the Foreign Exchange Control Law, the Law Concerning Establishment of Free Export Districts and the Science and Technology Promotion Law – were enacted in the late 1960s to govern the import of foreign technology into Korea. Only after 1979 were such regulations relaxed.

21 This law set forth that vocational school students must spend two to six months of their first two years training at an industrial site for on-the-job training and at least four months of their third year on the shop floor.

22 In January 1965, President Park made restructuring the educational system one of the major points in his State of the Nation address. It was Park's most emphatic call to transform education so that it would be directed toward economic development. "The current excessive liberal arts and science education . . . will gradually transform into advanced technology and vocational education.

(Seth 2002: 122).

But his goals was not achieved as academic high school education also expanded in parallel to vocational high school education. The percentage of vocational schools and students against that of academic counterparts, in fact, decreased somewhat. In short, the school system produced more students with vocational education but it did not become more directed to economic development. There were many obstacles to the government's push for vocational education, as Seth points out, "Many experts began to have doubts about the effectiveness of vocational education, finding it hard to match in-school training with the rapidly shifting needs of industry. The biggest single problem facing vocational education, however, remained public resistance. It was reflected by employers, who showed a preference in hiring non-vocational graduates, feeling that technical skills could be picked up on the job"

(Seth 2002: 127–128).

23 Joseph Stern and others write, "At the beginning of the 1970s, despite the earlier effort to remedy the situation, the research level in Korea was still very modest. In 1971, for example, only 2,477 persons were classified as researchers in science and technology, and total R&D expenditures were 10.7 billion won (US $29 million) or 0.3 percent of the Korea's gross national product (GNP). By 1975, the number of researchers had quadrupled to 10,275, and R&D expenditures had risen to 42.7 billion won (US$88 million). R&D expenditures were still a miniscule share of GNP1970s and all of the 1980s" (Stern et al., 1995: 26).

24 It later became the Korean Advanced Institute of Science.

25 While seeking foreign loans the government also decided to guarantee the reimbursement of all foreign loans, whether they were initiated by public companies or by private companies. This made it easier for entrepreneurs to borrow money from foreign countries and they actively sought foreign loans.

Additionally, in the absence of necessary technology and necessary capital the government also encouraged and helped Korean firms to find foreign firms to jointly invest and operate and provide necessary technologies and also find foreign loans when the concerned firms did not have enough funds to build a plant, the government formed two commissions – one for the United States and the other for Europe – to borrow loans or lure foreign capital investment to Korea.

26 "In the period 1972–76, for example, Japanese investment was more than four times the American total (US396 million to US$88 million)" (Cumings 1984: 35).

27 "The Vietnam War played for the ROK the role that the Korea War played for Japan. It accounted for as much as 20 percent of foreign exchange earnings in the late 1960s" (Cumings 1984: 33, see also Cole and Lyman 1971: 135).

28 Electricity, gas, railroads, highways, irrigation and the Seoul and Pusan subway systems.

Industrialization 157

29 Public enterprise share of GDP increased from 6.7 percent in 1963–1964 to 9.1 in 1971–1972 (Jones and SaKong 1980).
30 Among these laws were the Assembly and Demonstration Law, the Law Concerning Special Measures for Safeguarding National Security, Emergency Decrees, the National Security Law and the Anti-Communism Law.
31 One should also mention that the United States as an ally in the cold war had vested interest in South Korea becoming economically stable and stronger than North Korea (Cumings 1998: 18).
32 Park Ch'unghun, the EPB minister, stayed in his job for five years while not so able ministers lasted less than a year. Kim Chŏngnyŏm, widely known as the most brilliant "econocrat" during the developmental era, began as a bureau chief in the MCI, served as its minister for five years and then as the special economic adviser to Park for eight years. Altogether, he helped Park for nine years (October 1969– December 1978) consecutively. O Wŏnch'ŏl, a former engineer, assisted Park and Kim throughout the entire period of development under Park performing various tasks as a technocrat.
33 The group formed in 1966 at the request of the Korean government to look into the feasibility of the project and recommend to the IBRD to make a loan for it. It consisted of seven major steel companies from four countries.
34 The current remuneration system is a carry-over of the colonial past. The colonial government maintained the policy of keeping wage level and increase rate low throughout the entire period. Payments other than basic pays were devices introduced by corporate enterprises as a way of supplementing the low basic pay. The system continues to exist partly because it has been a long established-convention and partly because current corporate employers share the idea that the welfare of its employees is their responsibility.
35 Given the possible negative side of this practice, the government enacted the Public Servant Ethics Law in 2001. This act prohibits high-ranking officials from seeking employment with business firms related to their offices for three years before and two years after retirement. But it is frequently violated and the Public Servant Ethics Committee has not been strict in screening retiring officials' applications for reemployment with private firms.
36 How secret funds are created and used does not enter into the official accounting book, hence it is not reported to the Office of Taxation as gift-giving, and is a clandestine operation conducted by a small number of the group chair's hand-picked confidantes.

References

Akyuz,Yilmaz, Ha-Joon Chang and Richard Kozul-Wright (1998) "New Perspectives on East Asian Development." *Journal of Development*, vol. 34 no. 6, (November), pp. 4–36.
Amsden, Alice H. (1989) *Asia's Next Giant: South Korea and Late Industrialization*, Oxford: Oxford University Press.
An, Ch'unsik (1982) *Chūsingōyōsei no nikkan hikaku* (Comparison of Life-Time Employment in Japan and Korea), Tokyo: Ronsōsha.
Bae, Kyuhan (1987) *Automobile Workers in Korea*, Seoul: Seoul National University Press.
Ban, Sung Hwan, Moon, Moon and Dwight H. Perkins (1980) *Rural Development*, Cambridge: Council on East Asian Studies, Harvard University.
Brazinsky, Gregg (2007) *Nation Building in South Korea*, Chapel Hill: The University of North Carolina Press.
Chang, Dal-joong (1985) *Economic Control and Political Authoritarianism: The Role of Japanese Corporations in Korean Politics 1965–1979*, Seoul: Sogang University Press.
Cho, Chunghun (1996) *Naega kŏrŏon'gil* (The Path I Have Trodden), Seoul: Nanam.

158 Industrialization

Choi, Jang Jip (1989) *Labor and the Authoritarian State: Labor Unions in South Korean Manufacturing Industries, 1961–1980*, Seoul: Korea University Press.

Choi, Kwang and Young Sae Lee, 1990, "The Role of the Korean Government in Industrialization," pp. 53–69, in Lee, Chung H. and Ippei Yamazawa, (eds.) *The Economic Development of Japan and Korea*, New York: Praeger.

Chŏng, Chaegyŏng (1991) *Park Chung Hee sasang sŏsŏl: Hwihorŭl chungsimŭro* (The Introduction to Park Chung Hee Thoughts – Based on His Brush Writings), Seoul: Chipmundang.

Chŏng, Chuyŏng (1988) *Siryŏn'ŭn issŏdo silp'aenŭn ŏpta* (There May Be an Ordeal but There Is No Failure), Seoul: Chesamkihoek.

Chosŏn, Ŭnhaeng, 1948, *Chosŏn kyŏngje yŏnbo 1948* (The Yearbook of Korean Economy 1948), Seoul: Chosŏn Ŭnhaeng.

Clifford, Mark L. (1998) *Troubled Tiger: Businessmen, Bureaucrats, and Generals in South Korea*, Armonk: M.E. Sharpe.

Cole, David C. (1980) "Foreign Assistance and Korean Development," pp. 1–29, in Cole, David C., Lim, Youngil and Kuznets, Paul W (eds.) *The Korean Economy – Issues of Development*, Berkeley: Institute of East Asian Studies. University of California, Berkeley.

Cole, David C. and Princeton N. Lyman (1971) *Korean Development*, Cambridge, MA: Harvard University Press.

Cole, David C. and Young Woo Nam (1969) "The Pattern and Significance of Economic Planning," pp. 11–37, in Adelman, Irma (ed.) *Practical Approaches to Development Planning: Korea's Second Five-Year Plan*, Baltimore: The Johns Hopkins Press.

Cumings, Bruce (1985) *Korea's Place in the Sun: A Modern History*, New York: W.W. Norton.

Deyo, Frederic (1987) *The Political Economy of the New Asian Industrialism*, Ithaca: Cornell University Press.

Dore, Ronald P. (1971) "Modern Cooperatives in Traditional Communities," pp. 43–60, in Worsley, P. (ed.) *Two Blades of Grass: Rural Cooperatives in Agricultural Modernization*, Manchester: Manchester University Press.

Dornbush, Rudiger, Park, Yung Chul, Collins, Susan, and Corbo, Vittorio (1987) "Korean Growth Policy." *Brookings Papers on Economic Activity*, vol. 1, no. 2, pp. 389–454.

Enos, John Lawrence (1984) "Government Intervention in the Transfer of Technology: The Case of Korea." *IDS Bulletin*, vol. 15, no. 2, pp. 26–31.

Enos, John Lawrence and Woo-Hee Park (1988) *The Adoption and Diffusion of Imported Technology*, London: Croom Helm.

Ham, Yŏngjun (1990) "Kwŏllyŏkchŭng ŭi noemul kujo" (The Structure of Bribe of the Stratum of the Powerful). *Wolgan Chosun*, (May), pp. 156–181.

Hamilton, Clive (1986) *Capitalist Industrialization in Korea*, Boulder: Westview Press.

Han'guk kidokkyo hyŏpŭihoe (1987) *1970 nyŏndae minjuhwa undong 1* (Democratization Movement in the 1970s), Seoul: National Council on Churches of Korea.

Han'guk kidokkyo hyŏpŭihoe (1984) *Nodong hyŏnjang kwa chŭng'ŏn* (The Labour Situation and Testimonies), Seoul: National Council on Churches of Korea.

Han'guk kitokkyo sahoemunje, yŏn'guwŏn (1987) *Han'guk sahoe ŭi nodong tongje* (Labour Control in Korean Society), Seoul: Minjungsa.

Han'guk unhaeng chosabu (1957) *Kyongjeyŏn'gam 1957* (The Yearbook of Economy 1957), Seoul: Han'gukunhaeng.

Han'guk unhaeng chosabu (1960) *Kyongje tonggye yŏnbo 1960* (The 1960 Yearbook of Economic Statistics), Seoul: Han'guk unhaeng.

Industrialization 159

Hong, Wontack (1979) *Trade, Distortions, and Employment Growth in Korea*, Seoul: Korea Development Institute.

Hong, Yongbok (1979) "Chongsin koyongje ŭi yon'gu" (A Study of Life-Time Employment). *Chungso kiŏp yŏn'gu* (The Study of Medium- and Small-Size Enterprises), vol. 1, pp. 236–255.

Im, Chongch'ŏl (1975) "Haebanghu Han'guk'ui kongŏpbalchŏn" (Development of Manufacturing Industry in Post-Liberation). *Kyongche nonjip* (The Korean Economic Journal), vol. 3, no. 2 (June), pp. 1–21.

Johnson, Chalmers (1982) *MITI and the Japanese Miracle: The Growth of Industrial Policy 1925–1975*, Stanford: Stanford University Press.

Johnson, Harry G. (1967) *Economic Nationalism in Old and New States*, Chicago: University of Chicago Press.

Jones, Leroy P. (1975) *Public Enterprise and Economic Development: The Korean Case*, Seoul: Korea Development Institute.

Jones, Leroy P. and Il SaKong (1980) *Government, Business, and Entrepreneurship in Economic Development: The Korean Case*, Cambridge: Council on East Asian Studies, Harvard University.

Kim, Chongnyom (1990) *Han'guk kyongje chŏngch'aek 30 nyŏnsa* (A Thirty-Year History of Korea's Economic Policy), Seoul: Chung'ang ilbo, Chung'ang kyongche sinmun.

Kim, Kee Young (1984) "American Technology and Korea's Technological Development," pp. 75–96, in Moskowitz, Karl (ed.) *From Patron to Partner*, Lexington: Lexington Books.

Kim, Kwang Doo and Sang Ho Lee (1990) "The Role of the Korean Government in Technology Import," in Lee, Chung H. and Yamagiwa, Ippei (eds.) *Economic Development of Japan and Korea*, New York: Praeger.

Kim, Joon Kyung, Sang Dal Shim and Jun-il Kim (1995) "The Role of the Government in Promoting Industrialization and Human Capital Accumulation in Korea," pp. 181–200, in Ito, Takatoshi and Krueger, Anne O. (eds.) *Growth Theories in Light of the East Asian Experience*, Chicago: The University of Chicago Press.

Kim, Linsu (1988) "Building Technological Capability for Industrialization: Analytical Frameworks and Korean Experience." *Industrial and Corporate Change*, vol. 18, no. 1, pp. 111–136.

Kim, Linsu and Carl J. Dahlman (1992) "Technology Policy for Industrialization : An Integrative Framework and Korea's Experience." *Research Policy*, vol. 21, no. 5 (October), pp. 437–452.

Kim, Linsu and Youngbae Kim (1985) "Innovation in a Newly Industrializing Country: A Multiple Dicrimiation Analysis." *Management Science*, vol. 31, no. 3, pp. 312–322.

Kim, Sŭngyong (2008) *Inmaek kyŏnyŏng* (Personal Network Management), Seoul: Buk'oshon.

Kim, Taehwan (1981) "1950nyŏndae han'guk kyŏngje (Korean Economy in the 1950s)," pp. 157–255, in Chin, Tōkkyu and Others (eds.) *1950 Nyontae'ui insik* (Understanding the 1950s), Seoul: Han'gilsa.

Kim Yongch'ŏl (2010) Samsŏng ŭl saenggakhanda (Thinking about the Samsung), Seoul: Sahoe p'yŏngnon.

Kim, Yŏnghwa (2004) *Han'guk ŭui kyoyukkwa kyongche balchon: 1945–1995* (Education and Economic Development in Korea: 1945–1995), Seoul: Hanguk haksul chongbo.

Kuznets, Paul W. (1977) *Economic Growth and Structure in the Republic of Korea*, New Haven: Yale University Press.

Kwon, Taihwan (1977) *Demography of Korea*, Seoul: Seoul National University Press.

160   Industrialization

Lee, Kong Rae (2000) "Technical Learning," pp.170–292, in Kim, Linsu and Richard B. Nelson (eds.) *Technology, Learning, and Innovation*, Cambridge: Cambridge University Press.

Lyons, Gene M. (1961) *Military Policy and Economic Aid: The Korean Case, 19501953*, Columbus: Ohio State University Press.

Mason, Edward. S., Mahn Je Kim, Dwight H. Perkins, Kwang Suk Kim and David C. Cole (1980) *The Economic and Social Modernization of the Republic of Korea*, Cambridge: Council of East Asian Studies. Harvard University.

Nisbet, Robert A. (1953) *Community and Power*, New York: Oxford University Press.

O Kyŏnghwan (1995) *Pijagŭm, X pail* (Secret Fund, X File), Seoul: Moa.

O Wŏnch'ŏl (2006) *Park Chung Heenun ŏttŏkke kyŏngje kangguk Ŭl mandŬlŏtna?* (How Did Park Chung Hee Make Korea a Strong Nation?), Seoul: Dongsŏ munhwasa.

O Wŏnchŏl (1999) *Han'gukhyŏng kyŏngje kŏnsŏl: Nega chonjaengŭl hajanungŏtto aniji annŭnya [7]* (I Am Not Saying We Should Have a War), Seoul: Hanguk kyŏngje chŏngch'ek yŏn'guso.

O Wŏnch'ŏl (1996) *Han'gukhyŏng kyŏngje kŏnsŏl[2][3]* (Korean Style Economic Construction [2][3]), Seoul: Kia kyŏngje yŏn'guso.

O Wŏnch'ŏl (1995) *Han'gukhyŏng kyŏngjhe kŏnsŏl* [1], Seoul: Kia kyŏngje yŏn'guso.

Pack, Howard and Larry E. Westphal (1986) "Industrial Strategy and Technological Change: Theory and Policy." *Journal of Development Economics*, vol. 22, pp. 87–128.

Pak, Chŏng'ung (2015) *Ibwa, haebwatsŏ* (Hey You, Did You Try?), Seoul: Priikonomi.

Park, Chung Hee (1997) *Kukkawa hyŏngmyŏng kwa na* (The State, the Revolution and I), Seoul: Chikuch'on.

Park, Chung Hee (1962) *Uri minchok ui nagalkil* (The Path Our Nation Should Take), Seoul: Dong'a ch'ulp'ansa.

Reeve, W. D. (1963) *The Republic of Korea: A Political and Economic Study*, London: Oxford University Press.

Rhee, Yung Whee, Bruce Ross-Larson and Garry Pursell (1984) *Korea's Competitive Edge: Managing the Entry into World Markets*, Baltimore: Johns Hopkins University Press.

Rodrik, Dani, Gene Grossman and Victor Norman (1995) "Getting Intervention Right: How South Korea and Taiwan Grew Rich." *Economic Policy*, vol. 10, no. 2 (April), pp. 55–107.

Ryu, Sin-kei (1983) "Kanggoku ni okeru chūkakaku kōgyōka to seifuchito keizai no mondai" (The Development of Heavy and Chemical Industry and Problems of the State-Led Economy in Korea). *Ajia keizai*, vol. 24, no. 12, pp. 2–24.

Segye Ilbo 1996–05–04.

Seth, Michael J. (2002) *Education Fever: Society, Politics, and Pursuit of Schooling in South Korea*, Honolulu: University of Hawaii Press and Center for Korean Studies.

Song, Byng-Nak (1990) *The Rise of the Korean Economy*, Hong Kong: Oxford University Press.

Stern, Joseph, Ji-hong Kim, Dwight H. Perkins, and Jung-ho Yoo (1995) *Industrialization and the State: The Korean Heavy and Chemical Industry Drive*, Cambridge, MA: Harvard Institute for International Development, Harvard University.

Wade, Robert (1996) "Industrial Policy in East Asia: Does It Lead or Follow the Market?" pp. 231–266, in Gereffi, Gary and Wyman, Wyman (eds.) *Manufacturing Miracles: Paths of Industrialization in Latin America and East Asia*, Princeton: Princeton University Press.

Westphal, Larry E. (1978) "The Republic of Korea's Experience With Export-Led Industrial Development." *World Development*, vol. 6, no. 3, pp. 347–382.

Industrialization 161

Westphal, Larry E. (1990) "Industrial Policy in an Export Propelled Economy: Lessons From South Korea's Experience." *The Journal of Economic Perspectives*, vol. 4, no. 3 (Summer), pp. 41–59.

Westphal, Larry E., Linsu Kim and Carl Dahlman (1985) "Reflections on the Republic of Korea's Acquisition of Technological Capability," pp. 167–221, in Rosenberg, Nathan and Erischtak, Claudia (eds.) *Industrial Technology Transfer: Concepts, Measures and Comparisons*, New York: Praeger.

Westphal, Larry E., Yung W. Rhee, Linsu Kim and Alice H. Amsden (1984) "Republic of Korea." *World Development*, vol. 12, no. 5/6, pp. 505–533.

Westphal, Larry E., Yung W. Rhee and Gary Pursell (1979) "Foreign Influences on Korean Industrial Development." *Oxford Bulletin of Economics and Statistics*, vol. 4, no. 1, pp. 359–388.

Woo, Jung-en (1991) *Race to the Swift: State and Finance in Korean Industrialization*, New York: Columbia University Press.

Yi, Chongjae (1993) *Chaebŏl iryŏksŏ* (Curriculum Vitae of Chaebŏl), Seoul: Han'guk ilbosa.

Yi, Taegŭn (2002) *Haebanghu 1950 nyŏndaei kyŏngje* (The Post-Liberation Economy in the 1950s), Seoul: Samsung kyŏngje yŏn'guso.

Yi, Taegwan (2004) *Pak Taejun*, Seoul: Hyŏnamsa.

5 Democratization

The democratization project that began after port opening in 1876 and stalled by the colonial government was resumed in South Korea after Liberation in 1945.[1] Unlike the aforementioned two projects – educational expansion and industrialization – it was not led by the state but by the people. During the four decades after the birth of the First Republic in 1948 the state (with the exception of the Second Republic (1960–1961), it had largely been an anti-democratic authoritarian force against which the people had to fight to protect democracy from extinction.

The constitution and constitutionalism

South Korea officially became a democratic nation when the First Republic, born in 1948, adopted a democratic constitution. Although Korea's first-ever democratic constitution has been criticized for conferring excessive powers on the executive office, it was a remarkable (almost revolutionary) document in that it not only provided a new framework for democratic political order but also dictated a new system of political values – ultimately a total social transformation.

The constitution says Korea is a "democratic republic" and the sovereignty of the republic "shall reside in the people, and all state authority shall emanate from the people." Everybody becomes an equal and independent (autonomous) citizen – not a relational being in predominantly hierarchical society such as loyal subject to king or alien emperor, a filial son or daughter to his or her parents, a faithful wife to her husband, a devoted student to his teacher and a trusted friend or acquaintance.

The first and foremost of this constitution's two main objectives was to provide and guarantee each individual as a full-fledged citizen of the new republic a set of rights and responsibilities that epitomized universalistic democratic, not personalistic, values. Following T. H. Marshall's lead, I will group these rights and responsibilities into three categories: civil, social and political.

The civil category comprises the rights necessary for individual freedom:

> the freedom to individual corporeal liberty, the freedom to change residence, the right to privacy, the right to worship as one chooses, freedom of speech, freedom of assembly and the freedom of knowledge and art.

Democratization 163

The constitution grants citizens various forms of personal liberties of individual citizens: "All citizens shall enjoy freedom of faith and conscience. There shall be no national religion and religion shall be separated from politics" (Article 12). "The right of property of all citizens shall be guaranteed. It's content and limits determined by law) (Article 15). "Freedom of press, publication assembly and association of all citizens shall not be restrained except by law" (Article 13). All citizens shall enjoy freedom of learning and the arts. The right of authors, inventors and artists shall be guaranteed by law" (Article 14).

The social category concerns

> the whole range from the right to a modicum of economic welfare and security to the right to share to the full in the social heritage and to live the life of a civilized being according to the standards prevailing in the society.
>
> (Marshall 1950: 12)

These include the right to education, to the equality of men and women to equality before the law and to basic labour rights, namely the right of the employee not to be unfairly discriminated against by the employer (Marshall 1950: 12).

The constitution declares, "All citizens are equal before the law, and there may be no discrimination in political, economic, or cultural life on account of sex, religion, or social status" (Article 8). "All citizens shall have the equal right to receive education and primary education is compulsory and free of charge" (Article 16). "All citizens shall have the right and duty to work. The standard of working condition shall be determined by law" (Article 17). It added an additional provision for those who do not have the capacity to maintain livelihood owing to old age, diseases and other reasons of losing work capacity. They "shall be protected by the state as stipulated by law" (Article 19).

The political category includes the right to participate in the political process or the exercise of political power as "a member of a body invested with political authority or as an elector of the members of such body" (Marshall 1950: 11). It essentially refers to the right of the citizen to form a government that, in turn, guarantees these rights (Marshall 1950: 11).

Articles 25 and 26 of the constitution read, "All citizens shall have the right to elect public officials" and "be in charge of public duties as defined by law" (Article 26). Public officials are, therefore, "to be held responsible to citizens" and all citizens "shall have "the right to petition dismissal of a public officials who violated law" (Article 27). Thus, for the first time in history, ordinary citizens as subjects were granted the right to form the government by electing or appointing public officials or becoming public officials by themselves.

As such, the person as the citizen in the public domain has equal opportunities and liberties to participate in various social processes, including economic, political, educational and religious, according to his wishes and abilities as his conscience dictates. His right to realize himself as a respectable and valuable human being and to pursue his individual happiness is assured by the constitution (Yi Sŏkyŏn 2009). Citizens' equal opportunities and liberties are

164   *Democratization*

institutionally safeguarded by structural mechanisms built into the government system.

The other objective of the constitution is to get the people to form a government and to get rid of a government they dislike. Citizens as electorates could choose the government of their liking at each election every four years. No regime was to stay in power indefinitely. People had the right to choose a form of government. The constitution provided a competitive party system.

Political parties offer voters different policies to choose from. Opposition parties can freely criticize the incumbent government and ruling parties, and offer alternatives, thereby institutionalizing opposition.

Furthermore, the constitution prevents political power to concentrate in the hands of one man or a group by separating it into three branches: the legislative, the executive and the judiciary. The legislature enacts and revises laws, the executive governs according to laws and the judiciary interprets laws and apply laws to settle disputes between the state and the citizens or between citizens themselves.

And no individual is permitted to be a member of more than one branch at the same time. Each branch of the government, assigned with its own function, is independent of the other and not allowed to usurp or encroach upon the powers or the function of another but given the power to check upon others.

The power of the government is also spatially divided between the central and local administration. The local assembly was granted a degree of autonomy in administering local affairs and the authority to establish regulations.

Moreover, constitutionalism is the practice of politics according to the rule of law, not rule by man, which rendered the relation between the governor and the governed impersonal.

Under traditional dynastic and colonial authoritarianism, such relations were based upon personal loyalty of the subject to the ruler. Under constitutionalism, the relationship between the governor and the governed or the government and the citizen is determined by the rules and regulations stipulating the rights and responsibilities of both parties.

Democratic constitutionalism that confers citizenship to people with those rights and provides structural mechanisms to protect them directly challenges personalism. Personalism, as discussed earlier, places primary emphasis on the person as a relational being with primordial ties, attachments, loyalties and obligations, horizontal as well as vertical to close others.

Constitutionalism, by contrast, emphasizes the person as an independent and equal being with individual rights and responsibilities. As such, the personalist ethic is a code of conduct that governs the social interactions among people known to each other in a personal network, whereas the democratic ethic embedded in constitutionalism regulates wider social interactions among people, including strangers, in the public as well as personal network domain.

With the constitution, the traditional notion of the government as a unitary power and divine authority was swept away. The idea of government by consent with limited power divided into three branches was unfamiliar to Koreans at the time the constitution was proclaimed. The Confucian, especially neo-Confucian, idea of good government was based on the sovereign power of a king under the Mandate of Heaven serving devotedly on behalf of the people. But the people did not have control over the government. How the government protected the people was left to the government itself. Under the democratic constitution, a government that fails to protect people's rights and welfare could be dissolved by the people because the people empowered the government in the first place.

Such ideas of the citizen and the government, however, demanded Koreans, who had so long been nurtured with Confucian teachings, to make a radical break with the past.

The rise of an authoritarian regime

More than half a century has elapsed since the establishment of a republic with a democratic constitution, which has undergone a long and arduous process of taking root in South Korean political soil. There have been eight constitutional amendments, two major coups d'état, the rise and fall of some 500 political parties, no local autonomy (until 2006), many assassinations and assassination attempts of eminent political leaders, countless election improprieties, continuous student demonstrations, many declarations of emergency and martial laws and no peaceful succession (until 1987).

These strains and contradictions stem from the fact that the kind of political life or political culture that a democratic polity requires was not the one to which Koreans had been accustomed. Traditional norms re-cast the democratic political process. In the absence of established constitutional norms, democracy first became Koreanized rather than Korea becoming democratized. Constitutional norms emphasize the supremacy of the rule over the person, whereas Korean traditional norms tend to be predominantly person oriented.

The democratic process in South Korea has been mainly vitiated by successive incumbents of the executive office which has been occupied by three autocratic personalities who used it to build their personal power bases within the democratic political system for the continuation of authoritarian rule.

Syngman Rhee, the first president elected by the legislature, created a government which was almost completely dominated by the executive office and which he ran for 12 years until a student uprising brought it to an abrupt end.

Park Chung Hee seized power in 1960 after overthrowing the Second Republic of Chang Myŏn (June 15, 1960–May 16, 1961) through a coup d'etat and became the president of the Third Republic in 1963. He continued with and completed the authoritarian regime-building process that Rhee started. Park ruled the country for 18 years until he was assassinated by Kim Chaegyu, his right-hand man, the director of the Korean Central Intelligence Agency.

Chun Doo Hwan inherited Park's authoritarian government after he successfully staged a coup and stayed in power for seven years. Initially, Chun appeared to have every intention of staying beyond the first term in spite of his promise of not seeking a second term. But Chun succumbed to the pressure of organized opposition forces and was apparently persuaded by his colleagues within the

166   *Democratization*

ruling party to honour his words, thereby making a peaceful succession of power possible.

Altogether, nine-tenths of the four decades of the republican era have been under three authoritarian regimes, with two brief democratic interludes brought about by the downfall of the two presidents.

For the purpose of analysis, the development of the authoritarian regime within a democratic political framework will be understood as the process of a Caesarean leader coming to dominate parliamentary politics.

How, then, did an authoritarian regime evolve in the democratic frame of politics?

The Legislative Branch – Each president first established firm control over the legislature through his own party. The ruling party consisted of those people who pledged undivided loyalty to him. Such allegiance was reciprocated by the president's personal executive favour. The main objective of such close organization was to enable the president to dominate the legislature through obtaining a majority of party loyalists in the National Assembly. The president held the final authority to make party nominations and fully utilized his executive authority and influence to help elect the party nominees to the National Assembly.

It was, therefore, unthinkable for the ruling party National Assembly members to vote according to their own will in the legislative process instead of following instructions from the executive office. Going against the wish of the president was regarded as an act of defiance of his authority and of showing personal disloyalty to him. The ruling party thus became an arm of the executive office, and its assembly members became "built-in voting machines." The National Assembly was reduced to a "marginal or minimal" legislature (Kim 1990: 366). With the National Assembly dominated by government party members, the legislature's checks on the executive were rendered ineffective. More importantly, legislative initiative was usurped by the administrative office.

Park Chung Hee, however, wanted more and sought a more secure method of subordinating the assembly. Indirect control over the assembly through the ruling party left open the possibility of the latter revolting against Park. In 1972, Park suspended the legislature and ruled through the Emergency Council of State, issuing decrees that had the effect of law. He then revised the constitution to reorganize the structure of the government to solidify his position within it. Under the new constitution, the president was not elected by the people but by a newly introduced National Council for Unification (NCU), which dealt with all issues of unification. The chairman of the NCU, who was the incumbent president, nominated its fifty-member steering committee, which, then under an acting chairman whom it selected itself, conducted the election of the next president. The president so elected appointed one-third of the National Assembly with the approval of the NCU. In sum, the downgrading of the National Assembly in the new constitution reduced party politics to insignificance. Indeed, the president could dissolve political parties. When Park died, Chun Doo Hwan was elected president by the NCU and inherited the new government system that Park had built.

Democratization 167

The Judiciary Branch – If the legislative assembly became the "maid" of the (executive) power, the judicial branch of the government never had any constitutional autonomy in its operation. Initially, the president appointed a chief justice with assembly approval; judges' appointments were limited to ten years, with renewals subject to executive review. Subsequent revisions reduced the chief justice's term of office from ten years in 1962, to six years in 1972 and to five years in 1980, limiting it to a single term. Since the executive office controlled the legislature through his party, assembly approval of the president's appointment of judges became a mere formality. Executive control over the appointment of the top officials of the judicial branch gradually resulted in the ascendancy of the administration over the judicial branch. The administration gradually came to have power to determine appointment, firing, promotion, transfer and demotion of judicial officials, which translated into the subjugation of the judiciary by the executive and administrative power. The administration came to dominate the criminal justice system. Rarely were requests of arrest by the prosecutor denied by public judges. Prison terms for "political" cases (related to violation of the anti-communism law, the National Security Law) were usually determined by the Blue House, the office of the president. Judges were not expected to take an independent stance on trials of political dissidents critical of the government.

In the Fifth Republic under Chun Doo Hwan, a new system was introduced in order to avoid any possible conflict between the judiciary and administrative branch. This involved sending judges over to the presidential and intelligence offices. Their main task was to monitor the mood of the administration, the proper assessment of which would help the judiciary not to offend the administration in handling political cases. The administration also had security agents stationed in courthouses, monitoring and reporting on the trial process. Their reports on the performance of individual judges during the trial of important political cases served as a basis for the judges' promotion or demotion.

Once the legislature and judiciary were brought under the control of the executive office, the government came to be largely identified with the administrative bureaucracy, with the executive office at the top. The legislature failed to represent the masses of the people, and the judiciary failed to defend those dissidents who fought to regain their constitutional rights. The president and his administration came to loom large in the government process, with the president becoming a virtual despot within the democratic (or quasi-democratic) framework. It was the birth of what Tocqueville called administrative despotism (1948: 316–321).

Rhee, Park and Chun all tried to further strengthen his power base by establishing effective control over the police and the armed forces. This was done by cultivating loyalty to himself amongst the officers of the police and armed forces. High-ranking police and army officers were carefully screened, and anyone suspected of disloyalty to the president was dismissed under one pretext or another, while those who were unquestionably loyal were assured of their positions and promotion.

Park created the Central Intelligence Agency for surveillance of civilians. As the most powerful intelligence and investigation agency, with enormous extra-legal

168   *Democratization*

authority, the Korean CIA (KCIA) undertook a loyalty check, which involved the screening of all major political figures and high-ranking government employees, and played a key role in organizing Park's Democratic Republican Party, eliminating anti-Park elements inside and outside the power circle. The KCIA served as the eyes and ears of Park, and became the government organ most feared by the people. After the fall of Park, Chun replaced it with the Agency of National Security Planning, which performed more or less the same function as the KCIA.

The domination of the government process by the executive office was followed its effort to control the major civil organizations – namely, big corporate enterprises, labour unions, medias and universities,

Big Business Enterprises – The executive office reached out to the corporate sector, seeking financial contribution. From the beginning of the Republican era, it became necessary for the president to establish the link or coalition with the finance and business to generate additional informal funds to supplement election campaign funds, cover the government party's operational funds and to give gifts – mostly in the form monetary terms – to his supporters for their continuing loyalty and to others to make supporters out of them.

The Rhee government extended favors of various kind to selected business firms in anticipation of or direct exchange for donations.

Those firms acquired government-controlled foreign aid funds at favorable rates and purchased government-owned properties, mainly the so-called vested (enemy) property that included industrial plants, properties left by the Japanese residents in Korea, at a fraction of their market value, borrowed from the government without being pressed for repayment and evaded the payment of taxes (Oh 1968: 46). The government also reduced or completely exempted private firms, designated by the president and engaging in industrial production, from paying income tax, corporate profits dividend tax, business tax and corporate tax. These tax privileges not only help them do profitable business but also avoid paying taxes.[2]

The government controlled the flow of foreign aid and capital into capital-short Korea and the banking system itself. Thus it held firm control over business enterprises through management of capital allocation. It also had another weapon to control them – namely, tax auditing. Thus the government could easily use it to make or undo any business corporation.

Portions of the fortune made by businessmen were turned over to the government coffers as a form of gratitude or as a commission. Consequently, the state and business became inseparable partners.

High-ranking officers of the ruling Liberal Party played the role of mediator between the executive office and the business firms in exchanging favors and donation. It was common knowledge at the time that financial donations from business firms constituted the major sources of the party's managing funds.[3]

Park Chung Hee's approach to big business firms was somewhat different from that of Rhee. As discussed in the previous chapter, he had them join him in his development project as major partners. He helped them to do profitable business by providing numerous privileges and collected financial donations to establish private political funds.

Democratization 169

Chun Doo Hwan inherited Park's practices and methods of generating the "governance funds" (t'ongch'ijagŭm) when he assumed power in 1980. But he was more actively involved in collecting it than Park did. He directly asked chaebŏls to make informal financial donations directly to him and kept a substantial portion of it for his personal wealth. And he was unforgiving to those who were reluctant to oblige his request or gave less than what he expected.

Business became more reliant on political connections that would enable them to buy favours offered by the ruling party as the government came to control more of the flow of foreign aid and capital into capital-short Korea and the banking system itself. Consequently, the government held firm control over the business sector through management of capital allocation and tax auditing, two big weapons the government could easily use to make or undo any business corporation. Government and business thus became inseparable partners as Korea entered the development era of the 1960s. A large firm could not continue to prosper without maintaining amicable relations with the government through the ruling party or other government organizations.

The Labour Union – Following the constitutional stipulation of labour rights, the National Assembly of the First Republic legislated a series of labour laws in 1953. The Basic Labour Law stipulated labour conditions, guaranteed workers' minimum standard of living and promoted the development of a balanced national economy. The Trade Union Laws provided the three labour rights guaranteed by the constitution, thereby maintaining reasonable working conditions for workers and contributing to the promotion of their social standing and the development of the national economy. The Labor Dispute Regulation Law guaranteed the freedom of workers' collective action and regulated labour disputes fairly, thereby maintaining industrial peace (Kim Nakchung 1982: 168–173; Kim Sa'uk 1974: 86–88; Kim Yunhwan 1967: 278–308 and Sin Tubŏm, 1970: 18–21).

From the beginning, the Rhee government solicited support from the national union organization, the only collective civilian force. While closely monitoring its activities, the government established an intimate tie with it by cultivating the loyalty of the union leadership. It recruited high-ranking union officials into various government posts such as labour management councils, advisory committees and cabinet. Many labour leaders saw the union as a route to a political career. Consequently, the Korean Federation of Trade Union (FKTU) came to function more or less as a government organ while suppressing the democratic labour movement and concentrating on the promotion of labour management cooperation in accordance with government labour policy (Han'guk kidokkyo sahoemunje yŏn'guwon). In the words of one critic, "The national labour union distinguished itself for its patriotic anti-communist activities but failed to do its job in promoting the rights and welfare of industrial workers" (Han'guk kidokkyo sahoemunje yŏn'guwŏn 1987a: 34).

As discussed in Chapter 4, Park Chung Hee of the Third Republic was neither prepared to let a large-scale civic organization such as KFTU with a fair degree of autonomy have potential power to challenge his authority nor to let workers to freely protest against the employers demanding improvement of their working

170   *Democratization*

conditions. His government revised all four labour laws to make it difficult for industrial workers to form company unions and to engage in collective bargaining. Rhee Park solicited and received the KFTU's support for his development plans.

Chun Doo Hwan was equally hostile to labour unions. As a first step toward establishing a new labour control regime, his government eliminated those labour leaders who were considered responsible for labour protests in recent years. The Ministry of Labor, in accordance with the "new policy of cleansing labor unions," forced several selected national, industrial and company union leaders to resign. Those company union leaders who refused to resign were summarily dismissed, and some of them were sent to the infamous "cleaning education" center. At the same time, most of "democratic" company unions (created by company workers independently) were closed down by the police.

The Chun government, then, made it more difficult for workers to organize themselves and collectively take action against management by changing labour laws. The ultimate aim was to block the labour union movement itself (Yi Wŏnbo 2005: 272).

According to these new law the Office of Labor Affairs would approve of the request for union formation if at least 30 workers, or 20 percent of the workforce of a given plant or firm, agreed to become members (previously no such requirement existed); those who had not worked for the company more than one year did not qualify for union membership, and each union member could not serve on the union's standing committee for more than three years.

The new laws also did away with the union shop. Previously, the agreement, imperfect though it was, was that when there was a union representing a workplace, all the employees there would automatically become its members. But the new laws stipulated that regardless of the existence of a union in a unit workplace, one did not have to join it.

Furthermore, it was specified that bargaining could take place only at the enterprise level and ruled it illegal for the third party such as church groups, student activists and lawyers get involved in collective bargaining and action processes.

The Media – The next target was the mass media. The authoritarian ruler has a genuine dislike of the media, showing little tolerance for scrutiny and criticism by the media of his undemocratic regime building.

The Syngman Rhee government promulgated a constitution that guaranteed freedom of the press, among other freedoms. During the early period, Rhee publicly held the view that freedom of the press was at the very heart of the spirit of the new republic and that it was an idea he dearly respected (Choe Chun 1960; Song Kŏnho 1990). But he was also a staunch anti-communist and adopted anti-communism as a national policy, prohibiting the media from spreading information that recognized and praised the North Korean regime. His government first outlawed the few remaining left-wing[4] and did what it could to "curb or set bounds on these voices" (Henderson 1968: 58) through arrest of editors or reporters on the ground that their writings violated the National Security Law, obstruction of news gathering, hindrance of distribution of newspapers, police harassment of reporters, mob action, destruction of bill boards, discriminatory bank loans and so on (Song Kŏnho 1990; Choe Chun 1960; Chong T'aesu 1983). But they did not prove to be effective in subduing the media; the media continued to be critical of the regime and has continued to foment anti-government public opinion, which proved to be the major force sustaining democracy in Korea during this period.

Like Syngman Rhee Park Chung Hee disliked anti-government or pro-opposition party media and was determined to have the entire media on his side or silence those not favorably inclined to the government. His idea of the media, as clearly indicated in his speeches and writings, was that it should not be a critic but a participant in the government project of rebuilding the nation. He called for cooperation from the media in the economic development plan he launched shortly after he got himself elected as the president of a civilian government.

Over the 18 years of his reign, his government adopted various method of ensuring media cooperation. His junta government (1960–1963), the Supreme Council on Reconstruction of the Nation, first reduced the number of media by closing down selected media and imprisoning a number of so-called vicious or pseudo-reporters on the charge of blackmail, fraud, menace and forgery of official documents (Chŏng Chinsŏk 1985: 281). It then issued Declaration No 11, which enunciated the junta government's plan to reduce the number of daily newspaper from 115 to 39, of news agencies from 316 to 11, of weeklies from 485 to 32 and of monthlies from 464 to 178 (Kang Sŏngch'ae 1986: 267).

When he became the president of the Third Republic, his government announced the new press policy of allowing one daily newspaper in one province and enforced closure of one central and two local newspapers, and one news agency and merging of seven local daily newspapers into three (Chong Chinsŏk 1985: 320). Consequently, the total number of newspaper reporters decreased from 6,332 to 3,427 (Chŏng Taesu,1983: 197).

The surviving media were put under strict government control based on various restrictive measures.

A new system of press cards was instituted, allowing only those who held the card to do news gathering. The pronounced intent of introducing the press card system was to reduce the number of reporters since the government or Park Chung Hee personally felt that there were too many of them. But the cards were more readily issued to "those reporters who are cooperative to the government" than to "those who are not."

More directly, a new system of surveillance of the daily operation of the press was introduced by dispatching members of the KCIA to the media headquarters. They exercised their authority and power to ask media people, in connection with offensive articles, to accompany them voluntarily for inspection purposes to their headquarters (Kim Chinhong 1983:62).

The Ministry of Culture and Information freely requested or instructed the media through them how certain events should be dealt with – whether they should appear on the front page, whereabouts in the front page and in what type of print.

172 *Democratization*

The government also utilized its administrative influences or forces as a method of media control. The government denied uncooperative media certain financial privileges such as loans, allocation of media material and transmitting foreign currencies overseas. It also refused to issue visa to reporters from uncooperative media to travel overseas or limited the amount of foreign currency to carry when visas were issued.

Another powerful method of media control was putting pressure on giant corporations to withdraw advertisement from the targeted media. They were the major subscribers of advertisement space, and the income from advertisement constituted a major source of revenue of any media company revenue. Losing the income from their advertisement is a serious financial blow that any media company could not endure too long.

In the process of taming the media, the government apparently learnt the lesson that direct suppression of uncooperative media was bound to create negative public opinion, which would result in undermining the image of good government. So, at some point in the mid-1970s, it switched to indirect methods of control and introduced the policy of letting the media censor their own reporting.

The government deliberately helped major media organizations to strengthen their financial bases by arranging bank loans and extensions of loan payment periods.

In the early 1960s, most media organizations were considered struggling medium-size enterprises. In the 1970s, they grew rapidly as corporate business enterprises (for more on this point, see Song Kŏnho 1990: 160). With the help of the government financial aid, big newspaper companies expanded beyond newspaper publishing into publishing weeklies, monthlies, adolescent newspapers or co-owning electric wave media such as radio and TV. Some newspaper companies even entered the book publishing business. By the beginning of the 1970s, a few media organizations emerged as giant enterprises dominating the press industry.

Government support for them as enterprises became an essential element in continued growth and, consequently, they became cordial partners to the government. Most media owners were willing to cooperate with the government, as they were constantly seeking executive or government favors. The state was no longer the oppressor of the press. In order to maintain this solidarity, the press developed a built-in self-censor system as media owners did not want to jeopardize the good relationship with the government by criticizing the latter through their own media. Owners were no longer one with editors and reporters in carrying on the old tradition of being a public organ promoting public interest. The press, in the words of Choe Sokch'ae, "left the hand of the editor and reporter" (Song Kŏnho 1990: 87). The owner-publisher became the censor of his own publication.

This solidarity was further strengthened by the establishment of yet another link. While dealing harshly with the rebellious journalists – dismissed or jailed – some of those able journalists and media who remained un-rebellious and cooperative to the government were recruited into the administration as high-ranking officials, and others were directly rewarded with occasional cash payments for their conformity.

Gradually, criticism of the government became an expensive proposition. The pressure was increasingly built up on editors and reporters to protect the corporate interest of the press rather than the public interest of the people.

The power of media as a critical opposition force was rapidly undermined. The final outcome of this shifting loyalty of the media was the birth of the so-called establishment media (*chedo ollon*) – i.e., the media absorbed in the ruling system (Yi T'aeho 1984: 13–50 and Song Kŏnho 1987: 187–195). Media ceased being a public means of communication to become a government bulletin. The government served as the main source of information for the media and the media printed only the information which the government wanted people to know. Political affairs were no longer the dominant subject in newspapers or magazines. They had to develop a new taste for the subscriber. More space was allocated to telling the reader old stories and to columns on recreation, sports and health. Color pictures began to appear in media from the early 1970s. Readers' discontent with the media began to rise; students burned effigies of the press.

Succeeding Park Chung Hee, Chun Doo Hwan of the Fifth Republic more or less followed the footsteps of Park. Like Park, Chun regarded the role of public media "as a public organ that promotes the interest of all the people should devote themselves to the prosperity of the nation and the growth and development of the state." He also thought, "In our country, in comparison with various countries in Europe and America, there are too many newspapers and broadcast stations and we realize that they are inadvertently causing troubles to people and many social evils" (Im Ch'aejŏng 1984: 206).

His government prepared a list of reporters considered to be uncooperative with the government and ordered their employers to dismiss them and forced a number of medias to close down or merge with others. More than 1,500 reporters were released from their jobs, 172 periodical publications were discontinued and 62 media were reduced to 18.

In terms of control, reporting on the Chun administration was more direct and strict than Park's.

It then went ahead to have direct control over what the media reported instead of demanding their support and cooperation as the previous regime had done. The Public Information Room established in the Ministry of Culture sent out to each media everyday so-called the press guideline (bodochich'im) which instructed how the newspaper should be framed. The instruction covered a wide range of reporting: whether an article on a certain event should be printed or not, on what page a certain article should appear, whether a certain article should be printed with a picture or not, how to deal with the material provided by the government, etc.

As was the case under the Park's regime, the media functioned largely as a government mouthpiece. Media people might not have had much choice to do anything other than follow government instruction. But, in fact, the media did not simply follow the government instruction. They often became more cooperative with the government on their own than those reporters during the Park period. From the beginning, many major newspapers presented Chun Doo Hwan,

174 *Democratization*

the commander of Agency of National Security at the time of Park's death, who seized power through a coup, as the man who was clean, fair and could not tolerate injustice, and "the new leader in the new era." The Han'guk Daily compiled a book of Chun's sayings (Kim Chongch'an 1991: 465). They also supported, praised or wrote positively of various government policies and defended oppressive measures of suppressing mass demonstrations against the government.

For their self-motivated cooperation, media were handsomely rewarded with cash payment and invitation to high government positions. On the other hand, those reporters expelled from their jobs, suffered hardship. The government not only forced their employers to dismiss them but also prevented any media or other corporations from hiring them.

The University – University professors were of special concern to Park. When he came into power, he was mindful of the fact that during the Rhee era, professors enjoyed a considerable degree of intellectual autonomy, which permitted an independent stance on political affairs. The university community was quite vocal in criticizing undemocratic government policies and actions. A group of university professors played a decisive role in turning the major anti-government student demonstration in 1960 into a citywide civic protest when they took to the streets demanding that police not shoot innocent students.

Park did not want professors to have such public influence. In 1973 he introduced the reappointment system. Although reappointment was said to be based strictly on merit, the Ministry of Education used it to eliminate "problem" professors considered too critical of the government. In 1976, 416 faculty members, including many well-known academic scholars who were also outspoken critiques of the government, were denied reappointment (Kim Chŏngnam 2005: 224).

In the meantime, the government provided ample opportunity for faculty members willing to render "useful" service to the government by commissioning them to conduct policy-related research or inviting them to serve on committees evaluating various government policies (p'yongga kyosudan) and "give advice" to the government. Like those reporters who became ardent government supporters, many university faculty members did so too. Some – not a small number – university faculty members saw the opportunity to promote their academic or nonacademic careers by joining various government committees, undertaking government research and publishing articles and books praising government projects and the president (see Han'guk chongchi yon'guso (1988: 138–145)). They willingly became ŏyong kyosu (pro-government professors).

Park Chung Hee was also well aware of what dissident students could do to the regime they did not like: the student uprising in 1960 led to the fall of Syngman Rhee. From the beginning, he was critical of students going to the streets to demonstrate against the government "instead of studying" and deployed police forces to suppress them. He became even intolerant of their criticisms of and protests against his policy after amending the constitution to install the Yushin system in 1972. His government declared emergency decrees – Decrees 1 and 2 and Decree 9 in 1975, barring any act of "denying, criticizing, distorting and slandering" of the Yushin constitution and introduced various measures of protest control.

The government then authorized each university president to force those students who had been involved in organizing anti-government demonstrations in the past and were likely to do so again in the future to go on leave.

It was also eager to have faculty members do the job of guiding and policing activist students, and introduced the faculty guidance system (pundam chido kyosu chedo) in 1973. Under this system, all the students of each university were divided into a number of groups that corresponded to the number of faculty, and each group was assigned to a faculty. The job of each faculty was to meet with each of his students once a month to help them concentrate on studies and improve (or not to fail in) academic work as well as to give advice on other personal matters including advancement to graduate school, going abroad for further studies, job acquisition after graduation, etc. In addition, he was supposed to meet with students' parents once a month to discuss their children's school and extracurricular activities. At the end of each month, the faculty adviser was expected to submit a report on each advisee to the dean of his college. This system was apparently designed to minimize commotions on campus through active faculty advising.

There were other more direct control measures installed such as the decision to conscript those students released from jail after serving their prison terms into the army; legalization of the presence of police and security agents on college campuses whose job was to watch any anti-government activities, collect information on political orientations, research activities and content of lectures of faculty members and extracurricular activities of known activist students; forceful replacement of the existing Autonomous Student Government with the National Student Defense-Corps, which had been abolished by the Second Republic; and extension of students' military training and reduced extracurricular activities on campus.

Like Park Chung Hee, Chun Doo Hwan was equally afraid of the potential of student power and adamant about suppressing student protest. But unlike Park, he was more flexible in managing the student activism problem, and in the end, he succumbed to the pressure created by students to step down at the end of his term.

He began with the brutal suppression of the Kwangju uprising – a large-scale struggle initiated by university students for recovery of democracy in Kwangju – which ended up with casualties of some 200 deaths and several thousand wounded. He made it clear that he would not tolerate any form of opposition to his regime.

But he soon realized that he could not continue with the strong-arm policy given the fact that both the Asian (1986) and World (1988) Olympics were forthcoming, and such policy would negatively affect world opinions and more directly the Olympic Committees would have second thoughts on having the games in Korea.

The Chun government decided to shift the existing policy on university campus based on punishment to one on prevention with proper guidance. In December 1983, it adopted the campus autonomy policy. This policy had three main provisions: (1) all the police and intelligence forces stationed on campus legally as well as illegally were to be withdrawn, (2) all the students expelled from universities for their political (anti-government) activities would be allowed to return to campus in accordance with their wishes and (3) all the faculty members dismissed

176 *Democratization*

because of their political action – not because of their academic performances – would be allowed to resume their jobs.

The government also introduced the system of allowing universities to admit more students than before, but imposed fixation of the number of students graduating. The idea behind this system was to encourage students to concentrate on studies rather than nonacademic work – including demonstrations – so that they would successfully complete four years of undergraduate work.

The new reconciliation policies, however, did not have the effect of stabilizing university campuses as the government expected. Student activists became more active in organizing study groups to discuss student movement–related ideologies and protest tactics. Those students returning after years of absence resumed their leadership roles in the student movement.

The student movement became more radicalized. As will be discussed later, student activists demanded that Chun step down. They also shifted their focus from the recovery of democracy to liberating South Korea from US domination, thereby reunifying the two Koreas and protecting industrial workers from the exploitation by their capitalist employers. The movement openly adopted – in defiance of the law – leftist (Marxist) ideologies as the guiding principle.

The government responded by tightening control over campuses. They kept pressure on university administrations to monitor student activities closely and to punish politically active students by sending them to jail to serve long jail terms (five to seven years) or inducting them into military service.

The conflict between the government and student activists continued until 1987, when student demonstrations became a nationwide event; it gained a historical label, the June Struggle (Yuwol hangjaeng), which appeared to never simmer down, and eventually forced the government to grant what the opposition party demanded.

Political opposition and dissent: the development of the democratic movement

Authoritarian regime building eliminated a majority of citizens from the political process, thereby depriving them of many of their constitutional rights, including the one to create a new government through election creating discontent and making them aware of their constitutional rights and responsibilities.

Park Chung Hee offered the mandate of development combined with "Korean-style democracy" as a rationalization for the authoritarianization of the regime, yet he did not gain popular support. Discontent increased and political opposition and dissension against the government became widespread, consolidating into a strong anti-government force, which brought an end to the First Republic in 1960, the Fourth Republic in 1979 and the Fifth Republic in 1987.

Dissident students and Christian church leaders formed the major opposition force.

Student Activists – In 1960, the student uprising led to the overthrow of Rhee's government and paved the way for a new democratic regime. This revolutionary outcome enabled students to redefine their social role. University students conceived of themselves as "a symbol of rebellion and freedom" (Korea University Student April 18 Declaration, cited in Yi Che'o 1984: 169). They considered it their duty to "defend the people's freedom threatened with extinction by the dictatorship of the older generation" (Seoul National University Student Declaration cited in Yi Che'o 1984: 172) and took "pride in participating in the struggle against autocracy" (Korea University Student April 18 Announcement). They identified themselves closely with the new democratic Korea and assumed responsibilities for its future, expressing their distrust of the older generation whom they perceived to be representing traditional practices of corruption, opportunism and defeatism (Yi Che'o 1984: 172). Students thus rapidly established themselves as a powerful opposition force against the government and informed critics of society more generally, remaining so throughout the authoritarian era.

After a brief democratic interlude (the Second Republic), Park Chung Hee came into power in 1960. Students soon realized that the new regime, staffed with ex-military generals and colonels, was not intent on promoting democracy. They began to voice their views on political affairs, protesting against a government which had become increasingly undemocratic. Demonstrations continued to be held in protest against the negotiation and ratification of the normalization of diplomatic relations with Japan, the smuggling by the Samsung conglomerate of fertilizer from the United States using privileges given to it by the government, irregularities in the National Assembly member election and the proposed constitution amendment in 1971, which would clear a path for Park Chung Hee to run for president a third time.

From the beginning, Park stood firm against student protests. They represented an important internal challenge to government authority (Han 1980). Park seized upon it to eradicate what he considered to be the "demonstration-is-a-cure-all tendency" among students (Han'guk kidokkyo sahoe munje yŏn'guwŏn 1983: 29), fearing that "the arrogance and disrespect of a few rebellious students might cause political instability." "He was determined to change the students' bad manners" and to "uproot the student habit of demonstration" (Yi Sang'u 1985: 47). Government reaction was harsh, escalating repressive measures each time there was a massive demonstration. Park maintained that school is for study, not for organizing anti-government protests.

Despite severe measures against them, students' protested against the authoritarian government of Park continued. It was no longer directed to what they considered to be the government's undemocratic, un-nationalistic behaviour, but toward the government itself, which was viewed as undemocratic and un-nationalistic.

More specifically, students came to be concerned with such issues as the guarantee of freedom of the press and of dissent; release of jailed political dissidents; freedom to act according to one's conscience; restoration of the human rights of political prisoners; an end to torture, surveillance, political oppression; and the politics of intelligence – an end to the suppression of political dissidents and student activists under the National Security Law and the Anti-communism Law

178 Democratization

and the disbanding of the Central Intelligence Agency (or the Agency of National Safety Planning).

During the last five years of the Park period, the student activists went underground and indulged in ideological discussions on what student protest is about and why it should continue in spite of the government repression.

They arrived at the conclusion that the Yushin regime was a fascist one, sustained by police and intelligence force, depriving people of their basic human rights; the Korean economy was increasingly becoming dependent on Japan as evidenced by the extensive penetration of the Japanese capital into the South Korean economy, and the government economic policy was promoting inequality by rewarding a selected group of comprador capitalists with privileges and wealth while short changing ordinary people; accordingly industrial workers, the urban poor and rural farmers were suffering from severe poverty. In short, the Yushin regime is not only anti-democratic *pan-minju*) but also anti-nationalistic (*pan-minjok*) and anti-people (*pan-minjung*). The student protest against the government thus became a political movement with a clearly defined goal – defense of democracy, the nation's autonomy and the rights of the people, or three *min*s (Han'guk kidokkyo sahoe munje yŏn'guwŏn 1983: 139).

The student activists found Chun's administration no different from Park's and fought against it on three *min* fronts.

Two features distinguished student protest activities during the Chun period from the previous ones.

Firstly, students were divided into the undongkwŏn (movement circle) and piundongkwŏn (non-movement circle). The former refers to those students who were continuously and actively engaged in the movement or considered it their duty as student to participate in it and the latter to others who did not actively participate. The undongkwon students established a basis on campus by penetrating into the student autonomous government."[5] They were able to get themselves elected as key members of the new organization,[6] which, in turn, enabled them to engage in activism on an ever-more formal basis and with financial resources. The revival of the student government was an official recognition of student activism. It became integral part of the school system (Hwang Ŭibong 1986: 51–62). Those who are outside the undongkwon almost deliberately avoided competition against those undongkwon students in running for student government positions.

Secondly, the student movement became more leftist or socialist-oriented ideologically. Many undongkwon students chose the two new fronts – the people and the nation – to devote themselves to the struggle to "liberate industrial workers from their capitalist employers' exploitation" and "South Korea from American domination."

Some of them advocated of proletarian revolution. As a step toward achieving their goals, student activists formed alliance with labour in an effort to turn industrial workers into the major agents of people's revolution that would bring "true democracy" or people's democracy and an end to elite rule.

They adopted a Marxist perspective in explaining the poor condition of industrial workers. Low or "starvation" wages were regarded as inevitable in the capitalist

Democratization 179

economic regime because they were a result of profit-maximization efforts by the capitalists. Any system that demands the sacrifice of industrial workers who constitute the majority of the workforce is, they argued, an anti-people system.

In the early 1970s, some undongkwon students became factory workers without revealing their student identity (the government employers called them 'disguised employees') during summer and winter vacations in order to acquire factory life experience, thereby directly experiencing the reality of labour problems and sharing "the pains of people at the bottom of social hierarchy." Many of them actually quit school to become factory workers themselves. They formed unions at individual plants, including large (chaebŏl) enterprises, and district and industrial unions, organizing work stoppages and strikes (for more on this, see O Hana 2010 and Yu Kyŏngsun 2015). Toward the end of the 1970s, striking workers demanded more than pay increases and improvement of working conditions; they also demanded the end of the authoritarian regime and shouted anti-capitalist slogans. According to the estimate by the Agency for National Security Planning in the early 1980s, some 3,000 students left university to become labour activists.

Others became anti-American nationalists espousing unification of the two Koreas. Informed of the newly fashionable dependency theory originated from Latin America, they came up with a fresh interpretation of the political economy of South Korea. It goes as follows: the South Korean economy is increasingly dominated by foreign capital. It is becoming a branch office of giant conglomerates in Japan and the United States, and in South Korea, it is a dumping ground for American goods. Furthermore, the United States still holds a firm control over South Korea through its military presence. The Korean Army is still a part of UN forces under the command of a US general. The United States established a nuclear basis in South Korea in its attempt to contain the Soviet Union. South Korea is a testing ground for nuclear weapons. There is also a possibility that South Korea may turn into a battleground for a US-USSR feud. South Korea is not a liberated country; it is an American colony. Chun's regime is a puppet of the United States. South Korea has to be liberated from US dominion and reunified with North Korea. South Korea's close tie with or military dependency on the United States is a major barrier to reunification. The pro-American sentiment that had been built up since the Korean War began to change among student activists into anti-American sentiment.

The nationalist turn of the student movement began with the Kwangju student rebellion in 1980 against Chun Doo Hwan, who inherited Park's authoritarian regime through a coup d'état, ending "the Spring in Seoul" (the widespread popular expectation of the return of democracy) after Park's death. The Chun government brutally suppressed the student demonstrations by deploying one division of the army that resulted in more than 600 deaths of citizens. This event came to be viewed by student activists as an act of the United States supporting Chun's dictatorial government. Why, students asked, didn't the United States stop the army's massacre of innocent citizens? More specifically, why did the US commander of the US-Korean joint military force give permission to the parachute division

180   *Democratization*

under his command to suppressl the demonstration? Student activists held the United States responsible for the Kwangju killing.

Anti-Americanism that rapidly spread among them was expressed in various forms of protest against US officials stationed in Korea.

They refused to join military units stationed at the front for the compulsory weeklong military training with the reasoning that the Korean Army was an American mercenary and such military training was not for national defense. They burnt an American flag in a public place, set fires, threw rocks and bombs and even occupied United States Information Service and US Chamber of Commerce buildings in various cities, demanding apologies from the United States for its role in the Kwangju massacre and the withdrawal of its armed forces stationed in Korea.

Anti-Americanism was rising high on university campuses in the latter half of the eighties. "Expel US!," "No War, No Nuclear Armament!," "Yankee Go Home!," "Stop the Team Spirit US-Korea Joint Military Exercises" became favourite new slogans chanted at student demonstrations and rallies.

Viewed from the perspective this book has taken, the student movement became a direct challenge to the personalist ethic. To become an ideologue is to commit oneself to an abstract ideal. To fight for democracy becomes more important than maintaining personal or primary ties. Such an act, in an extreme case, required a severing of ties with some close others and strengthening ties with others who share the same ideal and risked formidable punishment. Many undongkwon students defied the National Security Law, the penalty of which was a lengthy jail term and sacrifice of a normal elitist career. Few parents wanted their children to become "revolutionaries' or members of a undongkwon. Instead, they hoped their children finish university and become judges, prosecutors, doctors, bankers and teachers. Many undongkwon students became ideologists against their parents' wishes. In 1984, one student wrote a letter from jail to his mother apologizing for becoming an un-filial son by choosing to become an activist and ending up in the law court as a defendant instead of becoming a judge or prosecutor after graduating law school and passing the judicial civil service examination as she had hoped (Hwang Ŭi-bong 1985: 231). Another jailed student wrote to her mother, begging her not to look at her daughter's radical action from the traditional women's view derived from "feudalistic value orientations," assuring her that her daughter's life was her daughter's and that she was fully capable of taking care of herself (Hwang Ŭi-bong 1985: 237–238). (For more on the student movement during this period, see Lee 2007.)

Progressive Church Leaders – Student activists were joined by dissident church leaders who represented the liberal segment of both the Protestant and Catholic Church communities. Both groups agreed that the revival of democracy meant the Liberation of the people. They advanced their conviction that liberal democracy was the best system for the realization of individual freedom and social justice.

The support of the Christian leaders for the democratization movement in the wake of the rise of an authoritarian regime was an indirect response to student activism. They reflected on their allegiance with Rhee's government and their inaction during the 1950 student uprising (Han'guk kitokkyo sahoemunje

Democratization 181

yŏn'kuwŏn 1983: 60–61), feeling ashamed for not reacting to the injustices, corruption and infringements of human rights they had witnessed. To join the democratization movement was for them a return to the original posture of the church and acting in accordance with religious conscience.[7]

For two decades – 1970s and 1980s – the dissident church leaders carried on their struggle for democracy, campaigning against the authoritarian regime through prayer meetings, all-night vigils, fasts, meetings and mass demonstrations. They dealt with numerous political and social issues, including abolition of the Yushin constitution, an end to police investigation on campus, release of arrested students and political prisoners, abolition of "bad" laws such as the National Security Law and abolition of torture, autonomy of the judiciary branches, guarantee of press and religious freedom, respect for human and civil rights, guarantee of the minimum wage and social welfare of industrial workers and guarantee of the three labour rights (Yi Su'ŏn 1984).

Dissident church leaders also took initiatives in organizing civilian anti-government groups in which they played a key role. They maintained close links with other democratization movement organizations. They readily supported other dissident groups or organizations and joined forces with them in various anti-government activities such as collecting one million signatures for the petition to demand revision of the constitution, boycotting the referendum of the Yushin constitution and forming a ballot inspection group in the thirteenth national election in 1967. They also offered their churches or cathedrals as places to hold meetings, prayers, vigils, fasts and sit-ins. Churches and cathedrals were one of the few places at the time to which the government hesitated to send in police and intelligent agents to arrest dissidents. Myŏngdong cathedral in Seoul, home of Cardinal Kim Suhwan and located in the heart of the city, is known as a sacred site for the democratization movement – a place where protest marches usually started and where dissidents could find sympathy and protection. Like other churches, the cathedral served as a rallying point for anti-government democratization forces. But what distinguishes this cathedral from other places is that the protest events that took place there drew more attention and had more symbolic meaning than what happened elsewhere (Mun Myŏngho 1986).

Both Protestant and Catholic dissident leaders lent support to other groups engaged in the democratization movement. For example, when young newspaper reporters staged sit-ins in protest against government interference with news making, the church readily lent moral as well as financial support. Conversely, when the press ceased to report on the events the government did not want the public to know about, such as student anti-government protests and demonstrations, police brutality, government corruption and election frauds, the church demanded that the press "wake up." The Council of Priests for the Realization of Justice, in particular, reported on the truth of the Kwangju citizens uprising, the sex torture of a female university student who worked as a labourer and the death by torture of a university student – truths the government was trying to underplay as best as it could. They also stood on the side of the students who set fire to the Pusan USIS office, recognizing the legitimacy of their action.

182 *Democratization*

Perhaps, the most notable of their activities was the support of factory workers' efforts to organize independent minjunojo (democracy union). Many dissident church leaders, both Protestant and Catholic, believed that the sufferings of God's people should not be neglected and that the church must act to protect their human rights as a gift of nature (Cho Sung-hyŏk 1981: 6–7). One Protestant clergyman said to the author, "To abandon workers is to abandon Jesus Christ."[8]

The Urban Industrial Mission on the Protestant side and the Jeunesse Ouvrière Chretienne (or Young Catholic Workers) on the Catholic side provided educational programs designed for the cultivation of workers' consciousness and training to help labourers to develop an organized capacity to protect their own interests and welfare to improve their working and living conditions.

They exposed poor working conditions and workers' suffering, as well as the corruption and inactivity of union leadership. They sent letters to the Office of Labour Administration protesting against their inaction in obtaining benefits for industrial workers. They made it their practice to investigate industrial disputes and produced reports in order make them available to a wider public; they held numerous symposia to discuss the content of new labour legislation and criticized intended revisions of labour law which they judged to be anti-democratic depriving workers of basic labour rights. If workers were forced to resign or expelled from their companies for their involvement in union activities, they protested against the companies for the unjust action, or they negotiated with the companies to help get the expelled workers reinstated. When these efforts failed, they made sure that the workers received due compensation from the companies. They also provided shelter to the expelled workers and collected donations for jailed workers.

Their efforts to oppose the regime publicly might not have accomplished their professed objectives. They were nevertheless important in that, while severe measures of government oppression silenced almost all oppositional forces, the progressive church continued to express displeasure at the weakening and attempted destruction of democracy.

One should bear in mind that the democratization movement described above was carried out under Emergency Decrees 1 and 2, which prohibited any act which negated, opposed, distorted or criticized the (Yushin) constitution and any act demanding proposing or requesting revision of the constitution. Anybody violating the decree faced a stiff jail term. Nevertheless, the church defied the government's warning and continued to criticize the government's undemocratic activities, demanding a return to democracy. The church's role as critic was doubly important since the press had already been silenced and was colluding with the government. The churches took it upon themselves to inform the people of government wrongdoings and corruption. They were determined to disclose publicly what the government did not want people to know. More importantly, in the eyes of the public, the church represented an opposition force at the forefront of the struggle for democracy. The church came to be accepted as a legitimate force in the political process.

Democratization 183

As the involvement of the churches in the democracy movement continued, their focus gradually came to rest on human rights.

In 1973, Han'guk kidokkyo kyohoe hyŏbŭihoe (the National Council of Churches of Korea) issued the "Human Rights Declaration" in which the concept of human rights was clarified and the aims of the anticipated human rights movement spelled out. Human rights were construed as individual autonomy. They argued that individual autonomy is bestowed on man by the creator; God created man according to his image and granted man the right to live on his own with what nature supplies; thus, the autonomy of man is a God-given right; the authority that deprives man's basic right of living and autonomy is considered a betrayal of God's will; therefore, Christ's church must oppose the secular authoritarian power that violates human rights. The dissident church leaders therefore considered it their duty to be on the side of the oppressed and to help them recover their human rights.

In 1974, Han'guk kidokkyo kyohoe hyŏbŭihoe established the Human Rights Committee to deal exclusively with the human rights issues (see Han'guk kidokkyo kyohoe hyŏbŭihoe 1987a: 18–19 and 470–485). It conducted prayer meetings, held lecture series, organized human rights study meetings and established a human rights week in order to enhance the political consciousness of people and encourage them to take action against human rights violations (Han'guk kitokkyo kyohoe hyŏbuihoe 1987: 18–19 and 487–497; Kim Yŏngil 1974). It also organized a human rights long march in 1974.

The committee specifically dealt with the incidents of human rights violations of "political prisoners" or those protesters who were arrested without a warrant, tortured and sent to jail without proper court procedures. It assembled information on political prisoner's cases and made it public, and it sent petitions to government authorities, urging them to stop human rights violation. In order to ensure that they receive a fair trial, the committee provided assistance in legal procedures. When they were convicted and sent to jail, the committee members visited them not only to give them moral support but also to ensure that they were properly treated. The committee also conducted what came to be known as the "Thursday prayer meetings," where the church members and prisoners' families prayed together for the safety and release of the prisoners, and expressed their criticism of the government for human rights violation (Han'guk kidokkyo sahoemunje yŏn'guwŏn 1987a: 487–497).

At the time, the church was the only public space where it was permitted to conduct prayer meetings and to make appeals to the authorities on behalf of political prisoners.

The student-church nexus gradually became a rallying point for opposition forces. Following their lead, other citizens subsequently protested against the authoritarian government or joined the many demonstration organized by them.

On many occasions, university professors issued public statements criticizing undemocratic actions of the government and the harsh treatment of opponents, including demonstrating students, by police and intelligence forces. Newspapers reporters demanded the freedom of the press by staging sit-ins, work stoppages, urging the withdrawal of secret agents from the press building. Some dissident

184 *Democratization*

lawyers formed the Lawyers Group for Democracy and devoted themselves to the defense of "democracy fighters," earning the label of human rights lawyers. The poet Kim Chi-ha published a poem calling larger enterprise owners, cabinet ministers and vice-ministers, National Assembly members, high-level bureaucrats and military stars the "five enemies" of the people. He was jailed on the grounds that he violated the anti-communism law, and the magazine *Sasanggye* (The World of Ideas), in which the poem appeared, was closed down by the government.

The opposition forces thus formed continued until the end of Chun's regime, culminating in the aforementioned June Struggle. It began with the news about the torture death of the undongkwŏn student Pak Chongch'ŏl of Seoul National University in April 1987 – the event the government unsuccessfully tried to cover up by making it look as an accident occurred in the investigation process. Public anger was aroused and large-scale demonstrations took place throughout the country in protest against government and continued until June. Demonstrators demanded explanation for Park's death and return to democracy through constitutional amendment. In response, Chun in April issued a statement saying that he will retire at the end of his term and find a successor through the existing selection process – i.e., the electoral colleges. He stressed that given the fact that Korea was to host the World Olympic Game in the following year it was not the time to talk about constitutional amendment. Chun thought that people would understand his reasoning for protecting the current constitution – the decision called the 4.3 Constitution Protection Measure – and delaying the discussion of constitutional amendment. The public reacted with mass protest. The protest became further fuelled by another death of student Yi Hanyŏl, Yonsei University student, who was hit by a tear-gas bomb shot by the police in a demonstration and died later in the hospital. Nationwide demonstration organized by the People's Movement headquarters began June 10 and continued for the next nine days during which more than a million citizens participated. It became apparent to the government the protest was not going to stop. On June 29, 1987, Chun's heir apparent, Roh Tae Woo, staged a quiet coup within the ruling party, accepted the opposition New Democratic Party's demands for constitutional revision and direct presidential election and further promised democratic reforms – the promise known as the June Twenty-Ninth Declaration, which marked the point of return to democracy.

Personalism and Political Opposition – The rise of administrative despotism described earlier was attributed to the personalist ethic that provided a moral justification to those administrators for personalizing the government process. How then, in this personalist society, did the democratic ideal find such a strong following, so much so that in the end the opposition forces prevailed? There is no doubt that the two dissident groups, student and church leaders, and those who joined them, came to value the virtues of the democratic political philosophy and institutions, committed themselves to them and were determined to fight for them. This process of democratization as a struggle for an ideology has now been well documented. What is not well known, however, is how this process actually came

Democratization   185

about and survived the harsh government repression. Was it merely ideology that drew the students to the movement and sustained them? Or was there something else? We think that as a widely shared code of social conduct, the personalist ethic also played an important role here. *The International Herald Tribune* of June 21–22, 1986, carried an article which described South Korean university student activists. It reads as follows:

> Radical thought is passed on in clandestine 'study circles,' groups of students who may come from the same high school or home town or church. These study circles . . . served as the basic organizational unit for demonstrations and other protests.
>
> (Quoted in Coleman 1988: S99)

Members of a study circle, as the reporter points out, had been friends since their high school days or before and formed friendship circles or became friends at the university partly because they shared the same interests. The label "study circle" is given to the group primarily because its members read and discussed books (usually banned) of their choice in accordance with their ideological orientations and in order to establish a theoretical rationale for their involvement in radical student movements. Commitment to a radical political ideology and action is usually a group decision arrived at by mutual consultation, persuasion, encouragement and criticism within a circle of close friends. They became more united when they took political action such as engaging in street demonstrations and occupation of targeted buildings (for example, a US information office or university administration buildings) and joining factory workers or farm workers in their protest actions. When one of the circle members got into trouble with the law because of his illegal anti-government activities, others in the circle helped him find a place to hide. A student activist serving a jail term could rely on his circle friends to visit him, to provide what he needed in his cell and to fulfil his duties outside of the jail, which he could not attend to. They felt strongly obliged to help, support, encourage and protect each other in order to promote their political goal. A sense of obligation to one's friends became an effective driving force in the student movement. The same mutual help ethic facilitated and kept alive "the democracy struggle" on the side of the dissident Christian church (see Chang 2003).

The Role of the United States in Korean Democratization – In one way or another, the United States has long been closely involved in the modernization process of South Korea. What is the US contribution of the democratization project?

The American Military Provisional Government (AMPG, 1945–1948) established by General Hodge, the commander of the American force that occupied South Korea, along with the Soviet counterpart in the north first, requested Korean political leaders to form parties and then in 1946 to set up the Korean Interim Legislature Assembly as South Korea's law-making body that, as Hodge declared, "would review appointment, be a forum for free discussion, 'foster free expression by the people and . . . be a sounding board for public opinion.'" The

186 Democratization

assembly was not, however, a completely independent organization in that its decisions were to be subjected to the review and veto of the AMPG. It was to have 90 members, half-elected by people and half-appointed by township heads (Henderson 1968: 153). During the Korean War (1950–1953), the UN military forces constituted largely of American troops prevented the take-over of South Korea by the communist north, thereby saving democracy in the peninsula from distinction.

But the after the Korean War (1950–1953) the United States became more concerned with economic rehabilitation and development, political stability and national security than with democratization. The active role the United States played in helping the Korean government to implement Korea's economic development plans distinctly is contrasted by the hesitance it showed in getting involved in political affairs. Though the Kennedy administration successfully insisted that Park return to civilian rule as promised at the time of coup, when he became the president, he received full support from the United States for his commitment to the economic development, strong leadership and anti-communist stance. The United States regarded opposition parties mainly as obstacles to development efforts led by Park and had little trust in opposition leaders' ability to take over power from Park. Park Chung Hee was thought to be the only person who could successfully carry out the development projects and maintain the political stability. When Park had to make unpopular decisions such as normalization of diplomatic relation between Korea and Japan, dispatching troops to Vietnam and devaluation of the Korean currency (won), the United States readily came to his aid by sending high officials or inviting Park to the States to show its support for the Korean government or offering special aid such as grains. When the former president Yun Posŏn, the eminent opposition leader, criticized Park's plan of sending troops to Vietnam, Winthrop Brown, the US ambassador to Korea, met with him in 1965 in an effort to persuade him to change his view. Requests for such tactical help sometimes also came from the Korean government. Prime Minister Chŏng Ilgwŏn requested from Ambassador Brown that the United States send either the secretary of state or secretary of defense to "assure the Korean public of continuing deep concern and support of US leadership for the ROK government," and also arrange a trip to Vietnam by Korean journalists and lawmakers so that they "could be indoctrinated in the need for ROK forces" (Brazinsky 2007: 139).

During the 1950s and much of the 1960s, the period during which the Korean economy rapidly expanded the US government showed little concerns with, "even encouraged the Park government to strengthen itself at the expense of civil society." (Brazinsky 2007: 148). The economic growth was accompanied by excessive concentration of power in the executive branch and nurturing of the coalition of ruling elites, high-ranking bureaucrats and big businesses. Washington began to "question whether by continually siding with Park against his opposition it had enabled him to become too strong" (Brazinsky 2007: 156).

In the mid-1960s, the US Operation Mission (USOM) in South Korea and tried to find ways to strengthen democratic institutions in South Korea and to integrate broader segments of the population into the existing power structure (Brazinsky 2007: 156). Together with other American organizations in Korea such as the USAID and the Asia Foundation, the USOM provided leadership training for union administrators by organizing workshops on collective bargaining and union administrative procedures for them and arranging visits of a group of South Korean judges, attorneys and prosecutors and the National Assembly members and assembly staffers to the United States to help them gain a better understanding of how the judiciary and legislative branch functioned in a democratic society. In making such attempts to strengthen democratic institutions in Korea Americans were cautious not to undermine the regime. At least the US Embassy in Seoul maintained informal contacts with the opposition. Paul M. Cleveland, the political and military officer at the embassy between 1973 and 1977, regularly met with opposition leaders including Kim Dae Jung and Cardinal Stephen Kim. The purpose of the visits was, among other things, to "alert the Park government that Washington had an interest in the welfare of certain dissidents and would take a dim view of arbitrary measure against them" (Brazinsky 2007: 227). When informed of the kidnapping of Kim Dae Jung by the KCIA from a Tokyo hotel in August 1973, Ambassador Philip Habib immediately met with President Park Chung Hee and demanded that Kim be kept alive, thereby saving his life.

The Carter administration's foreign policy, which put utmost emphasis on human rights and his actual meeting with Park in 1979 in which he raised the issue of human rights, had little impact on his government's anti-democratic tendency. The United States, with the withdrawal of economic aid in the late 1960s, no longer had the leverage to put pressure on the Korean government to change its policy on internal politics. Furthermore, there were "lingering concerns of US top administration officials that US intervention could endanger security or stability in the Korean peninsula" (Brazinsky 2007: 229).

Democratic reforms: dissolution the authoritarian polity and the rise of civil society

Roh Tae Woo's announcement of democratic reform or the June 29 Announcement (1987) consisted of eight points: granting amnesty to the opposition party leader Kim Dae Jung and reinstating his civil rights, releasing political prisoners, facilitating a direct presidential election within a year, revising the presidential election law, replacing the infamous Basic Press Law, with a more democratic regulation, establishing local assemblies and assurance of the autonomy of the university in particular and the educational process in general, guaranteeing freedom of political parties and introducing radical social purification plans. Accepting most of the requests made by the opposition party, Roh adopted this reform as a way of unlocking the political stalemate. Furthermore, it was a way of recognizing the opposition forces and could be viewed as a step toward further reform and consolidation of democracy (see Perez-Diaz 1993: 54–107).

Election – The first thing to note in the process of de-authorizing the political system is the peaceful transition of regimes through election. It appears that current incumbents of the executive office are not likely to refuse to accept the results of presidential election if they lost to another candidate in balloting.

188 *Democratization*

The Legislature – The control of the government process by the executive branch has been considerably reduced.

The National Assembly regained the right to investigate and audit the administrative organization. Although the president is not accountable to the National Assembly, as the administrative branch is represented by his minister, disclosure of wrongdoings, corruption, and irregularities in the administration by the legislature through annual investigation and inspection is likely to be taken as a reflection on presidential leadership and hence serve as a constraint on the president (Chang 2003: 118) The president no longer has the right to disband the legislature. And the National Assembly gained the power to ratify the Prime Minister, the Chief Justice of Supreme Court, and the Chief of the Constitutional Court appointed by the president.

The president does not remain the chief of the ruling party which, as a result, enjoys a considerable degree of autonomy. He does not monopolize the power to nominate candidates for National Assembly elections. Selection of candidates nowadays is done by the party's nomination committee. Accordingly, the ruling party's lawmakers appear to act fairly freely, without following instructions or orders from above on how to vote on certain issues in the legislative assembly – even though they do (or could) not completely ignore how the president wants his or her party's vote.

Unlike in the past, it has become eminently possible for an opposition party candidate to replace an elected president and an elected president may end up with the National Assembly with the representatives of the opposition party occupying more seats than those of his or ruling party. No president now can count on the National Assembly to serve as a maid of the executive office.

Furthermore, opposition party legislators freely express their discontentment with and criticism of the way the president governs the nation and use the National Assembly as an arena for debates on the forms that democracy should take without fear of getting punished by the president later on.

The Judiciary – The president still holds considerable control over the judiciary branch because of his or her right to appoint high officials, but the executive office does not or could not directly instruct the court on how to deal with the "crime" of opponents of the government as his or her authoritarian predecessor did.

Furthermore, the judiciary branch became more powerful with the revival of the Constitutional Court (CC) in 1988,[9] the main goal of which is to enhance the authority of the constitution, to assure basic human rights and to promote the ideas and values of the constitution, thereby providing a firm basis for peaceful integration of the nation.

Functionally, it purports to (1) judge the constitutionality of current laws, the legitimacy of which is questioned by individuals and groups; (2) rule whether impeaching high-ranking government officials indicted by the National Assembly is legitimate; (3) determine dissolution of political parties on the basis of their activities considered to be running counter to the constitutional order; (4) resolve disputes between the central government and the local government on the boundary of their respective administrative power; and (5) judge appeals brought by individuals or groups whose basic rights have been violated by the action or inaction of the state.

As of 2007, the CC has dealt with 635 out 787 cases of the constitutionality of laws, one impeachment case, one political party dissolution case, 62 out of 77 cases of disputes on the boundaries of administrative power and 20,478 out of 21,844 cases of civilian appeals of human rights violation (Wiki Korea Encyclopaedia). One notable decision was made in 2017. It ruled eight to zero that President Park Geun Hye be dismissed five months after the National Assembly impeached her.

Yet another big step that the government took toward promoting constitutionalism occurred in 2001 when the National Human Rights Committee (NHRC) was born. Like the CC, the NHRC has its major aim to "protect and promote human rights." But unlike the CC, which examines the constitutionality of specific laws, the NHRC directly deals with human rights violation appeals brought to them and offers relief measures. The NHRC's main functions are (1) to investigate the legal system relating to matters concerning human rights and offer reform measures, (2) to investigate and solve the cases of human rights violations experienced not only by Koreans but also foreigners residing in Korea and (3) to educate the public to enhance consciousness of human rights and disseminate human rights culture.

The establishment of the NHRC was well received by those people who did not know where to go when they suffered human rights violations. During its first 5 years, the NHRC received 21,598 appeals, 80 percent of which were classified as cases of human right violations, 12 percent as cases of discrimination, and the remainder as cases requiring legal or institutional reforms (Im Chibong 1993).

It recommended abolition of the National Security Law, which had been widely abused by the intelligence agencies, violating human rights of the political prisoners or "prisoners of conscience" for opposing the authoritarian government and the death penalty. It also recommended that an alternative to military service be introduced so that the constitutional right to object to military service and the duty of military service could coexist harmoniously. Their recommendations, however, were not made into laws. Perhaps, they were of too radical nature to many people.

The Regional Self-Government – Another notable change was the reinstatement of the local self-government system. Local residents now formed their own government by electing the governors, mayors, representatives and superintendents of educational affairs.

The autonomy of the local government, however, is still very much restricted. The regional government is not financially self-sufficient in that the regional tax revenue constitutes only 50 percent of its annual budget. It does not have the right to legislate its own acts and laws applicable to its own residents proper. Since a candidate for local government assembly is determined by his party, any assembly member who wishes to run again in the next election tends to remain as a loyal party member rather than acting as an independent lawmaker.

Nonetheless, many local self-governments make use of the limited autonomy in criticizing central government policies that they consider to be indifferent to or

190　*Democratization*

to undermine the interests of the regions they represent and in initiating various projects for regional developments In 2017, some of them even openly demanded President Park step down, as she, in their opinion, was unfit to govern the nation. The civil society is also going through democratic transformations in various ways.

Mass Media –The media now enjoys considerable freedom of the press. The government or the Ministry of Culture, Sports and Tourism does not openly instruct the media as to how news should be reported. Those intelligence agents and private clothed police officers that had been stationed at their office building have moved out. Most notably, criticism of the president for his policy and personal matters is not a taboo now. As will be discussed next, the post-Roh era witnessed the proliferation of digital newspapers with ordinary citizens freely commenting on the media content and sometimes in the news making itself.

Since Roh Moo Hyun assumed power in 2003, "subjecting the president to direct criticism and evaluation is not an exceptional thing any more" (Yi Chunŭng 2011: 374). According to one reporter who used to report on the Blue House, "In old days it took a great courage to write an article on the president. But during the Roh Moo Hyun administration one did not feel burdened in doing so" (quoted in Yi Chunŭng 2011: 374). Yi Chunŭng puts it another way:

> In the past even if the presidents made mistakes the media usually blamed his aides for them but it became a common practice to directly hold the president responsible for them from the time of the Roh (Moo Hyun) administration.
>
> (2011: 374)

Every move the president makes is subject to thorough scrutiny. The president is no longer a sacred being, as was the case during the authoritarian eras (Chŏng Chisŏng 2005).

Another notable change in the post-1987 media world is the birth of the *Hankyoreh Daily*. The Roh Tae Woo announcement that promised the maximum guarantee of press freedom lifted the legal restrictions on founding a new newspaper. Those reporters expelled from the two major dailies in the 1980s, *dong-A* and *Chosun*, immediately seized the opportunity opened up by the announcement and began planning to create "a newspaper for the people," an alternative to the existing "establishment media" – i.e., *Chosun, dong-A* and *Joongang* – that more or less served as spokesmen for the past authoritarian and conservative governments and big business enterprises. In August 1987, two hundred expelled reporters first formed a preparatory committee and chipped in 500,000 won each to establish the seed money (100 million won) for founding the paper. They then started selling stocks to ordinary citizens – 5,000 Won per unit – to create the total 5 billion Won needed for founding it. The idea behind such a fundraising project was "to institutionally guarantee the independence from the power and capital." The goal was reached by February 25 the next year. With the editorial committee consisting of expelled reporters, the first edition of *Hankyoreh* was printed.

With the publication of the *Hankyoreh*, a newspaper for the people founded by the people was born for the first time in Korean history, and clear lines came

Democratization   191

to be drawn between the newspapers friendly to, critical of and neutral to the government.

Netizens in the Cyberspace – The emergence of the pro- and anti-establishment newspaper was followed by the births of numerous digital newspapers such as *OhmyNews, Pressian* and *Media'onŭl*, and Internet broadcasting such as Newstapa and TV Chosun.

Anybody who has access to a computer can participate freely in cyberspace (Internet world); interact with other participants; form a club, group, or association; and discuss almost anything without identifying who they are. Cyberspace participants or netizens (citizens who use the Internet) are free, equal and anonymous. This is not a form of social interaction to which personalistic Koreans are accustomed. But cyberspace became a useful outlet for those interested in political affairs to express their opinions or criticisms and suggest reform measures. Koreans, especially younger ones, are increasingly becoming active cyberspace political actors. Cyberspace is rapidly emerging as a new political arena or public sphere in the Habermasian sense. "Netizens," those who participate in cyberspace, have proven themselves to be a powerful political group in recent years. It is widely recognized that Roh Moo Hyun's victory in the 2002 presidential election was largely due to the successful mobilization of voters through the Internet campaign by NOSAMO (No Muhyŏn'ŭl sarang hanŭn mo'im), the Internet group formed in 2000 by those people who "love" and felt sympathy for Roh Moo Hyun.

Many ordinary citizens in cyberspace are actively participating in the national politics as concerned political actors, becoming a formidable collective political force. The political establishment can no longer ignore the importance of cyberspace politics. Political parties are now trying to bring it into institutional politics. In an effort to coalesce netizen supporters, the Grand National Party (GNP Hannaradang) established "the Hannara Digital Propulsion Planning Committee," created the "Cyber Spokesgroup" and installed a corner entitled "Net-Pd" on the GNP home page. The Our Open Party decided to create an E-Party in cyberspace and invite netizens to join it as fee-paying members to whom membership cards would be issued, established an electronic political party committee, created online cafes that would function as district parties, and discussed the possibility of assigning a candidate to represent it in the next National Assembly election. In addition, the OOP inaugurated a netizen supporters group under the title "Together with People" in order to broaden the support base and appointed a well-known movie actor as its president. This move is interpreted as a strategy to embrace the experience and personnel resource of NOSAMO and a plan to utilize it as an arena for the politics of livelihood (*saenghwal chongch'i*) (*Han'guk NGO sinmun* 2004: 1–24).

In 2011, the CC ruled that the election law banning Internet election campaigning during the period of 180 days before election day was illegal on the grounds that doing so is "too restrictive of people's basic rights," and "prohibiting expression of opinions supporting or opposing a certain party is blocking criticism by people, thereby weakening the ideological basis of representative democracy,

192 *Democratization*

namely party politics." It then added, "the Internet is a political space which anybody can have access cheaply and lower the election campaign expenses" (Hankyoreh sinmun 2011–12–29).

The University – External surveillance by the police and intelligent agents has
also been removed from the university campus. Like the media people, university
employees and students enjoy the freedom of expression, can criticize the president and his or her administration. Perhaps, the most notable change is that both
students and faculty now can freely read Marxist literature.

The ban on reading and owning Marxist literature was lifted after the Roh Tae
Woo's Democratization Declaration. In 1989, *Capital, Volume One* by Marx was
newly translated into Korean in five volumes by the economist Kim Suhaeng of
Seoul National University. Many scholars now use Marxist theories in their analysis of the "ills" of the capitalist Korean society. Some of them openly identify
themselves as Marxist scholars. In 2003, Marxist scholars held the first international Marx Communale in Seoul. The prospectus of the communale formation
sates,

> All the progressive ideas do not convert to Marxist ideas. But it cannot be
> denied that Marxist ideas are the cornerstones of progressive ideas. In the
> wake of the intensification of contradictions of global capitalization and the
> deepening of social inequalities with the domination of the society by neo-
> liberalism and the massive production of global environmental crisis one may
> say the implications of Marx for the present age are the more great.
>
> (*Ohmynews* 2003–03–05)

Kim Suhaeng, a member of the organizing committee, was more specific about
the aim of the communale:

> In the 1980s Korean academics and student activists imported distorted
> socialism through Soviet Union and North Korea and there was no self-
> criticism of it since the fall of the Soviet Union. We will make this Marx
> Communale into a true arena of debate in search of a practical solution.
>
> (*Ohmynews* 2003–03–05)

It is clear that Marxist scholars try to bring back Marxism as a serious legitimate subject in scholarly discourse and offer a new model for a good society, an
alternative to the current capitalist one. Those scholars informed of the Marxist
literature had been critical of the North Korean version of socialism and Chuch'e
ideology by Kim Ilsung, which a segment of the student movement-circle group
advocated.

The student movement continued in the post-Chun period but with different
focuses. It became so radicalized and often violent that it began to lose support
from non-movement-circle students and the public. What happened to the student
movement after democracy returned needs to be discussed in some detail.

Democratization 193

The Chun announcement of the "Preserve the Constitution (Yushin) Decision" in April 1987 more or less forced student activists to concentrate on preventing Chun from carrying it out in collaboration with other democratization movement forces. In other words, the three-*min* struggle turned into a one min (democratization) struggle. Now that democracy is formally back with Roh Tae Woo's June 29 Democratization Declaration, the student movement has become a two-*min* – minjok (nation) and minjung (people) – struggle.

The undongkwŏn students, however, were sharply divided into two groups, NL (National Liberation) and CA (Constitutional Assembly), which later regrouped itself into PD (Popular Democracy). The former almost exclusively concentrated on achieving the independence and unification of the nation, whereas the latter focused on forming a working-class party and establishing a socialist society through the people's revolution.

Though the NL group did not abandon their anti-American sentiments, many of the NL members – some say, the majority – went one step further. They found that North Korea firmly maintained its independence from the Soviet Union and China and their leaders have the long history of fighting against the imperialist force, representing the spirit of self-reliance. Though they initially followed the Marxist-Leninist philosophy, they eventually developed their own line of principle, Kim Ilsung'ism or Chuch'e, ideas that guided their struggle against imperialism and served as the philosophical foundation of the Democratic People's Republic of Korea.[10]

They defended the north's manufacturing and testing of nuclear bombs as an inevitable act of self-defense under the threat of invasion from South Korea and the United States, and even took pride in the fact that North Korea was emerging as a nuclear power in the world.

Defying the National Security Law, the NL faction openly tried to establish contacts with the north. In 1988, one candidate for the chair of the National Student Self-Government proposed in his campaign speech entitled "Open Letter to the Students at the Kim Ilsung University" that students of both North and South do a pilgrim march together across the peninsula and students of both Seoul National University and Kim Ilsung University hold a sports event. In the same year, another student at the meeting commemorating the Kwangju student uprising held at the Myŏngdong Cathedral chanted "joint holding of Olympic," "expel American imperialists" and "fatherland unification" and killed himself by cutting his belly.

The National Council of University Student Representatives – controlled by the NL group – also formed the June 10 South and North Koreans Student Meeting and attempted twice to hold a meeting with North Korean students. The government blocked these attempts. In the latter half of 1988, the NL faction carried out the south-north joint holding of an Olympic campaign as a step toward unification. In 1989, it dispatched a student representative to the Thirteenth World Student Festival held in P'yŏngyang for the first time since the partition in 1948.

194　*Democratization*

Some NL faction members exchanged letters with North Korean students through fax. Listening to and recording the north's "Save the Nation" for the purpose of getting informed about current affairs in the north became a regular practice of this faction.

Meanwhile, the PD group became sharply critical of NL's adopting the North as a model for a new society, basing its movement on the Kim Ilsung's Chuch'e idea and following instructions from the Korean Labour Party and the Korean National Democratic Front of the North. They focused more on the issue of deepening class division resulting from the maturing capitalist economy.

They held that the capitalist class or bourgeoisies dominates the society, exploiting the working class or proletariat in pursuit of profits; hence, wealth is concentrated in the hands of a small group of top corporate business elites and the majority of the workers suffer from poverty and other forms of plight. In their views, liberation of the working class from the dominant capitalist class or proletarian revolution and establishment of an egalitarian socialist society is the urgent task that the student movement should undertake. Accordingly, they adopted the Marxist-Leninist theory of revolution as the guiding principle for their movement and the Soviet Union as the model to follow.

They largely concentrated on organizing workers into a collective political force, educating them to develop a working-class consciousness and forming a workers' party to lead a socialist revolution. Some of them advocated an armed revolt to overthrow Chun's 'fascist' regime and to build a socialist society (Ko Wŏn 2013: 117). Unlike the NL group, the PD group was extensively engaged in discourses on Marxist theories on class conflict and socialist revolution to establish firm ideological bases for their movement plans.

The student movement – much of what they did was unlawful – led by the NL and PD group, however, was short-lived after 1987. With the fall of the Socialist Bloc, the undongkwon students came to have doubts about the socialist-oriented movement for which the Soviet Union served as the model.

Moreover, the radicalization of the movement – leftist (socialist) and pro-north leanings, the rise of anti-Americanism and the violent nature of street demonstrations – alienated a large portion of the general public and student population.

The political climate of the college campus also changed after democratic transition began in 1987. It appears to be the case to many observers that students these days are more concerned with the problems they have to face individually than with social issues such as paying ever-increasing tuition, preparing for future careers, academic achievements, going abroad to improve their command of English or other foreign languages and leisure-time activities. But others maintain that many students are still holding onto the tradition established during the authoritarian period of devoting themselves to promoting public causes or siding with the poor and weak. They are actively participating in campus politics, addressing various issues within university organization, including school fees, student welfare within university organization, student rights, student participation in the university administration and sexual harassment of female students by male counterparts, and insist that the Student Self-Government address these issues. They also began to pay attention to larger issues such as fair elections (presidential, parliamentarian and regional), climate, environment, gender inequality and foreign workers, and some get involved in the citizen movement dealing with them (Choe Sŭngwŏn 2009: 113).

The Progressive Labour Union – The Korean Federation of Trade Union (KFTU) no longer acts as the right arm of the government, but more as an independent representative of the labour force. In 1994, the KFTU issued the "KFTU Development Declaration" which stated,

> Although the KFTU has continuously endeavoured to reform, there is still criticism about the autonomy and democratic character of our organization. We must prepare ourselves to carry out the historical task in the wake of changing situations surrounding the labour movement such as democratization and globalization. We will therefore pursue the four central tasks: enhancement of union autonomy, strengthening of democratic character, enhancement of moral character, and the grand solidarity of labour organization.
>
> (Quoted in Kim Chun 2001: 417)

More specifically, the Declaration mentioned that the KFTU would establish "labour unionism for the building of a democratic welfare society" as the guiding line for its movement, with an emphasis on union autonomy, participation in management and labour politics and structural reform of the capitalist economy, to promote the interest and welfare of employees. The KFTU then proposed to the National Labour Council (NLC), another national labour union federation, as yet to be officially recognized – that is, "a grand unity of labour." The NLC that had been critical of KFTU being too friendly to the government instead of protecting labour rights rejected the proposal and went on to establish the Korean Confederation of Trade Union (KCTU) in 1995, carrying out an aggressive campaign to persuade KFTU-affiliated unions to join it. More lower-level unions withdrew from the KFTU to join the NLC. The National District Union, the National Industrial Union and even some chaebŏl (conglomerate) group unions (including those at Hyundai, Kia and Daewoo) joined the KCTU. As of 1995, the KCTU had 420,000 members of 861 enterprise unions which are affiliated with 15 industrial unions and 10 district unions.

The two national labour union federations were slowly emerging as the representatives of enterprise union workers to the state and their employers. Both the KFTU and KCTU protested against the "nalch'iki" (snatching) passage of the "Labour Relation Law" bill[11] by the National Assembly under pressure from the Kim Young Sam government by separately organizing the first general strikes after Liberation, which lasted two months (December 26, 1996– February 28, 1997). Leaders of both ruling and opposition parties finally agreed to revoke the bill and came up with a new one, drafted by the latter and revised by the former, which the National Assembly passed. The new bill made it possible for selected categories of workers to belong to more than one upper level union (but not allowing teachers and civil servants to unionize themselves), limited the condition of

196 *Democratization*

dismissal of redundant labour to "acute management reasons", and prohibited workers to demand payment when they are fully engaged in union work and/or they are staging strikes (the decision based on the no work, no payment principle) (Cho Hyo Rae 2001: 505). Labour unions at the national level now participate in the national politics of labour law making as an independent power.

At the same time, the two unions came to be actively involved in labour management relations. Enterprise unions are increasingly delegating them to undertake collective bargaining with the employers for them. In the past, such joint collective bargaining method was confined largely to the textile, rubber, mining and transportation industries, but in 1993, it spread to the public sector and banking industries. Consequently, corporate employers tend to avoid direct confrontation with unionized regular workers and give them much of what they demand, except for the right to participate in enterprise management. Also to be noted are the changing causes of labour disputes. With the increase in wage levels, the focus of collective bargaining shifted to the improvement of working conditions (40 hours per week); the reduction of wage differentials by gender, type of work and educational level; the establishment of welfare funds within the company; and participation of employees in management. The involvement of upper-level unions in collective bargaining at the enterprise level appears to be closely linked with the new measures adopted by corporate employers in dealing with labour disputes. Instead of using physical force to suppress employees' demands, employers rely increasingly on taking legal action against the union, demanding compensation for damage caused by strikes and work stoppages, disciplinary punishment, dismissal and restraining union officials. (This section was based on Chang 2009: 110–111).

Another notable change in the national labour union federations is unionization of schoolteachers and civil servant. In 1999, the National Trade Union of Teachers, which was established with kindergarten, primary and secondary school teachers as members, officially recognized in 1999. In 2002, the National Union of Civil Servants was formed.

The Birth of the Progressive Democratic Workers Party – More importantly, in 1997 KCTU leaders formed a labour party, the People Victory 21, in cooperation with other labour leaders. The main objective of the party was to organize the workers, farmers and small- and medium-sized enterprise owners into a political force and build a new economic system in which they themselves will become main agents instead of the conglomerates (chaebŏl). But the immediate concern was to produce a labour candidate for the coming presidential election. Kwŏn Yŏng'gil as the People Victory 21 candidate ran for the seventeenth presidential election in 1997 and received 1.2 percent of the total votes. In 2000, the People Victory 21 was regrouped into the Democratic Labour Party (DLP) with labour leaders representing various labour movement groups joining it. In the third regional election in 2002, two DLP candidates were elected for municipal assemblies and 11 for provincial assemblies. Later in 2004, the DLP succeeded in occupying ten seats in the National Assembly – two by elected members and eight by proportional representatives (with the 13.1 percent of electorates voting for the DLP).

Initially, the DLP began as a political party representing the interest of the working class with those student-turned-union leaders of the PD group playing a major role in founding it. But later, more political activists of the NL group joined the DLP and emerged as the dominant faction. Accordingly, it could no longer remain as an exclusively labour party. Reunification became an added goal to be achieved by the party. In fact, the DLP increasingly came to be identified as a party friendly to the north. Thus the DLP was divided into "the Equality faction" (P'yŏngdŭngp'a) devoted to the promotion of the interest of the working class and the "Self-autonomy" faction (Chajup'a) committed to reunification of two Koreas by overcoming US domination. Many of the latter faction openly advocated adopting the idea of Kim Ilsung's Chuch'e idea as the ideological foundation for reunification. They called themselves the Chusa faction. Tension between the two factions became inevitable and unmanageable. The Pyŏngdung faction in 2008 broke away from the DLP and formed the New Progressive Party.

In 2011, by way of unifying opposition parties for the National Assembly election that year, some members of the New Progressive Party (NPP) left the party to form the Unified Progressive Party with the DLP, together with another opposition party, the People's Participation Party. A year later, NPP members again withdrew from the Unified Progressive Party and established itself as the Progressive Justice Party and the Justice Party a year later. Meanwhile, the NPP became the Labour Party in 2013. The Unified Progressive Party was disbanded in 2014 as the CC ruled it a party friendly to the north.

Big Business Enterprises or Conglomerates – With democracy returned and the subsequent rise of neo-liberalism that stresses the opening of the domestic market to the outside world, the state control over business has considerably weakened.

In the past, the chaebŏl groups collectively made financial contributions to the executive office and/or the government party – as a return payment for various privileges and favours bestowed upon them by the administration – to help them to create political funds as requested by them. But they had little influence on the making of government economic policies that would affect their business.

This one-sided relation between the government and chaebŏl groups changed after the Roh Tae Woo's 1987 announcement of democratization. Ku Chagyŏng, the president of the Federation of Korean Industries (FKI), one of the five leading business associations, stated in his New Year's greeting (1988) that "the free market system based on autonomy, competition, equity and efficiency is the only way to guarantee advancement of our economic society, and the progressive social climate in which the entrepreneur's spirits of creation and innovation is respected must be established" (quoted in Kim Kiman 1988: 385). As Kim Kiman points out, what Ku meant when he stressed autonomy and the entrepreneur's spirit was that government interference with the business world should be stopped, and the popular image of entrepreneurs should be revised or improved. Ku's statement was followed by the official resolution of the FKI next year to protect and develop a free-market economy and to raise and foster the enterprise loved and trusted by the people. Less formally, selected FKI leading members met and established the

198 *Democratization*

general rule on formation and distribution of political funds It is as follows: (1) In the past, the political fund (to be raised by the business world) consisted of the formal FKI deposition and informal shady donation of individual firms. From now on, the FKI alone will be responsible for raising and distributing political funds. (2) The FKI will collect donations from each member firm in proportion to their earnings. (3) Giving of political funds thus collected will be confined to conservative parties (Kim Kiman 1988). In short, chaebŏl groups wanted to be independent of government interference and to have the right to give money to the parties they choose. Later, in 2002, the leading five business associations together made their views on political funds more clear. They announced that they plan to examine and evaluate campaign promises of each candidate for presidential election to be held in March that year. One of them further clarified their view. Cho Namhong, the vice president of the Korea Employers Association, said in a press conference, "We are going to examine and evaluate whether what each presidential candidates promise will help foster the market economy and exercise our power to influence by conveying our views to the political world or presidential candidates" (Kim Yŏngbae 2002).

With wealth they have accumulated with the help of the government, chaebŏl groups are no longer under the thumb of the executive office. The government – both conservative and progressive – now advise (or entreat) chaebŏl groups to invest in job-creating development projects and heavily rely on their expert knowledge in establishing economic policies. The late president Roh Moo Hyun at one point declared, "Power now has shifted to the market (meaning chaebŏls)."

Personalism and Korean democracy

Democratization is steadily taking root in a personalistic political climate. Confucianism is no longer the main principle of state governance (kuksi). Moreover, references to Confucianism as the moral foundation of post-Liberation Korea are nowhere to be found in the constitution, the National Charter of Education, government offices or school classrooms (Koh 1996: 195). Nor are Confucian ethics formally taught, and knowledge of the Confucian classics has long ceased to be a requirement for sitting the civil service examinations (Chang 2006: 367).

The question still remains, "How democratic is South Korea?" Or what style of democracy is emerging in Korea.

Though officially dead, Confucianism continues to survive in the guise of the personalist ethic in Korean society. I have shown in the aforementioned that the kŭndaehwa process has had only a minor impact on the utilization of personal networks. Democratic values or principles have yet to become foundations for the code of conduct among citizens, even in the public domain.

In the absence of the democratic norm of social interaction, the personalist ethic has also penetrated into democratic institutional settings. Many Koreans tend to act personalistically in public offices. Consequently, the emerging South Korean polity is not taking the same form of liberal democracy that developed in the

Democratization 199

individualistic West. The Korean democracy contains a good deal of personalistic (illiberal) elements.

I will discuss how personalistic the Korean democracy is in the remainder of this chapter.

The Central Government – The president nominates and dismisses his cabinet members or ministers at will. With the exception of the prime minister, his ministerial nomination is not subject to confirmation by the National Assembly. While an appointment to the cabinet is based on qualification, it is often regarded as a personal favour or reward for the appointee. To distribute favours to those people to whom he owes political debt, the president makes ministerial changes fairly frequently. The average term of a minister has been about one year. This brief stay in a ministerial post does not allow the incumbent to exercise whatever power the post bestows on him or her or to engage in long-term planning. Presidential control extends to the administrative bureaucracy through exercise of his power to make appointments for what are known as "key" positions (*yojik*) – one hundred or more – in the administrative bureaucracy. Ministers make appointments for other high-ranking positions within his ministry with the understanding or approval of the president or his executive assistants.

Bureaucrats are recruited into administrative offices largely through open competition at various levels through civil service examinations. As society becomes more differentiated and complex through industrialization, urbanization and globalization, administrative offices require specialized and expert knowledge. Bureaucrats build up their careers within a government office and their performance is constantly evaluated, determining how far they can move up within the government. One cannot, however, readily assume that patronage is disappearing from bureaucratic organization. Who you know is still quite important in getting appointed to a preferred position or promoted. Civil servants are like other personalist Koreans in making efforts to create and expand personal ties.

The Judiciary – The Public Prosecution Office (PPO) is generally known to have a tendency to be lenient in dealing with corrupt practices by occupants of higher offices, including the president or the president's family members or close associates, since the people they investigate are likely to be the ones determining the career promotions of their bosses. Given the fact that the head of the PPO is appointed by the president or other top-level prosecutors, investigative independence or neutrality is bound to be restrained as results of an investigation that are unfavorable to the administration will likely have negative effect on their bosses' promotion.

The PPO has acted in a similar manner when investigating giant business group leaders suspected of illegal conducts. When the PPO investigated a number of conglomerate (chaebŏl) owners for their illegal contributions to the president, it publicly expressed the following view on how it should handle the case:

> In exercising the prosecutor's authority to investigate we should take into consideration the national interest. If our investigation is prolonged it will

200 *Democratization*

have a withering effect on the psychology of investors and consumers and eventually have a significantly negative effect on the nation's economy.

(Han Insŏp 2004: 337)

If the prosecutorial system is hesitant about indicting high-level public officials and big corporate owners for their corrupt practices, the penal system appears to be equally generous to them when they are indicted for corrupt practices (Yi Hon 2010). Courts tend to be lenient in sentencing the crime of high public officials for the same reason the prosecutors are in prosecuting them. Under the current appointment, system high judges, including those of the Supreme Court, are prone to be not harsh in making rulings on the crimes of high-level public officials, especially those who are closely connected with the president.

Some judges are also like prosecutors in deploying the nationalistic defenses in court trial of conglomerates.

A paper (cited in Nodong sahoe (2003: 11, 58–61)) by a researcher at the Supreme Court written as a defense of a Supreme Court decision on a labour contract – unfriendly to the labour union – stated,

> With the arrival of the global economic order rested on infinite competition, the international competitiveness of the business enterprise (which is the basis of nation's economy) becomes the international competitiveness of the nation itself. Therefore, the loss of the international competitiveness of the business enterprise will have significant negative effects on the nation's economy; and accordingly, it is not very desirable to promote the fixed idea, "the worker should be protected above all," the idea which would prove to be a significant obstacle to the development of national economy. Establishment and maintenance of the international competitiveness of the business enterprise may no longer be overlooked or ignored. It is even more true under our economic system in which international trade carries weight to a significant degree. The prevailing dominant opinions and judicial precedents cannot avoid the criticism that they are indifferent to the realistic imperative of the need to maximize entrepreneurial activities and contrive the creation of new jobs.
>
> (2003: 59)

One should not, however, fail to realize that such formal defense of big business enterprises by the judiciary offices is followed by informal appreciation by their owners in various forms, including monetary contributions.

Ordinary people, on the other hand, do not fully trust the judicial system that it will protect their interest when they are in trouble. Those who can afford it financially seek special informal legal service. They go after those lawyers who were formerly prosecutors or judges because of the practice known as *chonkwanye'u*. It literally means that public officials treat former (retired) officials with courtesy. It has been a long-established tradition, especially in the judiciary world, that the prosecutor or judge tends not to take lightly the personal request by the lawyer

Democratization 201

who was his former colleague (more likely a senior one) for favourable consideration for his client. Accordingly, prosecutors or judges turned lawyers are known
to be more successful than other lawyers in influencing prosecutors to go easy
in investigating, thereby not arresting or indicting their clients and judges, and
if they are indicted, to give a not guilty verdict or a suspended or light sentence.

The Legislature – Apparently, National Assembly men and women also frequently personalize their legislative roles. Many lawmakers are known for their
involvement in informal acts of receiving or demanding payments from certain
groups, usually business enterprises for voting for specific legislature concerning them. When the National Assembly debates and votes on bills aimed at formulating or revising economic policies, business firms intensify their efforts to
approach lawmakers with lavish gifts. National Assembly men or women usually
do not admit that their voting behavior is in any way influenced by lobbying. But
one reporter, Hwang Üibong, points out that they prefer to serve those committees – such as the Finance Planning Committee or the Political Affairs Committee – that attract lobbyists. Hwang's assumptions are that if lobbying did not affect
lawmakers' voting behavior, then there would not be lobbying, and where there
is lobbying, it is difficult not to be affected by it (Hwang Üi-bong 1989: 246). In
some cases, lawmakers invite lobbying or bribing. A lawmaker who is a member
of a certain standing committee may request information on specific firms from
the administrative office that monitors those businesses. That office in turn alerts
the firm to the lawmaker's request and the need to take proper action. This alert is
taken as a signal for lobbying. Another lawmaker makes a public statement expos-
ing the wrongdoings of a certain firm with the expectation that the firm mentioned
would approach him to negotiate rather than pursue the matter (Yu Yŏngŭl 1989:
422). According to one ex-journalist who became a lawmaker, "If you listen to
lawmakers' statements or questions in the assembly session carefully you will
be able to discern whether they do so in the hope of receiving lobbying or not"
(Hwang Üibong 1989: 244). In some cases, a lawmaker makes a phone call to a
business firm to inquire about a shady business deal it is suspected of; the firm
usually responds by offering some form of compensation for discontinuing such
inquiries (Yu Yŏngŭl 1989: 423).

Political Parties – The political party is formed of members seeking political
careers in the National Assembly and administrative offices. They are, in general,
attracted to party leaders with notable characters, not because of the political doctrine or policy lines the party adopts, but because of personal ties – friendship,
kinship, school and regional connections, among others. The central party tends to
be divided into factions along personal allegiance, each faction usually identified
with the name of its leader. Competition for the leadership often results in a split
in the party. Rarely does a political party last more than two national or presidential elections. Personal loyalty to a leader tends to persist through the formation
of a party to its breakup (Han 1972: 133). The party leader and the faction leader
are responsible for their close followers' career promotions, a portion of campaign
expenses and, sometimes living expenses. The leader tends to be possessive of
his party and to give it a strong personal stamp. Such a tendency makes the party

202 *Democratization*

a highly centralized and hierarchical organization which is unable to develop a wider subscription among lay citizens.

Each party nominates candidates for the National Assembly and local government elections. The party nomination is largely made by the party leader with the advice of a group of high-ranking officials (mostly faction leaders). Nominations for electoral districts (chiyŏkku) or local legislative assemblies are determined by personal loyalty to the party or faction leader and the perceived provability of candidates getting elected. Nomination for the national electoral district (chŏngukku) is mostly based on one's national reputation in the case of the ruling party and, national reputation and financial contribution to the party in the case of the opposition parties.

Gaining their party's nomination is the first hurdle to go through to become a candidate for legislative assembly elections and personal loyalty to party leaders plays an important role in the process both legislative assembly men and candidates are likely to be more attentive to what party leaders think of them than what their district voters do.

An Ch'ŏlsu, one of the presidential candidates in the 2017 presidential election, found this tendency so problematic that he promised to abolish – if elected – the party nomination of the election candidate system and return the nomination right to voters.

Election – As for the election itself, the chance of each candidate getting elected is largely determined by three factors: the candidate's personal reputation, constituency service and his or her political party's popularity in the electoral district. Of the three factors, constituency service is considered the most important. Ruling party candidates, with the advantage of support from local administrative offices and better financed campaigns, tend to focus more on constituency service and establishing informal, personal, face-to-face ties with their constituents. On the other hand, opposition party candidates are more likely to make up for the disadvantages they suffer by bringing to the attention of their constituents the failures of the current regime and corruption in the government (Park 1994: 9).

There is an increasing tendency for those who do not get party nominations to leave the party and run as independent candidates. They then join the party of their choice once they get elected.

It is no exaggeration to say that many National Assembly members appear to be more concerned with re-election through cultivating cordial relationships with their constituents than with engaging in legislative activities since the latter does not appear to contribute to their re-election as much as the former. Elected officials spend inordinate amounts of time on constituency service by visiting their electoral districts, writing letters to their constituents, receiving visitors from their electoral districts, finding jobs, obtaining bank loans, securing relief funds, bringing government public projects to their electoral districts, etc. Constituency service leaves little time for legislative work. Consequently, assembly members lack the information they need for devising legislation and rely instead on administrative officials. More importantly, many of them lack the professional knowledge to intelligently evaluate the content of the budget plans prepared by the Economic Planning Board and to formulate policies.

Mention was made in the earlier discussion of the fact that citizens regained the right to choose the president through election and indeed succeeded in electing two progressive presidents, ending what had appeared to be the enduring feature of the Korean democratic political system – namely, the one-party dominance of the government or no peaceful succession of power. But we need to be aware of the fact that election is not taken by many voters as a sacred duty or citizens do not take pride in participating in the political process of public decision making. One distinctive feature of voting behavior of Koreans is that a substantial proportion of voters – said to be around 30 percent – cast ballots to those candidates from the same home town and/or province. This so-called regionalistic voting is not likely to go away. Many others consider an election as the occasion to exchange their votes for material rewards from candidates. It appears to be common practice among candidates – the National Assembly and local government – to pay voters cashes or to make cash donations to the households in their district on the occasion of a birth, death and wedding in the family, or entertain or arrange sightseeing in anticipation of voters voting for them. They often pay those who could mobilize voters to vote for them, such as village headmen, chiefs of civic groups such as the Women's Club or the "men of wide foot (matangbal)." Or well-connected candidates often pay those voters who attend the meeting where they deliver a speech. In some cases, they manage to give gifts to members of the election supervisory committee. Under these circumstances, those candidates who could pay more money to each voter and to more voters will have a better chance of getting elected, although it is possible that those voters receiving payment may not vote for the gift-providing candidate. During the fifteenth National Assembly election it was believed that "twenty will win, ten will lose," that is to say, if you spend two billion won you will be sure to win in the election but if you spend only one billion you will probably lose (Pak Sŏngwŏn 1996: 138). Thus money often becomes the determining factor in elections, and candidates do their best to raise campaign funds and are likely to spend more than the limit of the campaign expense imposed by election law. One source indicates that the amount of campaign expense reported to the election supervisory committee is usually one-tenth of the actual amount expended (Pak Sŏngwŏn 1996: 150). Voter buying goes with voter selling. Many voters expect to get paid for their votes by the candidates.

Personalism continues to prevail in Korean democracy. I will demonstrate in the following chapter how deeply personalism penetrated into the urban life.

Notes

1 The government in exile in China during the colonial period drafted a democratic constitution (Kim Yŏngsu 1980).
2 It is difficult to measure the extent to which this occurred but the consensus is that "tax evasion was rampant and was one major reason why the entrepreneurs who made bids under the Rhee government were put on trial by Park's military government for illicit accumulation of wealth" (Hamilton 1984: 41; Kim Taehwan 1981: 191).

204   Democratization

3 It should be noted that the Rhee government also tried to establish a friendly relation with the corporate sector and adopted a pro-business policy. It installed a system of tariff exemptions on both aid and non-aid financed imports to help channel imports at reduced cost to selected domestic industries and to reduce undesired competition from imports and overvalued exchange rates (Hong 1979: 45–49). It also adopted a tax system heavily centered on indirect tax rather than on direct tax. Under this system, while those in the business of making money paid the same rate of commodity taxes as those who were not, their income tax did not increase progressively with increasing income. Furthermore, the Rhee government introduced a temporary land tax system mainly aimed at farmers during the Korean War to increase tax revenue. In short, the tax system was designed to reduce the tax burden of high income and corporate groups.

4 Most of leftist newspapers were suspended by the AMG.

5 In January 1985, the MoE abolished the Student Patriotic Association and admitted students to organize their own government on campus.

6 Piundongkwon students chose not to compete against them.

7 It should be pointed out that the political climate in the Christian church community was conducive to such a movement. The arrival in the 1960s of new theology, known as secular theology, participation theology, liberation theology and people's theology, encouraged a small number of young dissident Christian leaders to critically re-examine what role the churches had played in the past, and to redefine the relation between the church and the community (see Hanguk kidokkyo sahoe munje yŏn'guwŏn 1987: 64–66; Mun Tonghwan 1974; Sŏ Namdong 1983; Ham Se'ung 1984: 1–81 and Chi Myŏng-gwan 1972; Yun Ilung 1984: 172; and K'at'ollik chŏngŭi p'yŏnghwa yŏn'guso 1990: 47–75).

8 In an interview held in Chōngju, Korea, on May 24, 1991.

9 The CC was originally instituted by the Chang Myon government in 1960, replacing the previously established Constitutional Committee, a kind of constitutional court with limited function. With the fifth amendment of the constitution, the Park Chun Hee government was abolished in 1962.

10 The gist of the Chuch'e idea propounded by the "Great Leader" Kim Ilsung, the founder of the Democratic People's Republic of Korea, is as follows: People are the masters of everything and determine everything. People are self-reliant and creative social beings. Structural conditions based on material resources such as capital and power may be important to have to change the society but, ultimately, it is the self-reliant capacity of the people that determines the success of transformative efforts. The Chuch'e idea is not, however, an individualist political principle that emphasizes individual autonomy. Those who subscribe to Kim Ilsung's idea, forming the Chuch'e faction within the NL faction, are further expected to be unconditionally loyal to the "great leader" and to be ready to follow his teachings as faithfully as they can. Only by doing so will people's self-reliant capacity be made into unified collective revolutionary force to build a truly socialist society.

11 With this law, the Kim Young Sam government intended to address the demands from employers and employees. It did away with the old provision of the "three prohibitions" – prohibition of third-party intervention, of plural unions and of unions' political activities – but it also allowed employers to introduce the system of dismissal of redundant labour and flexible work schedules. The bill, however, stipulated the formation of plural unions at the national level could not begin until 2003, and at the enterprise level until 2002, while employers were allowed to go ahead with dismissing redundant workers, as this was necessitated by urgent management problems such as a continuing deterioration of business, the need of structural adjustments to improve productivity, technological innovation and changing the production line. The implication of this stipulation became immediately clear to the unions. Formal recognition of the KCTU had to wait six more years, which meant that the government had no obligation to respond to whatever demands the KCTU made.

Democratization 205

References

Brazinsky, Gregg (2007) *Nation Building in South Korea*, Chapel Hill: University of North Carolina Press.

Chang Yun-Shik (2009) "Industrial Workers, Corporate Employers and the Government in South Korea," pp.95-117, in Chang, Yun-Shik, Seok, Hyun-ho and Baker, Donald L. (eds), *Korea Confronts Globalization*, Oxford: Routledge.

Chang, Yun-Shik (2006) "Conclusion: South Korea in Pursuit of Modernity," pp. 345–373, in Chang, Yun-Shik and Steven, Hugh Lee (eds.) *Transformations in Twentieth Century Korea*, London: Routledge.

Chang, Yun-Shik (2003) "Mutual Help and Democracy in Korea," pp. 90–123, in Bell, Daniel A. and Hahm, Chaibong (eds.) *Confucinism for the Modern World* Cambridge: Cambridge University Press.

Chi, Myŏng-gwan (1972) "Han'guk kidokkyo-ŭi sahoe ch'amyŏ" (Social Participation of Korean Christianity). *Sindong-a*, (August), pp. 77–85.

Cho, Hyorae (2001) "Nodong hwangyŏng ŭi pyŏnhwa wa nodong undong ŭi saeroun mosaek [1996–99]" (Changing Labour Environment and a New Search for Labour Movement [1996–99]), pp. 477–682, in Choe, Yŏnggi et al. (eds.). *1987 nyŏn ihu Han'guk ŭi nodong undong* (The Labor Movement in Korea since 1987), Seoul:Han'guk nodong yŏn'guwŏn.

Cho, Sŭng-Hyŏk (1981) *Tosi sanŏp sŏn'gyo ŭi sahoe ch'amyŏ* (An Understanding of the Urban Industrial Mission), Seoul: Minjugsa.

Choe, Chun (1960) *Han'guk sinmunsa* (The History of Korean Newspapers), Seoul: Inchogak.

Choe, Sŭngwon (2009) "1990nyŏndae huban haksaeng undong'ŭi wigi wa daeung- sin yuhyŏng'ŭi ch'amyŏjawa undong pyŏnhwa" (Crisis and Confrontation of the Student Movement in the Late 1990s – the New Type of Participants and Movement Change). *Sahoe yon'gu* (Study of Society), vol. 2, pp. 101–142.

Chŏn, Chisŏng (2005) "Sabŏp p'adong ŭl t'onghae pon sabŏppu ŭi kaehyŏk kwaje" (The Reform Task of the Judiciary Branch Seen through Judicial Undulation). *Wŏlgan Ch'amyŏ sahoe*, no. 936, (1 October).

Chŏng, Chinsŏk (1985) *Han'guk hyŏndae ŏllonsaron* (A Study of the History of Modern Korean Press), Seoul: Ch'onyewŏn.

Chŏng, Taesu (1983) "Yi Sŭngman kwa Pak Chŏnghŭi ŭi ŏllon t'ongjesul" (Techniques of Press Control by Syngman Rhee and Park Chung Hee), pp. 175–227, in Song, Konho and Others (eds.) *Minjung kwa chayu ŏllon* ((The People and the Free Press), Seoul: Ach'im.

Coleman, James (1988) "Social Capital in the Creation of Human Capital." *American Journal of Sociology*, vol. 94 (Supplement), pp. s95–s120.

Ham, Se'ung (1984) *Konan ŭi ttang, kŏrukkan ttang* (The Land of Pain, the Land of Glory), Seoul: Turae.

Han, Insop (2004) "Ch'oekun Han'guk Ŭi chngch'i pup'ae e taehan kŏmch'al kwa tukkom ui tochon" (Challenging Political Corruption in Korea: The Conflicting Role between the Public Prosecution and the Independent Counsel), *Pobhak* (The Legal Study), vol. 45, no. 3, pp. 332–351.

Han, Sungjoo (1980) "Student Activism: A Comparison Between the 1960 Uprising and the 1971 Protest Movement," pp. 143–16, in Kim, Chong Lim (ed.) *Political Participation in Korea: Democracy, Mobilization and Stability*, Santa Barbara: Clio Books.

Han, Y. C. (1972) "Political Parties and Elections in South Korea," pp. 127–147, in Kim Se Jim and Cho, Chang, Hyun (eds.) *Government and Politics of Korea*, Silver Spring, MD: The Research Institute on Korean Affairs.

206 *Democratization*

Han'guk chŏngch'i yŏn'guso (1988) *Tokcheja ŭi k'al* (Dicator's Sword), Seoul: Tong-gwang ch'ulp'ansa.

Han'guk kidokkyo kyohoe hyŏpŭihoe (1983) *1970 nyŏndae ŭi minjuhwa undong* (The Democratization Movement in the 1970s), 5 vols, Seoul: Han'guk kidokkyo kyohoe hyŏpŭihoe.

Han'guk sahoemunje yŏn'guwŏn (1987a) *Han'guk sahoe ŭi nodong undong t'ongje* (Labour Control in Korean Society), Seoul: Minjungsa.

Han'guk sahoemunje yŏn'guwŏn (1987b) *Minjung ŭi him, minjung ŭi kyohoeŏ* (People's Power, People's Church), Seoul: Minjungsa

Han'guk sahoemunje yŏn'guwŏn (1983) 1970 *nyŏdae* minjuhwa undong kwa kidokkyo (The Democratization Movement in the 1970s and Christianity), Seoul: Minjungsa.

Han'guk NGO sinmun (2004) "Chŏnja chŏngdang, haeksim ŭn ch'amyŏ wa kaehyŏk" (The Electronic Party, the Essence Is Participation and Reform), January 24.

Hamilton, Clive (1986) *Capitalist Industrialization in Korea*, Boulder: Westview Press.

Henderson, Gregor (1968) *Korea: The Politics of the Vortex*, Cambridge, MA: Harvard University Press.

Hong, Wontack (1979) *Trade, Distortions, and Employment Growth in Korea*, Seoul: Korea Development Institute.

Hwang, Ŭibong (1986) *80 nyŏndae ŭi haksaeng undong* (The Student Movement in the 80s), Seoul: Yejogak.

Im, Ch'aejŏng (1984) "80 nyŏndae ŭi ŏllon chŏngch'aek kwa kŭ pip'an" (The Press Policy in the 80s and Criticism of It), in Song, Kŏnho and Others (eds.) *Minjung kwa chayu ŏllon* (The People and the Free Press), Seoul: Ach'im.

Im, Chibong (1993) *Han'guksahoe'wa kukka inkwŏnwiwŏnhoe* (Korean Society and the National Human Rights Committee), Google Korea.

Kang, Sŏngch'ae. (1986) "Pak chŏngkwon kwa ŏllon tanap" (The Park Regime and Press Suppression), *Shin Dong-a*, (April), pp. 400–419.

K'at'ollik chŏngŭi p'yŏnghwa yŏn'guso (1990) *Han'guk k'at'ollik kyohoe-sowoechŭng, kŭrigo sahoeundong* (Korean Catholic Churches, the Alienated Strata, and the Social Movement), Seoul: Pitgoul ch'ulpansa.

Kim, Chinhong (1983) *Ollon tongje ŭi chŏngch'ihak* (The Politics of Press Control), Seoul: Hongsŏngsa.

Kim, Chŏngnam (2005) *Chinsil, kwangjang e sŏda* (Truth, Standing in the Public Square), Seoul: Ch'angbi.

Kim, Chongch'an (1991) *6 Konhwaguk ŏllon chojak* (The 6th Republic, Media Fabrication), Seoul: Ach'im.

Kim, Chun (2001) "Nodong undong ui songjang kwa chwajŏl" (The Growth and Regression of the Labor Movement), pp. 477–682, in Choe, Yŏnggi and Others (eds.) *1987 nyŏn ihu han'guk ŭi nodong undong* (The Labor Movement in Korea since 1987), Seoul: Han'guk nodong yon'guwon.

Kim, Hojin (1990) *Han'guk chŏngchi ch'ejeron* (A Discourse on the Korean PoliticalSystem), Seoul: Pakyŏngsa.

Kim, Kiman (1988) "Chaegye ŭi ch'unggyŏk sŏnŏn," dŏ isang <tongne buk> il su ŏpta" (The Financial World's Shocking Announcement, We Cannot Be <Neighbor's Drum> Anymore). *Shin Dong'-a*, (November), pp. 376–389.

Kim, Nakchung (1982) *Han'guk nodong undongsa* (The History of the Korean Labour Movement), Seoul: Ch'ŏngsa.

Kim, Sam'ung (1987) *Kŭmso* (The Banned Books), Seoul: Paeksan sŏtang.

Kim Sa'uk (1974) *Han'guk nodong undongsa I, II* (The History of the Korean Labour Movement I, II), Seoul: San'gyŏng munhwasa.

Kim, Taehwan (1981) "1950 nyŏndae han'guk kyongje" (Kŏrean Economy in the 1950s), pp. 157–255, in Chin, Tōkkyu et al. (eds.) *1950 Nyontae'ui insik* (Understanding the 1950s), Seoul: Han'gilsa.

Kim, Yŏngbae (2002) "Dangdanghan chaegye 'pomnal i watta'" (The Grand 'Spring Day Has Come' for the Financial World), *Hangyŏre* vol. 21, no. 400.

Kim, Yŏngil (1974) "Han'guk kidokkyo ŭi sahoe ch'amyŏ" (Social Participation of Korean Christians). *Sin Dong-a*, (December), pp. 165–197.

Kim, Yŏngsu (1980) *Taehan min'guk imsi chŏngbu hŏnbŏpnon* (On the Constitution of the Provisional Republic of Korea), Seoul: Samyŏngsa.

Kim, Yunhwan (1967) *Han'guk ŭi nodong munje yŏn'gu* (A Study of Labour Problems in Korea), Seoul: Koryŏ taehakkyo ch'ulp'ambu.

Ko, Won (2013) "1970nyŏndaewa 1980nyŏndaeŭi haksaeng undong yŏn'gu: undongŭi hyŏngmyŏngchŏk kaejowa inyŏm ŭi toehaengsŏng, ijungsŏng Ŭi dilemma – minjung, minju (PD) p'a haksaeng undong'ŭi chiphapchŏk tŭksŏng yŏn'gu" (A Study of the Student Movement in the 1970s and 1980s: Revolutionary Remodelling of the Movement, Regressive-ness of the Idea, Dilemma of the Duality – A Study of the Collectivistic Nature of the Student Movement of the People, Democracy (PD)). *Ki'ŏk kwa chŏnmang* (Memory and Prospect), vol. 29, pp. 97–137.

Koh Byong-Ik (1996) "Confucianism in Contemporary Korea," in Tu, Wei-ming (ed.) *Confucian Traditions in East Asian Modernity*, Cambridge, MA: Harvard University Press.

Lee, Namhee (2007) *The Making of Minjung: Democracy and the Politics of Representation in South Kora*, Ithaca: Cornell University Press.

Marshall, Thomas. H. (1950) *Citizenship and Social Class*, Cambridge: Cambridge University Press.

Mun, Myŏngho (1986) "Minjuhwa undong ŭi sŏngso myŏngdong sŏngdang" (The Myŏngdong Cathedral, A Sacred Site for the Democratization Movement). *ShinDong-a*, (September), pp. 502–529.

Mun, Tonghwan (1974) "Haebang sinhak kwa han'guk ŭi kidokkyo" (Liberation Theology and Christianity in Korea). *Sindong-a*, (December), pp. 135–43.

Nodong sahoe (2003) no. 11, pp. 58–61.

O Hana (2010) *Hakch'ul: 80 nyŏndae, kongjang ŭro kan taehaksaengdŭl* (Hakch'ul: Those University Students Who Went to Factory in the 80s), Seoul: Imaejin.

Oh, John Kie Chiang (1968) *Democracy on Trial*, Ithaca: Cornell University Press.

Pak, Kiryong (1986) "Sabŏpbu yakch'eron" (A Discourse on the Weakness of the Judiciary Branch). *Wŏlgan Chosun*, (April), pp. 388–401.

Pak, Songwon (1996) "Son'gŏ kwalli wiwŏnhjoe kkaji p'ago dun tonpongt'u" (The Money Envelope that even Penetrated into the Election Managegent Committee). *Sindong-a* (June), pp. 174–179.

Park, Chan Wook (1994) "Home Style in a Developing Polity: How Korean Legislators Communicate With Their Constituents." *Korea Journal*, vol. 30, no. 5 (May), pp 4–15.

Perez-Diaz, Victor M. (1993) *The Return of Civil Society: The Emergence of Democratic Spain*, Cambridge, MA: Harvard University Press.

Shin, Doh C. (1999) *Mass Politic and Culture in Democratizing Korea*, Cambridge: Cambridge University Press.

Sin Tubŏm (1979) *Han'guk nodong chongch'aeknon* (A Study of Korean Labour Policies), Seoul: Sung'ŭisa.

Sŏ, Namdong (1983) *Minjung sinhak ŭi t'amgu* (An Exploration of People's Theology), Seoul: Han'gilsa.

Song, Kŏnho (1990) *Han'guk hyondae ŏllonsa* (The History of the Modern Korean Press), Seoul: Samminsa.

208 Democratization

Song, Kŏnho (1987) *Minju ollon, minjok ollon* (Democratic Media, National Media), Seoul: Turae.

Tocqueville, Alexis De (1948) *Democracy in America Vol II*, New York: Alfred A. Knopf.

Yi, Che'o (1984) *Haebang hu han'guk haksaeng undongsa* (The History of the Student Movement After Liberation), Seoul: Hyŏngsŏngsa.

Yi, Chunūng (2011) *Chongch'ichŏk sŏltŭk ŭi silpae* (The Failure of Political Persuasion), pp. 371–405, in Kang, Wontaek and Chang, Tŏkchin (eds.) *Roh Moohyun chŏngbu'ui silchŏng* (The Misadministration of the Roh Moo Hyun Government), Seoul: Hanŭl.

Yi Hŏn (2010) "Kowi kongchikcha piri silt'ae wa kŭnjŏlch'aek" (Conditions and Measures of Elimunation of High Ranking Government Officials' Irregulariies), paper presented to the Anti-Corruption Symposium organized jointly by the National Human Right Committee and the Korean Bar Association and held on December 7, 2009.

Yi, Sang'u (1985) *Pak Chonghŭi sidae* (The Park Chung Hee Era (2)), Seoul: Chungwŏn munhwasa.

Yi, Sang'u (1987) "Yusin ch'iha kidokkyo'ŭi banch'eje undong" (The Christian Anti-establishment Movement under the Yusin Regime), pp. 155–191, in Yi, Sang'u (ed.) *Kwŏllyŏk kundan* (The Regiment of Power), Seoul: Ŏmungak.

Yi, Sŏkyŏn (2009) *Hŏnbop chŏngsin kwa han'guk ŭi pŏpchi chu'ŭi* (The Spirit of the Constitution and Korea's Legalism). A Special Lecture Delivered at Mŭnchen University.

Yi, Su'ŏn (1984) "70 nyŏndae ŭi banch'eje moksadŭl" (Anti-establishment Pastors in the 1970s). *Shin Dong-A*, (September), pp. 168–193.

Yi, T'aeho (1984) "Chedo ollon kwa minju ŏllon" (Institutional Press and Democratic Press), in Song, Kŏnho et al (eds.) *Minjung kwa chayu ŏllon* (The People and the Free Press), Seoul: Ach'im.

Yi, Wŏnbo (2005) *Han'guk nodong undongsa 100 nyŏn ŭi kirok* (The History of Labour Movement in Korea: 100 Year Record), Seoul: Han'guk nodong sahoe yon'guso.

Yu, Kyŏngsun (2015) *1980 nyŏndae, pyŏnhyŏk Ŭi sigan chŏnhwan ŭi kirok* (The 1980s, The Hour of Reform, the Record of Transformation) Seoul: Pomnal ŭi pak.

Yu, Yŏng'ŭl (1989) "Chipchung yon'gu noemul" ("An Intensive Study of Bribery") *Sin Dong-A* (September), pp. 409–423.

Yun, Ilung (1984) "Yushin chŏnggwŏn kwa chŏngŭi kuhyŏn saje dan" (The Yushin Regime and the Catholic Priest Corps for the Realization of Justice). *Shin Dong-a*, (April), pp. 194–215.

6 Urbanization and the expansion of the public domain

The democratic constitution gave birth to the citizen, and the city provided him or her with the public space in which to meet and interact with other citizens, including a large number of strangers. How well, then, have personalist Koreans adapted to the expansion of public space brought about by rapid urbanization or to the building of public institutions that regulate interaction and protect the public (collective) interests of urbanites as citizens?

Compressed economic development accompanied by a rapid Urbanization

Slow but sustained growth of the urban sector began with the port opening in 1874, which brought in foreign traders (Western and Japanese) who hired Korean labourers to unload imported goods and continued with the growth of commerce and industry, which attracted the surplus agricultural population into the cities during the colonial period. The available government registration and census material indicate that in 1919, there were 13 bu (the administrative unit with 20,000 or more inhabitants) that accounted for 3.5 percent of the total population. In 1940, the year for which the last census information on city population is available, the number of *bu*s increased to 20 with 2,818,440 inhabitants, which constituted 11.6 percent of the total population. At the end of the colonial period (1945), it was estimated that city (bu) population accounted for about 12 percent of the total population of Korea. The corresponding figure for South Korea alone would be slightly higher than 12 percent since those Koreans returning from abroad and refugees from North Korea mostly settled in the cities.

When the first economic development plan was announced in 1962, the city population (those residing in administrative units designated as si with 50,000 or more inhabitants) accounted for 39.1 percent of the total South Korean population. Half a century later, this figure increased to 90.2 percent. Korea is now one of the most urbanized countries in the world. The city has become a representative residential administrative unit replacing the rural village.

Unlike the three major modernization projects characterized by abrupt discontinuity from the past that we discussed in the previous chapters, urbanization has not come as a result of state plan or deliberate efforts by citizens. Urbanization in

210 *Urbanization and the expansion of the public domain*

South Korea is a continuing process of transition from the traditional pre-capitalist to the modern industrial city – a process facilitated by capitalist economic growth.

A city, as Louis Wirth defines it, is a relatively large, dense and permanent settlement of socially heterogeneous individuals in contrast to a rural village, which is a relatively small, dense, and permanent settlement of homogeneous individuals (Wirth 1957: 50). Changes in the demographic and ecological nature of community inevitably call forth changes in the mode of existence in the city. The consensus among early sociologists was that "Urbanization leads to a decline of primary social networks" (Smith 1979: 73) and interpersonal relations in the city tend to be transitory, superficial, anonymous and segmentary (Wirth 1957: 54). Max Horkheimer declared that personal engagement with others "remains at best a hobby, a leisure-time trifle" (quoted in Giddens 1990: 116).

Empirical studies, especially on migration, by later urban sociologists, however, demonstrated that "primary-group social relations continue to perform important social, economic, and social-psychological functions" (Smith 1979: 173). Thus, primary social networks came to be perceived more as "indicators of creative adaptation of low-income migrants to the harsh conditions of economic security" than as "signs of social stagnations" (Smith 1979: 173).

Subsequently, many sociologists came to realize that primary group is alive and well in the cities. Claude Fischer declared that city dwellers live through network (1976). Bourdieu (1986) and Coleman (1988) recognized that personal ties function as a form of capital. Mark Granovetter differentiated strong from weak personal ties of urbanities and social roles they, respectively, play in circulating information within the network (1973). Since then, social network analysis evolved into a separate sub-field in sociology. Sophisticated though they may be, what social network analysts do, however, has limited applicability for explaining the structure and dynamic of personal network system in Korea. They tend to assume that 1) network more or less has a fixed structure – strong and weak, 2) what circulates in the network is mainly information and 3) a network member does not borrow other members' network.

In Korea, the role of primary social networks in the city is not of such limited nature. As will be shown below, primary social networks spread widely into the public domain and urbanites are actively engaged in creating and expanding their personal networks beyond their neighborhood through kinship, regional, school and work organizations and other ties, recreating the kind of close face-to-face interaction that prevailed among rural village neighbors. Traditional values of intimacy and solidarity continue to be strongly held among Korea's metropolitan residents. The old habit of or passion for intimacy and solidarity persists in the urban setting, resisting the depersonalizing tendency of the city. Korea is regarded as a network society (Hattori Tamio 1992; Kim Yonghak 2003: 121; Pak Sŭnggwan 1994: 20; Yi Chaeyŏl, An Chŏngok and Song Hogŭn 2007). Furthermore, personal networks not only get linked with but also deeply penetrate into public offices and organizations. Moreover, there is insurmountable tension between the network space and the public space. Personalism that governs the personal network space poses great obstacles to constitutionalism in establishing

Urbanization and the expansion of the public domain 211

itself as the moral principle guiding social interactions of citizens in the public space. More often than not, the former provides rationale or justification for violating rules and regulations in the public domain.

Networking in cities

This chapter demonstrates how widely personal networks are established in cities, how actively networking efforts are made, what effects they have on social interactions in the public domain.

Kinship Ties – Kinship ties, despite, or perhaps because of the decline of the extended family system and abolition of status distinction, continued to be valued by Koreans. Residential mobility in the wake of rapid urbanization dispersed members or households of the same name and the same bon[1] villages (tongjokch'on) and clusters, mostly of yangban aristocratic backgrounds, into various cities. Residential mobility, however, did not destroy kinship ties. Many urban Koreans continue to think kinship solidarity is good in itself and find it useful in pursuing practical goals – job seeking or career promotion – in the urban world.

Now those same names and same bon families scattered into various places divided into numerous p'a are forming lineage solidarity groups variously called chongch'inhoe, chongmunhoe, chonghoe, hwasuhoe, taechonghoe, tongchonghoe and tedongchongyakwon.[2] Efforts to form and expand chonch'inhoe (I will use this term to represent other titles of lineage solidarity groups) are widespread these days, and different surnames and bon groups are competing against one another in doing so. The size of chong'chinhoe groups varies widely. A large chong'ch'inhoe may have a half million registered members. These lineage solidarity groups have replaced small same surname and bon village communities.

The main purpose of forming chongch'inhoe is to promote clan unity and to maintain the family root or old yangban identity by remembering their ancestors and carrying on the family traditions built over generations. The home page operated by Chinyang Ha chongch'inhoe, for example, reminds its members of what one of their ancestors said about the importance of remembering ancestors:

> Ancestors are the lineage origin (chongwŏn) of their offspring and the roots that the offspring cannot forget. Therefore, each one should do his best to remember and revere his ancestors and embrace the noble ideal of becoming a fine person like his ancestors and try hard to become a figure to be admired by ten thousand men through big and clean action.

Many contemporary Koreans take pride in their yangban background and the accomplishments of their ancestors, and are not hesitant about identifying themselves with those eminent ancestors and differentiate themselves from other families without eminent ancestors. The old status element is still alive to the extent that their family background gives a competitive edge (even if only symbolically) and efforts will continuously be made to expand and strengthen kinship ties.

212 *Urbanization and the expansion of the public domain*

Chongch'inhoe is a nationwide organization with the headquarters located in the capital city[3] and branch offices in major cities. Each chongch'inhoe has its own office or building in Seoul, with branch offices in other cities and towns, and assets in the form of real estate, farmland and forests. Many chongch'inhoe have their own emblem, flag, song, by-laws, precepts (chonghun) and run an Internet home page that contains various sections, including its organizational chart, history, news of activities by members of public reputation, chongch'inhoe projects and events.

Unlike the munjung council, which is usually led by an elderly person of the eldest generation, the chongch'inhoe council (chonghoe) is almost always headed by a person of high social standing regardless of his age or generational standing.

The chonghoe organizes annual reverence ceremonies for the clan founder and other eminent ancestors. They are conducted at the pavilion erected at the house of the oldest grandson of the main family (chongson). There are other ancestor-related activities, including rewriting (through collection of new historical materials) the clan history (which sometimes traces back to the Three Kingdom period (BC 18–AD 918)), revising the genealogy of the entire clan (taedongbo), publishing the writings of well-known ancestors, rebuilding and beautifying the graves of selected ancestors and organizing group visits to graves the clan founder and other eminent ancestors. In addition to activities related to remembering ancestors, chongch'inhoe hosts sport events and picnics in which member families are encouraged to participate.

The chonghoe also records activities of current members of prominence such as cabinet ministers and other high-ranking officials, National Assembly men, corporate presidents, university professors and others. To ensure the continued flourishing of the clan, the chonghoe renders assistance by establishing a fellowship program for promising junior members.

Chonch'inhoe members take advantage of their linkage with prominent current members in enhancing their own social standing and count on their help when needed. At the same time, those prominent members actively participate in the chongch'inhoe activities in the hope that other members will give whatever support (vote, donation, service and others) to them when it becomes necessary.

Regional Ties – Village community solidarity also continues to flourish in cities in the form of home-town friendship societies (hyang'uhoe) based on regional ties. Those who leave home regions are likely to feel rootless or not to feel at home in another region and search for fellow home-town compatriots and form a circle of personal network or community.

The hyang'uhoe begins in a si (city) or kun (county)[4] where a sufficient number of migrants from another province or si (or kun) felt the need to create one. When migrants grew in number in a single city hyang'uhoe appeared in ku (borough, subdivisions of si) and even in dong (block, subdivisions of ku). At the same time, with the spread of hyang'uhoe activities, migrants from lower administrative districts, ŭp and myŏn (sub-county), formed hyang'uhoe. Another trend is that as hyang'uhohoe was established in various si, they were federated into provincial hyang'uhoe and national hyang'uhoe.[5] Similarly, Korean migrants in

Urbanization and the expansion of the public domain   213

a foreign country also formed hyang'uhoe in large cities (e.g., New York Yongnam Hyang'uhoe), regions (e.g., the Southern California Honam Hyang'uhoe) or countrywide (e.g., German Honam hyang'uhoe, the Philippine Honam Hyang'u hoe and others).

Whether there is a home-town friendship society in certain administrative district and what it does or can do is primarily determined by how large migrant population is in that area. If there is a sufficient number of migrants, even a village hyang'uhoe may form. Thus, hyang'uhoe formation is an ongoing process.

Each hyang'uhoe is open to all those who are natives of the area it represents. But not every migrant becomes a hyang'uhoe member or actively participates in hyang'uhoe activities. For example, of 250,000 Andong city natives estimated to be residing in the Seoul area in 2003, only 5,000 to 6,000 regularly attend Seoul Andong Hyang'uhoe Meetings (*Yongnam Ilbo* 2003–11–15). It is safe, however, to generalize that hyang'uhoe is a widely spread urban phenomenon and a substantial proportion of migrants in the cities maintain and strive to strengthen their home-town ties.

Most hyang'uhoe above the ku level have a ch'onghoe (governing council), members of which are democratically elected. Many of them have own office buildings, by-laws, organization emblems, manifestos, organization songs, flags, run home pages and publish organizational newspapers.

The ch'onghoe's job is to increase membership and encourage hyang'uhoe members to achieve its two main objectives – namely, strengthening ties among its members and their ties with the home-town. It calls a hyang'uhoe meeting annually toward the end of the year to which all members are invited to attend and informed of past year's activities and next year's plans. This formal procedure is followed by an informal recreation session intended to promote solidarity among members. The ch'onghoe constantly urges members to remember their hometown roots, help one another, take pride in what fellow home town compatriots have accomplished and help the home town to develop. It holds various events seasonally such as sport events (golf, tennis, marathon and soccer), picnics and parties to celebrate holidays together. Hyang'uhoe members indeed seek out other nearby members for help and support, and patronize their businesses. Using the Internet, they interact with members both far off and from the home-town, thereby forming a nationwide network of people in and out of the home town.

The ch'onghoe also undertakes various programs and projects by way of strengthening the ties with the home-town. It urges hyang'uhoe members to visit the home-town regularly, to buy home-town agricultural products, to help the disabled in the community or to find jobs for people in the home town, or simply to cultivate love of the home town (*aehyangsim*). It has become a normal practice for hyang'uhoe members to participate in home-town festivals and other events. The ch'onghoe often holds its annual meeting or solidarity meeting in a home province city. Group tours to home-towns are arranged for hyang'uhoe members. Creating a fellowship program to support able youths in the home town is another important hyang'uhoe program. One hyang'uhoe launched a drive to plant flowering trees on the home-town island (*Chŏnghaejin sinmun* 2007–07–30). Another

214 *Urbanization and the expansion of the public domain*

hyanguhoe tried to persuade the government to hold national as well as international events such as track-and-field meets or garden exhibitions in a home province city. Those who are well established at the national level such as cabinet ministers or National Assembly men do make efforts individually to persuade the government to construct highways to go through their home-towns or to move a division of the government organization to their home province cities.

Helping the home-town to develop can be a major official cause motivating its migrants to form a hyang'uhoe, but some home-town governments these days request the cooperation of hayng'uhoe and make deliberate efforts to expand hyang'uhoe networks. In 2012, designated as the Year to Visit the North Chŏlla Province, the North Chŏlla Province government requested Seoul Honam Hyang'ugoe to visit the home town (News 1 Korea 2012–04–04). It also signed with the All Country Honam Hyang'uhoe Presidential Group the agreement to cooperate with the home province government (hankookilbo.com 2012–03–15). The Yŏngyang County government conducted a census of Yŏngyang natives residing in other provinces in an effort to establish a nationwide network (*Kyong-buk Ilbo* 2012–05–11). In 2009, the governor of the North Ch'ungch'ong province gave a speech at the annual meeting of the All Country Ch'ungch'ong Province Hyanguhoe explaining why it is important to establish a new Sejong City in his province and asking for the help of Ch'ungch'ong migrants to do what they could for that project (*Hongju Ilbo* 2009–11–09).

Migrants from two regions, Honam and Yŏngnam, are more actively engaged in forming hyang'uhoe than migrants from other regions. The Honam migrants are most extensively organized into hyang'uhoes and active in promoting regional solidarity. The widespread anti-Honam sentiment appears to play an important role in strengthening their regional ties. The president of Ichŏn Honam Hyang'uhoe in his New Year greetings highlighted that the people from the Honam region have difficulty adjusting to the modern city and urges the hyang'uhoe members to help one another in doing so. In another case, one Honam hyang'uhoe president urged other groups to join his society in protesting against an anti-Honam remark made by a government official. According to Google Korea, Kwangju Hyang'uhoe is most active with its listing outnumbering any other group. Kwangju citizens share a collective memory of the brutal suppression by the Chun Doo Hwan government of the democracy movement in 1981. This unusual experience, together with the anti-Honam sentiment of people in the province to which Honam people migrated to, must have fostered clear solidarity among Honam migrants.

Yongnam hyang'uhoe solidarity is also strong but for different reasons. For more than two decades of the authoritarian regime, Yŏngnam people largely dominated elite worlds – government officials, administrators, military generals, corporate executives and others. They desire to retain the regional hegemony and privilege accorded to them. There is clearly nostalgia among Yŏngnam people about the heyday they enjoyed during the two decades of the Park Chung Hee reign; this is evident in the popularity of Park Geun Hye, his daughter, who eventually became the president of Korea in 2012.

Urbanization and the expansion of the public domain   215

But the solidarity of hyang'uhoe also implies mutual help and support at the personal level among members. Individual members may count on the support of other members in advancing their self-interest. Persons who intend to run for the National Assembly or the regional government tend to actively participate in their hyang'uhoe activities, even taking on managerial roles in an effort to garner their hyang'uhoe's support. The hyang'uhoe, moreover, appears to facilitate this process. For instance, the Seoul Andong Hyangu'hoe, as the sociologist Chŏng Byŏng'ŭn observes, does meet frequently, but when an election approaches, it comes up with various excuses for calling meetings and gives prominence to member candidates (Chŏng Byŏng'ŭn 2007: 267).

Likewise, some hyang'uhoe members try to establish personal connections with those influential members. Chŏng Byŏng-un quotes a hyang'uhoe official saying that many members are not very keen on participating in hyang'uhoe meetings or activities but keen on knowing about whether notable members will make their presence on such occasions (Chŏng Byŏng'ŭn 2007: 340).

School Ties – Even the public school, a modern institution, serves as a nesting ground for forming personal networks. One goes through four (formerly three) levels of school education – primary, secondary (middle school and high school) and tertiary (college and university) – and ties formed at each level continue to exist after graduation through reunions and the formation of alumni association.

At the primary school level, the alumni association is usually limited to only of those students graduated in the same year. At the secondary level, there are two types of alumni associations, one consisting of those students who graduated in a certain year and the other consisting of all the graduates. At the tertiary level, four types of alumni associations exist: one formed by class mates who entered an individual department in the same year, another by all the graduates of that department, a third by all the graduates of each faculty (liberal arts, law, commerce, engineering and so on) and a fourth by all the graduates of the university. Since primary school education is compulsory, secondary school almost universal and the majority of high school graduates are moving onto universities, many Koreans belong to alumni association at all three levels.

Additionally, school ties become the basis for high school and university graduates to form alumni associations in various cities in and out of the country – for example, the Ch'unchŏn High School Alumni Association in Pohang and the College of Nursing, Catholic University, Alumni Association in L.A. Those students who attended foreign universities also create alumni associations – for example, the Columbia University Alumni Association and the University of Michigan Alumni Association in Korea.

The initial objective of alumni association is to renew and strengthen old school ties among its members. They regularly meet, dine, picnic, play games, participate in sporting events, celebrate festive occasions and travel together. Furthermore, they exchange gifts and labour on holidays and at times of joy (such as birthdays, marriages, promotions and winning an award) and sorrow (such as accidents, divorces, deaths).

216   *Urbanization and the expansion of the public domain*

As the size of alumni association grows, it becomes more formalized. Many alumni associations have managing committees, officials who are elected by members, offices (usually provided by the alma mater),[6] by-laws and endowment funds donated by alumni and others. They also collect membership fees, run home pages, publish alumni newsletters and newspapers and compile a list of members with background information.

The managing committees of larger alumni associations such as the All Yonsei University Alumni Association, the All Seoul National University College of Engineering Alumni Association and All Kyong'gi High School Association undertake various projects as a way of paying back what they owe to their alma mater or helping alma mater to grow, including organizing visits of alma mater, launching fund-raising campaigns for construction of a new building, establishment of fellowship program and development fund.

At the same time, the managing committees are equally concerned with the promotion of alumni solidarity. They hold regular alumni meetings once or twice a year, host year-end parties, organize picnics and hiking, and sponsor *go*-tournaments and sports events. Another common practice is to collect and distribute various news through newsletters on activities and movements of members (usually those of note). News items can range from announcements of births, marriages and deaths in the family, or opening a new business enterprise, to appointments to high-level government posts or corporate executives, promotions, book publishing, and artistic performances and exhibitions. They are particularly keen to recognize alumni's individual achievements in various fields, such as those of artists, scholars, business leaders and politicians. It is a common practice for university alumni associations to give awards each year to those alumni selected as "the alumni we are proud of (*charang sŭrŏun dongmun*)" and to widely publicize and boast of having such luminaries among their alumni.

The association also eagerly promotes alumni solidarity. Each new president in his or her inaugural speech emphasizes the importance of strengthening the ties among alumni through loving, respecting, caring and helping one another. One high school association president promised to do his best to make the association play the role of creating opportunities for senior fellow alumni (*sŏnbae*) to meet fellow junior alumni (*hubae*) with whom they would like to work with ("Greetings of the 18th President of the Seoul High School Alumni Association" appeared on the association home page 2010–01–18).

Such bonding among alumni, in fact, is a widely practiced custom in Korea. As will be shown next, a highly placed senior alumnus may use his influence or authority to help a junior fellow alumnus to find a job; or a high-ranking government official may give priority to his junior fellow alumni in hiring new recruits and help him get promoted faster than others once hired. Given the role of those senior fellow alumni, it is almost natural for fellow junior alumni to try to establish personal ties with those senior alumni who could help their career. Accordingly, the alumni association plays an important role as a venue for junior fellows meeting influential senior fellows. In this regard, some alumni associations do better than others. Those associations with more accomplished alumni could do

Urbanization and the expansion of the public domain 217

more for junior members' career promotion than others with less accomplished alumni. Junior members receiving help from those senior members remain personally indebted to them and will readily give support them when it is required. Such practice of support and being supported may explain the statistical finding by the sociologist Kim Yonghak that associations tend to be more active with the increasing number of influential alumni (2003: 120).

Other Types of Group Ties – There are other forms of groups that resemble alumni associations. Those who meet and spend some time together in a group – anywhere from half a year or more – tend to form alumni-type associations after they leave the group. For example, graduates of an executive manager training course run by a major university and Judicial Training Centre continue to meet after finishing the course to maintain solidarity. Those who joined a certain government bureau in the same year or worked together for some period of time become a solidarity group and continue to meet after they moved into other positions or left the ministries and joined civilian corporate organizations (Seoul kyŏngje sinmun t'ŭkpyŏl ch'uijaeban 1992). The Christian church also has become a nest for breeding informal ties. There are also informal solidarity group like the Marine Comrade Society consisting of marines who fought in the Korean War in the same company and are proud of the tough training courses they underwent. Members of these groups meet regularly primarily for the purpose of promoting group solidarity but also help one another individually when needs arise.

All these societies formed on the basis of various ties have manifest aims of cultivating group solidarity and acting together to promote collective causes such as the development and welfare of the kin group, home town or home province, or alma mater. These groups also promote mutual help and support at the personal level among members. "Mutual help" is strongly emphasized as a virtue in the home page, newsletter, and the speech of the incoming president of any solidarity group. It stands out as an ominous objective in forming a solidarity group.

Creating new networks

As should be apparent by now, in Korea the primary social network survived as a society-wide phenomenon – not just confined to low-income groups – in the urbanization process. Furthermore, urban Koreans are eager to create more networks in various ways.

As we mentioned in Chapter 3, one of the main reasons for parents to make efforts to send their children to "prestigious" schools – at any level – is to make the right friends who could later help their sons' career. According to a survey conducted by Chui'ŏp p'otal (Employment Portal), 97.8 percent of a total of 767 office workers responded positively to the question "How important do you think management of personal ties are?" (quoted in Kim Sŭngyong 2008: 17–18). When they were asked for reasons why management of personal ties is important, 37.5 percent responded, "The help that could be received when they look for a new job or start a new business"; 19.6 percent said, "Getting help for promotion at workplace"; and 10 percent mentioned, "Making acquaintances with people

218   *Urbanization and the expansion of the public domain*

who would send donations on the occasions of wedding and/or funeral." Only 25.8 percent alluded to "affective solidarity" (Kim Sŭngyong 2008: 18).

Given the importance of building one's social network in the new urban industrial world, it seems no longer sufficient to rely on the traditional personal ties – kinship, school and home-town. Various attempts are deliberately being made to create new personal ties with others without such ties.

I already discussed the survival of the age-old practice used for forging new ties in the upper stratum of the society – namely, arranged marriage between two families in need of each other, and emergence of the new practice of business firms building ties with the people of power and influence.

Many people accept invitations to wedding or funeral from their friends and acquaintances or colleagues at workplace out of obligation engendered by personal ties. But some, especially young people, do so out of the expectation of making new acquaintances. Western-style parties where one meets strangers are also rapidly becoming fashionable (Kim Sŭngyong 2008: 20).

Breakfast meetings for managerial staff are frequently held for similar purposes. It is regarded as a must among CEOs to attend the afore mentioned high-level executive manager training course (Yang Kwang-mo 2008: 25).

Another new trend in this regard is the formation of friendship societies (tong'uhoe) by office workers (chikchang'in) doing similar kind of work or working or having worked for the same company. The former type includes such groups as KOFEN, a club formed by office workers working for branch offices of foreign business firms in Korea, Bankdajit, a club of current and retired bank workers, and Bohŏm nara, a society of insurance company employees. Example of the latter type are Kyo'uhoe (Friends of Kyobo), a friendship society of current and retired employees of the Kyobo Life Insurance Company, Samsung OB.com, a club of former executive directors of the Samsung Group, and Dae Woo Lŏbu (Daewoo Love), an association for former employees of the Daewoo Group. They are easily drawn together because they share the same work experience and become personal friends in the process of exchanging job or work-related information.

Perhaps the most notable development in networking is the formation of Internet friendship societies, variously called network communities, clubs, cafes or meetings. The Internet society invites netizens (Inter**net** citi**zens**) with varying personal backgrounds – hence varying interests and tastes and work experiences – to become members and provide an arena for them to interact by exchanging name cards, personal and other information. Networking through network communities is increasing rapidly. One network community called Kyoyuk inmaektang (Educational Network Party) has recruited 70,000 members within two years of its creation.

Forty thousand people have joined Inmaek Ŭnhaeng (Network Bank). Chikchang Inmaek Mandŭlki (Creating Workplace Network) was also able to invite 40,000 members in six months after the opening (Kim Sŭngyong 2008: 21).

Some of them organize in-person meetings or "meetups" of the members usually called *Inmaek festival* (personal network festival) (Yang Kwang-mo 2008: 55). The purpose of the festival is to provide opportunities for members to listen to a lecture by a feature speaker about networking, as well as to meet and interact

Urbanization and the expansion of the public domain 219

face-to-face with each other, exchange cards, get to know each other personally and possibly form personal ties. These events take place once a month, and each meeting usually lasts five hours (Yang Kwang-mo 2008: 55).

Another way of organizing meetings of strangers for the purpose of forming friendship networks is the open party. Parties are being held regularly by professional party organizers. Initially, a party organizer invites guests of his or her choice. One such party was attended by four guests – an engineer, a medical student, a civil servant and a member of an NGO. Each of those guests was then requested to bring a new guest among his or her friends, who would fit into the group formed, to the next party. This new breed of party is spreading rapidly among youths in their 20s and early 30s (Kim Sŭngyong 2008: 101).

As noted before, personal networks are increasingly recognized as social capital along with private property. One author claims that a transition is being made from "the age of know-how" to "the age of know-who" (Yang Kwang-mo 2008: 99). Another one says, "Ours is an age of personal network power" (Yi T'aegyu 2005: 6). Still another one predicts, "The 21st century is a war of personal network" (Chŏn Togŭn 2009: 14).

With the rising importance of personal networks, advising people on how to maintain existing personal networks and how to create new ones has become a booming business.

Research outfits on the study of networks are growing in number. They run public seminars on personal network management and organizing private clubs through the Internet, as well as hold parties for strangers to meet, interact and get acquainted.

In recent decades, numerous books have been published by self-claimed personal ties experts under titles such as *Inmaek kyŏngyŏng* (Human Ties Management), *Kwihan inmaek mandŭlgi* (Making Precious Personal Ties), *Hangugin sŏnggong ŭi chokŏn* (Conditions of Success of Koreans), *Hanguk ŭi pujainmaek* (Personal Ties of the Wealthy in Korea), *Pu rŭl purŭnŭn inmaekkwalli ŭi kisul* (Techniques of Human Ties Management that Will Bring Wealth), *Inmaek i saram ŭl umjiginda* (Personal Ties Move People) and *Sangsainmaek mandŭlgi* (Making of Personal Ties with the Superior).

While recognizing the important role of merit – inborn capacity and hard work – in career building, these personal-network experts all agree that the personal network is the key to one's success. They tell people not to be content with existing networks formed on the basis of blood, regional, school, marriage and other ties. Instead, they urge them to create as many new networks as possible and manage them effectively and scientifically, and provide techniques and methods for doing so. They also insist that one should try to make use of personal networks of one's close friends and acquaintances. One personal network expert refers to a highly successful network builder, a member of the Hay Group, a personal affairs consultant company. He is the managing officer for eight consulting groups such as Hanguk lidŏship skul (the Korean Leadership School) and Ikonomisŭtŭ yŏngu t'oronhoe (the Economist Study Group) has 1,005 names stored in his cell phone and 3,000 email addresses, and he has collected one apple boxful of business cards (Kim Sŭngyong 2008: 20).

220 *Urbanization and the expansion of the public domain*

Friendship and solidarity is not mentioned by personal network experts as a goal in itself in forming personal networks but merely as a means to sustain useful ones. Solidarity societies based on regional and school ties, as shown earlier, have the manifest aim of promoting the development of their home town and alma mater. Such function is not featured as an important aspect of networking in their business. Instrumentalization of personal networks is rapidly under way.

Formal organization and personal network

In the West, the principle of social contract is the philosophical and moral foundation for the formation of the government. In the urban industrial society, "People voluntarily cooperate to form and support a governmental agency, by implication people authorize it to impose on their respective activities," said Herbert Spencer (1960: 317). The idea behind the representative government is that the citizens rule and be ruled in turn. No one particular person stays in power indefinitely. Correspondingly, Ernest Baker said, "The theory of a contract of government is a theory that the State, in the sense of the government, is based on a contract between ruler and subjects" (1960: xii). The government that emerged with its goals so stipulated developed over a long period of time structural characteristics appropriate for attaining them. The outcome is a rational form of administrative organization known as bureaucracy. Main characteristics of bureaucracy identified Max Weber include 1) "a firmly ordered system of super- and subordination in which there is a supervision of the lower offices by the higher ones"; 2) segregation of "official activity as something distinct from the sphere of private life" 3) "entrance into an office" as "an acceptance of a specific obligation of faithful management in return for a secure existence," hence the public official's loyalty goes to the office (or impersonal and functional purpose), not to "a relationship to a person"; and 4) "the management of office based on general rules, which are more or less stable, more or less exhaustive, and which can be learned" (Weber 1946: 197–199). The bureaucracy, in essence, "approaches the complete elimination of personalized relationships and non-rational consideration (hostility, anxiety, affectual involvements, etc.)" (Merton 1957: 196). The bureaucrat in the West has been depicted as a machine-like person who strictly follows the rule without consideration of the person involved. Bureaucracy was likened by Weber to the "iron cage," which "traps individuals in systems based purely on teleological efficiency, rational calculation and control, and bureaucratization of social order as 'the polar of icy darkness'" (1994: xvi).

But formal organization, which is supposed to be impersonal and functionally specific, cannot be completely free from being personalized. Two contemporary American political scientists, Martin Landau and Russell Stout Jr. have offered a revised view. They write,

> Bureaucracies are fusions of artificially contrived and naturally developed systems. Apart from their formal properties, they are characterized by interest

Urbanization and the expansion of the public domain 221

groups, personal networks, patron, client relations, brokers, and derivative coalitions – informalities that rarely enter into the scheme of M-C designers.

(1979: 151, quoted in Johnson 1982: 55)

The degree and complexity of fusion, however, varies from country to country or from culture to culture. It is more likely to be higher and more complex in a personalist society such as Korea where the values of primordial and personal ties are more stressed than in an individualistic society where such ties are strongly valued.

As modern Korea is becoming a highly differentiated society in the wake of industrialization and urbanization, individual personal affairs are increasingly managed by formal organizations such as the government, military, corporate firms and labour union. But Korean government bureaucrats and corporate men are far from what Weber described. They don't act mechanically or strictly rationally because of the impersonal rules written in the codebook. Members sharing personal ties are bound to be drawn together and form informal personal networks, cliques or factions. Examples of such groups include the Yonsei Alumni Club in the Bank of Korea, the Koryŏ University Graduates Club in the Hyundai Group and the Seoul National University Club in the National Assembly. The tendency to form a clique among alumni goes beyond a particular workplace. The Seoul National Alumni Bankers Club, the Koryŏ University Alumni Journalist Group and Yŏnsei University Alumni Prosecutors Gathering are cases in point.

Group members interact (dining, drinking, weekend hiking, etc.) with each other more frequently than with others and tend to form identifiable factions or cliques within the office or organization. A faction or clique usually has a leader, and members of the faction identify themselves with their respective leader. Members of a faction support each other in getting promoted or transferred to a better position and in covering up misdeeds or wrongdoing. Mutual support among them extends into personal and family affairs through consultation, material aid and sharing pleasures as well as pains. They unite in expanding the size of the clique by recruiting new members sharing the same ties.

Factions or cliques within a formal group tend reproduce themselves as they effectively help people sharing personal ties with them to get recruited. As we discussed in Chapter 3, high-level government posts continue to be dominated by graduates of the three universities, Seoul National, Koryŏ and Yŏnsei.

Personal network in a formal organization is also created through appointment processes. Heads of public organizations (president, minister, university president) usually appoint people who are qualified and with whom they have personal ties (close relatives, friends, acquaintances, natives of their home town or home province, high school and university alumni) to posts considered to be "key positions" within the organization. When such candidates are not available, they appoint qualified people with whom they have no personal ties. But personal bondage spontaneously develops between them and the appointees as appointment is generally considered a personal favour, which should be returned with good performance and loyalty.

222 *Urbanization and the expansion of the public domain*

The State Public Official Act, together with the constitution, the State Organization Act and the Public Agency Management Act, authorizes the president to make appointments for more than 6,000 high-level posts – 236 posts at the deputy-minister level or above and other government officials at the third-degree rank or above. In practice, the president more or less makes direct appointments for posts down to the deputy-minister level, and approves of recommendations made by ministers and Supreme Court justices for positions below that level.

These appointees remain loyal personal confidantes and are recognized as "his or her men." Building a personal network within the office or organization one is heading is a way of fortifying one's formal authority. The power to appoint to and fire from high-level government posts gives the president enormous power to make the incumbents of those positions personally subservient and loyal to him. Indeed, almost all the presidents in the past have used this power to build a personal power basis within the government structure.

Also to be noted in this connection is so-called parachute appointment. It has long been customary for the president, cabinet ministers, provincial governors, city mayors or county chiefs directly appoint their close relatives, associates or retired high-ranking bureaucrats to top posts in state-sponsored enterprises, state-affiliated offices, various government committees and even (formerly state-owned) private enterprises.

In principle, their job is to approve or disapprove of candidates recommended by the personnel management committees of those public organizations. But it is widely known that the personnel management committees simply accept the people they appoint. The parachute appointment is another way of establishing a power basis within the administrative organization or paying back the loyal support received from their subordinates or what they personally owe to their close relatives or friends.

Top positions of public organizations are commonly considered as the place for high-ranking bureaucrats to go (or be sent) to after they retire. One source indicates that in 2002, 67.9 percent of head posts of government-affiliated organizations were occupied by retired government officials (Kim Yŏngjin 2000, quoted in Yi Chonghun 2005: 33). In fact, only 22.0 percent of public organizations have personal management committees. In other words, the majority of them do not even bother installing a personal management committee and, in the opinion of one researcher, if it exists it is a mere formality (Yi Chonghun 2005: xiv).

It is also known that presidents generally offer cash gifts – known as royal gifts (hasagŭm) – regularly to the people they appoint. This demonstration of personal attention and care strengthens both existing bonds and create new bonds with the appointees without such personal ties. This practice of cash offering was started by Park Chung Hee and made a common practice by Chun Doo Hwan and Roh Tae Woo.

As presidents, they also appeared to feel that it is necessary to give cash gifts of varying amounts to their close associates and aides and the people outside the

Urbanization and the expansion of the public domain 223

administrative office. Government party lawmaker, chiefs of local government, military commanders, high-ranking police officers and influential newspaper reporters would also receive gifts from the president on various occasions.

As party chairs, presidents considered it their responsibility to provide the ruling parties with financial support and to raise funds to supplement the election campaign costs of the party's presidential and National Assembly candidates. Each of them sent large sums of money to his party monthly to cover its operation costs and the salaries of party officials. Party officials also received bonuses on special occasions such as the New Year Day and the August Full Moon Day (August 15 by lunar calendar). When presidents made their annual visits to local party offices, they give party leaders cash gifts of certain amounts.[7]

President Chun even provided funds to the opposition party by way of pressuring it to appoint certain party members friendly to him or his party, or for inducing support for a bill submitted to the National Assembly by his administration or party. Presidential funds also covered the expenses for hiring thugs to suppress anti-government demonstrators.

It appears that cash offering became an informal ritual of presidential politics. Money was looked upon as a means of adding personal touch to the execution of official, hence impersonal, presidential tasks. Money buys personal support and loyalty from the recipient as it generates personal indebtedness and obligation to the president as a person, not merely as the incumbent of the executive office who comes and goes. Recipients of the president's personal attention readily form a buffer between the president and his opponents and critiques.

Such manner of maintaining and strengthening presidential powers has proven to be very expensive, requiring a large amount of disposable secret personal funds. One source indicates that the amount of secret funds Park Chung Hee accumulated during the nine-year period (1969–1978) with Kim Chŏngyŏm, the Blue House chief secretary, who admitted to having collected donations from corporate leaders on behalf of his boss, would be 60–70 billion won (equivalent to 500 billion won in 2012) (Pak Saeyŏl 2012–12–09). The amount collected by the next two presidents, Chun Doo Hwan and Roh Tae Woo, as estimated by the Public Prosecutors' Office in 1995 (when Kim Young Sam was president), were 950 billion won and 410 billion won, respectively (Kanghojiin 2008–10–29).[8] I will discuss later how they collected these informal political funds.

Personal linkage between the public office and the public

If public officials form personal networks within their organizations and with officials related to them, they are also under pressure to maintain personal linkages with individuals and groups outside their organizations, sharing personal ties. Furthermore, they are constantly being approached by outsiders who seek to establish informal ties in the hopes of receiving help from them in the future.

In personalist Korea, personal ties between the public agent and his friends and acquaintances are not easily impersonalized. Instead, the network formed

224   *Urbanization and the expansion of the public domain*

between the two expands as personal ties engender a sense of personal obligation to care and help one another, even though one of them is a public official.

A friend of someone who has close personal relationship with a public agent may also count on that connection when he needs a personal favor from the same agent. It is commonplace in Korea that one looks for a friend, or a friend of a friend, who can give him an introduction to the public agent in the office who could help him to get a permit or license from the office.

Those who are not personal friends or acquaintances, but connected with public agents through one of those other ties, may be differentiated from those who are without ties at all. "I graduated from the SNU (Seoul National University) in 1985," is likely to be the best way to personalize interaction with a public servant who also went to the SNU in order to get what one wants from his office. As soon as the fact that they went to the same university is known, the relationship between the two ceases to be one of the impersonal formal agent and client relationship, instead becoming a senior and junior fellow relationship (*sŏnhubae sai*). Doing homework or checking on the personal background of the public agent one is about to deal with often becomes a necessary step in dealing with the public office.

As discussed in Chapter 4, personal connection with the public agent may be bought by those who do not have one. Kim Sang-bong talks about clients looking for a lawyer who went to the same school as the presiding judge (2004: 209). It is widely believed that a lawyer's personal connection with the judge is often me important than his professional ability to defend his client (Kim Sang-bong 2004: 210). For example, a judge who twice rejected an application by an accused for bail made by an unconnected lawyer granted it when it when the application was then made by another lawyer who happened to be a fellow high school alumnus (Kim Sang-bong 2004: 210).

Public offices also get connected more directly with the general public through retired officials who then become private practitioners or lobbyists of nongovernmental organizations or private firms in the field related to their former office. It is almost customary for Supreme Court justices, judges and prosecutors to open private offices for lawyers' business in the city where they retired. Similarly, many retired tax officials also start new career as tax clerks. According to the Sabŏpkamsi 21 report issued by the People's Solidarity for Participatory Democracy, 89.9 percent of judges and prosecutors retired from the law court between 2000 and 2004 became independent lawyers (hani.co. kr 2004–10–03).

Retirees have advantages over those without official background in dealing with public agents. Though having left his job as a public agent, a retiree still has personal connections with the former colleagues in the office he retired from. In the case of judiciary officials, there is the aforementioned long-standing convention of chŏn'gwan ye'u. It is widely known that lawyers who were formerly judges or prosecutors do significantly better in acquiring favourable court decisions than those who were not. Consequently, the former tend to monopolize litigation cases and accumulate substantial personal wealth within a couple of years after retirement (Han Insŏp 1998: 166–168).

Urbanization and the expansion of the public domain 225

The possibility of retired public agents becoming private practitioners is, however, limited to a small number of professions such as prosecutors, judges and tax officials. The more common practice of post-retirement re-employment of high officials now is getting invited or scouted by groups either affiliated with the ministries to which they belonged (sanha tanch'e) or private corporate enterprises that have business relations with the offices they were part of before retirement.

Sanha tanch'e are organizations in which the government invested or provided financial support or managerial guidance. They include research institutes, corporations foundations, development institutes, committees, banks, etc. Yugwan tanch'e are private business enterprises and profit-making corporations (yŏngni pŏbin) that are related to the government. The System of Public Office Ethic specifies six types of relationships between yugwan tanch'e and government. Yugwan tanch'e either (1) conduct business for which they receive direct or indirect financial support from the government; (2) engage in business which requires government approval, permit, patent, recognition or where the mode, scale and management of production are subject to government inspection and audit; (3) engage in business directly related to the collection and levying of taxes; (4) conduct business where contracts or materials purchased require government inspection; (5) engage in business which the government directly supervises in accordance with law; or (6) conduct business that could directly influence investigations and judgments by the government regarding events with financial implications for their own firms or closely related ones.

Recently several National Assembly members reported on the basis of information collected from various ministries and lower administrative offices on numerous cases of re-employment of high-ranking officials by yugwan tanch'e after retirement. Linking or networking between the government and public/private corporations or enterprises by hiring former high-level officials is a widespread occurrence. I will cite three examples for illustration:

Forty-nine out of 60 officials above Grade 4 that retired from the Office of Prime Minister between 2008 and 2012 were offered employment by Sanha tanch'e such as Korea Consumer Agency, Korean Institute of Health and Social Affairs or private firms such as Samil Price Waterhouse Coopers, Dilloitkoria and Taepyŏngyang Law Firm (*Kyŏnggi sinmun* 2012–10–09); 72 out of 148 officials above Grade 4 that retired from the Ministry of Commerce, Industry and Energy over the five-year period from 2002 to 2007 were employed by yugwan tanch'e such as Kangwŏnland, Korea District Heating Corporation, Korea Gas Technology Corporation and Korea Energy Management Corporation (dong-A.com 2007–10–16); and 17 out of 28 high military officers retired from the Defense Acquisition Program Administration Enterprises between 2008 and 2012 went on to work at defense institutes such as Air Force Aerial Power Development Commission, Defense Agency for Technology and Quality and Agency for Defense Development and various civilian defense industry firms (*Kyŏnggi sinmun* 2012–10–09).

226   *Urbanization and the expansion of the public domain*

Re-employment of high officials is sometimes forced upon sanha tanch'e by their related government offices, a practice called "parachute personnel reshuffling" (*nakhasan insa*). Given the power and influence many top government offices have over their sanha tanch'e, the latter tend to serve as the places for high-ranking officials to go after retirement. In contrast, yugwan tanch'e compete against one another in attracting high officials retiring from related government offices.

We have already seen in Chapter 4 how actively private business firms are engaged in network building with public offices – directly as well as indirectly.

It should be apparent by now that urbanization in Korea has not been followed by the weakening of the primary social group. Instead, the role of the primary social group appears to have been strengthened in the process of urbanization. Personalist Koreans continue to live through personal networks, old and new. Moreover, the old norms of mutual help among friends and close acquaintances or the personalist ethic not only continue to prevail in the personal network space but also expanded extensively.

Urban Koreans in the public domain

How then do personalist urban Koreans interact with strangers with whom they have no personal ties or connections in the public domain? Are they prepared to revise rules of conduct to relate with strangers? How well do they as citizens cooperate with one another to promote common goods or to turn cities into communities of citizens? How willing are they to participate in community affairs or volunteer for community events or help those people unrelated to them who are poor, disabled, marginalized and alienated? In short, how civil and civic-minded are urban residents? These questions will be dealt with in the rest of this chapter.

The political scientist Torjesen writes,

> The public/political domain emerged as a separate sphere with its own morality and as a result of the development of the democratic polis or city state. . . . The notion of a public domain, of a public ethic (civility), of a public selfhood (the citizen), and the public good are valuable and important legacies of the Western political tradition.
>
> (1992: 111 and 113)

Clearly political philosophers and urban residents in the West have developed a civic way of living together in the public domain with both those to whom they are close as well as those whom are distant acquaintances or those whom they do not know (Calhoun 1992: 13). Simply put, Korea lacks this political tradition.[9] The sociologist Seol Tong-hun writes, "Korean society is saturated with disorderliness and incivility, and it is in a state of total anomie" (2004: 3). Foreign visitors who have lived long enough in Korea to observe Koreans in the public space have often pointed out their lack of manners or etiquette. The late chair of the Hyundai Group, Chŏng Chuyŏng, reminisced about what one foreign media correspondent

Urbanization and the expansion of the public domain 227

told him about his impressions of Koreans in the public sphere after a long stay in the country:

> Koreans are truly great people. They have a five thousand year-long glorious history and it is reflected in their diligent and sincere life pattern. But there is one thing that leaves to be desired. Koreans lack community (public) consciousness. He does well when he is left alone. But he does less well in public life where he breathes and lives together with a multitude of people.
>
> (1991: i)

Another visitor said, "People (Koreans) who have beautiful manners, and observe all the rules of etiquette in a family situation or a formal one, tend to be much less well-mannered in a public situation" (Smart 1977: 25). One Korean literary critic confirms these foreigners' observations stating:

> Although Koreans are affectionate and close to their friends, to strangers they are unexpectedly unfriendly and exclusive. We never greet people we don't know well. We don't make any concessions whatsoever to people we don't know. We fight easily. We are shameless. . . . Although we are so polite and affectionate to people we know well, to the general public we are completely cold and discourteous.
>
> (Lee Oyŏng 1963: 102, quoted in Smart 1977, his translation)

Equality – Strangers are, in theory, all citizens with equal rights conferred unto them by the constitution or equal human beings with natural human rights. But personalist urban Koreans often fail to treat strangers, both personally as well as institutionally, as equal human beings.

Older people often use the low form of language (banmal) in talking to younger people they meet in public places, causing unpleasant exchanges of words. Similarly, passengers often do not use the respectful language when addressing cab drivers. Adult customers rarely use the respectful language (chondaemal) when speaking to waiters in restaurants, hotels or i other service industries. The lowest form of language (haera) is the standard one used between customers and service girls at bars and lounges. Office phones are generally answered by an office errand girl/boy and callers usually do not address her/him as an adult.

The lack of common language spoken in the public sphere may be blamed for public incivility. But the traditionally held status consciousness of personalist Koreans is more likely to be the direct cause. A female newspaper reporter was once sexually harassed by a National Assembly man. When it became a public issue, he made a public apology, but with a partial justification for his behavior. He said his misconduct stemmed from the fact that he "mistakenly" thought she was a bar service girl. Serving customers at drinking places has been and is still regarded as a lowly job, and sexual harassment against these women appears to be a common practice.

There are more subtle forms of incivility based on status. If you arrive at a government office building in a chauffeur-driven car, the gate guard will not ask

228   *Urbanization and the expansion of the public domain*

you to show your identification. But if you arrive by a cab, however, the gate guard will be sure to ask you to produce your identification and leave it with him until your business there is done. The assumption the guard makes is that if you are driven by a chauffeur you must be somebody of a high social standing whose identity needs not be checked. In Seoul these days, the kind of a car one drives determines one's relative social standing.[10]

One also comes across people demanding to be treated differently from other citizens by virtue of the fact that they are themselves high-ranking or powerful government officers or closely related to someone who is; such people will insist on special treatment by saying, "Do you know who I am?" They often refuse to simply act as citizens but want others to know their social ranking and to be treated accordingly by them. The old status distinction based on occupational standing persists in modern urban Korea in a subtle form. Urban citizens tend to personalize their relations with other citizens in the public space; they are not ready to treat other citizens they meet in the public space as equal beings.

Sometimes, the rights of certain groups of people at the margins of society, such as mentally and physically disabled people, are not properly cared for by society. There are also reported cases of migrant workers and foreign brides from low-income countries, including China, the Philippines, and Bangladesh, suffering from unfair and inhumane treatment from their Korean employers and/or husbands (see Konggam 2013).[11]

Tolerance – Kim Dae Jung, the former editor-in-chief of the *Chosun Daily*, once wrote,

> The most lamentable aspect of public incivility is cursing and violence. Internet and the National Assembly is the representative arena for that. Readers' comments on articles in the Internet media are deluged with the kind of cursing and vulgar words which we learn for the first time and even wonder whether anything like that ever existed. . . . The National Assembly today is the place of anti-civility where cursing and violence frequently occurs.
>
> (Kim Dae Jung, 2009)

Disagreement between two parties on a bill under consideration may sometimes lead legislators to physical violence – e.g., shouting, fistfighting or throwing ashtrays.

Like debates in other areas, scholarly exchanges are often mired in personal attacks. Criticism of an academic paper or book does not end with the work under consideration; it frequently extends to critiques of the author's scholarly ability. Consequently, criticism of scholarly work is likely to be received by the author as a personal attack. Criticism of a noted scholar's work not only offends him but also his disciples.

Public debates taking place elsewhere, such as in the public media, law courts and public forums, have been similarly characterized. There is a wide consensus that the "debate culture" in Korea is "immature" and leaves a good deal to be desired. The most recurrent point made in the criticism of Korean debate culture is that debaters lack the courtesy to listen to the full argument of their opponents.

Urbanization and the expansion of the public domain 229

Debaters' emotion often takes over their reasoning capabilities, leading them to interrupt their debate partner. In other words, they have difficulty in separating the words uttered and the opinions expressed in debate from the debaters as persons and as such consider disagreement a personal attack. That debaters are not ready to listen to their opponents also means that they are not ready to admit the shortcomings of their argument and are not willing to revise or expand their argument. Furthermore, they are usually more concerned with criticizing or dismissing the opponent's argument than articulating their own. "In our society," said one scholar,

> the "optical angle" (sigak) of the people viewing the "of opinion" is too narrow. They do not recognize the fact that other people's thought may widen the horizon of their own. Instead they tend to develop the feeling of dislike, admonition, or abhorrence.
>
> (Hong Sehwa, 2005)

Hong Sehwa, the well-known social critic, speaks of his experience running the public forum "Debate and Discussion," which was sponsored by the *Hankyoreh* Newspaper, for three years (2002–2005). Hong commented in a table discussion held at the conclusion of the series that "the either-or mode of thinking appears to have been fixed in the mind of Koreans" and suggested that Koreans "should open their minds to the possibility that even though this is what I think . . . this may not be true" (2005). The American philosopher Bruce Ackerman similarly argued,

> somehow or other, citizens of a liberal state must learn to talk to one another in a way that enables each of them to avoid condemning their own personal morality as evil or false. Otherwise, the conversation's pragmatic point becomes pointless.
>
> (1989: 12)

The general consensus in Korea is that agreeing to disagree is yet to be accepted and the importance of disagreement is yet to be recognized in public debate.

These characteristics of Korean debate culture appear to reflect the absence of training in free and open discussion at school. Teaching is focused on memorizing information provided. Testing student knowledge is typically done via multiple-choice questions. Parents' primary concern is that their children ultimately enter university – a first-rate one, if possible – and put an emphasis on preparation for the entrance examinations. Unless debating skills were something to be tested at the entrance examination, parents would not bother to have their children develop the competency.

Students in Korea rarely raise questions about what teachers say or publish. A Korean sociologist told a French reporter, whose guest lecture to his students was followed by silence rather than by lively discussion, as is usual in France,

> In Korea it is deemed discourteous of students to ask a question in the middle of lecture by their professor or open up a debate on the topic dealt with by him. And the same is true when a foreign professor gives a lecture.
>
> (Sormant 1998)

230   *Urbanization and the expansion of the public domain*

If students rarely ask their teachers questions in the classroom, it is almost a taboo for a disciple to disagree with or criticize his or her teacher's ideas expressed in public lectures or published works. Once the author's American friend made a remark in a private group discussion, "Here in America, one's disciple is one's best critic." The same cannot be said about personalist Korea. Doing so is considered an act of disrespect of one's teacher.

Traditionally, orderly debate, discussion or criticism has not been a common feature of dialogue in a closed network as it is usually dominated by the senior person – who is either older or higher ranking – with little exchange of opinions. The Confucian norm as it was practiced in Korea did not encourage the junior to freely express his/her opinion to the senior. Filial sons or daughters or daughters-in-law are the ones who obey their parents faithfully. Children were not supposed to express opinions opposing what they were told by their parents. Responding negatively to one's parent, especially one's father, was an act of disobedience called "talking back" (maldaedap).

Law Abidingness or Respect for Law – Likewise, many Koreans who have visited foreign countries – mostly in the West – as tourists or have lived oversea have noticed and written about the differences between Koreans and foreigners' behaviors in the public. They usually point out how people in their host country keep their streets and public parks clean, patiently wait in line for their turn to purchase a theatre ticket, are kind to foreign visitors unknown to them, how efficiently the traffic police manage traffic jams, etc. Many Koreans are also impressed with foreign visitors in Korea who judiciously abide by the public rules and regulations, which Koreans easily violate.

Personalists tend to be keen on the rule of propriety in interactions with close personal ties but less sensitive to the observations of the rules of interaction with unknown and unrelated persons. In urban Korea, one's duty to abide by law as a citizen is in constant conflict with his loyalty to his close others as a person. The personalist Korean tends to deemphasize formal rules and regulations in interpersonal behaviors. According to the survey on trust conducted by the sociologist Ch'oe Hangsŏp, 60 percent of subjects (3,000) responded positively to the statement, "If you abide by the law, you are likely to suffer a loss" – "very true" (9.9 percent) and "true" (50.2 percent) – and only 6.3 percent responded negatively – "not true" (5.8 percent) and "not very true" (0.5 percent), with 30.5 percent remaining neutral. The statement, "It is still true that 'if you have money you will not be guilty of crime (you committed); if you don't, you will be'" elicited a positive response from the overwhelming majority – "very true" (36.5 percent) and "true" (49.2 percent). Negative responses accounted for only 1.8 percent – 1.5 percent not true and 0.3 percent "not very true" (2007: 81). Another study of law-abiding consciousness reports that 25.3 percent of the respondents chose the structured answer, "must abide by" to the question, "What is your thought on abiding by the law," while 74.7 percent responded "may not abide by." Only 19.9 percent of the respondents selected "the law" as an answer to the question, "What do you think is the most useful means of resolving disputes in our society now?" Answers to this question by other respondents were distributed between

Urbanization and the expansion of the public domain 231

"power" (39.6 percent), "money" (30.4 percent), "personal ties (6.3 percent), "common sense" (2.9 percent) and "others" (1 percent) (Korean Penal Policy Study Center 2000: 7, quoted in Yang Kŏn 2002: 196). Additional evidence for the tendency of personalist Koreans to put their loyalty to close others ahead of that to greater society is provided by a comparative survey on people's ethical consciousness. Oh Mansok, the political scientist, and his associates surveyed a sample of Koreans, Japanese and Americans about the statement, "Even if it is damaging to the society I will actively cooperate with my work mates if it proves to be advantageous to my workplace." They found that 71.9 percent of the Korean and 79.4 percent of the Japanese respondents answered affirmatively while 8.3 percent of Korean and 7.8 percent of Japanese respondents answered negatively to the statement. Conversely, only 3.78 percent of Americans surveyed responded positively and 85.3 percent negatively (quoted in Yang Kŏn 2002: 196–197). The same survey also found that, when presented with "If it is advantageous to me I will not oppose the construction of factory that is likely to pollute environment" 83.3 percent of Korean and 89.4 percent of Japanese respondents agreed, while 4.8 percent of Korean and 4.3 percent of Japanese respondents disagreed. Only 4.4 percent of American respondents answered positively while 85.2 percent of them negatively (quoted in Yang Kŏn 2002: 196–197).

Historically, personalist Koreans have had few occasions to acquire the norm of respecting law.

In Chosŏn Dynasty Korea, the judicial process was not separated from government administration. City mayors and district magistrates served as the judges in lawsuits brought to central and regional governments.[12] Their decisions were not subject to independent checks as there was no independent judicial branch in adjudicating laws. The judicial justice became a matter of the administrative heads' discretion. More importantly, the law was not applied equally. As mentioned earlier, during the Chosŏn period, slaves were punished more severely than people of good status or commoners for the same crimes and commoners who committed violations against slaves were punished less severely than if their crime had been against another commoner (Palais 1996: 255). The adjudication of the law was compromised by status distinction.

The law under the colonial authorities had different functions. It is generally agreed that they enacted various laws, ordinances and acts not primarily for the protection of the rights and properties of subjects of the colony but more as means to expedite their administration of the colony and suppress any acts that colonial subjects might commit aimed at returning to the independent past. Under these circumstances, violations of the law were often regarded by Koreans as acts of resistance against colonial authorities or as part of the fight for independence rather than as acts of disturbing the peace and order of the society as the colonial authorities would take them. Obedience to the repressive law was considered a pro-Japanese act. In other words, during the colonial period breaking certain laws and being sent to jail for it was legitimated on a moral basis. The colonial government differentiated the Japanese residents in Korea from Koreans. As discussed earlier, in the early part of the colonial period Korean students' primary schooling

232 *Urbanization and the expansion of the public domain*

lasted four years whereas Japanese students residing in Korea spent six years at primary school like their peers in Japan. In fact, the Japanese students in Korea were subject to the education law of Japan, not to that of the colony. There were also a an array of laws specifically enacted for the purpose of suppressing the political activities of Koreans; such laws included the Political Offender Punishment Law, the Preventive Detention Law, the Political Offender Protection and Monitoring Law, the Public Peace and Order Maintenance Law and the Press Law (Hŏ Yŏngnan 2010: 15). Koreans were also aware of colonial authorities' differential treatment of the Japanese residents in Korea and Koreans for the same crime. Their perception of the law was that not everybody were equal before the law. Under Japanese domination, the law was hardly an object of respect for Koreans.

Liberated Korea also did little to help new citizens to respect laws.

The new constitution promulgated by the Republic of Korea in 1948 prescribed the rule of law as the fundamental principle of governance. Yet, as discussed in Chapter 5 on democratization, the three authoritarian personalist presidents – Syngman Rhee, Park Chung Hee and Chun Doo Hwan – were not ready or refused to abide by it. Rhee and Park used their executive power to revise the constitution to remain in the office beyond the constitutionally prescribed two terms. They simply ignored the constitutional principle of the separation of powers by bringing the legislative and judicial branches under their control and used the judicial system as a means of suppressing critics and opponents as well as to protect supporters and friends of the regime. The judicial branch served the executive branch well in punishing opponents of the authoritarian government.

Those three authoritarian presidents with slim popular support relied heavily on "bad laws" such as the National Security Law, the Act on Assembly and Demonstration and emergency decrees to suppress those who opposed them and remain in power. In a manner similar to the colonial authorities, they used law as an instrument of governance. As many of the activities of the fighters in democracy movement were outlawed by the authoritarian regimes, it became necessary for them to break the law. Though breaking "bad laws" became a crime punishable by law, those who broke them gained moral support. Going to jail for anti-regime activities during the authoritarian period came to be regarded as a sign of courage for having stood up against undemocratic authorities that demanded people to obey the law. The question, "Should one obey a bad law?" continues to be debated by those who insist a bad law is still a law, hence it should be obeyed and those who argue that a bad law is not supposed to be obeyed.

Even after the return of democracy in 1987, the judicial system functions in such a way that it hardly helps to foster respect for the law among citizens.

Social Contract – The Sociologist Grace Goodell writes,

> It is when societies become as large and complex as states that the personalism of status interaction reaches its limits of effectiveness and begins to restrict rather than facilitate linkages, especially, linkages between strata. . . . But it is not enough to say that contract is the mode of interaction appropriate

Urbanization and the expansion of the public domain   233

to state-level societies. For participation in a state to be sustained with cumulative benefits to the society, contractual relations must replace status.

(Goodel 1980: 286)

Transition to contract from status is not, however, a natural course of societal evolution. Goodell goes on to write, "Contractual relations more appropriate for large-scale society did become institutionalized in the West and Japan during the long late agrarian period" – i.e., before the rise of capitalism (1980: 291).

A contractual relation is "a functionally specific relation in which the activities or considerations or rights and obligations or performances that are covered by the relation are precisely defined and precisely delimited" (Levy 1952: 256). In ordinary terms, contractualization is impersonalization of interpersonal relationship.

In Korea, such forms of relations were rare before the onset of capitalist industrialization. Even after the industrial urban transition, which was accompanied by a high degree of division of labour and increased functional dependence on others, including strangers, personalist Koreans displayed a strong resistance to contractualization of social interactions. Personalist Koreans are not as prepared to be impersonal in human relationships as in the pre-industrial West and Japan. Urban Koreans readily personalize contractual relationships.

The modern market in Korea, of course, is not without impersonal transactions in which one simply pays the predetermined price of goods and services. One does not bargain, for example, for goods with price tags at department stores, large stores or modern convenience stores; food at diners – including Western-style restaurants such as Macdonald's or Kentucky Fried Chicken; entrance tickets to theatres, parks and museums; fares for the bus, subway, train and taxi; stamps at the post office; new books at book stores; the use of public utilities, payphones and highway toll-gates; or hair-cuts at barbershops. Instead, one goes to a shop that offers goods and services more cheaply or discounts. Such transactions are now widespread; no haggling over the price of goods and services takes place. But there still is a good deal of negotiation between the seller and the buyer over the price on a personal level. Small- and medium -sized stores do not usually put price tags on the commodities they sell. Buyers usually don't pay what the store owners ask for these goods without trying to negotiate down the price. Sometimes the store owner offers a good at a price lower than what he originally quoted. Bargaining (hŭngjŏng) is a way of personalizing an otherwise impersonal transaction; it makes each transaction a negotiation with a particular customer.

Personalist Koreans resist living a contractual life as much as possible. Adam Smith wrote in the *Wealth of Nations*,

It is not from the benevolence of the butcher, the brewer and the baker, that we expect our dinner, but from their regard to their own interest. We address ourselves, not to their humanity, but to their self-love, and never talk to them of our necessities but of their advantages.

(Quoted in Dore 1987: 169)

234 *Urbanization and the expansion of the public domain*

This does not apply, at least not in part, to Korea. Korean buyers and sellers or patrons and clients do not readily accept Smith's advice. There is a good deal of benevolence or goodwill exchanged – disguised as it may be – between buyer – seller and patron-client.

When transactions between the same seller and buyer get repeated, the impersonal relationship transforms into a personal tie. A buyer turns into a tan'gol (steady client) to the particular seller. The word tan'gol originated from shamanistic practices but generalized to apply to other patron-client relationships. The steady client goes to his or her tan'gol tea room, tan'gol barber, tan'gol drinking place, tan'gol cook at a big restaurant, tan'gol doctor, tan'gol tailor, tan'gol shoe repairman, tan'gol shoeshiner and so on. Becoming a tan'gol is a way of building a trusting relationship which guarantees better, quicker service; removes the suspicion of getting cheated or being overcharged; and adds a personal touch to an impersonal commercial transaction. One buys an expensive bottle of imported whisky from a bar, puts one's name tag on it to keep it there and drinks a portion of it at each visit. One personalizes the doctor-patient relationship by paying extra for treatment, sending gifts regularly or playing golf together on weekends. There develops a certain feeling of obligation on the part of the tan'gol merchant to differentiate the tan'gol customer from other customers. He offers him better service, gives him a discount, and allows him to buy on credit. The tan'gol feels obligated to patronize his tan'gol merchant.

With the Labor Law enacted in 1948, the employer-employee relationship became one of contract. The Labor Law clearly differentiates it from the traditionally diffuse one of master and servant or employer and hired labour and defines its content (work to be done, skills required, employment period, pay, working conditions and insurance for industrial accidents). But as discussed earlier, employers were reluctant to abide by the specific rules. It took many years of struggle – strikes, sit-ins, refusal to work and other actions – for industrial workers to organize themselves into unions and collectively persuade employers to abide by the Labor Law and to convince the government to not get involved in labour conflict in support of employers.

More importantly, with the democratic constitution, citizens as voters elect the president and their representatives to the national and regional assemblies for the five-year terms. The elected official may be re-elected or replaced by new representatives at the next election. Elections are an example of a contract. The representative has no other way of retaining her status without relying on voters' support. Two presidents (the first and third), however, refused to abide by the constitutional rules of elections (i.e., the electoral contract) and abused their executive power to amend the constitution to allow themselves to run for election for a third term and beyond.

Personalizing Public Offices: Corruption – Personalists tend to help each other in pursuit of private or network interests, violating formal rules and regulations and sometimes demanding their friends and acquaintance do the same.

As shown earlier, gift-giving is a regular (almost institutionalized) practice closely associated with personal networks that include public officials. Though

Urbanization and the expansion of the public domain   235

gifts to public officials are usually given as an expression of goodwill intended as a way of strengthening personal ties, it is becoming increasingly difficult to differentiate gifts from bribes. When the gift is given more or less in the form of a bribe, the recipient of such a gift knows that he or she can not refuse future requests from the gift-giver for personal favours in the form of personalizing their roles or offices. Moreover, when public officials get used to receiving gifts for their services, they will expect to receive or demand payment for their services.

Widespread personal networks mediate both public officials within public organizations and public officials and the public. The prevailing personalist ethic greatly facilitates this process of personalizing public roles and offices, the practice known as corruption practices.

Personalization of public roles takes place extensively not only in administering laws but also in making and adjudicating them. The complexity of the subject prevents me from fully discussing it here. I will only briefly touch on the various types of corrupt practices, which I identified under the three headings: administrative, judicial and legislative.

i) Administrative Irregularities

a) Appropriation and Embezzlement – Act of public agents appropriating or embezzling properties and human or non-human resources in their offices for personal use or material gain.

b) Informal Service Charge – Acts of public agents charging informal fees, commonly known as "lubrication liquid (yunhwalyu)" or "express fee (kŭphaengryo)," in issuing copies of various documents to applicants such as resident certificates (kŏju jŭngmyŏng), family registers (hojŏk tŭngbon) and court proceeding records or assigning telephone numbers or for catching thieves, etc.

c) Permit Irregularities (In-hŏka piri) – Actss of public agents collecting payment – mostly monetary – from applicants in issuing various permits such as building permits, allowing increases of university enrollment or changes to the rank of colleges to that of university, licenses for driving automobiles or operating various machinery, licenses to open new business enterprises such as bars, restaurants, massage parlors, public bath houses and game stores and mines.

d) Turning a Blind Eye – Acts of public agents receiving or demanding cash or material payment for turning a blind eye to those not meeting requirements like building regulations or violating operating regulations such as restaurants and public bath houses failing to meet municipal hygienic standards or bars and lounges serving drinks to minors or rendering sexual services in barbershops, saunas and massage parlours.

e) Special Favours – Acts of the executive office or high government offices selecting preferred applicants or bidders as the recipients of special favours on the particularistic grounds of personal ties, lobbying skills, etc., in exchange for kickbacks in a) purchasing various goods and services such as office equipment, food, weapons and airplanes; b) awarding contracts for

236 *Urbanization and the expansion of the public domain*

government projects or bidding for the construction of highways, railways, subways, harbours and airports; c) allocating foreign aid money or goods; d) arranging foreign and domestic bank loans or auctioning off government-owned properties such as insolvent enterprises or properties left over by those Japanese who returned to Japan after the end of the Pacific War; e) distributing academic grants such as BK (Brain Korea) 21; and f) granting special permits to build new institutions such law schools.

f) Irregularities in Recruitment, Promotion and Transfer – Acts of public agents recruiting new members, promoting and transferring them from one position to another on the basis of personal ties or the amount of contributions received from them instead of open competition.

g) Avoidance of Civic Duties – Acts of of the National Tax Service (NTS) and the Military Manpower Administration (MMA) officers allowing certain citizens to evade civic duties on the basis of personal ties or in exchange for cash payments. Many taxpayers, both individual and corporate, bribe NTS officials in an attempt to avoid paying the full assessed amount in the tax notice. The bribe is exacted usually at the rate of 5 percent of the total amount of the tax to be paid. Some men of military service age pay MMA officials a large sum of money through brokers or other connections to avoid conscription or to be classified into the disqualified category in the military health examination – a designation that is supposed to be reserved for health or other reasons. Others may rely on their powerful or influential parents to put informal pressure on MMA officials for the same results.

h) Audit and Inspection Irregularities – Acts of the officials of the Board of Audit and Inspection and the Financial Security Service receiving payment from the organizations they audit for a) going easy in their audits, making the scale of wrongdoings appear smaller or completely ignoring them when detected; b) soliciting such payment by making secret documents available to the organizations to be audited; c) informing those organizations in advance of their plans to audit them; d) putting pressure on those organizations to provide favours of various kinds to their relatives or friends; or e) simply demanding cash or material payment for personal gain by virtue of the fact that they have the audit power over those organizations.

ii) Judicial Irregularities – Malfeasance practices committed by the members of the judiciary – i.e., prosecutors and judges – in adjudicating laws. As mentioned earlier, both prosecutors and judges tend to be lenient to crimes committed by high officials and conglomerates. Prosecutors may also receive bribes from the person suspected of breaking laws in exchange for seeking light sentencing from the judge or no indictment. Judges may be paid by the accused's lawyers for a not guilty verdict, bail or lighter sentencing than what they actually deserve.

iii) Legislative Irregularities – Informal acts of lawmakers of receiving or demanding payments from certain groups, usually business enterprises for voting for specific legislature concerning them.

Urbanization and the expansion of the public domain 237

The Low Trust Society – With personalist Koreans' low level of respect for laws and regulations and the ease with which rules governing the behaviour of the agents of public institutions and their relationships with the public are personalized or bent, South Korea cannot avoid being characterized as a low trust society. That is to say, that Koreans have little confidence that other individuals as citizens in public domains will always abide by the norms they are expected to follow and that agents of public institutions will apply them to the public in a consistent manner without differentiating a group of people from another. Not many Koreans believe that there is only one law for everybody.

Various surveys found Koreans distrusting others and public institutions. Consensus among those scholars who study the trust issue in Korea is that Koreans are apt to trust their close others – i.e., those personally known to them, while having little trust in distant others – i.e., strangers and public institutions. The results of the survey conducted in 2013, 2014 and 2015 by the Korean Institute of Public Administrative Studies (Han'guk haengjong yon'guwon) indicate that while the majority of respondents say they trust their family members, acquaintances and neighbours, more than half of them expressed their distrust of a large number of public institutions. Institutions most distrusted by Koreans include central and regional government organizations, the military, labour unions, the press, educational organizations, religious organizations and banking organizations. The only exception is medicine. Slightly more than half of the respondents (52.4 percent) trust medical doctors and hospitals. One cannot, however, say that the medical organizations, unlike other public institutions, are well trusted as still close to a half of the respondents indicated their distrust of them. The low level of trust in public institutions seems to reflect Koreans' perceptions of how these institutions generally function. The majority of respondents said that those institutions, including medical organization, are neither "clean" nor "fair." That is to say, the agents of these institutions lack integrity and fail to be impersonal and consistent in managing them. Many public agents tend to treat those who offer to pay differently from those who refuse or could not pay for their service. (Han'guk Han'guk haengjŏng yŏn'guwŏn 2015).

This is almost unavoidable for personalist Koreans who are more prone to trust their close others with personal ties or members of their networks than unrelated persons or impersonal institutions. Personalist Koreans, in general, areconfident that their close others – kin members, friends and acquaintances – would not do something that would disappoint them or negatively affect their personal relationship. Personal ties or *ŭiri* is valued so strongly that one does not easily refuse to oblige requests from close others, including bending rules. Thus the personalist citizen or public agent cannot easily say no to his close others' requests to cooperate in bypassing rules. The former prosecutor and law professor Kim Tusik and the former Supreme Court Justice Kim Yŏngnan spoke of the "request that cannot be refused" (*kŏjŏlhalsu ŏpnŭn ch'ŏngt'ak*) (1999: 84–91). The personalist citizen also knows other citizens are not likely to be astute rule abiders. The public agent is well aware that many other agents receive bribes for bending rules.

238 *Urbanization and the expansion of the public domain*

Accordingly, both personalist citizens and public agents are constrained by their awareness of the widespread practices of personalizing rules since bending rules is more of convention than exception: "Since everybody is doing it I become a loser by not doing it." Urban Koreans readily trust close others but haven't developed the habits of trusting remote others. They are more "personal trusters" than "social trusters."

Public concerns have been expressed about the absence of the rule of law and low levels of social trust, and almost all presidents have promised to clean up corruption when they began their terms. Many personalist Koreans are aware of this issue. They tend to criticize others for not abiding by the law, but they themselves often fail to be law-abider themselves.

One should be ready to refuse to cooperate with close others in conspiring against rules and regulation if he or she wants to become a rule-abiding person. Such act may entail severing ties with friends and close acquaintances. In a society where uiri is highly valued, it is a hard – if not impossible – decision to make. This is the dilemma that the personalist frequently faces.

On the basis of his long-term study of the "great historical experimental project of installing a regional assembly system in Italy," Putnam concludes that those who acquired the habits of trusting persons in small civic networks such as soccer clubs, credit rotation associations, bird watching societies or bowling leagues may find themselves more willing to trust strangers (1993: 175). His conclusion is based on the following reasoning: In interacting with strangers, individuals may draw upon their past experiences of cooperating with other members of their personal networks for mutual benefit. Personal trust readily becomes a basis for creating social trust. Accordingly, those who are members of personal networks can more easily and more readily learn to trust strangers than those who are not (Putnam 1993: 175). This observation does not apply to Korea. As discussed earlier, personal trust is trusting others as persons whom one has known and interacted with over a long period of time, whereas social trust is trusting others as role players or agents of public institutions about whom one knows little and with whom one has no personal ties. Personalist Koreans commonly believe that, like themselves, others lack respect for rules and regulations and easily violate them; as such, they are not likely to trust strangers that easily, let alone cooperate with them. Furthermore, for personal trust to become social trust, the emphasis put on personal ties has to be replaced by an emphasis on obeying impersonal rules, or when loyalty to a person is in conflict with loyalty to rules or institutions, the latter should prevail. Personal trust cannot be converted to social trust as easily as Putnam expects – at least, not in Korea.

Putnam also states that networks of civic engagement have beneficial effects of promoting mutual help among members and for the common good. The logic behind this claim is that in networks, individuals learn to cooperate for mutual benefit and thus choose to cooperate to benefit the community. Hence networks of civic engagement become "an important part of a community's stock of social capital" (Putnam 1993: 175) as the education people receive becomes their human capital. His findings, he claims, contradict Mancur Olson's claim that "small

Urbanization and the expansion of the public domain 239

interest groups have no incentive to work toward the common good of society and every incentive to work to engage in costly and inefficient 'rent seeking' – lobbying for tax breaks, colluding to retrain competition, and so on" (quoted in Putnam 1993: 176). But we cannot dismiss Olson's thesis or hypothesis simply on the grounds of Putnam's research findings. Putnam did not consider the possibility that members of a small network largely cooperate with one another to promote their personal or network interests rather than the common good. Personalist Koreans are prone to be actively building networks primarily for the purpose of exchanging help in their pursuit of self-interest and enhancing network solidarity. Olson's statement more aptly describes the social function of the network in Korea than Putnam's. Personal networks promote mutual aid among its members, but not necessarily a common good. Often personal network promotes personal interests at the expense of the public good.

Learning to advance common goods in public domains is not like learning to cooperate for mutual benefit in networks. It implies putting priority on public interests over personal interests or shifting one's loyalty or commitment to close others to abstract principles or imagined communities. In personalist Korea, the network is largely personal capital and only rarely becomes social capital. Utilizing personal networks for fostering common goods is a recent phenomenon. During the authoritarian period, the personal network proved to be a basis for democracy movement of student activists and the "democratic union movement" by young factory workers. After democracy returned, the personal network served as the basis for former undongkwon students to form NGOs to promote common goods. They have demonstrated that networks can be utilized for advancing common goods. In other words, they turned their personal networks into social capital. It takes great courage and determination to shift one's loyalty from specific persons to abstract principles or public causes. As discussed earlier, undongkwon students gave up being filial sons to become democracy fighters, causing displeasure and pain to their parents whose prime, long-term concern is to see their sons get university degrees and become doctors and lawyers, not get involved in student movements at the risk of getting expelled from university and going to prison. But they are a minority. For the large majority of Koreans, their personal network still is personal capital.[13]

Low Level of Civic Engagement – Close attachments to private persons – friends and acquaintances – heavy involvement in closely knit personal network and the amount of time and energy spent on managing personal ties are not likely to not make personalists socially active public men or women.

Personalist urban Koreans are not prone to join civic associations established for the purpose of promoting public causes or interests other than those aimed at enhancing private or network interests.

The 1994 Democratization Survey conducted by the political scientist Do C. Shin indicates that the majority (64 percent) of respondents were members of fraternal associations formed on the basis of personal ties, such as alumni (school) and clan (kinship) ties. Meanwhile, less than 10 percent of respondents were affiliated with "the three modern types of civic association, which directly involve

240 *Urbanization and the expansion of the public domain*

those citizens without personal ties, economic interest groups (e.g., agricultural co-ops and labour unions), social groups (e.g., charity and environmental protection) and cultural organizations (e.g., arts, hobbies and sports clubs" (1999: 107–108).

The Korean Institute of Public Administration Studies (Han'guk haengjong yon'guwon) came up with similar findings in the aforementioned surveys (Han'guk haengjŏng yŏn'guwŏn 2015). As Table 6.1 indicates, the proportion of the respondents who are members of the civic association, such as political parties, civilian movement groups or public regional societies or voluntary service groups and charity organizations, is less than 10 percent, whereas that of fraternal associations, such as amateur clubs of like-minded people, alumni associations and home-town fraternal societies, is 54.4 percent (Han'guk haengjŏng yŏn'guwŏn 2015: 6).

It is noteworthy that almost one out of three respondents is a member of a school alumni association and home-town friendship society, while one out of 50 respondents is affiliated with a political party. Had the survey estimated the extent of respondents' involvement in clan organizations and other forms of personal networks the participation rate of the fraternal associations would have been much higher.

On the whole, Koreans are rather politically inactive. It is true that free elections were reinstated in 1998, and voters replaced the incumbent of the executive office with the candidate of the opposition party. The peaceful transfer of power through an election took place for the first time in Korea's republican history. They also sent a small number of opposition party members, including former undongkwŏn students, to parliament. The rate of voter participation in the election was relatively high. Voting rates reached the high point in the thirteenth presidential and parliamentary elections in 1988 with 89.2 percent and 75.8 percent, respectively. Since then, the rates declined somewhat, reaching 75.8 percent in

Table 6.1 Types of Social and Civic Participation, 2013, 2014, 2015(%)

	2013	2014	2015
Political Party	2.0	2.2	1.6
Labour Organization Business Owners Association, Occupational Cooperative	3.1	3.1	3.0
Religious Organization	17.9	18.2	17.7
Amateur Club of Like-Minded People	19.8	23.6	20.0
Citizen Movement Group	2.4	2.4	2.2
Regional Society Public Association	11.9	7.7	7.8
Alumni Associations, Home-Town Fraternal Society	34.8	36.5	31.3
Others	8.3	6.3	15.9
Total	100.0	100.0	100.0

Source: Han'guk haengjong yon'guwŏn (2015: 6)

Urbanization and the expansion of the public domain   241

the eighteenth presidential election in 2012 and 54.2 percent in nineteenth parliamentary election.[14]

But electing the president and national and local assemblymen, Shin points out, is the only political activity "in which more than one-half of the Korean electorate has ever been engaged as citizens of a democratic state"(1999: 102). In his survey, Shin found that a relatively small portion of his respondents had ever engaged in other types of political activity such as "attending political meetings or assemblies," "submitting or signing petitions," "working with others on community problems," "campaigning for political parties or candidates," "taking part in demonstrations," "making contributions to political organizations or candidates," "contacting joining strikes," "contacting government officials or politicians" and "affiliating with political organizations" (Shin 1999: 102–103). His survey results also reveal that while close to 70 percent of the respondents said that they did discuss political or social issues with people around them, less than 30 percent said they did not "express their opinion on political and social issues on on-line," "presented opinions to the government or the press," "participate in signature collecting campaigns," "submit petitions," "join demonstrations or rallies," "deliver civil appeals to public officials or politicians" or "participate in commodity boycott campaigns" (1999: 7).

Returning to the question raised at the beginning of this chapter, "How well do urban Koreans live with strangers and are they successful in building a community within the city?," one may argue that they are not doing well in interacting with strangers or establishing an impersonal universal order in the public domain of modern urban society. While urban Koreans find it easy to work with or trust persons dear and near, they tend to distrust persons who are unrelated and far removed. The personalist ethic that survived sweeping kŭndaehwa (modernization) does not serve as proper guiding rule for social relations in the ever-expanding impersonal public domain.

Equally visible is the lack civic virtue in actively cooperating one another to promote common goods. Personalist Koreans have not been accustomed to taking seriously abstract ideas that embrace the interests and welfare of people – human rights, equality, social justice, fellow feeling toward humanity, etc. – beyond the confines of their personal networks. In the personalist society, the utilitarian idea of the greatest happiness of the greatest number of people is not likely to be a dominant thought. The prevailing concern is the happiness of close others with little attention paid to distant others. Often public interest is sacrificed in the interest of his or her personal network.

Lack of concern for or indifference toward others beyond their personal network and the low degree of participation in communal affair is the problem that the new urban Korea has to combat. Urban Korean citizens continue to remain as personalist network men and women rather than becoming fully civil and civically virtuous public men and women. The culture of citizenship is slow to evolve.

Comparatively speaking, what is absent in Korea is forceful super beings that demand loyalty from people over and against their loyalty to their close others. In

242 *Urbanization and the expansion of the public domain*

the individualistic Christian West, loyalty to the almighty God always comes ahead of loyalty to friends, acquaintances and even kin members. In fact, according to Calvin, God demands an exclusive trust in him and exhorts to trust no one, even one's closest friend. Other human beings were not only useless to him but also might be positively dangerous (Parsons 1949: 525). During the feudal period, beyond kinship ties, there were the lord-vassal ties (Bloch 1964). In collectivistic (groupish) Japan, although people are closely tied with their kin members, friends and acquaintances, their loyalty to the group to which they belong preceded their loyalty to close others, and when there was conflict between being loyal to their close others and being loyal to their feudal lords, the latter prevailed (Levy 1955). In other words, almighty God and feudal lords served as moral bases for building communities larger than the small face-to-face rural villages. Nationalism often unites Koreans. But personalist Koreans become nationalists when the nation faces crisis or competes against other countries in sports or other games. In peacetime, the nation does not loom large in their minds. In South Korea, the moral basis of the personalist ethic has yet to be seriously challenged. It is worth noting that in the north, under the totalitarian system, personalist Koreans were forced to shift their loyalty from their close others, including kin members, to the party or the single "Great Leader."

Notes

1 The birth place of the clan founder or the place where the clan has lived over generations.
2 To give some examples: Haenam Yunssi Chongch'inhoe, Kossi Chongmunhoe, Doksu Yissi Chonghoe Yech'on Kwonssi hwasuhoe, Ulsan Kimssi taejonghoe, Tongnae Chongssi *tongchonghoe,* or Chonju Yissi taedongjongyangwon.
3 In some cases, Seoul district chongch'inhoe serves as the headquarters of the national chongch'inhoe.
4 We use the bracket since city and county are at the same administrative level.
5 When a national federation of hyang'uhoe is born, it, in turn, tries to help those cities or countries without a hyang'uhoe to create one.
6 Some university's general alumni associations own their own high-rise office buildings.
7 In principle, as the political party law states, any political party should manage itself as an independent organization on its own with five sources of income: (1) membership fees, (2) donations by party sponsors, (3) the party trust fund, (4) support from the national budget and (5) income generating activities of its own. No political party, however, has been able to create enough funds from these sources to be self-sufficient. From the beginning of the history of political parties in Korea, leaders of parties – ruling as well as opposition – have been expected to be responsible for fund raising not only for the parties but party officials. One of the major qualities of party leadership has been the capacity to raise funds.
8 When President Roh Tae Woo's secret fund that deposited under fictional or borrowed names was made public in 1995, he admitted that it was what was left over from the political funds (in the amount of 500 billion won) he accumulated while in office. Having spent 35 billion Won of what he called governance funds (t'ongch'ichakŭm), 150 billion Won still remained.
9 Dallmayr (2003) points out that the Confucian ethic failed to provide a social norm for citizens.
10 In general, more prestigious model of car is a foreign import, not a Korean brand.

Urbanization and the expansion of the public domain   243

11 It should be noted that urban Koreans tend to be uncivil only to those strangers who appear or are regarded socially (status-wise) lower than themselves and those foreign strangers who are from the countries considered less advanced than Korea (see Konggam 2013).
12 The idea of judicial independence was introduced during the Kaehwa period when the modern court system was established in 1895 as part of the Kabo Kyŏngjang (Kabo Reformation).
13 The distinction between the network as social capital and the network as personal capital is not clearly made in the sociological analysis of networks. In many cases, the network is treated as social capital (Coleman 1988; Putnam 1993; Nan Lin 2001). Moreover, network sociologists have rarely dealt with the network as personal capital used for advancing personal or network gains even at the expense of public interests entailing the violation of laws and regulation.
14 In the first regional election in 1995, 68.8 percent of the electorate elected their representative to local assemblies. The rate in the sixth election in 2014 was 56.8 percent.

References

Ackerman, Bruce (1989) "Why Dialogue." *Journal of Philosophy*, vol. 86, no. 1 (January), pp. 5–22.
Baker, Ernest (1960) *Social Contract: Essays by Locke, Hume and Rousseau*, Oxford: Oxford University Press.
Bloch, Marc (1964) *Feudal Society 2*, Translated by Manyon, Chicago: University of Chicago Press.
Bourdieu, Pierre (1986) "The Forms of Capital," pp. 241–258, in Richardson, John G. (ed.) *Handbook of Theory and Research for the Sociology of Education*, New York: Greenwood Press.
Calhoun, Craig (1992) *Habermas and the Public Sphere*, Cambridge, MA: MIT Press.
Ch'oe, Hangsŏp (2007) "Chŏngbo sahoe Ŭi sillnoe wa sahoejŏk chabon" (Trust and Social Capital in Information Society), 2007 nyon sahoe chabon tukpyol simpochiun (Proceedings of the 2007 Social Capital Special Symposium). *Han'guk chongbo hakhoe* (Korean Information Society), September 5, pp. 74–92.
Chŏn, Togŭn (2009) *Pu rŭl purŭnŭn inmaek kwalli ŭi kisul* (Techniques of Management of Personal Net that Brings in Money), Seoul: choŭn mandŭlgi.
Chŏng, Byŏng'ŭn (2007) "Hyang'uhoe sahoe chabon kwa chiyŏk chu'ui – chaegyŏng Andong Hyang'uhoe rŭl chungsim'ŭro" (The Home town Fraternal Association Social Capital and Regionalism – With Reference to the Andong Fraternal Association in Seoul), *Sahoe kwahak yon'gu* (The Social Science Study), vol. 23, no. 3 (December), pp. 331–358.
Chŏnghaejin sinmun (2007–07–30).
Chung, Chuyŏng (1991) "Preface" in Asanchedan (Ed.) *Tŏburŏ sanŬn saramdŬl* (People Who Live Together), Seoul: Chayuch'ulp'ansa.
Coleman, James (1988) "Social Capital in the Creation of Human Capital." *American Journal of Sociology*, vol. 94 (Supplement), pp. s95–s120.
Dallmayr, Fred (2003) "Confucianism and the Public Sphere: Five Relationships Plus One," *Dao*, vol. 3, no. 2, pp. 192–212.
dongA.com (2007–10–16).
Dore, Ronald P. (1987) *Taking Japan Seriously*, Stanford: Stanford University Press.
Fischer, Claude S. (1976) *The Urban Experience*, New York: Harcourt Brace Jovonovich.

244   *Urbanization and the expansion of the public domain*

Giddens, Anthony (1990) *The Consequences of Modernity*, Stanford: Stanford University Press.

Goodel, Grace (1980) "From Status to Contract: The Significance of Agrarian Relations of Production in the West, Japan, and in 'Asiatic' Persia." *European Journal of Sociology*, vol. 21, pp. 285–325.

Granovetter, Mark (1973) "The Strength of Weak Ties." *American Journal of Sociology*, vol. 73, pp. 1360–1380.

Han, In-sŏp (1998) "Pŏpcho biri: munje wa che'an"(Judiciary Malfeasance: Problems and Proposals). *Pŏphak* (The Journal of Jurisprudence), vol. 39, no. 1, pp. 164–188.

Han'guk haengjŏng yŏn'guwŏn (2015) *Silnoe sahoe kuhyŏn kwa hyŏmnyŏkchŏk gŏbŏnans kuch'uk* (Embodiment of Trust Society and Establishment of Cooperative Governance), The Proceedings of 2015 Korean Institute of Public Administration Study Social Research Center Discussion Meeting held on December 22, 2015, Seoul: Han'guk haengjŏng yŏn'guwŏn.

Hattori, Tamio (1992) *Kankoku (Korea)*, Tokyo: Tokyo taigaku shuppanbu.

Hŏ, Yŏngnan (2010) "Haebang ihu sikminchi bŏp'yulŭi chŏngniwa t'alsikminhwa" (Sorting Out and Decolonization of the Colonial Law after Liberation), pp. 13–40, in Han'il yŏksa kongdong wiwŏnhoe (ed.) *Han'il yŏksa kongdong yŏn'gu bokosŏ che 5 kwŏn*, Seoul: Kyŏng'in munhwasa.

Hong, Sehwa (2005) "Han'guk'ŭi t'oron munhwa rŭl t'oronhanda" (Debating the Korean Debating Culture)," hani.co.kr (2005–05–09).

Hongju Ilbo (2009–11–09).

Johnson, Chalmers (1982) *MITI and the Japanese Miracle*, Stanford: Stanford University Press.

Kangjiin (2008) "Chŏnjik taetongnyŏng pijakŭm ŭi ch'uŏk [The Memory of Former Presidents' Secret Funds]." (2008–10–29). http://blog.daum.net/always 330/157711271.

Kim, Dae Jung (2009) "Tongbang murye chiguk" (The Eastern Country of Incivility), *Chukan Chosun*, no. 2038 (January 6).

Kim, Sang-bong (2004) *Hakpŏl sahoe* (Academic Sectarian Society), Seoul: Han'gilsa.

Kim, Sŭngyong (2008) *Inmaek kyŏnyŏng* (Personal Network Management), Seoul: Buk'oshon.

Kim, Yonghak (2003) "Han'guk sahoe ŭi hagyŏn – sahoejŏk chabon ŭi ch'angch'ul esŏ inchŏk chabon ŭi yŏkhwa" (School Ties in Korea – The Role of Human Capital in Social Capital), pp. 99–127, in Kim, Sŏngguk et al. (eds.) *Uri ege yŏngo nŭn muŏsinka – Hanguk ŭi chiptanchŭi wa* netŭwŏkŭ (What is Human Ties to Us – Korean Groupism and Network), Seoul: Chŏntong kwa hyŏndae.

Konggam (2013) *Uri nun himang Ŭl pyŏnho handa* (We Defend Hopes), Seoul: Buki.

Kyŏngbuk Ilbo (2012–05–11).

Kyŏnggi sinmun (2012–10–04).

Levy, Marion (1952) *The Structure of Society*, Princeton: Princeton University Press.

Levy, Marion (1955) "Contrasting Factors in the Modernization of China and Japan," pp. 496–536, in Kuznets, Simon, Moore, Wilbert E. and Spengler, Joseph (eds.) *Economic Growth: Brazil, India, Japan*, Durham, NC: Duke University Press.

Lin, Nan (2001) *Social Capital: A Theory of Social Structure and Action*, Cambridge: Cambridge University Press.

Merton, Robert K. (1957) *Social Theory and Social Structure*, Glencoe: The Free Press.

News 1 Korea (2012–04–04).

Pak, Saeyŏl (2012) "Kim Musŏng chŭng'ŏn ch'ujŏk haeboni chongch'ak yŏk Ŭn 'Pak Chŏnghŭi pimil kŬmgo" (The Tracing of Kim Mu-song's Testimony Led to the Terminal Station Which Was 'Park Chung Hee's Secret Safe). *Pressian*, (2012–12–09).

Urbanization and the expansion of the public domain 245

Pak, Sŭnggwan (1994) *Dŭrŏnan ŏlgul' kwa boiji annŭn son – Han'guk sahoe'ŭi kommyunikeishon kujo* (The Revealed Face and the Invisible Hand – The Structure of Communication in the Korean Society), Seoul: Sinyewŏn.

Palais, James B. (1996) *Confucian Statecraft and Korean Institutions: Yu Hyŏngwŏn and the Late Chosŏn Dynasty*, Seattle: University of Washington Press.

Parsons,Talcott (1949) *The Structure of Social Action*, Glencoe: The Free Press.

Putnam, Robert B. (1993) *Making Democracy Work*, Princeton: Princeton University Press.

Seol, Tong-hun (2004) *Han'guk'inŬi simin uisik* (Citizen Consciousness of Koreas), Seoul: Songsukhan sahoe gakkugi moim.

Seoul, kyŏngje sinmun t'ŭkpyŏl chuijeban (1992) *Hanguk ŭi inmaek* (Personal Network in Korea), Seoul: Han'guk ilbo.

Shin, Doh C. (1999) *Mass Politics and Culture in Democratizing Korea*, Cambridge: Cambridge University Press.

Smart, Clifford E. J. (1977) "Manners Private and Public." *Korea Journal*, vol. 17, no. 12 (December), pp. 25–27.

Smith, Michael. P. (1979) *The City and Social Theory*, New York: St. Martin's Press.

Sormant, Guy (1998) "Han'guk'un 't'oron munhwa k'iwŏra." *Munhwa Ilbo*, (1998–01–07).

Spencer, Herbert (1960) "Militant and Industrial Societies," pp. 292–335, in Mills, C. Wright (ed.) *Images of Man*, New York: George Braziller.

Torjesen, Karen J. (1992) "Public Ethics and Public Selfhood: The Hidden Problems," pp. 110–113, in Runzo, Joseph (ed.) *Ethics, Religion and the Good Society*, Louisville: John Knox Press.

Weber, Max (1946) *From Max Weber: Essays in Sociology*, Translated, edited, and with an Introduction by Gerth, H. H. and C. Wright Mills, New York: Oxford University Press.

Weber, Max (1994) *Political Writings*, Lassman, Peter (ed.) Peter, Ronald and Spoeirs, Ronald (trans.), Cambridge: Cambridge University Press.

Wirth, Louis (1957) "Urbanism as a Way of Life," pp. 46–63, in Paul K. Hatt and Albert J. Reiss, Jr (eds.) *Cities and Society: The Revised Raeder in Urban Sociology*, New York: The Free Press of Glencoe.

Yang, Kŏn (2002) "Han'gyk ŭi bŏp munhwawa bŏp'Ŭi chibae" (The Culture of Law asd the Rule of Law in Korea). *Bŏphak yŏn'gu* (The Study of the Philosophy of Law), vol. 5, no. 1, pp. 185–202.

Yang, Kwang-mo (2008) *Tangsinman ŭi inmaek* (Create Personal Network that Is Only Yours), Seoul: Ch'ŏngnyŏn chŏngsin.

Yi, Chaeyŏl, An, Chŏngok and Song, Hogŭn (eds.) (2007) *Netŭwŏkŭ sahoe ŭi kujo wa chaengchŏm* (The Structure and Problems of Network Society), Seoul: Seoul taehakkyo ch'ulpanbu.

Yi, Chonghun (2005) *Kwŏllyŏk hyŏng piri chŏkkyŏl ŭl wihan chedo kaesŏn pang'an yŏngu* (A Study on Institutional Reform Devices to Eliminate Corruption), Seoul: Kukhoe pŏpche sabŏp wiwŏnhoe.

Yi, T'aegyu (2005) *Han'guk ŭi puja inmaek* (Personal Network of the Rich in Korea), Seoul: Ch'ŏngnyŏn jŏngsin.

Yŏngnam ilbo (2003–11–15).

Conclusion

This book began with the observation that there were two Confucianzation projects – Confucianization of the state and Confucianization of the family – during the Chosŏn Dynasty period, and in the end, the latter prevailed over the former.

The Confucianization of the state project was aimed at building a state led by the hereditary king with officials recruited on the basis of merits through the competitive civil service examinations open to all adult males regardless of status distinction – except slaves. The prime of this project was to revive the "ultimate form of politics of the Three ancient Chinese dynasties – Hsia, Shang, and Chou," that is, building the government for the people, ensuring the welfare of the people – "hangsan" and "hangsim"

The Confucianization of the family project initiated by yangban aristocrats in opposition to Confucianization of the state system was to sustain the old ideology of status distinction and focused on building the family system based on ancestor worship and paternal succession with sophisticated rituals according to the *Family Rites of Zhu Xi (Chujakarye)* by way of establishing the yangban culture that would clearly distinguish the people of yangban status from those of commoner status.

With yangban dominating the bureaucracy and royal politics of the central government who were more committed to protecting and promoting the interest of the yangban class the Confucianization of the family emerged as the main historical project of the Chosŏn Dynasty, while the Confucianization of the state system or building the government for the people remained merely an ideal without ever being made into a solid political tradition. Consequently, Chosŏn Dynasty Korea in the end became a particularistic or personalistic hierarchical society rather than an equal universalistic one,

Sustained change of Confucian Korea or kŭndaehwa (modernization) of Korea did not begin until 1876 when the hermit kingdom was forced to open its ports to foreign traders and launched various reform measures under the name of kaehwa (enlightenment).

Viewed in historical perspective, the kŭndaehwa project, as it should be apparent from the earlier discussion, is a process of abandoning the Confucianization of the family project and moving in the direction of the Confucianization of the state project.

Confucianism as the official principle guiding politics has long been dropped. The Confucian ethic, the base of the moral system of the Chosŏn Dynasty, is no longer a major focus of the family and school education. Confucian ethic texts merely survive as part of the Confucian classic.

The kŭndaehwa project, in fact, has gone much beyond the scope of the Confucianization of the state project. The main objective of the democratic system adopted in South Korea after Liberation is to build the government not only for the people but also of and by the people. It elevated the status of the people from subject to citizen who were called to participate in the political process. The democratic constitution says power resides in people. The distinction between the "good" (yang) and "base" (ch'on) people is the thing of the dynastic past. There are no slaves now. Women are not confined to the inner court anymore. They moved into men's world, often out performing men in various roles.

Kŭndaehwa is basically the process of learning from and catching up with the West and Westernized Japan or more specifically importing various institutions from them.

Men's top knots were cut. Women's long hair shortened and permed. Men wear Western suits most of the time, switching to Korean costumes only on special occasions, while women normally clad themselves in Western dress (yangjang), though they have not abandoned Korean dresses as men have. Men and women wear Western leather shoes (yanghwa) and have almost completely replaced the straw woven shoes. They live in Western houses (yang'ok) and apartments instead of thatched roof houses. Coffee and tea have become preferred drinks after meals instead of traditional teas. Western medicines pushed aside traditional herbal medicines and acupuncture in health care. Western music – both classic and popular – has become the dominant form of performing art for which the public is willing to pay to watch.

The field of technology witnessed breathtaking progress – be it production, construction, communication, industrial manufacturing, electronics, digital industry or weapon manufacturing.

The mode of building the society also went through drastic transformation. The Chosŏn Dynasty was a predominantly closed, status-oriented agrarian society. The contemporary South Korea is a predominantly open, pluralistic and highly differentiated market society.

The breakaway from the past began with the opening of the educational market after the port opening in 1876. The traditional educational system was mainly concentrated on learning the Chinese characters and reading the Confucian classics. The prime objective of this system was to cultivate princely personalities with a deep understanding of Confucian moral and political philosophy, and thereby produce such personalities for civil – service or scholarly careers. Though the formal school education was officially open to any male who could afford to pay and spare time for it, it remained more or less a privilege accorded largely to male yangban elites, Women were categorically denied access to it. The democratic constitution adopted by South Korea states that it is the right of every citizen to receive school education and that the elementary education should be provided free of charge.

248 *Conclusion*

A compulsory education plan was implemented in 1950 with the proclamation of the Compulsory Education Act. The response of the citizens was overwhelming, and the government made noteworthy efforts to build more schools. By the end of the decade, more than 90 percent of school-age children were attending primary schools. The middle school education was also made compulsory first in the surrounding islands in 1985 and completed in 2004. Although the high school education is not compulsory, the large majority (90 percent) of high school-age children (13–18) was enrolled in 1985. Some 80 percent of high school graduates, both male and female, are now advancing to colleges and universities. Few drop out of school at all levels.

South Korea transformed itself from a rural agrarian to an urban industrial society. Unlike in the Chosŏn period, the overwhelming majority (95 percent) of able-bodied men and women are now engaged in non-agricultural work, and the non-agricultural work is highly differentiated in terms of skills required to perform it, and the job market in industrial Korea is free of status and gender discrimination. The Basic Labour Law promulgated in 1953 stipulated minimum standards for working conditions for all employees, banned discrimination on the basis of sex and provided special protection of working conditions and maternity leave for female workers. The women's constitutional right to work meant their right to make a living through their own employment (Shin 1994). The right to work became an inalienable right possessed by all human beings. In other words, the constitution guaranteed women the right to live on their own, without necessarily being dependent on men. Occupational choice is now more closely related with the level of one's educational attainment. There are numerous jobs to choose from in the job market. With qualifications acquired, one enters the job market to choose a job or career through competition. The traditional status dimension has more or less disappeared from the employer and employee relationship as it became one of contract. The employee begins working on a new job with the understanding of how much he or she will be paid for the work rendered for the employer for the time period he agreed to work for the employer. The Basic Labour Law entitles employees to organize themselves into a union, negotiate with or strike against employers about their working conditions.

With industrialization, the structure of the job market changed considerably, and the scope for individual mobility expanded accordingly. The decline of the agricultural workforce from 70 percent of the total workforce in 1960 to 5 percent in 2010 may be taken as a rough measure of the extent of occupational shift that took place during that period. The rapid growth of the non-agricultural sector has also been accompanied by a considerable upgrading of educational levels of workers, a high degree of specialization and professionalization, corporatization and income differentiation. Accordingly, differentiation of social position proceeds in terms of property, prestige and power, with a notable relative growth of the middle strata through reshuffling of the workforce (Chang 1991: 113).

Until the end of the Chosŏn Dynasty period, yangban men married yangban women, commoner men married commoner women and slaves married each other at early ages – around 18 – through arrangement by parents. Women, especially,

Conclusion 249

yangban, were prohibited from remarrying, even if they became widows at young ages, while men were permitted to divorce or abandon their wives on the following seven grounds: disobedience to parents-in-law, inability to procreate, debauchery, jealousy, malignant disease, gossippyness and thievery.[1] Men were also allowed to have concubines. The growth of the educational and job markets directly confronted the traditional marriage norm and gave birth to a marriage market. School education and job experience outside the home produced a delay in the age at first marriage, provided freedom and opportunities for women to get to know men and form close relationships – relationships which were allowed only to kin members previously. Girls and boys nowadays go through a prolonged adolescent period to enable young women to meet and interact with male counterparts in a wider community. They marry at a mature age – mature enough to know their preference for marriage partners and to act on their own judgments. With the increasing nucleation of the family, what parents-in-law to be want from their future daughters-in-law has become less important than what the two persons marrying each other want. Even though many parents, especially of the upper class, are still involved in their children's marriages, they do not insist on their children marrying girls or boys they themselves choose for them in the way parents did during the Chosŏn period. Youths these days tend to think of marriage primarily as a matter of their own decision. In the words of two sociologists Lee Dongwon and Cho Sungnam (1986), "Individualism, or the pursuit of self-interest, increasingly prevails in the process of mate selection, gradually replacing the traditional emphasis on the family" (unpublished manuscript). The pursuit of self-interest resonates with the importance of romantic love in marriage. Youths, like their parents, of course, have other concerns in selecting a lifetime partner such as personality, health, family background, occupation, income and so on. But they consider love as a necessary condition for marriage. Marriage based on self-interest and romantic love presupposes a freedom of choice in mate selection; the marriage market provides that choice. One can meet potential marriage candidates at school, at the workplace, at church or through friends. The new idea of basing marriage on love has an additional meaning for married life. If there is no love between husband and wife, they may choose to end the marriage and return to the market again, instead of resigning themselves to their "destiny" and continuing the loveless marital relationship. The divorce rate has been steadily rising in urban Korea. Moreover, one also has the freedom not to marry. Remaining single is now considered to be an alternative to marriage. Korean parents particularly do their best to marry off their daughters in time, but if they are unable to do so, or if daughters are adamant about not getting married, their parents are willing to live with them.

"As the income level goes up," wrote Veblen (1953[1899]: 72), "consumption becomes a larger element in the standard of living in the city than in the country." The self-sufficiency that characterized the traditional peasant economy is quickly replaced by the urban market economy that emphasized consumption. In the latter part of the twentieth century, South Korea has rapidly developed into a consumer society. During the Chosŏn Dynasty period, most peasants largely lived at the

250 *Conclusion*

subsistence level. Their basic needs were barely procured, and their consumption of goods produced outside of their communities was minimal. They went to periodic markets to sell a minor portion of what they were able to produce, such as grains and fruits, in order to purchase what they needed but could not produce by themselves such as farm equipment, woven materials (e.g., rice bags), products made of wood, bamboo, stone and brass, herbal medicines and marine products (Mun 1941). In the cities, licensed shops supplied goods other than basic necessities, including luxury items, to a small number of limited customers including the government office, the royal house and yangban residents. Commoners went to open markets to purchase what they needed for daily living: foodstuff and fuel supply. In general, luxury living was discouraged; frugality, not consumption, was considered a virtue.

With the economic growth based on the expansion of the manufacturing industry and rising income levels, the consumer market grew rapidly in post-Liberation South Korea. Numerous goods, produced domestically or imported are sold in stores and shops of varying types, ranging from street vendors, corner grocery stores, convenience stores and supermarkets to department stores and shopping malls and, recently, the electronic market. Similarly, various forms of services – transportation, news, information, delivery, domestic help and others – have been made available in the form of commodity. There are also movie theatres, amusement parks, exhibition halls, opera houses and music halls offering various forms of entertainment. Information on consumer goods has been aggressively distributed by business enterprise through advertising and media channels. Those who advertise also create constantly changing fashions for consumers, arousing curiosity and fostering motives to purchase new products. Credit cards were introduced in the 1960s, enabling Korean consumers to purchase goods on credit at any time they desired. As more Koreans travel overseas these days, they gained access to foreign markets for shopping. Unlike other forms of markets (marriage, education, job and political) the consumer market is open to everybody who has money to spend. As many Western consumer behavior researchers have predicted (for example, Slater 1997), consumers in Korea are becoming more individualized. Entering the market, consumers have to know what they want in order to choose from a wide range of goods and services. Consumption in the market, therefore, helps consumers to become more aware of their own tastes, preferences, talents and aptitudes. In short, the consumer market helps people to discover themselves and to act according to their own will and need in choosing commodities and services. (This section was adapted from Chang 2006: 358).

The political market is a modern concept. Until the Republic was born in 1948, most people remained passive subjects, not active participants, in the political process. They were ruled by the rulers without any right to check the power of the latter. The constitution granted the right to citizens to participate in the political process both at the national and regional levels as voters or politicians. It stipulates that any citizen above age 18 can vote to elect his or her representatives to the legislative assemblies for a limited time period or to stand as a candidate for all levels of election to become a politician. Having the voting right to choose

Conclusion 251

their legislative representatives means they have the right to get rid of them if they are not satisfied with their performances in the assembly at the next round.

Voters are invited to assess the competing candidate's campaign promises, views on building a good society and records, personalities, political parties' records and orientations and election's salient issues (Lane 1979: 457). The constitution gave citizens or voters the right and duty to make individual decisions about political issues without relying on others. Ideally, they are supposed to cast ballots according to the dictates of their own reasoning. Voters are equal in that each one has one vote like everybody else. Thus citizens, as Weber put it, may become "politicians who live off politics and politicians who live for politics" The former strive to make politics a permanent source of income or a vocation, whereas the latter does not (Weber 1958: 84). That women – single or married – can seek a career or becoming representatives in the legislative assembly in the world of politics, which had been exclusively dominated by men, is a distinct mark of modernity that destroyed the traditional image of women as submissive beings. Although small in number, women are increasingly becoming members of the National Assembly and regional governments. The first woman president was born in 2013. Voters – men or women – appear to be accepting women as capable of leading the nation.

The ideological front also is experiencing slow tranformation. Until recently, South Korea has been an ideologically monolithic conservative nation. Since the partition of the Peninsula after Liberation, the authoritarian regimes of Syngman Rhee and Park Chung Hee adopted anti-communist policy that placed the utmost emphasis on national security. Any praise or advocacy of leftist ideology or political pluralism was considered an act "beneficial to the enemy" (i.e., North Korea) in violation of the National Security Law – a crime punishable by the law court. After the 1987 Democratization Declaration by Roh Tae Woo, the political (or ideological) climate of South Korea began to change. Roh's government made serious attempts to establish peaceful relations (through negotiation) with the north, and anti-communism and the National Security Law became less powerful as ideological forces. In 2000, President Kim Dae Jung held a historical summit meeting with the president of North Korea Kim Jong Il and signed an agreement on mutual cooperation. Exchanges increased sharply between the north and south in various forms: talk, trade, goodwill visits, tourism, information and knowledge. The two Koreas became more reconciliatory to one another than before, and expectations of reunification, at least in the South, rose considerably.

This development posed a challenge or threat to those South Koreans who were not ready to accept the idea of a reunification of the two Koreas that would recognize the north's sovereignty. South Koreans began to be divided into those who insisted on preserving the South Korean national identity in reunification – meaning reunification by absorbing the north, and those who advocated reunification first and negotiation on the identity of unified Korea later. The former coalesced into a conservative or rightist force, while the latter turned into a progressive or leftist force.

This ideological division may be taken as a sign of tacit recognition of the leftist ideology. In 1995, the progressive labour union movement with a socialist

252 Conclusion

agenda led by the Korean Confederation of Trade Unions (KCTU) was officially recognized by the Kim Young Sam government. The KCTU went on to create the Democratic Labour Party, and eventually seized seats in the National Assembly in 2000. Also to be mentioned is the gradual acceptance of Marxism by the government and the public as a legitimate political theory. Reading and translating Marxist literature is no longer considered an offence of "benefitting the enemy" in violation of the National Security Law. Courses on Marxism are being offered at universities. Marxist scholars are increasing in number.It is difficult to tell how far the ideological market will open up. Ther is no attempt to form a Communist political party. The anti-North sentiment is very strong. Even progressive politicians are cautious in expressing their political views in order not to be branded as pro-North (chongbuk).

At the beginning of the Chosŏn Dynasty, Confucianism replaced Buddhism, which had been the official religion of the previous dynasty, Koryŏ (918–1392). Confucianism, as it was practiced in the Chosŏn society, was a more worldly system of belief providing guidelines for proper human conduct. It did recognize the authority of the Heaven as the king ruled his kingdom with his mandate, and it was believed that the Heaven closely monitored the king's governance. However, Heaven did not send an apostle as a savior to the world, teaching the gospel, drawing followers and commanding their loyalty. Confucian scholars and politicians in Chosŏn Korea did not officially recognize any belief system that sought life after death and divine assistance and blessing in pursuing worldly fortune or success and thus condemned Buddhism as a heterodox, self-centered doctrine (Chung Chai-sik 1995: 171) and shamanistic practices as superstition (umsa) (Choe Chongsŏng 2002). Both Buddhist monks and shamans were banished from the capital and yangban elites were prohibited from seeking their help (Buswell 1992 and Choe Chongsŏng 2002). On similar grounds, the Chosŏn court denounced Christianity (Catholic) – when it came to Korea in the late eighteenth century – as a "barbarous, beastly and heterodox" religion (Chung Chai-sik 2002: 35) and urged those Koreans who converted to this alien religion to forsake it. When they refused to do so, they were persecuted.

The religious market began to develop with the port opening in 1876. In 1884, the first foreign Protestant ministers – mainly American and Canadian – reached Korea, following the traders and diplomats, and launched missionary work (Moffet 1962: 32–35). Unlike their Catholic predecessors, they carried out their missionary work freely without the fear of prosecution, since their governments protected their citizens residing in Korea under the Korean–American Trade Agreement. Thus Christianity – Protestant as well as Catholic – came to be accepted by the Korean government as a legitimate faith. Both Protestant ministers and Catholic priests continued their missionary work throughout the Japanese period, and Christianity now became a well-established religion in Korea with Christian converts – Protestant and Catholic – constituting the largest religious group (29.2 percent of the total population according to the 2008 Population and Housing Survey).

Another notable religious movement that occurred concurrently with the spread of Christianity was the coming of Japanese Buddhists, who had goals to

Conclusion   253

(1) provide religious service to Japanese Buddhist residents in Korea and (2) to convert non-Buddhist Japanese residents to Buddhism and Buddhist Koreans to Japanese Buddhism and (3) to incorporate Korean Buddhism with Japanese Buddhism, thereby creating a religious tie to help the government-general to carry out the assimilation policy easily (Hur 1999; Song Chuhyŏn 2004; and Kim Kyŏng-chip 2005). The more wide-ranging and historically important impact of the Japanese Buddhist missionaries was the request by the Japanese monks to the colonial government to lift the ban on Buddhist monks entering the capital. In 2008, Buddhists account for 22.8 percent of the total population.

There is also a small but growing religious Islamic community in Korea. It began during the Korean War (1950–1953), when a Turkish Imam succeeded in converting a small number of Koreans into Islam. In 1955, those Korean converts formed the Korean Imam Society and began missionary efforts to propagate the new religion in Korea and built a temporary Islamic temple in the following year. In the same year, there were reportedly 208 Korean Muslims; by 2007, the number increased to 140,000.

Apart from the landing of great foreign religions and the revival of Buddhism in the twentieth century, a less notable but significant development is taking place – namely, the birth of indigenous new religions. There are three types of new religions:

1   Those founded by former Christians and Buddhists, who abandoned their respective religions to create new versions such as the Unification Church and Chondokwan (Christian breeds) and Wonbulkyo (Buddhist related);
2   Those founded by Korean civic leaders on the basis of indigenous belief systems in combination with Confucianism, Buddhism and Zen Buddhism; and
3   Those imported from Japan (Sōkagakkai and Tenrikyo) and China (Ilkwŏndo).

These new religions combine Buddhist, Confucian, Taoist, Christian and shamanistic elements and "promise the advent of a savior – none other than the founder of each sect – with the coming of the new world" (Grayson 1989: 240). Each sect has a relatively small number of followers and will likely remain a minority religion.

Indigenous shamanistic practices have survived for thousands of years of numerous attacks from officially adopted great religions (Buddhism, Taoism, Confucianism, Christianity and Islam) and are still doing well, caring for the people whose religious needs are not met by the those religions. An estimated three million Koreans regularly consult modern-day shamans (fortune tellers), whose establishments are found on virtually every corner – there were reportedly more than 600,000 fortune tellers in 1997 in South Korea (Kukminilbo 1997, quoted in Kim 2002). Moreover, this folk belief system is being elevated to the level of religion, mugyo (shaman religion), from the old rank of musok (shaman folkways) or superstition. Clients of shamanistic service have traditionally been almost exclusively women; however, in urbanized Korea, men, especially businessmen and politicians, actively seek their help in pursuit of profits or fortune. (The religious market section was drawn from Chang 2009).

254 *Conclusion*

After a century of kŭndaehwa, South Koreans now look or live more like contemporary Westerners than Koreans at the time of port opening in 1876. Those pictures taken by Western visitors at the end of the nineteenth century clearly testify it.

The extensive marketization of the society, through importation of Western public institutions, however, as I have already discussed, has had little impact on the traditional personalist ethic. It did not make individualists out of personalist Koreans, or did not liberate personalist Koreans from their personal networks. Instead, they continue to strengthen their personal ties with close others and build new personal networks. Even Protestant churches became bases for building personal networks among their members. And personalist Koreans successfully adapted themselves to the new market development. In impersonal market situations that arise in the process of kŭndaehwa, they are expected to and do give and receive help from their close others. The age-old collectivist norm uiri is still widely valued in Korea today (Chang 1991). In the marketized society, Koreans continue to remain personalists or network builders.

That Koreans continue to remain personalists and adapted themselves well to market situations means that the kŭndaehwa process has taken place largely in the public domain in which various institutions imported from the West, and Westernized Japan replaced Confucian ones borrowed from China. Let's look at the democratization closely. It entails the import of Western political institutions and organizations – political parties, presidential, national assembly, independent judiciary system and local autonomous government, elections, a free press and citizens' volunteer associations – in which people participate as free and equal citizens. If we look back at the democratization movement during the pre-1987 authoritarian era, it was a struggle to regain the freedom in the public domain or a war against the government that restricted the freedom in the public domain – freedom of the press (or expression), the freedom of assembly (or protest), the freedom of association and the freedom of election. It was not a struggle to protect individual autonomy – the freedom of not being prevented from choosing as I do by other people – including close others – or the freedom to be his or her own master making decisions about his or her own affairs. One cannot say that the informal interpersonal network domain went through democratization to the same extent.

Universalistic values that democracy espouses has yet to have much impact on the interpersonal face-to-face sphere. In both public and personal domains, Koreans continue to be particularists or personalists in their hearts. Democratic values or norms embodied in constitutionalism – including human rights, human dignities, freedom, equality, tolerance, plurality or diversity – have not been firmly or fully established as the moral basis of the public domain. They have not been internalized by the public as the general principle guiding interpersonal interaction in both the public and private domains. Democratic ethics is not being taught as widely at home or school as the Confucian ethics were taught during the Chosŏn period.

Conclusion 255

Personalists have found personal ties or networks or the personal capital useful in promoting personal or network interests, and eagerly expanded their tightly knit networks.

Public roles and offices are frequently personalized. Consequently, the public interest, or the interest and welfare of the people, is often pushed aside by those who help one another for private gains. Public officials who apply rules and those whom the rules are applied to often negotiate or cooperate on a personal basis to bend the rules for mutual benefit. Personal network largely turned into personal capital, not social capital. In a personalist society such as South Korea, it is difficult to say that everybody is equal before the law or entitled to receive equal public service. Citizens are differentiated into two groups, those who can and those who cannot pay officials for their services or those who are well connected and those who are not. The quality of life is significantly different between the two. The poor and powerless are considerably marginalized by the government and the rest of the society. They constitute the so-called Eul (B) class – that is, constantly being personally bullied by "Kap" (A) class of the rich and powerful in what is supposedly impersonal contractual relationship.[2] Contractualism, or legalism, has not been fully established as a major social norm in urban life.

The city has yet to become a larger community (imagined) in which citizens scrupulously abide by rules and regulations, help each other – whether they are related or not – and actively participate in community events and form civic groups instead of building informal networks on the basis of various personal ties and strengthening their solidarity for personal aims.

People, lay and specialist, increasingly are coming to a realization that Korea has modernized and joined the club of developed countries, but has not fully become an "advanced nation" (sonjin'guk). It is still backward in many ways. Some of them consider Korea as a sick society. "Korean diseases" (Han'guk byŏng) include diverse strands: widespread corruption, lack of respect for law, the deep participation of the military in civilian politics, treatment of the former (retired) public officials with courtesy by current ones (chŏnkwan ye'u), parachute appointment, big corporate firm first-ism (over medium and small firms), polarization in income distribution, deepening gaps between the rich and the poor, conspicuous exhibition excessive consumption, high suicide rates, high unemployment rates, the historical nihilism and excessive ideological disputes. Others go even further to call it "Hell Korea" and advise people to get out.

Efforts have been made or attempted to cure these Korean diseases by both the government and citizen groups. The three governments of the civilian presidents, Kim Young Sam, Kim Dae Jung and Roh Moo Hyun introduced a number of reform measures – bureaucratic reforms (the real name deposit, opening personal wealth of public officials to public, prohibition of money laundering), legal reforms (abolition of "bad laws" including the National Security Law, the Social Safety Law, the Press Law), judiciary reforms (replacing the bar examination with law school, abolition of the Central Investigation Bureau of the Prosecution office, establishment of the Bureau of Investigation of High Official),

256 *Conclusion*

political reforms (investigation of illegal presidential campaign fund), political party reforms (separation of political party and administration and the executive office), electoral reforms (introduction of primary election and small donor system), press reforms (severing ties between the media and politicians and high-ranking bureaucrats, abolition of the Press Club), educational reforms (enactment of the Private School Law) and others.

Some public-minded citizens organized themselves into citizen groups or nongovernmental organizations on the basis of personal ties to promote public causes or common goods – human rights, gender equality, extension of citizen rights to foreign workers, environmental protection and others. Like undongkwon students in the 1970s and 1980s, they try to make social capital out of their personal network.

It is not clear, however, how these public-minded personalists firmly will resist the temptation of personalizing their public roles for private gains and how they will be able to form strong unified collectively forces to serve as an effective check on rule-bending tendencies of the network-oriented personalists – especially the huge elite cartel consisting of politicians, bureaucrats, judiciary officials, big corporate leaders and owners and reporters of major media. They are small in number, and their movement is largely led by intellectuals – university professors and lawyers. Though they call themselves citizen groups, the general public does not participate and support them actively. In that sense, conflict between the two Confucian projects still continues in altered forms.

The related issue is how much effect the reform efforts by the progressive governments and citizens groups have had in curing the Korean diseases and how far reform efforts will eventually go. At the moment, there is little sign that they are being eradicated. I will not make an attempt to analyze those diseases here, for there is no space left for me to do so. But I won't hesitate to say that at the root of the Korean diseases lies personalism or the personalist lack of respect for laws and regulations, and a tendency to put personal and network interests ahead of public interest; this fact is not well recognized by public officials or scholars. Unfortunately, I am more or less alone in talking about personalism. Even those NGO scholar-activists who successfully facilitated their personal networks in promoting common good, thereby proving that personalists could become common good promoters, instead of remaining as network interest protectors, failed to address the problems of the traditional ethic of mutual assistance.

I end this book with the hope that this time-old normative orientation, personalism, or the personalist ethic, will receive the wider attention, analytical as well as reflective, that it deserves from scholars as well as politicians.

Notes

1 But even if a wife committed one of the seven, men were not allowed to abandon their wives.
2 The recent widely publicized event that occurred in December 2014 illustrates the point well. The vice president of Korean Airline, a daughter of its chair, ordered the captain to

Conclusion 257

return the plane she boarded at the New York international airport as a passenger back to the departure point from the runway and had the plane manager apologize to her on bended knee, for she was displeased with the way a stewardess served her a bag of nuts.

References

Buswell, Jr. Robert E. (1992) *The Zen Monastic Experience*, Princeton: Princeton University Press.

Chang, Yuns-shik (1991) "The Personalist Ethic and the Market in Korea." *Comparative Studies in Society and History*, vol. 33, pp. 106–129.

Chang, Yun-Shik (2009) "Introduction: Korea in the Process of Globalization," pp. 1–38, in Chang, Yun-Shik, Seok Hyun-Ho, and Baker, Donald L. (ed.) *Korea Confronts Globalization*, London: Routeledge.

Chang Yun-Shik (2006) "Conclusion: South Korea: In Pursuit of Modernity", pp. 345–373, in Chang, Yun-Shik and Lee, Steven Hugh (ed.) *Transformation in Twentieth Century Korea*, London: Routledge.

Choe, Chongsŏng (2002) *Chosŏnjo musok kukhaeng Ŭirye yon'gu* (A Study of Shamanistic National Rites in Chosun Dynasty Korea), Seoul: Ilchosa.

Chung, Chai-sik (1995) *A Korean Confucian Encounter With the Modern World: Yi Hangno and the West*, Berkeley: Institute of East Asian Studies.

Grayson, James Hyntley (1989) *Korea: A Religious History*, Oxford: Clarendon Press.

Hur, Nam-lin (1999) "The Soto Sect and Japanese Military Imperialism in Korea." *Japanese Journal of Religious Studies*, vol. 26, no. 1–2, pp. 107–134.

Kim, Andrew Eungi (2002) "Characteristics of Religious Life in South Korea: A Sociological Survey." *Review of Religious Research*, vol. 43, no. 4, pp. 291–310.

Kim, Kyŏng-chip (2005) "Kaehwagi Hanll pulgyo'ŭi kyoryu (Exchanges Between Korean and Japanese Buddhism in the Enlightenment Period." *Tongyanghak* (Oriental Studies), vol. 38, pp. 172–184.

Lane, Robert (1979) "Political Observers and Market Participants: The Effects on Cognition." *Political Psychology*, vol. 1, pp. 3–20.

Lee Dongwon and Cho Sungnam (1986) "Changing Patterns of Marriage in Korea" (Unpublished).

Moffet, Samuel Hugh (1962) *The Christians of Korea*, New York: Friendship Press.

Mun Chŏngch'ang (1941) *Chōsen no sijō*, Tokyo: Nihon hyōronsha.

Shin, Inryung (1994) "Legal Rights of Women As Workers," in Cho, Hyoung and Chang, Pil-wha (eds.) *Division of Labor in Korea*, Seoul: Ewha Womans University Press.

Slater, Don (1997) *Consumer Culture and Modernity*, Cambridge: Polity Press.

Song, Chuhyŏn (2004) "1910 nyŏndae Ilbon bulgyo'ŭi Chosŏn p'ogyo hwaltong" (Japanese Buddhist Propagtion Activities in Korea in the 1910s). *Munmyŏng Wŏnji* (Origins of Civilization), vol. 5, no. 2, pp. 61–91.

Veblen, Thorstein (1953) *The Theory of Leisure Class*, New York: New American Library.

Weber, Max (1958) *From Max Weber: Essays in Sociology*, Translated, Edited, and with an Introduction by Hans H. Gerth and C. Wright Mills, New York: Oxford University Press.

Index

Academic Clique in Korea – is it Another Caste? 97
Agricultural Land Reform Law 111
agriculture: growth of 35–6, 75–7, 116–17; as the root (pon) of the kingdom 29
Akyuz, Yilmaz 124
Allen, Horace 2
Alumni association (Tongch'anghoe) 215, 216
American Military Provisional Government (AMPG) 110, 111, 117, 185, 186
Amsden, Alice 2, 123, 128, 135
An, Ch'unsik 110, 148
An, Hosang 92
anti-Americanism 180
anti-Communism 93, 177
Artisans, in Choson Korea 30–1
August the Third Settlement (P'alsamchoch'i) 133
Austria-Korea Treaty 81 1n
authoritarian regimes: defined 165; subjugation by the executive office of legislative and judiciary branches by the executive office 165–8; and of universities, media, press, labour union, and big business enterprises 168–76

Bae, Kyuhan 138
Baejae haktang 58
Baker, Donald L. 12
Ban, Sung Hwan 111
banking 60, 68, 74, 114
Barclay, George 77
base job (ch'ŏnŏp) 32
base people (ch'ŏnin) 28, 247
basic labour law 148, 169, 248
Belgium-Korea Treaty 81 1n

big business enterprises 168–70
Bloch, Marc 242
Brain Korea (BK) 21, 99
Brazinsky, Gregg 133, 186, 187
Brown, Winthrop 186
Brown Memorandum 131
Buddhism 252
Building Educational Korea 58
Buswell, Robert 252

Calhoun, Craig 226
Calvin 242
campus autonomy policy (Hagwŏn chayulhwa chongch'aek) 175
Capital, Volume 1, 192
capital city river merchant *see* merchant
Chaebŏl 147; *see also* big business enterprises
Chang, Chinho 96
Chang, Ha-Joon 132
Chang, Myŏn 165
Chang, Yu 26
Chang, Yun-Shik 75, 77, 80, 185, 188
Chant, Dal-joong 129
chastity 25–7
China: and Imo mutiny 53–5; and Kapsin coup; Korea-China Trade Agreement; and Tonghak rebellion 56–7; trade with 42
Chinese Land Tax Law (Kongbop) 17–18
Cho, Chunghun 131
Cho, Hyorae, 196
Cho, Kanghwan 93
Cho, Namhong 198
Cho, Sŭnghyŏk 182
Cho, Sungnam 249
Cho Chaegŏl 105
Ch'oe, Chonghyŏn 153
Ch'oe, Hangsŏp 230

Index 259

Ch'oe, Ikhyŏn 52
Ch'oe, Kangsik 96
Ch'oe, Myŏnggil 26
Ch'oe, Sŏkch'ae 172
Choe, Young-ho 34
Ch'oe Chongsŏng 252
Ch'oe Chun 170, 171
Ch'oe Yun'gyu 68, 75, 78
Choi, Jang Jip 137, 138, 139
Chŏn, Pongjun 55–6
Chŏng 5
Chŏng, Chaegyŏng 119, 134
Chŏng, Chinsŏk 171
Chŏng, Chisong 190
Chŏng, Manjo 20, 21
Chŏng, T'aesu 171
Chŏng, Yagyong 26
Chongjo 17
Chŏng Tojŏn 11
Chŏn'gwan ye'u 200, 224
Chonji (Small token of good will) 11
Chōsen sōtokufu (The Japanese
  Government of Korea) 73
Chosŏn dynasty: as an agrarian society'
  34–45; as a Confucian society 10–28;
  as a hierarchical society 28–34
Christianity: as a belief system 252; and
  education 58–9
Chuch'e idea 192, 193, 197
Chun, Doo Hwan 88, 89, 153, 165, 166,
  167, 170, 173, 175, 178, 179, 192
Chung, Chaisik 11
Chung Chu Young 142, 144, 145, 146,
  153, 226
Chungjong 16
Civil Relief in Korea (CRI) 113
Cleveland, Paul 187
Clifford, Mark 142
Code of Administration (*Chosŏn
  kyŏnggukchŏn*) 11
Cole, David C. 111, 112
Coleman, James 185
commerce: as the branch (mal) of the
  kingdom 29; change 36–43, 59–60;
  joint-sales decree (sinhae tonggong)
  39; supplementing the branch
  (pomalmubon) 42; suppression of the
  'branch (ŏkmalmuabon) 36, 42
commoners (p'yongmin or sang'in) 30
Compulsory Education Act 84
Confucianism 198
Confucianization projects 10, 246; of the
  family 13–15; of the state 17–28

constant hearts (hangsim) 11
constant means of support (hangsan) 11
Constitutional Assembly (CA) 193
Constitutional Court 2, 188, 189, 191, 197
constitutionalism 162–5
consumer market 249–50
corruption: defined 234; and a typology
  234–6
Council of Priests for the Realization of
  Justice 181
Cram school (hagwon) 101, 102, 113; *see
  also* education
Cumings, Bruce 131, 157 33n

Dallmayr, Fred 242 9n
Dalman, Carl 156 23n
Democracy and Education 91
Democratic Labour Party 196, 197, 252
Democratic Life 93
democratic reform: and birth of the
  Democratic Workers Party 196–7; of
  election 187; emergence of the cyber
  space of university 192–5; of the
  judiciary 188; of labour unions 195–6;
  of the legislature 188; of the mass
  media 190–1; the revival the regional
  government 190
democratic union (Minju nojo) 182
Denmark-Korea Treaty 81 1n
Deuchler, Martina 14, 15
developmental autocracy (kaebal tokche)
  120; *see also* Developmental state
developmental state 119–24
Dewey, John 91
Deyo, Frederic 132
diploma disease 93–4
Direct Foreign Investment (DFI) 125, 126,
  132; *see also* economic development
Doctrine of the Mean 11
Dore, Ronald P. 6, 7, 14, 34, 89, 144
Dornbush, Rudiger 133
Duus, Peter 2, 4, 53, 54, 69

East-Asia Co-Prosperity Area 77
Eberhard, Wolfram 11
Eckert, Carter 77
economic bureaucracy *see* economic
  development
Economic Cooperation Administration
  (ECA) 112
economic development, in South Korea:
  financing of 130–4; in the First
  Republic 112; Park Chung Hee factor

260 Index

in 141–2; role of corporate leaders in 144–7; role of economic bureaucracy in 120–1; role of economic nationalism in 139–41; role of industrial workers in 137–9; role of public and private enterprises in 134–9; role of technology in 124–30; in the Third and Fourth Republic - Five-Year Development Plans of 120; under the APMG 110–11
economic miracle 119; *see also* economic development
economic nationalism *see* economic development
Economic Planning Board 120, 121, 141, 142
education (new or Western) : adult education 88–9; de-Confucianization of 90–1; and diploma disease and meritocracy 93–100; Educational Ordinances 71; financing of 89–90; growth 57–9, 64–6, 71–4, 84–90; and job 94–100; parental desire for their children's education 102; primary education 84–5; supplementary education 100–7; tertiary education 87–8; and wage 96; Westernization of 90–3
educational market 247–6
Ehwa haktang 58
enlightenment (Kaehwa): as a social campaign 51–64
Enlightenment Party (Kaehwadang) 54
Enos,John 127, 141, 144
entrepreneurs, Korean: in Japanese period 70, 80; in Kaehwa period 59–60; in post-Liberation period
Equal Service Law (Kyunyokbop) *see* Tax reform
establishment media (Chedo ollon) 173
Experience and Society 91

Family Rites of Zhu Xi 246
Federation of Korean Industries (FKI) 197
financing, of South Korean development plans: direct foreign investment (DFI) 132; domestic resource mobilization 132–3; foreign loans 131; overseas adventures 131–2; private loans 133–4; stock market 133–4
Fischer, Claude 210
Five-Year economic development Plans: first plan (1962–1966) 120, 128; second plan (1967–1971) 120; third plan (1972–1977) 120

Food and Agricultural Organization 113
Foreign Capital Inducement Law 156 20n
Foreign Exchange Control Law 156 20n
Foreign Operations Administration (FOA) 112

Germany: financial aid 131; Korea-Germany Trade Treaty 81, 1n
Gibney, Frank 2
Goodel, Grace 232, 233
good people (yang'in) 28, 247
Government Appropriations for Relief in Occupied Area 111, 112
Grand National Party 191
Granovetter, Mark 210
Great Code of Adminisration of 1498 11, 25, 35
Grossman, Gene 136

Habib, Phiip 187
Hamilton, Clive 115, 118
Ham Yŏngjun 150, 151, 152
Han, Chunsang 90
Han, Insŏp 200
Han, Insuk 103, 104, 106
Han, Sungjoo 177
Han, Ugun 11
Han, Wansang 100
Han,Y. C. 201
Han, Yŏng'u 12
Han'guk chongch'l yŏn'guso 174
Han'guk kidokkyo kyohoe hyŏpǔhoe 138, 183
Han'guk kidokkyo sahoe munje yŏn'guwŏn 178, 180, 183
Han'guk ǔnhaeng 111, 116, 117
Heavy and Chemical Industry (HCI) Declaration 122, 125, 128
Henderson, Gregory 170, 186
Hicks, George 79
High School Equalization Plan 87
Hŏ, Suyŏl 80
Hobsbawm, Eric 2
Hodge, John R. 185
hometown friendship society (hyang'uhoe) 212–13
Hong, Sehwa 229
Hong, Wontack 115, 118
Hong, Yongbok 148
Hong, Yŏngnan 96, 107 5n
Hong'ik in'gan 91
Hong Yŏngsik 54
Hori, Washo 76
Horkheimer, Max 210

Index 261

Huang, Zun Xian 51, 52
Human Rights Declaration 183
Hur, Namlin 254
Hwang, Ŭibong 178, 180, 201
Hyojong 20
Hyŏn, Ju 97, 105
Hyundai Construction 117

ideological market 251
Im, Ch'aejŏng 173
Im, Chibong 189
Im, Chongch'ŏl 116
Im, T'aebo 105
Imjin War 17, 18, 20
Imo Mutiny (Imo kullan) 53
Independence Club (IC) 60–4
Independent Party (Tongniptang) 54
indigenous new religions 253
industry, handicraft, in Chosŏn Korea
    42–3, 59–60
Injo 20, 26
Inoue, Kaoru 56
International Cooperation Administration
    (ICA) 112
international trade 42–3
Italy-Korea Treaty 81 1n
Ito, Hirobumi 65

Janelli, Dawnhee 14
Janelli, Roger 14
Japan: colonization 71–81; financial
    aid 131; and Imo Mutiny 53–4; and
    Kabo-reform 56–7; normalization
    of diplomatic relation 131; and port-
    opening 2; and protectorate government
    64–9; technology transfer 127–8; trade
    with 76
job market 248
Johnson, Chalmers 124
Johnson, Harry G. 140
Johnson, Lyndon 131
joint assembly of all people (manmin
    kongdonghoe) 62
Jones, Leroy 135, 136, 138
June 29 Democratization Declaration 187,
    192, 193, 197
June Struggle 184
Justice Party 197

Kabo reform (Kabokyŏng jang) 57
Kang, Chunman 96, 97, 98, 99, 100, 103,
    106, 108 7n
Kang, Sŏngguk 88
Kanghwa Treaty 51

Kang Man'gil 32, 38
Kapsin Coup (kapsin chŏngbyŏn) 54, 56
Kim, Ch'angsŏn 148
Kim, Chiha 184
Kim, Chinhong 171
Kim, Chongch'an 174
Kim, Chŏngnam 174
Kim, Chŏngnyŏm 133
Kim, Chunsŏk 16
Kim, Hogyŏng 79
Kim, Kiman 197
Kim, Kyŏng'il 81
Kim, Linsu 124, 126, 127, 155 23n
Kim, Misuk 102
Kim, Nakchung 169
Kim, Okkyun 54
Kim, Samung 192
Kim, Sangbong 224
Kim, Sauk 170
Kim, Sŏkhyŏng 23
Kim, Sŏnhi 42
Kim, Stephan 187
Kim, Suhaeng 192
Kim, Sŭngyong 154
Kim, T'aegil 40
Kim, Taehwan 115, 116, 118
Kim, Tonghun 97
Kim, Uchang 2
Kim, Ujung 142
Kim, Yangbun 102
Kim, Yŏnfbae 198
Kim, Yŏngho 39
Kim, Yŏnghwa 85, 87, 129
Kim, Yŏng'il 183
Kim, Yongsŏp 35, 36
Kim, Young Sam 100
Kim, Yuk 16
Kim, Yun'gon 17
Kim, Yunhwan 169
Kim Chaegyu 165
Kim Dae Jung, columnist 228
Kim Dae Jung, President 187, 251
Kim Ilsung 141, 192, 193, 197
Kim Jongil 252
Kim Kyŏngchip 253
Kim Young Sam 152, 153
Ko, Wŏn 194
Koh, Byongik 198
Kojong 52
Kong Unbae 90
Korea –England Trade Treaty 81 1n
Korea-France Trade Treaty 81 1n
Korean Central Intelligence Agency
    (KCIA) 167, 168, 171, 178, 187

262   *Index*

Korean Confederation of Trade Union (KCTU) 195, 196, 252
Korean disease 255
Korean Federation of Teachers Association 107, 195
Korean Federation of Trade Union (KFTU) 169, 170, 195
Korean Institute of Science and Technology 129
Korean Interim Legislative Assembly 185
Korean Oriental Development Company 43–4
Korean War 85, 112, 125, 253
Koryŏ University 98, 99
Kozul-Wright, Richard 132
Ku, Chagyŏng 197
Kuznets, Paul 120, 122, 154 8n
Kwanghae 18–19
Kwon, Taihwan 110
Kwon, Yŏnggil 196

labor mobilization, forced 79
Landes, David 46
Landow, Martin 220
landownership 32–3; land reform 16–17, 111
land survey 74
Land Tax Law (Kongbŏp) *see* tax reform
Law Concerning Establishment of Free Export Districts 156 20n
Learning from the North (Pukhak Ŭi) 46
Lee, Dongwŏn 249
Lee, Ki-baik 18, 20, 21, 22, 23, 31, 52, 53, 54
Lee, Kong Rae 126, 130
Lee, Namhee 180
Lee, Oyŏng 227
Levy, Marion J. 223–42
lineage group (Chongmun) 14
lineage solidarity group (chongch'inhoe) 211–12
Lyons, Gene M. 112

MacArthur, Douglas 3
Mandate of Heaven 11
marriage market 249
Marshal, T. H. 162, 163
Marx Communale 192
Mason, Edward S. 112
McGinn, Noel F. 89
merchants, in Chosŏn Korea: capital city river merchants 37–8; city shop merchants (sijon sang'in) 31–2;

itinerant peddlers (haengsang) 42–3; Kaesong merchants meritocracy 93–4
Merton, Robert K. 220
middle strata (Chung'inch'ŭng) 30, 33
Min, Queen 54
mining 44–5, 69
Ministry of Commerce and Industry 120, 121, 129, 141, 142
Ministry of Education 88, 90, 93, 104
Ministry of Finance 120, 12, 234
Ministry of Science and Technology 129, 130
Miracle on the side of Han River 110; *see also* economic development
Miyajima, Hiroshi 74
modernization (Kŭndaehwa) projects: and democratization 60–4, 162–208; expansion of new (Western) education 57–9, 65–6; industrialization 66–70, 77–80
Moffet, Samuel 252
Moon, Pal Yong 111
Mun, Chŏngch'ang 250
Mun, Myŏngho 181
Muslims, Korean 251
Myŏngdong Cathedral 181, 193

Nam, Young Woo 112
National Charter of Education (Kungmin kyoyuk hŏnjang) 92–3
National Council for Unification 166
National Human Rights Committee 2, 189
National Liberation (NL) 193, 194
National Security Law 177, 189, 252
Nation First Theory (Ilmin chŭi) 92
Native religion
Nisbet, Robert 143
Nodong sahoe 200
non-governmental organizations (NGO) 256
Norman, Victor 136
Nossamo (No Muhyŏnŭl sarang hanŭn moim or the Meeting of those who Love Roh Mu Hyun) 191
Nothoi or sedondary son *see* Occupational hierarchy

O, Ch'ŏnsŏk 91, 107
O, Hana 179
O, Kyŏnghwan 153
O, Miil 59, 68
O, Sŏngch'ŏl 74
O, Wŏnch'ŏl 125, 129, 131, 137, 139, 141, 142, 143, 144

Occupational hierarchy, in Choson Korea: artisans (kong) 30–1; chung'in 30; government officials and scholars (sadaebuor sa); merchants 31–2; and outcasts or low –born 32; peasants (nong) 30
Oh, John Kie- Chiang 75
Ohkawa, Kazushi 75
Organization for Economic Cooperation and Development (OECD) 1, 141
Oriental Development Company 69
Our Open Party 191

Pack, Howard 134
Pak, Chansŭng 80
Pak, Chindong 74
Pak, Chiwŏn 46
Pak, Chongch'ŏl 184
Pak, Chongch'ŏn 28
Pak Chong'ŭng 146
Pak, Ch'unghun 121, 134, 142
Pak, Ch'unho 103, 104, 106
Pak, Kyusu 54
Pak, P'yŏngsik 35, 36
Pak, Taejun 141, 144–5, 146
Pak, Yŏnghyo 5
Pak Siyŏng 16
Palais, James 17, 18, 20, 21, 22, 23, 24, 27, 30, 34, 46
parachute appointment 222
Park, Chung Hee 85, 87, 91, 119, 121, 122, 124, 134, 137, 138, 140, 141, 142, 143, 144, 153, 154 7n, 166, 170, 176, 177
Park, Woo-Hee 127, 141, 144
Parsons, Talcott 3
Perez-Diaz, Victor 187
periodic market (changsi or hyangsi) 39–42
Perkins, Dwight 111
personalism see personalist ethic
personalist ethic: defined 3–7; and democratization 198–203; and educational expansion 104–7; industrialization 141–54; and political opposition 184–5; and urbanization 210–43
personal network: in formal organization 220–3; of kinship ties 211–12; making of 218–19; of other ties 217; of regional ties 212–15; of school ties 215–17
Pictorial Books o Three Relations (Samgang haengsilto) 15
Pohang Steel Company (POSCO) 144, 146
Policy for Korea 52

political fund (chongch'I jagŭm) 153
political market 250–1
political opposition: by others 184; by progressive church leaders 180–4; by student activists 176–80
Popular Democracy (PD) 193, 194
press guideline (Podochich'im) 173
Private School Act 66
Private School Ordinance 87
private tutoring 100–5; *see also* education
Progressive Justice Party 197
Progressive Labor Union, 195–6
public loans (PL) 480, 113, 116
Pursell, Gary 124, 126
Putnam, Robert B. 5
Pyŏn, Kwangsŏk 31

railways 68, 74
Redfield, Robert 4
Reeve, W. D. 112
Regional Self-government system 189
rehabilitations plans 111–19
religious market 252–4
Rhee, Syngman 85, 140, 171
Rice-cake money (ttŏkkap) 152
Rice Inrease Plan 75–7
Riesman, David 5
Robert's Rule 61
Rodrik, Dani 13
Roh, Moo Hyun 78, 107 6n, 108 7n, 190, 191
Roh Tae Woo 153, 184, 242 8n
Rosovsky, Henry 75
Russia 53
Russo-Japanese War 54, 64

SaKong, Il 135
Same Family Name Village (tongchokch'on) 48 4n
School and Society 91
secret fund (Pijagŭm) 153
Science and Technology Law 156 20n
Seoul National University 98, 99, 100
Sequel to the Great Code of Administration of 1498 (Sok taej ŏ n) 12
Seth, Michael 85, 88, 106, 128, 285
Shamanism: as a belief system 253–4; and education 106
Sin, Tubŏm 169
Sin, Yongha 62
Sino-Japanese War 54, 64
six articles (Honŭiyukcho) 62
slave (nobi): and outside-resident slave (oegonobi) 23 ; private slaves (sanobi) 22;

264 *Index*

public slave (kongnobi); reform efforts of 22–4; resident slaves (solgo nobi) 23
Smart, Clifford E. J. 227
Smith, Adam 233
Smith, Michael P. 227
Sŏ, Chaep'il 54
Sŏ, Kwangbŏm 54
Son, Insu 66
Song, Chuhyŏn 253
Song, Jun-ho 34
Song, Kŏnho 170, 172
Song, Pyŏngnak 119
sprout of capitalism 45–7
state-run ability test (Sunŭnggosi) 100, 106
Status distinction, in Choson Korea: yangban, middle strata (chunginchung) and nothoi, commoners (pyŏngmin) 30; slaves (nobi) 22–4
Stern, Joseph 121, 122, 156 23n
Stout. Jr., Russel 220
Sunjo 24
Suzuki, Takeo 77

Tae, Wansŏn 142
Takezoe, Shinichirō 54
tax reform: in Chosŏn Korea –Land Tax Law (Kongbŏp) 17–18; and Equal Service Law 20–2; in Korea under Japanese control 67; in post Liberation South Korea 115, 132; Uniform Land Tax Law 18–20
technology 77; human resource development 128–9; promotion of scientific research 129–30; technology transfer 125–8
Three Ancient Chinese Dynasties: Hsia, Shang and Chou 11
three min 178
Tonggyech'ong (Korean National Statistics Office) 102, 103
Tonghak pesant rebellion 55–6
Torjesen, Karen J. 226
Toward a Democratic Education (Minju kyoyukul chihyang hayŏ) 107 4n
trade: in Choson Korea 42–3; in Korea under Japanese control 75–6; in post-Liberation South Korea 120–4
Tu, Weiming 12

ŭiri 4
undongkwon 178, 179, 180
Unified Progressive Party 197
Uniform Land Law (taedongbop) *see* tax reform

United Nations Children's Fund (UNICEF) 113
United Nations Civil Assistance Command Korea 113
United Nations Educational and scientific Cultural Organization (UNESCO) 113
United Nations Korea Reconstruction Agency (UNKRA) 113
United States: American Military Provisional Government 185; foreign aid 112–13; Korean-American Trade Agreement; role in Korean democratization 185–7
United States Information Service (USIS) 181
University Student Quota Ordinance 87
Urban Industrial Mission 182
urbanization 209
Urban Koreans: and civic engagement 239–42; and corruption 234–6; and respect for law 230; and social equality 227–8; and social trust 237–9; and tolerance 228–30
U.S. Chamber of Commerce 180
U.S. Foreign Aid 112
U.S. Information Service (USIS) 180
U.S. Operation Mission (USOM) 186

Veritable Records 15, 26
vested properties 114
Vietnam 135
Vietnam War 131–2

Wade, Robert 128
Webb, Sydney 2
Weber, Max 220
Westphal, Larry E. 124, 126, 127, 140, 155 23n
Wirth, Louis 210
women, Korean: in Choson dynasty 24–8; consumption 250; and education 84–9, 218; and job 248; and politics 250–1
Woo, Jung-en 132, 141

Yang, Kŏn 231
yangban: and civil service examination 32; defined 13–14; and landownership 33; local self-governing body (yuhyangso) 13; local yangban register (hyang'an) 5; occupation of 29–30; and recommendation (munŭm) 29; tax duty of 16–21
Yi, Che'o 177

Yi, Chonggyu 96, 107 5n
Yi, Chongjae 117
Yi, Chunŭng 190
Yi, Hanyŏl 184
Yi, Huiju 104
Yi, Hurak 155 11n
Yi, Hwang 12
Yi, I 18
Yi, Ik 24
Yi, Kwangnin 53
Yi, Kyuyong 96
Yi, Nŭnghwa 25
Yi, Pyŏngguk 170
Yi, Sang'u 177
Yi, Songgye 11
Yi, Sŏngmu 29, 30, 32, 34
Yi, Suon 181
Yi, Taegŭn 113, 115, 116, 117
Yi, Taeho 173

Yi, Taehwan 145
Yi, Tuhyu 107
Yi, Wŏnbo 170
Yŏngjo 21, 24
Young Catholic Workers (Jeunesse
    Ouvriere Chreienne) 182
Yonsei University 98, 99, 100
Yu, Hyŏngwŏn 17, 23, 27
Yu, Kyŏngsun 179
Yu, Suwon 24
Yu, Wŏndong 36
Yu, Yŏng'ŭl 201
Yu Kyŏngsun 179
Yun, Posŏn 186
Yushin 174, 182
Yu Sŭngju 45

Zenshō, Eisuke 48
Zhu Xi 24

Printed in the United States
By Bookmasters